# CLEAN
# SWEEP

OSPREY
PUBLISHING

# THOMAS
# McKELVEY CLEAVER

# CLEAN
# SWEEP

## VIII FIGHTER COMMAND
## AGAINST THE LUFTWAFFE, 1942–45

OSPREY PUBLISHING
Bloomsbury Publishing Plc
Kemp House, Chawley Park, Cumnor Hill, Oxford OX2 9PH, UK
29 Earlsfort Terrace, Dublin 2, Ireland
1385 Broadway, 5th Floor, New York, NY 10018, USA
E-mail: info@ospreypublishing.com
www.ospreypublishing.com

OSPREY is a trademark of Osprey Publishing Ltd

First published in Great Britain in 2023

A catalog record for this book is available from the British Library.

ISBN: HB 9781472855480; PB 9781472855459; eBook 9781472855466;
ePDF 9781472855473; XML 9781472855497

23 24 25 26 27   10 9 8 7 6 5 4 3 2 1

Maps by www.bounford.com
Index by Fionbar Lyons

Typeset by Deanta Global Publishing Services, Chennai, India
Printed and bound in Great Britain by CPI (Group) UK Ltd, Croydon CR0 4YY

Osprey Publishing supports the Woodland Trust, the UK's leading woodland conservation charity.

To find out more about our authors and books visit www.ospreypublishing.com. Here you will find
extracts, author interviews, details of forthcoming events and the option to sign up for our newsletter.

# CONTENTS

# LIST OF ILLUSTRATIONS AND MAPS

Major Robert S. Johnson, first Air Force pilot in the ETO to officially equal Eddie Rickenbacker's World War I score, with his crew chief Sergeant J.C. Penrod, in Johnson's last P-47D, "Penrod and Sam." The aircraft was named for the two of them in May 1944, on the occasion of Johnson's 28th victory. (USAF Official)

Chesley Peterson (left) was the first American to command an Eagle Squadron (No. 71) and the third American to become an ace in World War II. When the Eagles transferred to the USAAF, he became deputy group commander until June 1943, when he became group commander. Oscar Coen (right) was another original Eagle Squadron member and replaced Peterson as commander of the 334th Fighter Squadron (ex-71 Eagle Squadron). (USAF Official)

Captain Charles E. "Chuck" Yeager with his P-51D, "Glamorous Glen II," in November 1944. Shot down over France in March 1944, Yeager got to Spain with the help of the French Resistance and returned to the 357th Fighter Group, where he managed to stay on-base until after the invasion, when he was allowed as an "evader" to fly operations again. In November 1944, he scored five to become an "ace in a day." He was later the first man to fly faster than Mach 1. (USAF Official)

Major George Preddy of the 352nd Fighter Group, photographed with his P-51D-5, "Cripes A Mighty III," after scoring four victories during one mission in August 1944. Preddy was the top-scoring Mustang pilot with 26.83 victories in the P-51 when he was shot down on Christmas Day, 1944, by Allied flak while chasing a German fighter at low level. (USAF Official)

Colonel Donald J.M. Blakeslee, commander of the 4th Fighter Group. Unable to qualify for the USAAF, Blakeslee joined the RCAF. Following the Morlaix disaster in September 1942, he was transferred to 133 Eagle Squadron to make up the losses and became commander of the 334th Fighter Squadron in 1943. When he scored the P-47's first victory in April 1943, diving on two Fw-190s, he said, "By God it ought to dive, it certainly won't climb!" He championed the P-51 and promised to have his pilots transition to the new fighter from the P-47 within 24 hours, telling his pilots, "Learn to fly 'em on the way to the target." He flew the equivalent of over five tours without a break, doctoring his logbooks; he and Hub Zemke are considered the best American fighter leaders in Air Force history. (USAF Official)

Major Duane Beeson was the leading ace of the 4th Group's 334th Squadron and was one of the original Eagle Squadron members who formed the group. He was shot down in early April 1944 while strafing a German airfield in his P-51B, "Boise Bee." (USAF Official)

Captain Don S. Gentile of the 336th Fighter Squadron with his crew chief, Sergeant John Ferra, in March 1944, with his famous Mustang, "Shangri-La." (USAF Official)

As an aviation cadet, Gabreski was advised by his instructor to "seek another line of work" because of his lack of aptitude for flying. Gabreski persisted and eventually became the top-scoring ace of the ETO with 32 victories before crashing in July 1944 during a low-level strafing run on a German airfield when his propeller tip hit the ground. He had been on his way back to the States and marriage when he decided to make "one last mission." (USAF Official)

In April 1944, Supreme Commander General Dwight Eisenhower came to Debden to award Don Gentile (left) and Don Blakeslee (right) the Distinguished Flying Cross for their achievements in the Battle of Germany, famously calling Gentile a "one-man air force" for being the leading VIII Fighter Command ace at the time. The difference between Gentile, with his "100-mission look" and casual appearance, and Blakeslee's "thoroughly GI" appearance, was symbolic of their personalities and approaches to the business at hand. (USAF Official)

Captains Don Gentile (left) and Steve Pisanos (right) were best friends from their days in the Eagle Squadrons. Gentile was a first-generation son of Italian immigrants and Pisanos had "illegally immigrated" from Greece to become a pilot in America, "where all things are possible." His immigration status was discovered when the Eagle Squadrons transferred to the USAAF and Pisanos became the first immigrant to take advantage of the new rule that serving in the US armed forces would gain immediate US citizenship. (USAF Official)

James A. Goodson survived the sinking of the *Athenia*, the first Allied ship sunk in World War II, traveling back to Canada to join the RCAF. He flew in the RCAF before being transferred to the Eagle Squadrons and was commander of 336th Fighter Squadron and the group's leading ace when he was shot down over a German airfield in July 1944. Strafing would be responsible for the overwhelming majority of VIII Fighter Command losses during the war. (USAF Official)

"Hairless Joe" was the P-47D-25 Thunderbolt flown by 56th Fighter
Group deputy group commander Lieutenant Colonel Dave
Schilling. The 56th created "camouflage" for Thunderbolts that
arrived in unpainted aluminum finish, which identified the airplane
by squadron. (USAF Official)

Robert S. Johnson's P-47C-5, "Half Pint," after he landed at Manston,
July 1, 1943. Shot up when the squadron was attacked over
France because the canopy was jammed shut, Johnson survived an
encounter with JG 2's Major Egon Mayer, who fortunately had no
20mm ammunition when he spotted Johnson trying to make it
across the Channel and shot him up with 7.72mm bullets. When
Johnson got out of the Thunderbolt, he counted 200 bullet holes in
the fuselage without having to move. (USAF Official)

Hollywood star Jimmy Stewart fought the Air Force to get in, and to be
assigned to a combat unit despite being in his mid-30s. He became
first a squadron commander and later deputy group commander
of the 447th Bomb Group, flying 35 missions over Germany.
His wartime experience colored his later choice of roles when he
returned to Hollywood; from then on, he eschewed the "sunny"
stories he had appeared in before the war. (USAF Official)

Described as "the Huckleberry Finn of the Fourth Fighter Group," Ralph
Kidd Hofer joined the RCAF on a whim and scored on his first
mission after joining the 4th Fighter Group in 1943. He was lost
in an air battle over northern Yugoslavia during the group's shuttle
mission to the USSR and Italy in July 1944. (USAF Official)

First Lieutenant John T. Godfrey (left) and Captain Don S. Gentile (right),
photographed on March 3, 1944, at Debden in front of Gentile's
"Shangri-La." They were the subjects of an VIII Air Force publicity
campaign as "Damon and Pythias," leader and wingman. Godfrey
recalled in his memoir, *The Look of Eagles*, that they flew together on
fewer than half of the missions they flew. (USAF Official)

Colonel John T. Landers (center) in his P-51D, "Big Beautiful Doll,"
when he commanded the 78th Fighter Group in 1945. Graduating
from flight school the Monday after Pearl Harbor, Landers went
to Australia with the 49th Fighter Group, where he became an ace
over Darwin and New Guinea. He arrived in England in September
1943 with the 55th Fighter Group; later he served as a commander
of the 357th, and then took over the 78th Fighter Group when
it transitioned to the P-51. Landers is 26 years old in this photo.
(USAF Official)

P-51B "Snoots Sniper" of the 486th Fighter Squadron, 352nd Fighter Group in summer 1944. The British-designed bulged "Malcolm hood" vastly improved pilot visibility in the P-51B as compared with the "coffin lid" framed canopy. (USAF Official)

"Spokane Chief," the P-47C of Major Gene Roberts, CO 84th Fighter Squadron of the 78th Fighter Group, who led the group on the July 29, 1943, mission in which the Thunderbolts used a tail wind and stayed low to use all the fuel in their unpressurized ferry tanks in order to surprise the Luftwaffe 50 miles inside Germany, saving the bombers they were there to escort and proving that VIII Fighter Command could take on the enemy over their own territory. Roberts scored the first VIII Fighter Command "triple" on this mission. (USAF Official)

Group commander Lieutenant Colonel Jack Jenkins brought the 55th Fighter Group to England in 1943. Their P-38H Lightnings, like his "Texas Ranger" here, were vulnerable to the cold over Europe and to having an engine explode when the throttle was advanced too quickly after flying at a lower power setting. Serving with VIII Fighter Command in the ETO was the one time the P-38 didn't provide outstanding service. (USAF Official)

Though he is indelibly associated with the P-47 as the first commander of the 56th Fighter Group, the first P-47 unit, Colonel Hubert "Hub" Zemke was not wedded to any particular type. In June 1944, he suggested to General Kepner that successful group commanders be sent to less successful units to help turn them around. When the 479th Fighter Group's commander was lost in August, Zemke left the 56th to lead VIII Fighter Command's final fighter group and help it transition from the P-38 to the P-51. He was lost in October 1944 when his P-51 broke up in a thunderstorm over Germany, becoming the Senior Allied Officer at Stalag Luft III for the rest of the war. (USAF Official)

## MAPS

# FOREWORD
## BY BRIGADIER GENERAL USAF (RET.)
## CLARENCE "BUD" ANDERSON

The air war over Europe was hard and demanding. Between the first mission on August 7, 1942, and the final combat mission on April 29, 1945, the Eighth Air Force lost more men killed and wounded than the US Marines did between the first landing at Guadalcanal that same August 7, and the declaration the enemy was defeated on Okinawa in mid-June 1945.

VIII Fighter Command scored its first victory on August 19, 1942, over Dieppe. Between then and the final missions in late April 1945, two-thirds of all the enemy aircraft shot down by Air Force fighter pilots in World War II in all theaters were shot down in the skies over Europe. The command's struggle to become an effective fighter force that could provide the crucial protection for the bombers was epic on all levels – personal, organizational, and technical.

I was proud to be a member of that organization, most particularly a pilot in the 357th Fighter Group, "The Yoxford Boys" as we called ourselves after being welcomed to Europe in a broadcast by Lord Haw-Haw. In those first days of our war, the P-51 Mustang we flew was not the airplane it became: there were problems with the engine, the guns, and other operational difficulties we had to overcome as we took the battle to the enemy in the skies over Berlin and other cities.

Thomas McKelvey Cleaver tells this story in detail, with accounts from both sides of the battle that illuminate the struggle and put it on the human level of young men fighting like none before had ever fought – or ever would again. I am pleased to recommend *Clean Sweep: VIII Fighter Command Against the Luftwaffe 1942–45* as an honest account of our war.

Clarence "Bud" Anderson
Brigadier General USAF (Ret.)
357th Fighter Group, 363rd Fighter Squadron

# AUTHOR PREFACE

Here are some facts you should know: between August 19, 1942, when the first enemy airplane was shot down by a pilot in an VIII Fighter Command unit, and the end of operations over Germany on May 5, 1945, the 15 fighter groups fielded by that command were credited with the destruction of 9,000 enemy aircraft, in the air and on the ground. Twelve of the top 15 aces of the US Army Air Forces (USAAF) in all theaters served in VIII Fighter Command. Also, during that period, the Eighth Air Force suffered more casualties, killed and wounded, than the US Marine Corps did between the invasion of Guadalcanal on the 7th of that month in which the Eighth flew its first mission, through the entire Pacific campaign to the end of June 1945, when Okinawa was declared secure.

When I decided to become a screenwriter, a writer a bit further down that road told me that the way to get noticed and start one's career was to "Write the movie *you* want to see." This advice was quickly followed by the admonition, "Just know you'll never see it on the screen."

I chose to follow that advice and decided I would write the fighter pilot movie I had always wanted to see. The result, *Little Friends*, did get optioned by a then-hot young actor who was also a pilot, and he did show it around, and it did get me noticed. And it never got made. But researching it led me to meet some very remarkable people. A fellow aspiring writer read an early draft and told me he knew a producer who had been a fighter pilot, and provided me an introduction.

Jackson Barrett "Barry" Mahon grew up in southern California and learned to fly while in high school. In 1941 he joined the Royal Canadian Air Force, and a month before Pearl Harbor he arrived in

England, where he was assigned to 121 Eagle Squadron. By the end of July 1942, he was credited with shooting down four Fw-190s. On August 19, 1942, the three Eagle Squadrons flew together for the first time in the war, as part of the cover for the Dieppe Raid. At 0830 hours, he shot down his fifth Fw-190, then turned on the wingman and hit him before the element leader he hadn't spotted shot him up and he was forced to bail out, unluckily being fished out by the crew of a German torpedo boat who made him prisoner. At Stalag Luft III, he was the real "cooler king," and only missed taking part in what came to be known as "the Great Escape" because after 60 days in the cooler, punishment for his third escape, he wasn't in condition to go. In the years after the war, he entered the movie business as Errol Flynn's last agent, later making low-budget films. Barry took a liking to me, and proceeded to introduce me to his fellow Eagles and 4th Fighter Group pilots. It was the door into the world of the people whose stories populate this book.

Most prominent of these was the amazing Steve Pisanos, who lived up to Walter Cronkite's description of him as "the single most interesting individual I ever met in all of World War II," and became my friend for the next 34 years; top 4th ace Jim Goodson, the epitome of the "dashing fighter pilot" 40 years later; and Jim's "Sancho Panza" wingman Bob Wehrman – never an ace, Bob was a close observer of people, who provided insights into the pilots he flew with that brought the Eagles alive to me. Eventually, after putting me off for 15 years, their legendary leader Don Blakeslee gave in after I was recommended to him by my friend and his former neighbor, Air Apaches strafing king Vic Tatelman; he finally opened up on the realization that he'd run across a historian who really wanted to hear what he had to say.

Steve's introduction to his long-time friend Walter Cronkite gave entry to a productive afternoon's conversation learning the politics of the air war from an astute observer. Gladwyn Hill, who was Cronkite's opposite number for the Associated Press, turned out to live five miles from me; his stories of being a war correspondent with the Eighth Air Force also provided great insight.

Meeting and talking with Generals Adolf Galland, Gunther Rall, and Walter Krupinski opened the door to the "other side." Krupinski's story of his feelings just before ordering a "Twelve O'Clock High" attack into the American bombers was invaluable to understanding the Jagdwaffe's war. My long-time friendships through Planes of Fame with Me-262 pilots Jorg Czypionka and Hans Busch helped me gain understanding of the lives of the front-line pilots.

Forty-five years ago, Elmer E. "Mac" McTaggart taught me aerobatics and told me the story of how he set the record for escape and evasion back in 1943. His fellow 78th Group pilots Dick Hewitt, Ernie Russell, Hughie Lamb, and Wayne Coleman were each founts of information.

I was also fortunate, from my involvement at the Planes of Fame Air Museum, to know "Bud" Mahurin for 30 years. Bud always opened his presentations at the museum by saying, "I've crashed every plane I flew." That wasn't an admission of lack of ability, but rather the fact that this bold and aggressive pilot flew to the limits every time he climbed in a cockpit. Bud's never-ending supply of risqué humor brightened every meeting and his near-photographic recall of his fellow Wolfpack pilots was irreplaceable. His introduction to "Hub" Zemke allowed me to interview the other leading American fighter leader of the war.

Major "Chili" Williams was also a friend out at Chino, which was the only way I could ever have discovered his remarkable story as a photo-reconnaissance pilot.

Getting hired as the unit publicist's assistant on *The Right Stuff* led to meeting and becoming friends with one of my childhood heroes, Chuck Yeager. He was the only person I ever interviewed for whom I ran out of questions, we spoke so long!

It wasn't until years later that I realized I had grown up immersed in stories of the Eighth Air Force. Mr. Smith, who lived on the far corner from us on our block, had flown 30 missions in Liberators. My high school physics teacher, Mr. Kusel, flew 35 missions as a B-17 pilot. Mr. Allen, one of the leaders of Boy Scout Troop 242, flew 25 missions as a navigator. All three eventually relented and answered the questions from the curious kid who wanted to know about their war. Bert Stiles grew up around the corner and down South York Street from where I grew up 23 years later. I took piano lessons from his mother, and once – after I had given a good performance at a recital – she let me see the room she kept exactly the way he left it in 1944. I may well have been the only student at South Denver High School who looked up at the big brass plaque on the wall outside "Senior Hall" that held the names of students who died in the war, and was in awe of his. I think I am the only other writer to graduate from that school.

It is shocking to me to realize as I review this that every one of the people named here who told me their memories of this war is no longer with us. The world is a lesser place without them, and it is my privilege to be able to bring them "back to life" here.

Thomas McKelvey Cleaver
Encino, California
2022

# I

# THE MOST IMPORTANT DAY

The sky over the English Channel at midday on July 28, 1943, was partly cloudy, an early indicator that the past week of clear weather over northwestern Europe was coming to an end. Fifteen miles west of the Dutch coast, the 40 olive drab and gray, white-nosed P-47 Thunderbolts of the 78th Fighter Group eased their slow climb out of England behind them to 23,000 feet and leveled off to cross into enemy airspace ahead. Each big fighter carried a bulbous tank attached to its belly beneath the semi-elliptical wings. Standard Operating Procedure was for the fighters to make their entry into the enemy's air at 29,000 feet, above the flak. But this time, 84th Fighter Squadron commanding officer (CO), Major Gene Roberts, who led the formation, was attempting something new. He recalled:

> We started with the usual 48 fighters – three squadrons of 16 fighters per squadron. However, two of the pilots reported mechanical problems and had to abort as we crossed the English Channel. In each case, per our standard procedure at that time, I had to dispatch the aborting airplane's entire flight of four to provide an escort back to base. That left us with 40 fighters for the mission by the time we reached Holland.

Brand-new group commander Lieutenant Colonel Melvin F. McNickle flew beside Roberts as White Three element lead on this, his first mission. Deputy group commander Lieutenant Colonel James Stone was Red One of the second flight while Captain Jack C. Price, who had scored his first Fw-190 on July 14, was Blue One of the third flight. First Lieutenant Quince L. Brown – victor in his first air combat 30 days earlier – led the fourth flight as Yellow One; his wingman, Flight Officer Peter Pompetti, also a one-victory pilot, was known in the group as a "maverick."

Above Roberts' squadron, the 83rd Fighter Squadron flew high cover, led by Captain Charles P. London, Red One, the group's top scorer with three. Major Harry Dayhuff, another single-victory pilot, led the 82nd Fighter Squadron in the low position.

At this altitude, Roberts reckoned the Thunderbolts could draw the last of the fuel from the unpressurized ferry tanks they carried. For a fighter that was as thirsty for fuel as the P-47, every gallon mattered, as the pilots attempted to get as far into enemy territory as possible. The Thunderbolts crossed the coast north of Rotterdam, high enough that the sound of their roaring Pratt & Whitney R-2800, the P-47's powerplant, was unheard on the ground below. They flew past Nijmegen, where all the pilots switched to their internal fuel tanks as they pulled back on their sticks and followed Roberts up to 29,000 feet, where they leveled off and entered German airspace over Kleve. From this altitude, they could see the city of Haltern on the horizon. Roberts thanked the lucky tail wind they must have found for pushing them so far east. This was the deepest penetration of Germany yet made by VIII Fighter Command fighters. Only the day before, the 4th Fighter Group had used the troublesome, unpressurized belly tanks for the first time to set a new penetration record, making it as far east as the German border. Roberts' decision to delay climbing to penetration altitude as long as possible was proven right as – for the first time ever – American fighter pilots looked down from their cockpits on western Germany. Their mission was withdrawal support to bring the bombers out of Germany, after which the Debden Eagles of the 4th would provide final cover across the Channel.

Good summer flying weather in the latter part of July 1943 had allowed VIII Bomber Command to mount 14 strikes ever deeper into Germany since July 24, the first sustained air offensive by the Eighth Air Force against Germany proper since the Americans had commenced operations from southern England a year earlier. Eighth Air Force leaders saw it as the opening blow of the Combined Bomber

Offensive that would over the next ten months prepare the way for the cross-Channel invasion and the liberation of Europe. The seven days of good weather would be known among the aircrews afterwards as "Little Blitz Week." Today, July 28, the "blitz" would end with three missions against the Focke-Wulf factories at Oschersleben, Warnemünde, and Kassel, respectively. They were deep penetration missions beyond the range of escort fighters, and drew maximum opposition from the German defenders.

One group of bombers executed a feint in the direction of much-bombed Hamburg-Kiel, then swung inland toward Oschersleben, 90 miles south-southwest of Berlin. Despite a cloud deck over the target, 28 B-17s bombed the A.G.O. Flugzeugwerk – a major Fw-190 constructor – when a small hole in the nine-tenths cloud cover opened and the lead bombardier was able to recognize a crossroad only a few miles from the aiming point. Calculating quickly, he dropped by timing the flight to the group's ETA. The next day, reconnaissance photos showed a tight concentration of hits on the target. British intelligence estimated that the attack, despite being only 67.9 tons, resulted in four weeks' loss of production. The Flying Fortresses were able to head into the westerly wind at 22,000 feet, thankful that the wind allowed them to continue straight on for home. As the bombers came out of the flak field over the city, defending German pilots in Bf-109 and Fw-190 fighters slashed through the bomber boxes. Defending gunners in the bombers fired at the gray fighters as they streaked through the formations, cannon flashing. Three Fortresses were hit, catching fire and heading down. The sky filled with blossoming parachutes. A B-17 in the lead box took hits in an engine and dropped below, out of formation; the pilot added power to the three engines left as he desperately tried to keep up with the squadron for protection.

The bombers neared Haltern, where rocket-armed Bf-110G twin-engine fighters attacked from the rear, firing their missiles outside the range of the bombers' defensive fire. The missiles were far from accurate, but if one rocket found its mark and the B-17 it hit exploded in the middle of the formation, it might take down a second and damage others.

At that moment, the 78th arrived on the scene. Roberts spotted the enemy fighters. "We were outnumbered by at least three-to-one odds but were able to maneuver into attacking position with very little difficulty. The main reason for this success was that the German fighter pilots didn't believe we could possibly show up that far inland and were not expecting to see a defensive force at all."

The American pilots took full advantage of German confusion. Roberts remembered:

> There was one B-17 beneath the main formation, and it was being attacked by around five German fighters. The bomber was pouring smoke and appeared to be in deep trouble. From my position in the lead of the group, I dove down on the enemy fighters that were attacking the cripple. However, the Germans saw us, broke away, and dived for the ground. There wasn't much more we could do to help the crippled B-17, so I pulled up on the starboard side of the main bomber formation, about 1,000 yards out. I discovered on reaching this position that my second element – Lieutenant Colonel McNickle and his wingman – had broken away and was no longer with me. I had only myself and my wingman, Flight Officer Glenn Koontz. We immediately saw enemy aircraft ahead of us and above the formation. I judged that there were over 100 enemy aircraft in the area, as compared with our 40.

Unknown to Roberts, McNickle had suffered an oxygen system failure and collided with his wingman, First Lieutenant James Byers. Incredibly, McNickle survived the resulting crash, regaining consciousness to find the airplane upside-down, with members of the Dutch Resistance attempting to free him. With two broken shoulders and other serious wounds, he was turned over to the Germans, who denied him medical care for several days in an attempt to get information. McNickle survived two years' imprisonment and emerged from captivity in 1945. With his loss, Jim Stone – who had been in command prior to his arrival – once again became group commander. He would hold the position over the next year.

Roberts and Koontz came across a gaggle of Focke-Wulfs:

> Dead ahead of me was a single Fw-190, at the same level as Koontz and me, about 1,000 to 1,500 yards ahead. He was racing in the same direction as the bombers so he could get ahead of them, swing around in front, and make a head-on pass. The bombers were most

vulnerable from dead ahead. The Germans referred to this tactic as "queuing up."

Roberts dived slightly below the enemy fighter to avoid being spotted, then closed to 400 yards and opened fire, hitting the German heavily with a three to five-second burst. "The Focke-Wulf's wheels dropped and it spun down in smoke and flames." Roberts spotted two more. "They were about 2,000 yards in front of me, heading out so they could peel off and come back through the bomber formation." Roberts closed so fast he had to pull up and roll in on his second victim to avoid a collision. "I opened fire from dead astern. I observed several strikes and, as before, the enemy fighter billowed smoke and flames, rolled over, and spun down." Amazingly, Roberts and Koontz were still in the middle of the action:

After the second engagement, we were about two miles ahead of the bombers, about 500 feet above them, and still well out to their starboard side. Koontz was on my right wing. About this time, I observed a '109 on the port side and ahead of the bomber formation. I dropped below the bomber formation, crossed over to the port side, and pulled up behind him, again at full throttle.

As Roberts closed on this third enemy fighter, the 109 suddenly executed a starboard 180-degree turn to attack the bombers head-on. Roberts followed as the bomber formation loomed beyond the German. "I closed to within 400 or 500 yards and opened fire. He was in a tight turn, and that required deflection shooting. My first two bursts fell away behind him, but I continued to close. I fired my third burst as he straightened out to approach the bombers." This caught the enemy fighter from dead astern within 150 yards of the bombers; it fell over into a spin, trailing smoke and flame. While Roberts dispatched his third victory, wingman Koontz flamed the wingman Roberts had failed to spot.

"We were now at the same level as the bombers and approaching them from head-on. We had no alternative but to fly between the two main formations, which were about two miles apart. Bless their hearts, they did not fire." Roberts then spotted two 109s attacking a P-47:

They were all heading 180 degrees to me, so I couldn't close effectively to help. I did fire a burst at the leading German, but without enough deflection. The P-47 dove and took evasive action. I didn't see him or the Germans again. I headed out and joined up with a loose element from the 84th, and we headed home together.

Gene Roberts had just scored the first triple victory by an Eighth Air Force fighter pilot.

Everyone else was equally busy. Top-scorer Charles London caught two Fw-190s at 26,000 feet, flaming the leader and diving to avoid the wingman. Zooming back up to 28,000 feet he spotted a Bf-109 and hit it in its engine, setting it afire. With this victory, London was the first VIII Fighter Command ace.

Quince Brown and Peter Pompetti spotted a flight of four Bf-109s and hit them from the rear; Brown damaged the leader while Pompetti fired on the remaining three. As he made a high-G turn, five of Brown's eight guns jammed; with only three still working, he hit the wingman on the right in the cockpit, killing the enemy pilot before breaking off to avoid a collision.

Captain Jack Price came across a flight of Fw-190s and flamed the leader. He turned into the enemy element leader and opened fire with his wingman, Second Lieutenant John Bertrand; each hit one of the three remaining 190s, which both went down out of control.

Lieutenant Colonel Stone hit a Bf-109 that blew up so close that his wingman, Second Lieutenant Julius Maxwell, flew through the explosion.

82nd Squadron commander Dayhuff spotted a Bf-109 making a beam attack on the bombers; closing astern, the German blew up under his fire.

Suddenly, the sky was clear of enemy fighters.

The battle had been an intense ten minutes and the Thunderbolts broke off while they still had gas to return to their Duxford home. No more B-17s were lost after the 78th's P-47s engaged. The B-17s were soon picked up by the 4th Fighter Group and taken home safe.

For a cost of seven P-47s lost in the melée, the 78th was credited with 16 victories. Added to the eight credited to the 56th and 4th groups, the day's battles doubled VIII Fighter Command's total score to date. Charles London had become an ace, while Gene Roberts had scored the first "triple."

Overall, the missions cost 22 B-17s and their crews, with the force sent to Oschersleben losing 15 of the 39 that bombed the target. Leutnant Heinz Knoke's 5.Staffel, Jagdgeschwader 11 (5./JG 11, 5th squadron of Fighter Wing 11) employed W.Gr.21 rockets and scored the first real success with them. One rocket hit a B-17 with a direct hit that caused it to crash into two others, with all three going down. Claims by the defending gunners bore witness to the intensity of the fighting, with the Oschersleben force claiming 56 enemy aircraft destroyed, 19 probably destroyed, and 41 damaged; all claims from both groups totaled 83/34/63.27. The Jagdwaffe's actual loss was 15, which was primarily due to the intervention of the 78th's P-47s.

July 28, 1943, is the most important date in the history of VIII Fighter Command. For the first time, American fighters found and attacked superior enemy fighter forces over Germany, scored heavily with minimal losses, and protected the bombers. It was a sign of things to come.

# 2

# WAR ON THE HORIZON

In April 1936, Brigadier General Stanley D. Embick, one of the US Army's rising stars, opined that it was inadvisable to have a long-range bomber "since this would give rise to the suspicion, both at home and abroad, that our GHQ [General Headquarters] Air Force was being maintained for aggressive purposes."

Embick was specifically referring to the result of the Air Corps Request for Proposals issued on August 8, 1934, for a multi-engine bomber to replace the Martin B-10. It was to be capable of reinforcing the air forces in Hawaii, Panama, and Alaska, with a suggested range of 2,000 miles and a suggested top speed of 250 miles per hour, while carrying a "useful bomb load" at an altitude of 10,000 feet for ten hours. Significantly, the design circular did not specifically mention the number of engines.

Douglas Aircraft responded with the DB-1, a military version of its successful twin-engine DC-3 airline, while Martin Aircraft put forth the Model 146, which was an improved B-10. Boeing Aircraft in Seattle presented the Model 299. The then-enormous design would be of all-metal construction, with retractable landing gear and a bomb load of an astounding 4,000 pounds, and would be powered by no fewer than four engines. All three produced prototypes at their own expense, which flew in 1935. Boeing demonstrated the capabilities of the Model 299 by flying it non-stop from Seattle to Wright Field in Dayton, Ohio, on August 20, 1935, in nine hours and three minutes at an average cruising speed of 252 miles per hour.

At the fly-off, the Model 299 was clearly superior to the DB-1 and Model 146. GHQ Air Force commander Major General Frank Maxwell Andrews (a man so important in Air Force history that he is the only individual who gave his name to two Air Force bases, Maxwell and Andrews airfields), believed that the Model 299 was better suited to the emerging Air Corps doctrine of strategic bombing. The Air Corps agreed with him and before the competition finished, it was suggested the Air Corps purchase 65 of the aircraft, to be known as the YB-17.

On October 20, 1935, test pilot Major Ployer Peter Hill and Boeing employee Les Tower took the Model 299 on a second evaluation flight, but forgot to disengage the "gust locks" that locked the control surfaces in place while parked on the ground. The Model 299 lifted off and entered a steep climb, stalled, nosed over, and crashed, killing Hill and Tower, while the other observers aboard survived with injuries.

With the crash, the Model 299 was disqualified since it could not finish the evaluation. The design was not at fault in the accident, and the Air Corps remained enthusiastic about the big bomber. However, Army procurement officials were daunted by its cost. Douglas quoted a unit price of $58,200 ($1.1 million today) for a production order of 220 aircraft, compared with $99,620 ($1.88 million today) for 65 Model 299s. Army Chief of Staff General Malin Craig canceled the order for 65 YB-17s, and ordered 133 Douglas DB-1s as the B-18.

Regardless of the 299's crash, the GHQ Air Force remained impressed. While the Model 299 never received a military serial, the B-17 designation appeared officially on January 17, 1936, when the Model 299 was retroactively termed "XB-17." General Andrews had found a legal loophole in the Army procurement regulations and convinced the Air Corps to order 13 YB-17s (designated Y1B-17 after November 1936 to denote special "F-1" funding) for service testing on that day. The YB-17 incorporated a number of significant changes from the Model 299, including more powerful engines. Twelve of the Y1B-17s were delivered between March 1 and August 4, 1937, to the 2nd Bombardment Group at Langley Field in Virginia for operational development and flight tests, where crews immediately adopted the suggestion that a preflight checklist be used to avoid accidents such as the one that had befallen the Model 299. In one of their first missions, General Andrews sent three of the bombers – directed by lead navigator First Lieutenant Curtis LeMay – to "intercept" and photograph the

Italian ocean liner *Rex* 610 miles off the Atlantic coast. The mission was successful and widely publicized, leading to a renewed battle between the Army and the Navy over which service bore responsibility for coastal defense, with the result that in early 1937 now-Major General and Deputy Chief of Staff Embick issued a second statement that "Our national policy contemplates preparation for defense, not aggression. Defense of sea areas, other than within the coastal zone, is a function of the Navy. The military superiority of a B-17 over the two or three smaller planes that could be procured with the same funds remains to be established." Following that, Secretary of War Harry H. Woodring canceled planned production of more B-17s in fiscal year 1939 on the grounds that they cost too much and were not needed.

At the time that General Embick first declared the role of the Army Air Corps, the service's pursuit squadrons were equipped with the Boeing P-26, the service's first all-metal monoplane, still with an open cockpit, and spatted landing gear, armed with two .30-caliber machine guns and capable of a top speed of 234 miles per hour, carrying fuel for a combat range of 360 miles; some squadrons still flew P-6E and P-12E biplanes. In May 1935, Willi Messerschmitt's new Bf-109 fighter, with an enclosed cockpit and retractable landing gear, had first flown in prototype form, also armed with two rifle-caliber machine guns, its British Kestrel engine powering it to a then-blistering 280 miles per hour. That November, Sir Sidney Camm's Hurricane fighter took to the skies; still fabric-covered, it used retractable gear, had an enclosed cockpit and was designed to carry no fewer than eight .30-caliber machine guns; it produced a speed of nearly 300 miles per hour from its new Rolls-Royce P.V.12 engine, soon to be called the "Merlin." A month before Embick defined American military aviation, R.J. Mitchell's amazingly graceful Type 300, another all-metal monoplane with enclosed cockpit and retractable landing gear, also powered by the new Rolls-Royce engine, flew on March 5, 1936. The next month, the Hawker prototype received the name "Hurricane" while Mitchell's fighter received the name "Spitfire," which he detested only slightly less than the alternative, "Shrew."

Not everyone in the Air Corps was as blind to the world situation and its possibilities as General Embick. In 1934 – the same year that the German Air Ministry ordered Focke-Wulf, Arado, and (belatedly) Messerschmitt to design modern fighters for a competition to equip the then-secret Luftwaffe, while the British Air Ministry issued Specification F.5/34 to Sir Sydney Camm for his proposed "interceptor" and agreed to finance R.J. Mitchell's private venture Model 300 for 10,000 pounds sterling – the Air Corps' Air Materiel Division had issued a circular requesting design proposals for a new fighter to replace the P-26. It specifically required retractable landing gear and all-metal construction, the prototypes to be tested in a fly-off competition in 1935, which was delayed to 1936 to allow the respondents time to construct their prototypes. The result had been all-metal monoplanes with enclosed cockpits and retractable gear from Northrop Aviation, the Seversky Aircraft Corporation, and the Curtiss-Wright Corporation; the Northrop design did not compete due to its loss in company testing, while the designs from Seversky and Curtiss became, respectively, the P-35 and P-36. While the P-35 "won" the competition and received an order for 76 aircraft, the P-36 became the recipient in 1938 of an order for 200, the largest Air Corps order for a fighter since World War I.

On January 28, 1938, President Franklin D. Roosevelt launched a program for the buildup of airpower in reaction to a secret report by Charles A. Lindbergh of the growing Axis threat and expansion of the Luftwaffe as a result of his well-publicized visits to Germany. At a remarkable meeting that day, the president ordered the Air Corps to develop a program for the production of 10,000 airplanes, stating that "he didn't want to hear about ground forces, that a new barracks at some post in Wyoming would not scare Hitler one goddamned bit."

In response to the president's order, the Air Corps approached Consolidated Aircraft Corporation in San Diego with a proposal for the company to produce the B-17 under license. After company president Reuben Fleet and his senior executives visited the Boeing factory in Seattle, Washington, Fleet instead directed his design staff to submit a more modern design. The Model 32 was designed around David R. Davis's high-efficiency airfoil wing design, with the twin-tail design from the Consolidated Model 31 flying boat, and a new fuselage that was intentionally designed around twin bomb bays, each one being the same size and capacity as the B-17's single bomb bay. In January 1939, the Air Corps asked Consolidated to submit a formal design study for a bomber possessing longer range, higher speed, and greater ceiling than the B-17. The Air Corps specification was written in such a way that the Model 32 would be the winning design, receiving the designation B-24.

The Davis wing gave what Consolidated called "the Liberator" a high cruise speed, long range, and the capability of carrying a 10,000-pound bomb load. However, although the thick wing could provide increased fuel tankage while providing increased lift and higher speed, the wing made the airplane unpleasant to fly when operationally equipped at heavier wing loadings. At high altitude and in bad weather, the Davis wing was also more susceptible to ice formation than that of the B-17, which caused distortion of the airfoil section with a resulting loss of lift; it drew comments such as "The Davis wing won't hold enough ice to chill your drink." However, when the RAF received early models of the Liberator, they became the first aircraft to fly the Atlantic non-stop as a matter of routine.

In comparison with both the B-17 and the RAF's Lancaster heavy bomber, the B-24 was physically difficult to fly, with heavy controls and poor low-speed performance. Once armed and armored to operational requirements, it had a lower operational ceiling and was more susceptible to battle damage than the notoriously tough B-17. Aircrews preferred the B-17, while the USAAF General Staff favored the B-24; eventually, 18,500 B-24s – including 8,685 manufactured by Ford Motor Company in its massive River Rouge factory in Detroit – were produced, making the B-24 in all its sub-types the most-produced bomber, heavy bomber, multi-engine aircraft, and American military aircraft in history.

Just before the president's 1938 instruction, but still adhering to the official position that the purpose of the Air Corps was defensive, Circular Proposal X-608, a set of aircraft performance goals authored by First Lieutenants Benjamin S. Kelsey and Gordon P. Saville for a twin-engined, high-altitude "interceptor" for "the tactical mission of interception and attack of hostile aircraft at high altitude" – was issued in February 1937.

Born February 27, 1910, in the remote mining town of Ishpeming, Michigan, where his Swedish-immigrant father ran a construction company, Clarence Johnson was ridiculed for his name in elementary school, with some boys calling him "Clara." While waiting in line one day to get into class, one boy started up the name-calling and Johnson tripped him so hard the boy broke a leg. The others then started calling him "Kelly," from a popular song at the time, "Has Anyone Here Seen Kelly? (Kelly from the Emerald Isle)." He was Kelly Johnson ever after.

Smitten by aviation when an airplane landed in his town in 1916, he won a prize at age 13 for designing a rubber-band-powered airplane that flew further than other entries.

Majoring in aeronautical engineering at the University of Michigan, Johnson conducted wind tunnel tests of Lockheed's proposed Model 10 airliner and found it lacked adequate directional stability; however, his professor – who had been hired by Lockheed to conduct the tests – felt it was stable and informed Lockheed accordingly. After completing his master's in 1933, Johnson joined Lockheed as a tool designer for a salary of $83 a month. Soon after, he convinced Chief Engineer Hall Hibbard that the Model 10 was unstable. Hibbard sent Johnson back to Michigan to conduct more tests; he eventually changed the wind tunnel model to have twin rudders directly behind the engines, to address the problem. Lockheed accepted his change and the Model 10 went on to become successful as the "Electra," while Johnson was promoted to aeronautical engineer. After assignments as flight test engineer, stress analyst, aerodynamicist, and weight engineer, he became chief research engineer in 1938. The first project he was handed was designing the proposed high-altitude interceptor in response to Circular Proposal X-608.

In 1975, then-retired General Ben Kelsey explained that when he and Saville drew up the specification, they used the word "interceptor" as a way to bypass the inflexible Army Air Corps requirement for pursuit aircraft to carry no more than 500 pounds of armament including ammunition, and to avoid the restriction of single-seat aircraft to one engine. Kelsey and Saville were looking for a minimum of 1,000 pounds of armament and wanted to get a more capable fighter, better at dog fighting and at high-altitude combat. The circular's specifications called for a maximum airspeed of at least 360 miles per hour at altitude, and a climb to 20,000 feet within six minutes; at the time this was the toughest set of specifications the Air Corps had ever put forward.

Since it was only expected that any order for a successful prototype would involve no more than around 60 aircraft, Kelly made no bargains with ease of production in the design he created. Working under Hibbard's overall management, he considered a range of twin-engined configurations, including putting both engines in a central fuselage with push–pull propellers as the Luftwaffe ultimately did with the Do-335. Eventually, he chose a design featuring twin booms to accommodate the engines, turbosuperchargers, and tail, with a central nacelle housing the pilot and armament.

The XP-38 was designed to be armed with two .50-caliber M2 Browning machine guns with 200 rounds per gun, two .30-caliber weapons with 500 rounds per gun, and an Army Ordnance T-1 23mm cannon with a rotary magazine substituted for the non-existent 25mm Hotchkiss aircraft cannon specified by Kelsey and Saville. Armament was changed in the 12 YP-38s to a 37mm M9 cannon with 15 rounds in place of the T1; the M9 did not perform reliably in flight, and further armament experiments between March and June 1941 resulted in the final configuration of four M2 Browning machine guns with 500 rounds per gun and one Hispano 20mm cannon with 150 rounds. Putting the entire armament in the nose meant that the guns did not have their useful range limited by pattern convergence; a P-38 pilot could reliably hit targets at any range up to 1,000 yards with a combined rate of fire of over 4,000rpm with every sixth projectile a 20mm shell.

The design featured two 1,000hp, turbosupercharged Allison V-1710 liquid-cooled engines fitted with counter-rotating propellers to eliminate torque, with the turbochargers positioned behind the engines, exhausting along the dorsal surfaces of the booms. It was the first Army aircraft to feature a tricycle landing gear, and also the first American fighter to make extensive use of stainless steel and smooth, flush-riveted, butt-jointed aluminum skin panels. To top things off, the XP-38 was also the first military airplane in the world to fly faster than 400 miles per hour in level flight.

Lockheed's Model 22 design was declared the winner on June 23, 1937, and the Air Corps commissioned a single prototype, the XP-38, for $163,000. Construction began in July 1938 in an old bourbon distillery in Burbank, California, purchased by Lockheed to house expanding operations. Johnson later designated this secure and remote site the first of five Lockheed Skunk Works locations. Ben Kelsey made the XP-38's first flight on January 27, 1939. The prototype demonstrated such outstanding performance that Kelsey proposed a long-distance speed record flight to Wright Field to relocate the XP-38 for further testing. The record attempt was approved by newly promoted Air Corps commander General Henry H. "Hap" Arnold, who recommended a flight to New York City. On February 11, 1939, Kelsey flew from Burbank to New York in seven hours and two minutes, not counting two refueling stops. He flew conservatively, working the engines gently and even throttling back during descent to remove the associated speed advantage. During his final refueling stop at Wright Field, General Arnold congratulated Kelsey and said, "Don't spare the horses" on the next leg. After reaching altitude, Kelsey pushed the XP-38 to 420 miles per hour. As he neared his destination at Mitchell Field, the control tower ordered Kelsey into a slow landing pattern behind other aircraft, which resulted in the prototype crashing short of the runway due to carburetor icing. Although the prototype was a total loss, the Air Corps ordered 13 YP-38s on April 27, 1939, for $134,284 each, on the basis of the record flight.

At the same time that they had produced Circular Proposal X-608 for a twin-engine "interceptor," Kelsey and Saville had hedged their bet with Circular Proposal X-609 for a single-engine high-altitude interceptor. One company had responded, Bell Aircraft, with a proposal for a radical fighter with its engine buried in the fuselage behind the pilot, allowing the nose to accommodate a heavy bomber-destroying armament of a 37mm cannon and two .50-caliber machine guns, with a turbocharger in the rear fuselage and using a tricycle nose-wheel landing gear for the first time in any single-engine fighter. With the turbocharger, Bell promised a top speed of over 400 miles per hour at 25,000 feet. The proposal was quickly accepted by the Air Corps with an order for a prototype designated XP-39, to which Bell gave the emotive name "Airacobra." Unfortunately, during the detail design of the prototype, less-imaginative Air Corps officers, still committed to the idea of the "defensive-only" air force, ordered Bell to remove the turbocharger, since they saw the airplane with its heavy armament as a useful ground attack fighter to oppose an invading enemy army. Thus, the fighter Bell created – which was later lauded by pilots who flew it such as Chuck Yeager, who recalled it as his "favorite" for its excellent performance below 10,000 feet altitude – was defective from the beginning and would be cursed by the pilots forced to try to fight in it at higher altitudes where air combat increasingly occurred. The need of an effective high-altitude single-engine fighter remained unfulfilled, but this would soon change.

By 1939, Seversky Aircraft had become Republic Aviation. As with many visionaries, Alexander P. Seversky was not a successful manager. Following the "victory" at the fighter fly-off in 1936, he had purchased three factories and an airfield and hangar, with a seaplane assembly base, at Farmingdale and Amityville on Long Island. When it became known that Seversky had negotiated a secret contract with the Japanese for 20 SEV-2PA fighters, the Air Corps stopped procurement of the P-35 at 76 aircraft. Bankruptcy was avoided in 1938 when Paul Moore, brother and heir of Edward Moore who had been the source of Seversky's initial financing, refinanced the company with the proviso that Seversky would have his budget cut as president, with day-to-day control by managing director Wallace Kellett. When Seversky made a European sales tour, the board of directors reorganized the company in his absence as Republic Aviation Corporation with Kellett the new president on October 13, 1939.

Seversky's most important decision had been to hire Alexander Kartveli as a designer. Born Alexander Kartvelishvili in Tblisi, Georgia, on September 9, 1896, he moved to Paris shortly before the outbreak of World War I to study aeronautical engineering and graduated in 1922 from the Highest School of Aviation in Paris. Between 1922 and 1927, he designed the Bernard and Ferbois aircraft for the Louis Blériot company; one of his aircraft established a world speed record in 1924, demonstrating his gifts as a designer. Following this success, in 1928 American millionaire Charles Levine invited him to come to New York and join the Atlantic Aircraft Corporation. He met Seversky in 1931 and went to work for his fellow Georgian, "Americanizing" his name to Kartveli. He designed the SEV-3, from which he created the P-35.

Kartveli was interested in increasing the altitude capability of the P-35, and convinced the Air Corps to approve turning the last P-35 into the XP-41, powered by a Pratt & Whitney R-1830-19 engine equipped with a two-speed supercharger and revised, inward-retracting landing gear. At the same time, he created the AP-4, which was rolled out shortly after the company's reorganization and name change to Republic. Powered by a Pratt & Whitney R-1830 engine with a belly-mounted Boeing-developed turbocharger, the AP-4 had excellent high-altitude performance and an effective oxygen system. The Air Corps ordered 272 as the P-43, naming it "Lancer."

All Kartveli's designs to that point had excellent range, due to Seversky's demand that they use a "wet wing" as a gas tank. The P-35 had a range of 1,000 miles, and the P-43 not much less. The newly named United States Army Air Forces canceled further production in 1942 due to leakage in the wing tanks, though this problem was solved in the field when the P-43 arrived in China, where it served effectively in combat with the Republic of China Air Force until replaced in 1944.

At the time that the Air Corps bought the P-43, Kartveli was already at work on the P-44 "Rocket," a development of the P-43 with a more powerful engine. In late 1939, in answer to complaints that his designs weighed too much, he commenced design of the AP-10, a lightweight fighter powered by the Allison V-1710 liquid-cooled engine, armed with an astounding eight .50-caliber machine guns. The Air Corps became interested and backed the project, giving it the designation XP-47. But by the spring of 1940, both Kartveli and the Air Corps had concluded that both the XP-44 and the XP-47 were inferior to Luftwaffe fighters. Kartveli tried improving the XP-47, proposing the XP-47A, which failed to gain interest. Then, looking to the 1938 specification in Circular Proposal X-609 for a single-engine, high-altitude interceptor, which had yet to be fulfilled, he offered a new design.

The Air Corps ordered a prototype in September 1940, designating it XP-47B, though it had virtually nothing in common with either the XP-47 or the XP-47A. The design was all-metal save for fabric-covered elevators and rudder, with a semi-elliptical wing that went back to the P-35 and had been used on the P-41 and P-43. Significantly, because it was to be a point-defense interceptor, the wing was not designed as a gas tank; fuel was carried only in the fuselage with main and auxiliary self-sealing fuel tanks placed under the cockpit with a total fuel capacity of 305 US gallons, deemed more than sufficient for its intended role as an interceptor. An armament of eight .50-caliber machine guns with 500 rounds per gun filled the wing outboard of the wheel wells for the wide-track landing gear.

The powerplant was the brand-new Pratt & Whitney R-2800 Double Wasp two-row, 18-cylinder radial engine producing 2,000hp, using a four-bladed Curtiss Electric constant-speed propeller, 12 feet, two inches in diameter. The engine cowling ducted cooling air for the engine, the left and right oil coolers, and the turbosupercharger intercooler system. Engine exhaust gases routed into a pair of pipes running along each side of the cockpit provided power to drive the turbosupercharger turbine located in the lower rear fuselage. When operating at full power, the pipes glowed red at their forward ends, spinning the turbine at

21,300rpm. The ductwork and turbosupercharger gave the XP-47B a deep fuselage, requiring the wings to be mounted in a relatively high position. This in turn meant using long-legged main landing gear struts to provide ground clearance for the enormous propeller. In order to assure sufficient room in the wings for the guns, the gear legs were fitted with a mechanism that telescoped the strut nine inches when extended. The resulting XP-47B had an empty weight of 9,900 pounds, 65 percent more than the P-43; it would be the heaviest single-seat fighter used operationally during the war.

Republic test pilot Lowry P. Brabham first flew the XP-47B on May 6, 1941, by which time it had been given the name "Thunderbolt." The prototype proved impressive in early trials, with only minor problems, but was lost in an accident on August 8, 1942; by then it had shown a level speed of 412 miles per hour at 25,800 feet and demonstrated a climb from sea level to 15,000 feet in five minutes. However, while the XP-47B gave the Army Air Forces cause for optimism, the airplane had its share of teething problems that caused an equal amount of apprehension.

The president's message to Congress on January 12, 1939, issued in the aftermath of the Munich Conference the previous September, with conflict now threatening in Europe and an undeclared war raging in China as the result of Japanese aggression, asked for a much larger appropriation to strengthen the military establishment. This time, funding for Air Corps requirements constituted more than half the total requests and marked the beginning of a period of Air Corps expansion which did not reach its peak until 1944. Asserting that "increased range, increased speed, increased capacity of airplanes abroad have changed our requirement for defensive action," President Roosevelt strongly urged that $300,000,000 be appropriated for the purchase of aircraft for the Army and Navy.

At the outbreak of World War II in September 1939, the United States was well down on the list of military powers. The US Army, with a strength of 174,000, was 19th in the rankings of ground forces, putting it – according to historian Eric Larrabee – "ahead of Bulgaria but just behind Portugal." The US Army Air Corps was rated fourth or fifth in the relative standings.

The National Defense Act adopted in April 1939, following the German takeover that March of what was left of Czechoslovakia and the British issuance of a guarantee to Poland which convinced a sufficient number of Members of Congress that an emergency was indeed on the horizon, had approved a strength of 5,500 airplanes for the Air Corps, with a top limit of 6,000. At the outbreak of war on September 1, 1939, the Air Corps had a personnel strength of only 26,000 and possessed some 1,200 bombers and fighters, the majority of them obsolete and none – other than the P-36 that had entered service in 1938 and also been ordered by the French Air Force – capable of entering combat against a European air power like Germany. Pilots in first-line operational units in Hawaii and the Philippines were still flying the open-cockpit P-26.

In May 1940, the president called for an air force of 50,000 airplanes – 36,500 airplanes for the Air Corps, 13,500 for the Navy – and production of 50,000 airplanes a year. Eddie Rickenbacker, America's "ace of aces" from World War I, said that the United States was ten years behind Germany in military aviation development. The only edge the Air Corps could claim was the B-17, but there were only 42 of those.

To take advantage of approved increases in aircraft and personnel, the Air Corps in the spring of 1939 formulated a plan calling for 24 tactical groups to be combat-ready by June 30, 1941. Before this objective was reached, however, the trend of events abroad urged further expansion, and in May 1940 the Air Corps projected a force of 41 groups. By July, the goal was again revised upward in the 54-group program, which foresaw an air force of 4,000 tactical aircraft, 187,000 enlisted men, 15,000 aviation cadets, and 16,800 officers. In September 1941, an 84-group program was announced in anticipation of the vast expansion contemplated in the as-yet unapproved Victory Program for munitions.

The aircraft industry was asked to expand from its normal capacity of some 2,000 planes a year to more than 4,000 a month. Aircraft production in 1940 showed an increase of 250 percent over 1939.

By the summer of 1941, with the clock ticking down toward Pearl Harbor, the personnel strength of the Army Air Forces was 152,125, and the service possessed 6,777 aircraft, of which 120 were heavy bombers, 903 were light and medium bombers, and 1,018 were fighters. Even that total was inflated with substantial numbers of obsolete bombers and fighters.

While the general public was largely isolationist in sentiment at the time that war broke out in Europe, between then and Pearl Harbor it had, for the most part, come to recognize the threat. Many young Americans, sensing that a war was coming, chose to enter the military during this time, when the possibility of choice of service was still available. Both the Navy and the Air Corps built up their flight training programs and more young men became aviation cadets or joined for the opportunity of technical training. This change in public opinion was in reality a psychological preparation for war; it was brought about by the sheer logic of events abroad, particularly the fall of France in June 1940, which led to passage of the Selective Service Act and institution of the country's first peacetime draft that summer, and the Battle of Britain that followed. This psychological preparation was the most important single factor in improving national defense before the outbreak of war.

Pilot training goals were successively raised to keep pace with the anticipated progress of other defense programs. From a 1939 plan calling for the training of 1,200 pilots a year, the figure was raised in 1940 to 7,000, then to 12,000, and in February 1941 to 30,000. By September 1941, when the 84-group program was under discussion, the Army Air Forces contemplated training 50,000 pilots a year by mid-1942.

At the time of Pearl Harbor, no one in the upper reaches of the Army Air Forces paid much attention to the two fighters that had been delivered to Wright Field by North American Aviation; they had been designed and built for the Royal Air Force (RAF), who called them "Mustang." In the summer of 1940, the British Purchasing Commission had approached James H. "Dutch" Kindelberger, president of North American Aviation (NAA), with a proposal for the then little-known company to produce license-built copies of the Curtiss P-40, a fighter developed from the P-36, with which the British planned to equip the RAF. Kindelberger turned them down, saying he didn't want to produce an "obsolete airplane" and suggesting to them that his company could deliver a world-beating fighter of original design.

The myth of the Mustang's creation is recurring in aviation history. In October 1981, at a conference honoring the 40th anniversary of the prototype's first flight, designer Edgar Schmued was asked about the story that the airplane had been designed and built within 100 days. "The first Mustang was indeed built in a hundred days," he replied, "but I had been designing it for five years before."

Born in 1901, Edgar Schmued fell in love with aviation when he saw an airplane fly in his native Germany at age eight. From then on, he was dedicated to the idea of becoming an aviation engineer. Self-taught, he became an apprentice in a small aircraft engine manufacturing company during the last year of World War I. With the Versailles Treaty having crippled aviation development in postwar Germany, he left for Brazil in 1925 and took a job with the General Aviation Company, the aviation branch of General Motors Corporation's Brazilian subsidiary. He built a reputation for solid work, and in 1931 he was brought to the United States by General Motors (GM), where he achieved his dream of becoming an aircraft designer at the Fokker Aircraft Corporation of America, now owned by GM. In 1934, GM sold Fokker to the North American Aviation holding company, which had been founded in 1928 to buy and sell interests in airlines and other aviation-related companies. The Air Mail Act of 1934 ended such companies; NAA became an aircraft manufacturer with the acquisition of Fokker, with James "Dutch" Kindelberger recruited from Douglas to run the new company.

Kindelberger moved the company headquarters from Maryland to Los Angeles. At that time, Schmued – whose wife did not wish to move to California – took a position with Bellanca in New York. A few months after the death of his wife in a car accident, Schmued rejoined NAA, hired as a preliminary design engineer since Kindelberger was looking for young designers. Over the next several years, he was involved with design of the GA-16 trainer that became the BC-1 and led to the famous T-6 Texan trainer series. Schmued's first foray into fighter design was the NA-50, a single-seater based on the T-6 trainer, 50 of which NAA sold to the Peruvian Air Force.

Kindelberger managed to convince the Army Air Corps to let his design team inspect and disassemble the first Messerschmitt Bf-109 to arrive in the United States following its capture in the Spanish Civil War. This connection to the Bf-109, and the later similarity of the early P-51 to the German fighter, led to an urban myth that Schmued had worked for Messerschmitt. Although this was untrue, Schmued did put the knowledge he gained from studying the Bf-109 to use in his ongoing "side hobby" of designing a fighter that would be "right," as he explained later.

When the British Purchasing Commission came calling with the offer to build P-40s under license and Kindelberger offered a totally new fighter instead, he knew all about Schmued's "hobby." The result was an airplane that equaled the performance of the Spitfire, with the range to fly into Germany from Britain on internal fuel. Its only problem was that it was powered by an Allison engine without a supercharger, limiting its high-altitude performance.

As war clouds loomed in the fall of 1941, all thought of the Army Air Forces as a solely defensive organization had long been cast aside. On December 7, 1941, a total of 70 tactical groups had been activated, including 14 heavy bombardment, nine medium bombardment, five light bombardment, 25 pursuit, 11 observation, and six transport groups, though most were at cadre strength only, and few had been equipped with suitable aircraft. On December 10, 1941, when the US Congress declared war on Germany in response to Hitler's declaration of war against the United States, all the major types of airplanes with which the Air Force would fight World War II were in production. There were now 198 B-17s, with 93 more coming off the line that month as production of the B-17E, the first version capable of offensive combat, began to grow. The B-24 had also entered production but the first ones were only just entering service. The P-38 had been brought to operational status in one fighter group for roughly six months, but of some 60 produced, there were only 20 P-38Es, the first sub-type capable of combat, and the airplane had demonstrated dangerous tendencies in flight as its performance took it into areas of aeronautical knowledge that were little understood, the primary one being compressibility. The P-47 had flown as a prototype, but there were still numerous problems to be worked out with that airplane, compressibility being only one. And two Mustangs sat in the back of a hangar at Wright Field.

As US military power grew and expanded during the years between the Nazi invasion of Poland and Pearl Harbor, the military establishments of Britain and the United States grew closer and expanded cooperation. This was most notable in the exchange of military intelligence and – more significantly – in the joint creation and development of war plans by US and British officers. This began following the defeat of France in June 1940, with the effort expanding as the British demonstrated they could prevail in the Battle of Britain. Over the following year, US war plans drafted in 1941 went far beyond the academic exercises of earlier years. US planners began to accept the fact of military cooperation with Britain and other Allied nations which were already at war; British officers paid more frequent visits to Washington, where they worked in close and frequent coordination with their American counterparts in the brand-new Pentagon. With the US public still largely ambivalent – at best – over the issue of American involvement in the war, and for obvious security reasons, these planning sessions and their results were not publicized, outside of occasional public statements by Roosevelt and Churchill, supplemented by less intentional disclosures through leaks to the press by those still opposed to the process, in order to give the public some notice of the increasingly close rapport between the two nations. Isolationist political opponents of the Roosevelt Administration talked constantly of the existence of "secret agreements for war."

At the staff level a due regard for legal limitations had to be strictly maintained. The plans being developed involved what would happen "if" the United States should enter the war, with no mention of "when." Regardless, the result of this broad military strategy that evolved in 1941 remained after Pearl Harbor without radical modification as the basis for the new Anglo-American alliance.

This all began with a series of conversations between a US Joint Chiefs of Staff committee and a delegation representing the British Chiefs of Staff that began at the end of January in Washington, with a goal of developing a broad overall agreement regarding mutual goals. This was embodied in a final report that was submitted on March 27, 1941, known by its short title, ABC-1. The report laid out the best means by which the United States and the British Commonwealth could defeat Germany and her allies "should the United States be compelled to resort to war." The report included broad plans involving the employment of forces and cooperation between the two militaries. This included delineation of areas of responsibility, principles of command, and the forces likely to be involved. The primary point on which the planners agreed was that the United States would continue aid to Britain and other Axis opponents. This would later be enunciated by President Roosevelt when he called on the country to become "the arsenal of democracy," and recognized that the greatest thing the United States brought to the alliance was its unparalleled economic power. The offensive strategy adopted was known as

"Germany First," based on the belief that since Germany was the preeminent member of the Axis, "the Atlantic and European area is considered to be the decisive theater." Thus, the main US and British effort would be concentrated on the defeat of Germany. The long-term pattern of offensive action against Germany was described: economic pressure by blockade and other means; "a sustained air offensive against German Military Power, supplemented by air offensives against other regions under enemy control which contribute to that power"; early elimination of Italy; raids and minor offensives against the continent; support of all neutrals and belligerents who opposed the Axis; and the build-up of forces for an eventual liberation of German-occupied Europe. As regarded aviation, "it would be the policy of the associated powers to achieve as rapidly as possible superiority of air strength over the enemy, particularly in long-range striking forces." In operations in the Atlantic area, "US Army air bombardment units [would] operate offensively in collaboration with the Royal Air Force, primarily against German Military Power at its source."

In light of subsequent events, ABC-1 is one of the most important military documents of the war.

Since October 1939, the War Plans Division of the General Staff had been working on five basic war plans for possible use against potential enemies. Each plan, bearing the generic code name RAINBOW and its own numeral designation, assumed a different situation and course of action in regard to the Atlantic and Pacific areas. RAINBOW No. 5, which contemplated an offensive in the Atlantic–European areas and a strategic defense against Japan in the Pacific, fitted most accurately the strategy outlined in the United States–British staff conversation; consequently, that plan was developed in detail in the spring of 1941, and by the end of April the Joint Army and Navy Basic War Plan RAINBOW No. 5 had been adopted as the primary strategy. RAINBOW No. 5 accepted all the major theses of ABC-1; the assumptions, overall strategy, and principles governing strategic direction and theater command were identical. In the European theater, where the United States was to exert its principal effort, initial operations were to be preponderantly naval protection of shipping and aerial bombardment of Germany. Hence, the Army forces set up for early deployment included a token ground force to aid in the defense of England; and the bombardment force for the air attack on Germany.

RAINBOW No. 5 was approved by the Joint Board on May 14, 1941, and within three weeks by the Secretaries of War and the Navy. During the next six months, no change was effected in the basic principles of the plan, but in view of developments in the international situation and in US forces available, modifications in detail were necessary. On November 19, the Joint Board approved Revision No. 1, which among other things established a more substantial initial increment for the air force in the United Kingdom.

Further discussions of joint strategy and policy at the Argentia Conference between Roosevelt and Churchill and staff negotiations afterward revealed a basic disagreement between American and British war planners. The British held to the belief that Germany was too strong to attack frontally without a preliminary undermining of the foundations of the Nazi war machine and German national morale. Their policy was to accomplish by blockade, subversive activities and propaganda, and aerial bombardment. The bomber offensive should be carried out on a scale far beyond any previous attempts, limited only by the number of aircraft which could operate from the United Kingdom; to that end production of heavy bombers should be given highest priority. By concentrated bombardment of transportation centers and the industrial areas surrounding them, it was thought that cumulative efforts would seriously weaken the German ability and will to resist. Since the British war planners were all veterans of the Western Front of World War I, there was always hope that a direct military confrontation at the old front could be avoided and that these methods alone might induce Germany to sue for peace, with the role of the British Army limited to that of an army of occupation. Nevertheless, a land army should be prepared to invade the continent and Germany itself.

Among the immediate reactions of the US leaders in the memorandum of September 25, 1941, that constituted the formal reply to the British statement, the attitude of the Air Corps leadership was important: they rejected the British idea of area bombing of the enemy population and recommended the strategic bombardment of specific industries, which would be carried out by daylight bombing, with the statement that they believed the attack on civilian morale implied by area bombing was actually counterproductive. (Had the RAF leaders taken the time to consider the response of the British public to the German "blitz" of 1940–41, they would have seen that the Americans were correct.) They also stated their belief that too much faith was placed in the "probability of success solely through the employment of a bombing offensive," whereas "dependence cannot be placed on winning important wars by naval and air forces alone." The air leadership joined the rest of the Army in stating that the British gave too little attention to the build-up of large ground forces which would be needed completely to defeat the German war machine. In substance, the US Joint Board was not inclined to believe that American entrance into the war, with initial cooperation limited to air and naval action, would ensure an early victory, and it was convinced that overall strategy should adhere more closely to that described in ABC-1.

The British, surprised by the strong tone of rejection in the US memorandum, responded in November that their review had been misunderstood. They gave a reasoned explanation of what they meant by morale bombardment and their choice of target objectives. They affirmed that their emphasis on the bomber offensive did not preclude a final land offensive. They then went on to present what would become the British position on delay of the cross-Channel invasion until Churchill was forced by his two stronger allies to formally commit to a 1944 invasion at the 1943 Tehran Conference: they had been studying the problems of landing operations and had found many difficulties, and expressed interest in American views on the detailed aspects of such an operation.

The Pearl Harbor attack three weeks later postponed the American reply; the implied differences in outlook were to be debated repeatedly over the next two years. More importantly for the immediate future, while both ABC-1 and RAINBOW No. 5 scheduled air attack from the United Kingdom as the earliest American offensive action, neither plan contained any detailed statement of how that mission should be accomplished.

All the military considerations flowed from the assumption that if America became embroiled in war with Germany, such a conflict would inevitably involve Italy and very probably Japan; this was based on Allied understanding of the Triple Alliance that had created the Axis powers, which had been signed by the three nations in November 1940. Gaining knowledge of the specifics of this treaty through the breaking of the Japanese "Purple" code used for diplomacy by a small team in the State Department was the first great US contribution to the eventual Allied supremacy in signals intelligence. The Triple Alliance required the other two parties to declare war on any opponent that came into conflict with the third party, whichever that would be. There was initial disagreement among diplomatic and political experts over how likely it would be, if either Japan or Italy came into conflict with the United States, that Hitler would live up to the agreement and declare war in support of the others, with many pointing to his failure to live up to any other political agreements he had made since coming to power in Germany. This would be resolved to the Allies' benefit on December 10, 1941, when Hitler, for the only time in his career, acted in accordance with an agreement he was party to and unilaterally declared war on the United States following the Japanese attack on Pearl Harbor. Had he not done so, it was politically unlikely that the Roosevelt Administration could have brought the Congress to unilaterally declare war on Germany in the absence of any warlike actions by the Germans.

3

# FLEDGLING FIGHTERS

It has been an article of faith in most histories of the strategic bombing campaign that the Army Air Forces (AAF) believed so strongly in the doctrine of Douhet and Trenchard – "the bomber will always get through" – that all plans for the coming campaign were based on the "fact" that Eighth Air Force could operate over Germany with "self-defending" bombers, until losses proved otherwise in the summer of 1943. The truth is radically different.

While indeed there was a substantial prewar belief among AAF leadership that "the bomber will always get through," AAF planners studied the massacre of 18 unescorted Wellington bombers in December 1939 that led the RAF to abandon daylight bombing; additionally, Air Corps observers in England had reported what happened to unescorted Luftwaffe bombers during the Battle of Britain. Thus, by the time serious planning for the creation of a strategic bombing force to operate from the United Kingdom began in 1941, a force of fighter escorts was seen as integral for the force and its operations in Europe.

Only one American fighter was considered competitive with German fighters: the P-38 Lightning. Originally designed as a short-range high-altitude point defense interceptor, in September 1941 a P-38D equipped with two 160-gallon drop tanks had demonstrated potential as a long-range fighter capable of operating over distances of 600–800 miles. The 1st Pursuit Group had only received the first 13 pre-production YP-38s in June, but production tempo expanded as the following airplanes were modified at the Burbank production line with operational equipment. The 36 P-38Ds delivered in September were equipped with self-sealing fuel tanks and armor plate. The 210 P-38Es that began rolling off the line in November were close enough to combat standard that a squadron of these early Lightnings served in the Aleutians throughout that campaign.

Almost as soon as squadrons received it, the P-38 demonstrated "gremlins" not heretofore experienced in combat aircraft; its high performance took it into previously unexplored areas of aeronautical science. What pilots found most disturbing was a tendency to tuck the nose under in a dive, thus increasing the dive angle while controls stiffened to the point that a pilot could not pull back on the yoke even bracing his feet on the instrument panel. If the dive was started high enough, there was a possibility of successful recovery as the fighter entered thicker air that slowed its rush toward the ground, but if the airplane had nosed over beyond vertical, there was no hope of avoiding the inevitable crash. Additionally, there was an unfortunate tendency for the Fowler maneuver flaps to deploy differentially, resulting in the airplane flipping over due to the differential lift of the wings and going inverted without notice.

On Friday, December 5, 1941, there were 69 P-38s of all sub-types in the AAF, only 12 of which were considered fully equipped and capable of operational use.

The AAF had begun creating new pursuit groups as rapidly as possible in 1941 through a process of subdividing an existing group to create new groups with an experienced cadre providing leadership for the new organization. For pilots who had joined the Air Corps over the previous two years, this led to phenomenal promotion as former lieutenants moved up in the unit structure to captain positions, and those who demonstrated flying skill and leadership potential could end up in command of a unit and promoted to major within a year of having first been commissioned. This process only accelerated after Pearl Harbor thrust the country into the war.

Between mid-December 1941 and early January 1942, the 1st Pursuit Group – which was the group with the most experience on the P-38 – lost over half its trained pilots and ground crews, as personnel were assigned to the newly formed 14th and 82nd groups. On January 7, 1942, Second Lieutenant Robert Eby was transferred from the 94th Pursuit Squadron of the 1st to the 49th Pursuit Squadron of the

14th Pursuit Group, which was commanded by newly assigned First Lieutenant Arman Peterson, who had been an Air Corps pilot since graduating from flight school in the fall of 1940; Eby was promoted to captain two weeks later. Eby later recalled, "That day, we transferred to Long Beach Airport to check out in P-38s. Of the other two squadrons in the group, one flew a mixture of P-38s and P-43s, while the third was equipped with Vultee P-66 fighters, which were terrible."

Groups equipped with the Bell P-39 and Curtiss P-40, which had entered production in 1940–41 and were available in greater numbers than the more-capable P-38 and P-47, were quickly expanded and sent on to the Pacific as rapidly as possible. Despite the P-39's lack of high-altitude capability after the turbocharger originally planned for the airplane was removed by Air Force decision, Bell's speedy increase in production meant that it became an important type by sheer availability.

Most units were sent to the Pacific, where the airplane's lack of performance was quickly discovered in combat over New Guinea. However, the 31st Pursuit Group, which had been the first to equip with the P-39, flying its airplanes during the important 1941 War Games that were the Army's "dress rehearsal" for the coming war, was assigned to air defense of the West Coast, operating from Paine Field, Washington. Shortly after New Year, the 31st gave up pilots as cadre for the newly formed 52nd Pursuit Group. In February 1942, the 31st started over when the unit was divided in half, with the original 39th, 40th, and 41st squadrons transferred to the 35th Pursuit Group, for immediate transfer to Australia. The "new" 31st set up with the 307th, 308th, and 309th Pursuit Squadrons in New Orleans, where they flew P-40Bs for three months before their complaints resulted in re-equipment with the P-39 in early May.

By the end of January, the 14th Group had flown its 14 P-38s and an assortment of P-43 and P-66 fighters from Southern California to Hamilton Army Airfield in Marin County, across the Golden Gate Bridge from San Francisco. Eby recalled, "We trained new pilots and prepared for overseas duty. Twice a week the call came down from Fighter Command to ship a certain number of pilots overseas the next day, which was done by drawing names out of a hat. We were one of two groups defending the northern West Coast, with the other at Paine Field." The number of P-38s in the group grew as pilots were sent to Burbank to pick up new airplanes from the factory. The inexperienced pilots soon discovered the gremlins lurking in the Lightning. Eby remembered, "We were soon averaging more than one crash a week in the P-38, with most of those being fatalities. Pilot morale was low."

On February 7, 1942, two weeks after the 14th had transferred to Hamilton, the new 78th Pursuit Group, composed of the 82nd, 83rd, and 84th Pursuit Squadrons, was formed and took half the pilots of the parent 14th Group. The 82nd Squadron had 24 enlisted men and seven pilots, commanded by First Lieutenant George Nash; by March 27, the squadron had expanded to 92 men and six pilots, now commanded by a second lieutenant. First Lieutenant Frank Wagner was made group commander at the end of the month.

The 14th and 78th groups operated as one unit while the pilot ranks were quickly filled out with new flight school graduates, none of whom had any twin-engine training. Newly promoted Captain Gene Roberts, assigned to the 84th Squadron, remembered, "A high-time P-38 pilot in this period was one who could record his total P-38 time in low double digits." On May 7, 1942, Captain Arman Peterson, the 14th Group's 49th Squadron commander, was promoted to major and transferred to the 78th as group commander. That day also saw the official AAF designation change from "Pursuit Group" to "Fighter Group," with squadrons becoming "Fighter Squadrons." First Lieutenant Harry Dayhuff arrived from Naval Air Station (NAS) North Island on May 15 with three of the four P-38s that had originally taken off. Second Lieutenant Wendell Seppich had been lost off La Jolla when he flew into a cloud bank, became disoriented, and spun out of the cloud and crashed. Dayhuff soon became the 82nd Squadron's new commander.

On June 23, the three squadrons began operating from Hamilton Field, Oakland Airport, and South San Francisco Airport. Dayhuff recalled, "Our training was hit or miss until Major Peterson organized the group, unified our goals and set it all down in writing." Eby, who had been transferred to the group staff, remembered:

During this period all squadrons were constantly on alert with one flight of four pilots in readiness with the planes warmed up and ready to scramble on receipt of orders from Fighter Command. One night I was out on a flight and we were notified that a Japanese submarine had been spotted off the Golden Gate. We managed to identify the submarine as a fishing boat that was heading back to harbor.

The P-38 was such a handful that accidents could happen quickly in the air or on the ground. Group operations officer Morris Lee would never forget a visit he made to the 83rd Squadron at South San Francisco Airport (today's San Francisco International). As he walked through the main hangar, he happened to look out the open doors, spotting an out-of-control P-38 that was headed straight at the building. He yelled for everyone to evacuate the hangar as the airplane ran into the structure:

> I ran around to where the P-38 had crashed into the door frame of the maintenance hangar. The pilot was a new trainee who had been shooting landings. He managed to open the canopy and raised up from the cockpit, crying "Help me!" Before anyone could do anything, he was engulfed in flames and the fire caused the ammo to start cooking off. Boxes of .50-caliber and .30-caliber ammunition stored nearby in the hangar started going off. Several planes under repair in the hangar were soon aflame. Fire units from nearby communities took several hours to contain the major conflagration. I can still hear the pilot's helpless cry as he slumped back into the seat behind a wall of flames.

This was only one of many fatalities. Lee also recalled:

> At this time, we were losing approximately a pilot a week to fatal crashes. One I had to investigate north of Hamilton Field had gone straight in from a vertical dive. The two engines required a backhoe to retrieve them from ten feet in the ground. A jellied mass the size of two basketballs was all that was identifiable of the pilot.

While squadrons on the West Coast struggled to tame the P-38, Republic's P-47 had begun to come out of the production line at Farmingdale, on New York's Long Island. The USAAF had ordered 171 P-47Bs, with an engineering prototype YP-47B delivered in December 1941, followed by the production prototype in March 1942. The first production P-47B rolled off the production line that May.

Originally designed to meet the X-109 specification for a single-engine high-altitude point-defense interceptor, the amenability of the airplane to take on roles unforeseen when the prototype XP-47B rolled out of the factory in early 1941 – which would guarantee it a place in history as one of the truly outstanding aircraft of World War II – was then unknown.

Among the problems pilots soon identified was that the Thunderbolt's sheer size limited ground-propeller clearance after raising the tail into a fuselage-level attitude, which made for challenging takeoffs requiring long runways. This meant that pilots had to learn to hold the tail low until close to takeoff speed on the initial run, unlike the procedure for other tailwheel aircraft. Also problematic was the gun installation's tight fit and cramped ammunition belt tracks, which led to jamming, especially during hard maneuvering. Additionally, at high altitude the ailerons "snatched and froze" while control loads were excessive at higher speeds. Power was affected by arcing in the ignition wiring, which was fixed when Republic fitted a pressurized ignition system. This problem would continue when the airplanes were shipped by sea to England, where it was discovered that the engine packing cases had not been sealed tightly, allowing salt air corrosion in the wiring.

Teething problems continued. A Republic test pilot was killed when the fifth production P-47B lost control in a dive on March 26, 1942, and crashed due to tail assembly failure after its fabric-covered tail surfaces ballooned and ruptured. This was the first indication that the Thunderbolt's performance brought pilots into the transonic flight regime approaching Mach 1, where they experienced "compressibility," a problem never encountered before the P-47 and P-38 flew.

Changes on the production line gradually addressed the P-47B's problems; the USAAF quickly followed the initial order with an order for 602 improved P-47Cs. Importantly, metal-covered control surfaces were introduced on the production line to the P-47C in early 1943.

Initially authorized on November 20, 1940, the 56th Pursuit Group "stood up" at Hunter Field, Georgia, on January 14, 1941, with three officers and 150 enlisted men. Its component units were the 61st, 62nd, and 63rd Pursuit Squadrons. Following the arrival of more pilots and ground support crews, in May 1941 the 56th transferred to Charlotte Army Air Base, North Carolina, where it received six AT-6s, three Bell P-39Ds, and five Curtiss P-40Bs; pilots concentrated on building flight experience that summer and fall. Following Pearl Harbor, the group went to Charleston Army Airfield in South Carolina, where it was equipped with a full line-up of P-36s. In January, the 56th flew to Mitchell Field, Long Island, to provide air defense for New York City.

It soon took possession of ten Curtiss P-40Es and four P-38Es. By April 1942, the group was equipped with P-40F Warhawks.

By May 1942, group headquarters was at Teaneck, New Jersey, while the 61st Squadron took up station at Bridgeport Airport in Connecticut; the 62nd at Bendix Airport, New Jersey; and the 63rd at the Republic Aviation factory on Long Island. With a squadron at Republic's airfield, it was unsurprising when the newly renamed 56th Fighter Group was selected as the first group to be assigned the new P-47, with the first received in June. The group's proximity to the factory allowed it to serve as an operational evaluation unit for the new fighter. As its members gained experience over the course of the summer, Republic made numerous modifications as a result of unsatisfactory reports from 56th pilots and engineers.

The pilots soon found that while the rate of climb was not impressive, high-altitude performance was; runs at 400 miles per hour were easily obtained at 30,000 feet. It could also dive faster than nearly every other fighter due to its weight. However, diving from high altitude needed caution; two pilots were killed when they failed to recover from high-altitude dives.

Among the pilots reporting to the group that summer was Second Lieutenant Robert S. Johnson. Born in Lawton, Oklahoma in 1920, at age eight he had seen the Air Corps flight demonstration team The Three Musketeers, led by Captain Claire Chennault, perform a routine with their P-12s roped together. He later wrote, "I turned to my father as we walked back to our car and told him I was going to be an Army fighter pilot when I grew up, and I was going to be the best one." On November 11, 1941 he was sworn into the Air Corps as a member of Class 42F and was commissioned with his wings on July 9, 1942. Though he had requested assignment to fly the A-20 and was classified as a bomber pilot on graduation, he found himself assigned to the 56th Fighter Group.

While the four P-38-equipped groups spent the first half of 1942 in training, the 31st Fighter Group was notified that it was going to England on May 17, becoming the first US fighter unit to arrive in England in June.

AAF planners planned to send fighters to England by air, and determined the P-39 could fly trans-Atlantic in stages from Newfoundland to Greenland, then on to Iceland and then northern Scotland. All that was needed was for the diminutive fighter to strap on the new 175-gallon ferry tank recently developed for the P-38. The idea was daunting enough that the leaders of the 31st managed to convince AAF Headquarters that further research and testing was needed. It was found that the tank could be attached under the fighter, but that there was less than a foot of ground clearance. This meant that the airplanes could only operate from smooth paved runway – Bluie West One in Greenland didn't qualify. With a long-enough takeoff run, the P-39 could get airborne, with a climb rate that almost touched 200 feet per minute. The big problem was in the air: the tank had no internal baffles, which meant that fuel sloshed fore and aft or side to side with the slightest movement, and such sloshing amplified the maneuver that had caused it. Control was marginal, at best. One experienced pilot flew into a cloudy patch where the oscillation of the fuel caused the airplane to maneuver wildly enough to topple his artificial horizon; the resulting out-of-control crash was fatal. A second, similar event was almost fatal, but the pilot was able to force open one of the cockpit doors and bail out at the last moment. It was decided that P-39s would travel by ship.

The group's ground echelon arrived in Scotland on June 9 after a five-day voyage from New York aboard the *Queen Elizabeth*. The next day they took a 14-hour train ride to their new airbase, Atcham in Shropshire, where they were surprised to discover 48 Spitfire Vb fighters waiting for them, rather than the familiar P-39s. RAF Fighter Command had managed to convince VIII Fighter Command's leader Brigadier General Frank O'Driscoll "Monk" Hunter that the P-39 could not survive in the European combat environment. The pilots were buoyed by a telegram from Hap Arnold that read: "You have been chosen to be the spearhead of the United States combat forces in the European Theater of operations. Congratulations and good luck." Traveling aboard HMS *Ramapura* over 13 days, they arrived a week after the ground echelon.

The conversion did not go easily; several Spitfires were soon written off, including four on June 28, 1942. The first flying fatality was recorded the next day, the cause being engine failure on takeoff. The week after a celebration of Independence Day on July 4, the group and squadron commanders were sent to fly with the 412 Squadron of the Royal Canadian Air Force (RCAF) for operational experience.

While the 31st found its feet in England, the 52nd Group arrived in Northern Ireland. Its men needed more training and remained there while they too were given Spitfires rather than the Airacobras they had spent the previous five months mastering.

By July 14, 21 of the 31st's Spitfires had been written off in training. Fortunately, enough replacements arrived to present the group in full when King George VI and Queen Mary arrived for a visit on July 16. On August 1, after the group leaders returned from flying with the Canadians, the group moved to Tangmere in East Anglia, where it would finally go to war. A further reorganization saw the group broken up, with the 307th Squadron sent to Biggin Hill and the 308th to Kenley, while the 309th remained at Tangmere. Each squadron became a fourth squadron in the three-squadron RAF wing based at the three different fields, to gain more experience before operating together.

While the 31st learned the Spitfire, an event occurred that would have a profound effect on the way that VIII Bomber Command would operate in the coming air campaign. To date, the Americans had been following RAF experience and basing operational decisions on that information. As a result, RAF Bomber Command expected that VIII Bomber Command would join them in the nightly air war over German cities, while RAF Fighter Command expected VIII Fighter Command to reinforce their efforts. This thinking came to an abrupt halt with the arrival on June 18 of Major General Carl "Tooey" Spaatz, with orders to establish the headquarters of the Eighth Air Force at High Wycombe. Spaatz had demonstrated his combat command ability over the Argonne Forest in the fall of 1918, during which he shot down several German airplanes despite flying a Salmson 2A2 bomber. Throughout the interwar years, he had been at the leading edge of technical development in the Air Corps, setting several records along the way. He had the full confidence and backing of his closest friend, "Hap" Arnold, Chief of Staff of the Army Air Forces. Spaatz was one of a handful of USAAF leaders with the moral authority to win the fight over an independent role for the AAF against the RAF leadership and Churchill. His assignment from Arnold was to integrate the American daylight offensive as an equal to the British night offensive, not in a subordinate role. This was a battle that would continue through the next 17 difficult months as VIII Bomber and Fighter Commands struggled to make the daylight offensive successful.

While the pilots of the 31st were getting ready to go to war, the 1st and 14th groups, the most experienced of the four P-38 groups formed, were notified that they were moving to England now that two B-17 groups were there and close to being operational. Given the P-38's range with one normal 160-gallon tank and one 175-gallon ferry tank underwing, it was planned that they would fly to Europe. The 1st Fighter Group began flying aircraft to England on June 27, 1942, with formations of six to eight P-38s, each escorted by a B-17 providing navigation over the North Atlantic Route, which started at Presque Isle, Maine, flying on in stages to Goose Bay, Labrador; then to Bluie West One in southern Greenland; on to Reykjavík, Iceland; with final destination at Goxhill, England. On July 15, six P-38Fs from the 94th Squadron and their two B-17 escorts were forced down on the Greenland ice cap. Although all personnel were recovered safely, the aircraft were left behind and the plan to send fighters by air was abandoned. The 1st Group moved to England by ship in late July, followed by the 14th in August.

The 309th Squadron became the first USAAF fighter unit to see action in the European Theater of Operations (ETO) on August 9. The squadron was on a training flight when it was notified that there were Fw-190 fighter-bombers in its area. Squadron commander Major Harrison Thyng spotted one German fighter when it streaked past and chased it, pressing the trigger to become the first USAAF fighter pilot to open fire on the enemy in the ETO. Later that afternoon, the squadron accompanied the RAF wing it was assigned to on a sweep over France, where the enemy ignored it.

August 17 was a red-letter day in the history of the Eighth Air Force. Eighteen B-17Es from the 97th Bomb Group – six each from the 340th, 341st, and 342nd Bomb Squadrons – took off from their bases at Polebrook and Grafton-Underwood in Northamptonshire at 1530 hours, on the first bombing mission mounted by the USAAF in the ETO.

VIII Bomber Command leader General Ira C. Eaker had originally ordered the mission be flown on August 10, the day after the 97th Group was declared operational after training for a month following its arrival in the United Kingdom in late June. The general was immediately confronted by an enemy the bombers would contend with to the end of the war: English weather. The field was covered in fog so dense one could not see the runway from the hardstands. The fog hung around for the next six days, only clearing unexpectedly on August 17.

The target for the dozen bombers of the "main force" was the Sotteville-lès-Rouen railroad yards in Rouen, the largest and most active railroad yard in northern France, while six more made a diversionary strike. The lead ship was B-17E 41-2578 "Butcher Shop," flown by 340th Squadron commander Major Paul Tibbets (who would fly a second historically important mission three years later in the Pacific as commander of the B-29 "Enola Gay"), with 97th Group commander Colonel Frank A. Armstrong, Jr. Flying B-17E 41-9023 "Yankee Doodle," lead ship of the 341st Squadron, was Brigadier General Ira C. Eaker. The 340th and 341st squadrons arrived over Rouen at 23,000 feet and dropped 19 tons of bombs on the target between 1739 and 1746 hours, while the six B-17s of the 342nd Squadron flew along the French coast as a diversion. Accuracy was good. One of the aim points, the locomotive shops, was destroyed by a direct hit. The overall results were moderate.

First Lieutenant Levon L. Ray aboard "Butcher Shop" was the group lead bombardier. He later recorded the mission in his diary:

Twelve ships with Colonel Anderson and our crew in the lead ship took off from Grafton-Underwood on the first all-American high-altitude daylight raid of this war. Target was Rouen marshalling yards, which received a very good pasting. Opposition was very weak. Surprise was apparent and what few fighters did get up caused very little damage, one ship exchanged fire with a fighter and one of our ships was hit with a stray piece of flak.

Among the German pilots who intercepted this first mission, but did not attack the heavily armed bombers, was Oberleutnant Egon Mayer and his wingman, Leutnant Georg-Peter Eder of Jagdgeschwader 2 (JG 2, 2nd Fighter Wing). Mayer later recalled that he was surprised by the "great size" of the American bombers, though both he and Eder noticed that the B-17's formidable defenses did not extend to the bomber's forward quarter. They would both make use of that knowledge in other observations of the early VIII Bomber Command missions that fall to devise what they called the "company-front attack" and American aircrews would remember as the terrifying "Twelve O'Clock High" head-on attack.

For the Luftwaffe, the advent of the American bombers was different from the threat it had faced during the RAF's 1941 offensive. Where the RAF had sent Blenheim light bombers, which carried a maximum bomb load of 1,000 pounds, generally in the form of four 250-pound bombs, the American B-17 carried 4,000 pounds of bombs, and the B-24 a load of 5,000 pounds. Whereas the British bombers had been distinguished by an inability to create serious damage to their target and could often be ignored, the American bombers could carry sufficient heavy 500-pound or 1,000-pound bombs to punish their targets. Thus, the Jagdwaffe could not ignore them. The German fighters were forced to confront every raid, losing the tactical initiative they had maintained over Europe since the Battle of Britain. Fortunately for the fighter pilots, American strength was slow to develop, which gave them time to experiment with tactics and equipment with which to oppose the new enemy. Because JG 2 "Richthofen" and JG 26 were positioned so close to the Channel coast, they needed more warning than the German controllers had been used to giving, if they were to have time to climb to the bombers' altitude over 20,000 feet. In several of the early missions, the defenders failed to intercept due to a late warning. This incurred the wrath of both Reichsmarschall Göring and General der Jagdflieger Galland, who was finally promoted to *Generalmajor* (major general) on November 1, giving him military authority equal to the responsibility assigned to him for organizing the fighter defenses.

Leutnant Karl Borris, *Staffelkapitän* (squadron commander) of 8./JG 26, later wrote of the psychological impact of the B-17s and B-24s on German pilots:

Pilots were now facing the most formidable challenge of their lives. The size of the heavy bombers and their formations, and their unprecedented defensive firepower, could not be adequately described to the green pilot; they had to be experienced firsthand. The classical stern attack, which at the time was the only approved method, was frequently initiated and broken off too soon to cause damage. Range estimation proved difficult. The Revi gunsight was sized for attacks on fighters; the wings of a typical fighter filled its sighting circle at 100 yards range. The bombers loomed large in the Revi long before reaching effective range.

By August 18, the 31st's three squadrons had each flown several missions over enemy territory, escorting A-20s and B-17s, as well as several two-plane "Rhubarbs" and some RAF "Circus" sweeps. (Rhubarb involved two aircraft at low level attacking targets of opportunity, usually in bad weather to preclude interception; Circus was an escorted bomber mission into Europe in the war's early days.)

That evening, the group was declared operational; its pilots would fly their first mission as a full American-only group the next day, when their baptism of fire would find them flying cover for the Dieppe Raid.

The pilots were called to readiness at 0320 hours on August 19. At 0717 hours, RAF wing commander Peter Wickham led 308th Squadron commander Major Fred M. Dean and Lieutenants Hill, Van Reed, Ingraham, Smith, Dahlrymple, Baker, Fleming, Corrigan, Reichert, and Waltner when they took off from Kenley and flew into history as the first USAAF fighter pilots to join combat with the Luftwaffe. When they arrived over the fleet off Dieppe, the enemy was waiting for them.

The Germans were first aware of the Allied force offshore when shelling began around 0600 hours. Two Fw-190s from 5./JG 26, flown by Oberleutnant Horst Sternberg with Feldwebel Peter Crump as his wingman, arrived over Dieppe at about 0620 hours and saw the Allied ships offshore firing on the town, and landing craft headed toward the shore. Avoiding several Spitfires that Crump called out, the *Rotte* (two-fighter formation) flew over the town and then returned to Abbeville to report what they had found.

The Luftwaffe was not really able to engage the Allied force. The only "day bombers" on the Channel Front were the two *Jabostaffeln* (fighter-bomber squadrons) of Fw-190A-4/U-3s operated by JG 2 and JG 26, which had at the time some 18 fighter-bombers operational between them. There were 220 Ju-88 and Do-217 night bombers in Belgium. The first German fighter response was a formation of ten Fw-190s, followed by another of 16 from I./JG 26 at St Omer-Arques, which spotted 12 Spitfires orbiting over Dieppe – the Americans from the 308th Squadron.

The JG 26 Fw-190s dived though the 12 Spitfires, which immediately broke formation to evade the attack. Lieutenant Hill found himself behind the German lead fighter and fired his 20mm cannon. The Fw-190 smoked and turned away, but Hill was not able to confirm his victory when he was set on by the wingman. A moment later, Lieutenant Ingraham was forced to go over the side from his burning Spitfire, which had been set afire by the Fw-190 that latched onto his tail; his parachute streamed and only filled moments before he touched down in the water, right next to a pair of German E-boats; he became the 31st's first prisoner of war (POW). Ingraham's wingman, Lieutenant Smith, was able to make it back to Kenley despite a big hole in his right wing made by the explosion of a 20mm cannon shell, while the Spitfire's fuselage was recorded as being "well ventilated" with 7.62mm bullet holes. The 11 survivors were all back at Kenley by 0900 hours.

Twenty years later, Frank Hill provided a full account of his experience over Dieppe to historian Eric Hammel:

As we neared the French coast, we could see a number of ships near Dieppe harbor, and a large number of aircraft were flying in the general area. At our altitude, it was hard to tell if the ships or planes were friend or foe... We had been over Dieppe only a few minutes when the RAF operations center reported that a dozen or so enemy aircraft were approaching Dieppe from the direction of the big German aerodrome at Abbeville. A few minutes later, a flight of aircraft arrived above us, at about 12,000 feet, and immediately rolled over and commenced an attack on my flight. I could see they were Fw-190s... I wanted to keep my flight together and avoid giving up the advantage. As the Germans attacked, their formation broke up into pairs. I turned and flew at them head-on, which made it hard for them to keep their sights on us and forced them to attack us head-on.

After about three minutes of trying to keep my flight from being hit – by constantly breaking and turning into the Germans – I found myself in a position to get a good shot at one, and I fired everything I had. He swung out to my left, and I got in another good burst, firing at his left side from 300 yards down to about 200 feet. He started pouring black smoke, then rolled over and went straight down. I followed him to about 3,000 feet but had to pull out because the ack-ack coming from the ground was really intense. The last I saw of him, he was about a thousand feet over the Channel, north of Dieppe, still smoking and in a deep dive.

Since neither Hill nor anyone else saw the Fw-190 crash, he would receive credit for a "probable." In fact, Oberleutnant Schmidt had attempted to break away using a split-S (a diving turn to reverse direction); with insufficient recovery altitude he crashed into the Channel, the first German fighter shot down by an American pilot in a USAAF fighter.

Major "Pips" Priller's III./JG 26 at Wevelgem in southern Belgium sent two *Staffeln* (squadrons) off at 0700 hours, but they failed to make contact with any Allied fighters. II./JG 26 launched the first large response, with the entire *Gruppe* (group) taking off from Abbeville and Amiens at 0750 hours. The *Staffelkapitän* of 5.Staffel, Leutnant Wilhelm-Ferdinand "Wutz" Galland – Adolf Galland's middle brother – was in the lead, upset that his regular *Schwartze 8* Fw-190A-4 had been damaged earlier by flak when flown by Crump on the initial reconnaissance. The *Gruppe* arrived over Dieppe at approximately 0830 hours, where it broke into *Staffel* formations and took on the orbiting Spitfire cover.

The 309th Squadron's first mission of the day set off from Tangmere at 0754 hours. They arrived on the scene at around the same time as the II./JG 26 formation and were immediately engaged by enemy fighters in the middle of what was shaping up to be the biggest air battle of the war to date. The 309th's First Lieutenant Junkin scored the first officially credited US victory, an Fw-190 that was among the *Staffel* of *Würgers* that dived on the star-marked Spitfires. All US Spitfires survived the fight and returned safely by 0930 hours. II./JG 26 returned to their bases at 1040 hours with the pilots claiming a total of 27 Spitfires shot down in the various individual battles that had raged over the invasion fleet.

The 307th took off from Biggin Hill at 0950 hours, with wing commander Thomas leading squadron commander Major Marvin L. McNickle and ten other Americans. Arriving over the fleet at 1015 hours, they split into elements of two and chased German fighter-bombers from 10.(*Jabo*)/JG 26 that were diving on the ships below, but the Fw-190A fighter-bombers were diving on the ships from the seaward side, dropping their bombs at minimum altitude and maximum speed, and heading straight inland at high speed; the Spitfires had no chance of catching them. When the 309th returned to Biggin Hill at 1120 hours, Lieutenants Tovrea and Wright were missing and Lieutenant Mitchell's Spitfire was heavily damaged.

The 308th sent off its second mission of the day at 1002 hours. When they returned at 1130 hours, Major Dean's Spitfire, and the fighters of Lieutenants English, Robb, and Johnson, were all damaged to varying degrees; none had seen their attackers. Dieppe was a hard "graduation test" for brand-new fighter pilots.

At 1130 hours, the II./JG 26 Abbeville-Drucat airfield was bombed by 24 B-17s from the 97th Bomb Group on its second mission. Bombing from 23,000 feet, the B-17s met no fighters since the Germans were busy elsewhere, but flak holed several of the bombers. The bombers reported a successful drop, and the radio on the airfield went off the air following the attack. The German air operations were not affected, since II./JG 26 was able to operate from the satellite airfields at Cambrai-Epinoy, Liegescourt, and Amiens. Lieutenant Ray recorded the mission in his diary that night:

> Twenty-four ships attacked Abbeville airdrome in support of the Dieppe Commando Raid. It was very successful, some flak, but few fighters. We hit the radio station and knocked it out and diverted the fighters from Abbeville further inland. Two enemy ships taking off disappeared in the smoke of one bomb. Colonel Anderson flew with us again as lead ship.

Further missions were flown throughout the day. The British radio monitors were impressed by how calm the German controllers sounded as they vectored the Fw-190s and Bf-109s onto the Allied fighter formations. The Germans did not consider it necessary to involve any other units but JG 26 and JG 2. After the initial *Gruppe*-strength mission, II./JG 26 operated at *Staffel* strength through the rest of the day. The *Jabostaffeln* of both *Geschwadern* (wings) made repeated attacks on the ships offshore, with two Fw-190A-4/U3s from 10.(*Jabo*)/ JG 2 hitting and sinking the Royal Navy destroyer HMS *Berkeley* with 500-kilogram bombs.

The 307th's final mission took off at 1605 hours, with Major McNickle leading Captains Zimlich, Robertson, and LaBreche, and Lieutenants Collinsworth, Throop, Whisonant, Wooten, White, Dugen, Mitchell, and Leggett. The fleet was already turning away from France, having evacuated the Canadian survivors of the raid that made it off the beach. Four Fw-190s attacked the Spitfires, and Whisonant and Wooten chased after them, opening fire on the leader, who caught fire and disappeared, pouring black smoke. Captain Robertson and Lieutenant White chased a second 190. After several bursts, the enemy fighter went straight down on fire, though neither American could stick around to witness the final outcome when four more Fw-190s showed up.

At the end of the day, Lieutenants Tovrea, Collins, Wright, and Dabney were missing, and Lieutenant Wells had been fished out of the Channel by an RAF rescue launch, drowned after having struck his head when he attempted to ditch his Spitfire into the water. Lieutenant Junkin, the first official American victor, had been badly wounded in a fight on a later mission. The final credits gave the 307th's Captain Robertson one Fw-190 destroyed; Lieutenant White one Fw-190 probable; and Lieutenant Whisonant one Fw-190 probable. For the 308th, one Fw-190 probable was credited to Lieutenant Hill. The 309th's Major Thyng was credited with a probable, while Captain Thorsen and Lieutenants Biggard and Payne shared a Do-217 damaged, and Lieutenant Junkin had one Fw-190 destroyed. Overall, the results of the 31st's participation in what had become indeed the biggest air battle of the war to date was a good first show for an inexperienced unit.

At 1724 hours, Wutz Galland, with Peter Crump forgiven for damaging his fighter and now flying as his wingman, led 5.Staffel on a *freie Jagd* (Free Hunt – a fighter sweep, similar to a US "Ramrod," a fighter sweep by a squadron or group looking for targets of opportunity) to Dieppe. Crump remembered that the town was now deserted, with some British tanks and other equipment abandoned on the beach following the withdrawal of the Canadian troops earlier that afternoon, with the only other evidence of the day's battle being the destroyed houses along the beach and the corpses of British soldiers floating in the water. Minutes later they spotted an RAF rescue launch headed west and strafed it. The boat evaded the first run, zigzagging at top speed. On the second run, its bow wave disappeared under the hail of fire and the boat quickly sank; no survivors were spotted. Overall, all three *Gruppen* of JG 26 had flown 377 sorties during the day in 36 missions. They claimed 40 Spitfires that were later confirmed, and 11 probables. JG 2 claimed 42.

The Allies claimed 47 Fw-190s, three Bf-109s, 33 Do-217s, eight Ju-88s, and five He-111s shot down; actual German losses were 14 fighters from JG 2 and six from JG 26 with a total of 14 pilots lost. The RAF recorded 71 pilots and ten aircrew killed or missing and 106 aircraft failed to return, including 88 fighters. The German claims were much closer to reality.

The next day, Major McNickle led Circus 206, a diversionary sweep that flew as far inland as St Omer, I./JG 26's main base. Unfortunately, after the big day before, the Jagdwaffe was uninterested in the 20 Spitfires. On August 21, wing commander Thomas led the 31st on

Circus 209, a sweep to Ostend. Nothing was seen until the end, when six Fw-190s were spotted below just before it was time to turn for home. Pilots called them out as the four fighters ran away inland, but Thomas came on the radio and pointed out 60-plus Fw-190s that were climbing to their altitude from inland. Clearly, the first six were bait to draw the Spitfires back inland while the large formation cut them off from getting home. As they followed Thomas back toward the Channel, Lieutenant Whisonant's flight of four reefed around and pointed their noses at the trailing Germans, who all turned and ran while out of range.

Over the rest of the month, the American Spitfires, again flying with their British mates, made several appearances over the Channel and northwestern France, but the Germans refused to be goaded into action. September saw more of the same, with escort missions flown for raids by RAF Boston bombers (the British version of the A-20) and several diversionary Circus missions flown. In mid-month, the group was told to pack its gear for a major move. After that was completed, there was no move, and operations continued, though the increasingly cloudy fall weather forced several aborts and outright cancellations.

The first shoot-down of a B-17 by a German fighter happened on September 6, when Hauptmann Conny Meyer, *Gruppenkommandeur* (group commander) of II./JG 26, shot down a Flying Fortress from the 97th Bomb Group near Amiens at 1855 hours, after the *Gruppe* had dispersed the Spitfire high cover of 133 Eagle Squadron, which lost three of its airplanes and pilots. Several minutes after Meyer's victory, another B-17 from the 92nd Bomb Group under attack by four Fw-190s of 4./JG 26 crashed into the English Channel near Le Treport. The ability of the B-17 to absorb damage and keep flying was already becoming legendary among German pilots. Oberleutnant Kurt Ruppert of 9./JG 26 repeatedly attacked a damaged B-17 that had fallen out of formation. In repeated passes, he knocked out three engines, one of which fell off the bomber and crashed in the Channel. He watched, amazed, as the B-17 remained airborne on one engine while the crew threw out equipment and guns; he followed it across the Channel and witnessed its successful crash-landing on the beach at Ramsgate.

By the first week in October, the 31st Group loaded gear on lorries that disappeared out the gate, destinations unknown. On October 13 the 31st was declared "non-operational." All flying ceased on October 16. Between October 19 and 23, the group departed Wethampnett airfield in separate groups. They boarded trains and after overnight trips ended back where they had started, in the Firth of Forth, where the first group went aboard a transport on October 22. By October 24, all were aboard ship. On October 25, the large troop convoy departed England. Once at sea, the pilots and ground crew were called to meetings where they were informed they were about to take part in the invasion of North Africa. The 31st would not see England again for the rest of the war.

The 97th Bomb Group flew its final mission from the UK on October 21, against the U-boat pens at Lorient harbor on the Bay of Biscay. Lieutenant Ray recalled that "Major Tibbets led the mission. Three other groups turned back because of the weather, but we bombed from 14,000 feet, just under the overcast." With that, the 97th and the 301st Bomb Groups, the two most experienced VIII Bomber Command units, were transferred to the newly formed Twelfth Air Force to take part in the North African invasion.

By the end of October, the 31st and the 52nd groups, both equipped with Spitfires, and the P-38-equipped 1st and 14th groups that had also come to England over the summer and had been about to fly their first escort missions for the B-17s, were transferred to the North Africa-bound Twelfth Air Force. The 82nd Group's P-38s arrived in England in November and the unit was immediately transferred to join the others in North Africa.

VIII Fighter Command would now start over.

In September 1942, while the men of the 31st Group were honing their skills in their Spitfires over the English Channel, back on Long Island the 56th Group welcomed a new commander, Major Hubert Zemke. Born in Montana in 1914, Zemke had never exhibited any interest in airplanes or flying as a youth. Graduating from the University of Montana in 1936 with a degree in engineering and with few employment prospects in the midst of the Depression, he allowed two friends to convince him to join them in the Air Corps as flying cadets. After graduating with his pilot's wings from Randolph Field in 1937, he was assigned to the 36th Pursuit Squadron, based at Langley Field, Virginia, just in time to see its ancient Curtiss P-6E open-cockpit biplanes replaced with the then-new Curtiss P-36A a few months after his arrival. In 1940, the squadron was among the first units to re-equip with the new P-40B fighter.

Promoted to captain, Zemke was sent to England in September 1940 as a combat observer with the Royal Air Force, where he studied the tactics of both the RAF and the Luftwaffe. The next year, he was sent to the Soviet Union to instruct Russian pilots on flying Lend-Lease P-40s. After his return to the United States in February 1942, he was one of the first Air Corps pilots to fly the XP-47B that spring. His experience with the P-47 and knowledge of European air combat made him a natural choice to take over the 56th.

On November 1, 1942, the 78th Group set out for England, departing Oakland on November 10, bound for Camp Kilmer, New Jersey. Major Morris Lee later recalled:

> We were not in cattle cars, but the old coaches they had pressed into service were anything but comfortable for sleeping. The baggage car used as a mess hall was cold and windy. I saw several guys step through the passageway back to their car, only to find their plates empty upon entering the coach. Those strange air currents between the cars could take the sauerkraut and wieners right off the plate. The poker games ran all night and all day through the five days of the trip.

Robert Eby remembered their arrival at Camp Kilmer on November 15:

> Colonel Arman Peterson believed in advance planning. Before we left, we salvaged two large crates used for film developing machines. The pilots and crews all chipped in and bought enough American booze to fill the crates, which were cleverly marked and shipped off with the other equipment. There must have been some breakage en route, as only one crate was eventually delivered in England. We voted not to open it until Christmas.

Pilot Earl Payne recorded in his diary:

> 20 November, 1942. Had my last typhus shot today, the worst of the three. The most painful! They gave the whole barracks a five minute physical today. It is a prerequisite for overseas shipment and they do everything they can to NOT find anything wrong with a person. Two *ahh*s, a cough, and a bend over forwards spreading the buttocks.

On November 23, the men went aboard RMS *Queen Elizabeth*, with 12,000 other American soldiers, sailors, and fliers; French fliers; British fliers; and 300 nurses. Pilot Jack Miller remembered:

> The big disadvantage to being on a Limey ship was the chow. It would take hours to sweat out a chow line which wound its way down four flights to the mess deck. When the line got far enough that the familiar smell of mutton would waft upstairs, I'd just return to the cabin. My main diet was Nestle bars and Pepsi-Cola. At night one of the cooks would come around with a box of ham sandwiches, just two slices of bread and a slab of ham. I never tasted better sandwiches in my life. No one asked any questions about where he got the ham, they were so glad to get edible food. He must have made a fortune off us.

The group arrived in Scotland on November 29 and the next day headed for their new base. Jack Miller was amused by the English railways:

> Every station we came to, smiling ladies came along the cars passing out hot tea and crumpets, which tasted mighty good after living on chocolate bars and Coke for five days. The afternoon was bright and sunny and we passed through some very beautiful country of rolling hills and woodland. Everyone started to think this wasn't going to be half bad, but we learned later, when the sun shines here, it is a rare occasion.

The 78th arrived at Goxhill at 0130 hours, November 30, 1942. Unofficially named "Goat Hill," Eighth Air Force Station No. F-345, Goxhill Field, had been built by the RAF in 1941 and new USAAF units received ETO indoctrination there beginning in August 1942. Earl Payne recalled Nissen hut-living as "sixteen beds and one teeny-weeny coal stove, no latrines or water within a mile, with 25-watt bulbs for 'illumination.' The sun hardly ever shone and the days were short and lately it was very cold and windy." Mutton was soon replaced by Spam. Morris Lee remembered, "One group member got a Christmas present from home. When he opened it, he found a ten-pound can of Spam. He was said to have contemplated suicide but was talked out of it. To add insult to injury, his friends and family had to pool their ration coupons back home to buy it for him."

While the 78th was traveling to England that November, the 56th's Bob Johnson was one of the pilots who learned about the P-47 and compressibility "the hard way." As he later wrote, he was at 33,000 feet when he decided to find out why the pilot's manual expressly forbade power dives from high altitude:

> I pushed over, and in a matter of moments, the airplane was shaking so hard the stick came out of my hand. I grabbed it and tried to regain control, but things only got worse. As I passed through 10,000 feet with no sign of any change, I literally placed my feet on the instrument panel to give myself leverage to try and pull the stick back. Suddenly as the altimeter went through 5,000 feet, the shaking stopped and suddenly the nose came up so sharply I had to push forward to avoid stalling out!

Badly shaken, he flew back to Farmingdale and landed, hoping no one would notice. The event was discovered when the crew chief found the fabric elevators nearly destroyed. Since the group was short of pilots and now under orders to prepare to move to England, group commander Zemke didn't throw him out of the group.

Around the same time that Johnson had his near-death experience, Lieutenants Harold Comstock and Roger Dyar of the 63rd Fighter Squadron got into similar compressibility dives while flying two of the first P-47Cs equipped with metal rudders and elevators, which allowed them to reach unprecedented speeds in the region of 500 miles per hour. Republic's publicity department took advantage of the incident to proclaim that they had come near to the speed of sound.

By the end of 1942, most of the P-47's troubles had been worked out. The 56th was alerted for overseas movement on November 26, 1942, and ceased flying operations. On December 28, it moved to Camp Kilmer, New Jersey, and on January 6, 1943, it sailed from New York City aboard the RMS *Queen Elizabeth* for Scotland, arriving seven days later on January 13, 1943.

# 4

# YANKS IN THE RAF

September 29, 1942, saw a driving rainstorm cover East Anglia. At Debden, a prewar RAF base, 65 young Americans lined up in formation in the soaking rain. Over the previous month, they had exchanged their former RAF blues for new tailor-made "pinks and greens" while in London to take their officers' oath of allegiance to the United States. James A. Goodson, who had only recently joined what was now the 336th Fighter Squadron, later recalled, "We couldn't understand why they had to have us out in the rain when we could have held the ceremony inside one of the hangars. It was the first of many run-ins we would have with the strange and unexplained ways of the US Army's bureaucracy." For the USAAF, and VIII Fighter Command specifically, these men were a godsend, since the one thing America's industrial plant couldn't provide was an entire fighter group composed of pilots with combat experience on the crucial Channel Front.

Previously, the pilots had been members of 71, 121, and 133 squadrons, RAF, known to the public as "the Eagle Squadrons." In the mythology of aerial warfare, the Eagle Squadrons – "the Yanks in the RAF" – rank with the Lafayette Escadrille and the American Volunteer Group (AVG) for mystique. The Eagles were far more in the mold of the young pilots of the Escadrille Lafayette: like them, none were professionals before joining the RAF, while the AVG was formed with professional Army, Navy, and Marine Corps pilots, their mission underwritten by the US government. The closest any of the Eagles had gotten to service in the US military was as aviation cadets who were flunked out for various reasons, while many had been rejected before getting that far, primarily for lack of the proper educational background; they had found an air force willing to take them in and train them in Canada. All they had to do was risk the loss of their US citizenship for violating the Neutrality Act if they were caught by the Federal Bureau of Investigation (FBI) when crossing the border.

Several of the men who became original members of the Eagles were prewar pilots who had originally come to Europe after the outbreak of war to join the French Air Force as their forbears of the Lafayette Flying Corps had, or to volunteer to fight with the Finns. Since the Finnish war with the Soviet Union was over quickly, with France defeated a matter of months later, they found themselves in Britain, where the RAF was glad to take them into service. Ten flew in the Battle of Britain, though none of them were still alive to stand in the rain at Debden this day.

During the Battle of Britain, Charles Sweeny, a wealthy American businessman in London, persuaded the British government to form an RAF squadron manned completely by Americans. Once the idea received Churchill's approval, Sweeny's group joined with World War I ace Billy Bishop and the US aviation artist Clayton Knight, to form the Clayton Knight Committee in New York City to recruit Americans for the RAF. Sweeny and his rich society contacts provided over $100,000 for the cost of processing and sending the volunteers to Canada and the United Kingdom for training; such financial support to individuals was in the form of "loans" that were never repaid, and as such were legally "gifts to encourage foreign service," making such support a crime. While the Knight Committee's activity was unofficially supported by President Roosevelt himself, and thus "tolerated" by the Department of State, the Committee was constantly harassed by the Federal Bureau of Investigation on the orders of J. Edgar Hoover himself, regardless of any support for this by the president since Hoover considered his authority independent of anyone else in government; as the likelihood of the United States entering the war became more obvious during 1941, the Bureau began to desist in their enforcement of the Neutrality Act. By the time the United States entered the war, the Knight Committee had processed 6,700 applications from Americans to join the RCAF or RAF, though 86 percent of the applicants were rejected, with only about 1,000 actually joining the RAF. Of those 1,000 volunteers, only

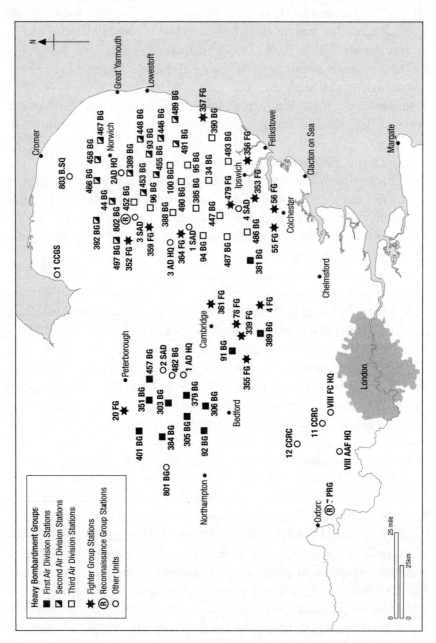

MAP I: US VIII AAF Installations in the UK – June 6, 1944

244 served in the Eagle Squadrons. A unit like the Eagle Squadrons attracted "adventurous types," and the Eagles – in both their RAF and USAAF editions – had more than their share of "memorable characters" in their ranks.

The minimum requirement for acceptance by either RAF or RCAF was a high school diploma, age 18–31, minimum eyesight of 20/40 correctable to 20/20, and 300 hours of flight experience. As then-19-year-old Barry Mahon recalled:

I had about 70 hours actual time in Piper Cubs, and "padded" my logbook with 230 hours in a Spartan Executive as 'complex aircraft' experience to get to 300. When I got to Canada, the first day I was on the field they told me that with my experience they'd just send me off in a Harvard. I was convinced I was going to die, but somehow I managed to climb up into that cockpit, got airborne, flew around the pattern and put it back on the ground in one piece. Fortunately, they noticed my lack of ability and decided I was in need of more training, though my instructor later told me he admired my guts for trying.

The first Eagle Squadron, 71, was formed in September 1940 at Church Fenton. Originally, it was considered that the squadron might fly the American Brewster Buffalo fighter, and several were delivered to the field; fortunately, the poor performance of the export version of the Buffalo obtained by the RAF was quickly apparent and the squadron re-equipped with hand-me-down Hurricane I fighters that had served in the Battle of Britain in November. In January they were issued new Hurricane IIs and became operational for defensive duties on February 5, 1941. Among the original pilots was Chesley G. Peterson, who found his way to the RAF after being flunked out of Army Air Corps pilot training during ground school in early 1940. While working at Douglas Aircraft, he learned of the Clayton Knight Committee and applied for the RAF that spring. Following flight training, he arrived in the United Kingdom in December and was immediately assigned to 71 Squadron.

Demonstrating talent in the air, Peterson was promoted to flight lieutenant in May with command of B Flight, the first American in the squadron to join the RAF leaders in a command position. By June, they had shown themselves capable and joined the Hornchurch

Wing in 11 Group on the Channel Front. By August 1941, the Hurricanes were exchanged for hand-me-down Spitfire IIs. Peterson was promoted to command the squadron at the end of August, only weeks past his 21st birthday, the first American to command an Eagle Squadron. When the Eagles were taken into the USAAF 14 months later, he was promoted to group executive officer as a 22-year-old lieutenant colonel and became group commander six months later, promoted to colonel that summer of 1943 at age 23, the youngest full colonel ever in US service.

The second Eagle Squadron, 121, was formed in January 1941 at Kirton-on-Lindsey and was declared operational in July. The third and final Eagle Squadron, 133, was formed that July at Coltishall and became operational in August. By that fall, 71 had re-equipped with the Spitfire V, followed by 121 in November, after both squadrons had briefly flown hand-me-down Spitfire IIs for a month each. 133 re-equipped with Spitfires in January 1942. The three squadrons only flew together for the first time during the Dieppe Raid on August 19, 1942. 71 Squadron claimed one Ju-88; 121 an Fw-190 (with victor Barry Mahon shot down moments later while shooting down a second 190, to become a POW); 133 – now operating with the Debden Wing – claimed four Fw-190s, a Ju-88, and a Do-217, with Pilot Officer Don S. Gentile claiming the Do-217 and one Fw-190 to open his score. Six Spitfires were lost, with one pilot taken prisoner and one killed.

In light of its excellent performance at Dieppe, 133 Squadron was "promoted" to flying the new Spitfire IX, while the pilots completed their transfers to the USAAF. Unfortunately, on September 26, 1942, 11 of 12 brand-new Spitfire IXs were lost while escorting B-17s to bomb Morlaix, France. Unforecast strong winds reaching 40 knots blew them further south in the cloudy skies than expected. After failing to rendezvous with the bombers in the poor weather and short of fuel, the squadron let down through the clouds to find themselves directly over Brest, where they were intercepted by Fw-190s from JG 2 and the many German flak batteries below opened up. Four Eagles were killed: First Lieutenant William Baker and Second Lieutenants Gene Neville, Leonard Ryerson, and Dennis Smith; and six became POWs after bailing out of their stricken fighters. One Fw-190 fell to Captain Marion Jackson before he parachuted into captivity. Only

Second Lieutenant Richard Beaty made it back to England, where he was badly injured when he crash-landed on the Cornish coast. Second Lieutenant Don Gentile was left at Debden; as the "spare," he had turned back when the squadron reached the French coast and none of the other 12 aircraft had aborted the mission. The escort was also composed of 64 Squadron RAF and 401 Squadron RCAF, which never rendezvoused with 133 in the poor weather. Australian ace Tony Gaze, 64's commander, was relieved of command following the mission for insufficient preparation of the mission and mistakes during its execution.

Negotiations between the RAF and USAAF over transfer of the three Eagle Squadrons had commenced shortly after Ira Eaker had arrived in the UK in January 1942; interservice bureaucracy took nearly nine months to straighten out. President Roosevelt had to formally pardon each pilot for violating the Neutrality Act in order for them to meet the qualifications for an American commission. Since none of the pilots had completed USAAF flight training, there were additional negotiations for the USAAF to certify that the RCAF and RAF flight training standards met US standards so they could be issued USAAF pilot wings. A seemingly minor point regarding authorization for the pilots to wear RAF wings on their US uniform took three months to resolve in favor of a slightly smaller version of the RAF symbol being worn on the right breast of the uniform jacket, opposite the silver USAAF wings. The RAF received extra aircraft through Lend-Lease to compensate the loss of three experienced fighter squadrons.

In the meantime, the RAF scoured their squadrons to find enough experienced American pilots to completely fill out the squadron tables of organization. Among the Americans who involuntarily became Eagles, three would become prominent in the 4th Fighter Group. Foremost among the three was 23-year-old Flight Lieutenant Donald J.M. Blakeslee. Born in Fairport, Ohio, in 1917, his father had taken him to the Cleveland Air Races, where he fell in love with airplanes. After learning to fly in 1938, he and a friend purchased a Piper Cub, which the friend crashed in 1940. Unable to meet the educational requirements to join the Air Corps, Blakeslee joined the RCAF through the Knight Committee and trained in Canada. Arriving in the United Kingdom in May 1941, he was assigned to 401 RCAF Squadron. He proved to be a gifted pilot though not a good shot; he would later joke with the other aces of the 4th that "you dead-eye shots take all the fun out of it – the fun is when a guy like me comes motoring up behind them and has to open fire to see where the bullets are going." Scoring his first victory in November 1941, he shot down two Fw-190s in April 1942, by which time he had demonstrated gifted leadership that was cited in the Distinguished Flying Cross (DFC) he received that summer. He resisted transfer to the Eagle Squadrons because he considered them "pampered prima donnas" who "played sister with their claims." Only after learning that he would be transferred to instructor duty on completing his combat tour in August 1942 did he change his mind about the Eagles.

On a personal level, Blakeslee was remembered by those he flew with as "intense and committed"; he was also described as "thoroughly GI" – in almost all photos taken of him in the USAAF, his officer's hat was always completely regulation with the wire frame inside, unlike the "100-mission look" with the hat frame removed, which had been adopted by Air Force pilots up to General Carl Spaatz. Blakeslee was destined to achieve legendary status as the 4th Fighter Group's leader at the high point of the battle with the Luftwaffe in 1944, and would be tied with Hub Zemke of the 56th Group as the finest fighter group commander in Air Force history.

Another reluctant "volunteer" was Flying Officer James A. Goodson, who was transferred from 403 Squadron RCAF. Born in New York City of British parents and educated in Canada, making him a "passport American," Goodson traveled to England shortly after graduating from high school in the summer of 1939, working his way on a freighter as a pantry boy. Once there and realizing that war was coming, he tried to join the RAF but was told there was a six-month wait. Told he would have a better chance joining in Canada, he booked passage aboard the SS *Athenia*, which departed Liverpool for Montreal at 1300 hours on September 2, the day after the Germans began World War II with the invasion of Poland. At 1630 hours on September 3, five and a half hours after Britain had formally become a combatant, the ship was spotted off the Hebrides by *U-30*; her commander, Leutnant Helmut Lemp, tracked the liner until 1930 hours, when he fired two torpedoes, one of which hit *Athenia* in her engine room. Goodson, who was on deck when the torpedo struck, later recalled assisting with rescue efforts as

*Athenia* listed and her lights went dark. He later wrote in his memoirs, "I went to see if there were people trapped in the main section, and I saw dead bodies swooshing around in the water. I was plunged into the whole war thing in a matter of minutes." More than 100 passengers and crew were killed, including 28 Americans; their loss so concerned Hitler that the United States might enter the war, that the Germans denied sinking the ship until Lemp confessed to having done so after the war. Rescued by a passing ship and taken to Galway, Ireland, Goodson met the son of the American Ambassador to Britain, who had come to Ireland to assist the surviving Americans; Goodson and John F. Kennedy would renew their friendship after the war, until Kennedy's assassination. Completing training in May 1941, Goodson was sent back to Britain that fall, where he underwent operational training. He joined 416 RCAF squadron in June 1942, and participated in the Dieppe operation where he scored a probable Fw-190. Once in the 4th Fighter Group, Goodson would later command the 336th Fighter Squadron, formed from 133 Eagle Squadron, and would become the group's leading ace by the time he was shot down on a strafing mission on June 20, 1944.

Goodson later recalled in his memoirs that Blakeslee was not fond of authority: "While no one questioned his talent in the air, many in the top command had less confidence in his behavior on the ground." He recounted that the night before the Eagles' official turnover to the United States, Blakeslee entertained two female Women's Auxiliary Air Force (WAAF) officers in his room. When Brigadier General Frank "Monk" Hunter, commander of VIII Fighter Command and a nine-victory ace during World War I, arrived to visit Debden the next morning prior to the turnover, the two WAAFs just had time to scramble out the barracks window, right into the path of the general and his staff. When told that Blakeslee would be demoted and transferred, Hunter responded, "For one, maybe. But for two, he should be promoted!"

The third pilot sent to the Eagles was later recalled by Walter Cronkite, who covered the air war as United Press's "Man with the Eighth," as "the single most interesting individual I ever met in all of World War II."

Born November 10, 1919, in Athens, Greece, the son of a poor streetcar motorman with a large family, young Spiros Pisanos grew up expecting he would follow his father in work. In 1935, however, he met his destiny. "I was out in the country, when I heard a noise and when I looked up I saw two airplanes practicing aerobatics." Transfixed, the boy forgot about everything else as he watched the two fighters. Minutes later, they flew to what turned out to be a nearby Greek Air Force base. "They let me close to the airplanes and explained them to me. I thought they were wonderful, and said I wanted to be a pilot and fly airplanes like these." One pilot quickly disabused him of the idea, telling him that, in Greece, a boy like him could never fly airplanes; Pisanos left, but the officer had not destroyed his dream. "When I got home, I told my father I was going to America, where all things are possible, to become a pilot." His father had no argument that would change his son's mind; he did, however, manage to elicit a promise that his son would not leave home until he completed school.

In 1938, Pisanos was ready to leave for America. Too poor to pay for passage, he signed aboard a freighter as a cabin boy, planning to jump ship on arrival at his destination. "It took me three trips, because I didn't know there was a North and South America." After trips to Buenos Aires and Rio de Janeiro, Pisanos finally arrived in Baltimore, where he went on shore leave and never returned, becoming what would be called today an "illegal immigrant." He found a restaurant owner in the Greek community there who hired him to wash dishes until he could earn enough to take the train to New York City, where he found work shelling oysters in Delmonico's Restaurant for ten dollars a week and "Americanized" his name to "Steve." "I knew I had to learn English before I could fly, so each day on the streetcar, I would read the *New York Post* with a Greek-English dictionary." Within a year, he began flight training at Floyd Bennett Field. A one-hour lesson cost $5; by this time his pay was $15 a week. "I moved to Plainfield, New Jersey after I soloed, when I found a better job and a cheaper flight school."

By May 1941, Greece had fallen to the Nazis. Pisanos, with all of 80 hours in light planes, bumped that total to 300 hours with an hour's work on his logbook and snuck across the Canadian border to join the RCAF. He was a newly minted pilot officer when he completed training in April 1942 and arrived in England in May, where he was assigned to 402 Squadron, RCAF, from which he was assigned to 71 Squadron that August. When his paperwork was being processed for transfer to the USAAF, the fact that he was not an American citizen came out. American Ambassador John Winant learned that Congress had just passed a law allowing an immigrant who joined the armed forces to gain immediate citizenship. On September 10, 1942, Spiros "Steve" Pisanos became the first immigrant to take advantage of that law; immediately after he took the Oath of Allegiance to the United States as a citizen, he was sworn in as a second lieutenant in the USAAF. The son of the poor Athens streetcar motorman was not only a pilot, but an American citizen and "an officer and a gentleman by Act of Congress."

Lieutenant Colonel Edward Anderson, who at age 39 was definitely "old" for a fighter pilot, became group commander, though the 4th was considered "the Debden Wing" in RAF Fighter Command, with an RAF station commander and wing leader Duke Woolley leading the group in the air, until January 1942 when Debden became an official USAAF base and VIII Fighter Command assumed official control. Major Gus Daymond, a former set decorator at MGM in Hollywood before he joined the RAF and became the first Eagle Squadron pilot "officially" credited as an ace in August 1941, led the 334th Squadron; Major William Daley, who had transferred to the group from the RAF just before the turnover to the USAAF, was appointed commander of the 335th Squadron; Major Carroll W. "Mac" McColpin – the second American ace of the war after setting a record of shooting down five enemy aircraft in five weeks and fighting leading German ace Werner Mölders to a draw, the only pilot to serve in all three Eagle Squadrons, and the second American to command an Eagle Squadron in the RAF when he was sent to 133 after the Morlaix disaster – commanded the 336th Squadron. For the pilots, the main change as a result of transferring to the USAAF was a pay increase. A pilot officer in the RAF made 70 pounds a month (US$350 then), while a USAAF second lieutenant drawing both flight and combat pay received $550 per month, a significant difference.

With white stars rather than RAF roundels now on its Spitfire Vs, the 4th Fighter Group flew its first USAAF mission on October 2, 1942, escorting B-17s to Dunkirk. The Luftwaffe decided to contest the mission, and the 334th and 335th squadrons engaged Fw-190s from JG 26, with Captain Oscar Coen and Lieutenants Gene Fetrow and Stanley Anderson each credited with an Fw-190 and Second Lieutenant

Jim Clark sharing an Fw-190. All missions flown over the rest of the month failed to entice the Luftwaffe to show up.

Finally, Lieutenants Jim Clark and Bob Boock found some action flying a Rhubarb on November 16 in poor weather. When they strafed Saint-Valery-en-Caux in Normandy, Clark flew so low avoiding the defending flak that he hit a tree, returning to Debden with branches in his radiator intake. On November 19, the 335th's Second Lieutenant Frank Smolinsky added to the group's score when he shot down an Fw-190 over the Channel.

On November 22, Major Daley completed his operational tour. Don Blakeslee, who had managed to keep his commission as a captain despite the incident with the WAAFs, was promoted to replace Daley. The weather then closed in for the rest of the month, precluding operations until early December.

The 4th flew a group-strength "Rodeo" (a non-escort mission by a squadron or group) fighter sweep along the French coast on December 4, which the Luftwaffe again ignored. Two days later, flying escort to B-17s that bombed the Lille/Fives locomotive works, Gene Fetrow spotted an Fw-190 as they headed back to England and shot it down. The weather closed in again over the rest of December, and the only action seen were a few low-altitude Rhubarbs flown in the poor weather.

The first major missions of 1943 were two bomber escorts flown on January 13, 1943. The next day, Lieutenants Anderson and Boock flew a Rhubarb to Ostend, during which they were intercepted and bounced by a pair of Fw-190s. Chopping his throttle and skidding violently, Anderson managed to get the two Germans to overshoot; quickly straightening out, he caught the wingman from a range of 200 yards, setting the enemy fighter on fire and sending it into the Channel below. In the meantime, Boock spotted two more Würgers closing in on Anderson and opened fire on the leader, who reared up before crashing into the Channel in a shower of spray.

After other uneventful missions, some of which were canceled due to weather, the group escorted B-17s to bomb St Omer on January 22. This time, JG 26 intercepted the Spitfires over the coast. The Fw-190s turned onto the Spitfires and one shot up Bob Boock badly, a bullet actually clipping his goggles and knocking them off. He managed to return to Debden, where his Spitfire was written off. In the fight that followed, 336th Squadron CO Captain Oscar Coen and Lieutenant Joseph Matthews each claimed one Fw-190.

Four days later, Coen led the squadron on a Ramrod fighter sweep to Bruges, Belgium. As the planes crossed the coast, Boock's new Spitfire was hit by flak and caught fire. Boock turned out to sea to put as much distance between himself and the enemy as possible. When the fire started to melt his flying boots and burned through some control cables, he was finally forced to go over the side, six miles off the Belgian coast. While four of his fellow pilots orbited overhead, he got in his raft and began paddling toward England. Fortunately, 20 minutes later he was picked up by a British ship.

# 5

# STARTING OVER

Just as VIII Fighter Command's groups were beginning to demonstrate their ability, Eighth Air Force lost its most experienced units to the North African invasion. Just before this was announced, the command flew its most important and ambitious mission to date. Mission 14, target Lille, flown on October 9, 1942, would be the first opportunity to demonstrate the four-engine bomber as a war-winning weapon, and the first time the Luftwaffe would get a taste of the battles to come.

Lille was in range of the fighters based in southern England. A complicated schedule of fighter sweeps and diversions was planned, through there would be no close escort for the bombers, which were considered capable of self-defense. The operation would also involve 36 Spitfire squadrons of the RAF's 11 Group. A total of 432 fighters would be involved in the two target support forces that would cover the force's entry into France, two rear support forces to cover withdrawal, and three diversionary forces which were to distract the defenders. Both target support groups would reach Lille just before the bombers' arrival and orbit until they arrived and hit the target. As the target support groups disengaged when low on fuel, the two rear support groups would cover the return of the bombers out of France and across the Channel.

The bombing force was composed of 108 heavy bombers of the 92nd (B-17), 93rd (B-24), the veteran 97th (B-17), 301st (B-17), and 306th (B-17) Bomb Groups. It would be the debut mission for the B-24Ds of the 93rd and the 306th Group's B-17s. The B-24s would fly at 23,000 feet while the B-17s flew at 25–26,000 feet, in 18-plane "box" formations.

Opposing them would be the three *Gruppen* of JG 26, all equipped with the Fw-190A. The *Würger* (Butcher Bird), as it was known, was superior to any Allied fighter at low to medium altitudes, while its heavy armament of two MG 151 and two MG-FF 20mm cannon gave it hitting power to knock down a bomber. This would be the first time Fw-190s would attack B-17s flying at 25,000 feet or higher, which would reveal the fighter's poor performance above its rated altitude of 23,000 feet.

The bombers began taking off from their East Anglia airfields at 0830 hours. The point of penetration into German-controlled airspace was just south of Dunkirk. The German Y-Service intercepted radio traffic from bomber radiomen testing their gear before the takeoff, while the *Würzburg* radars spotted the bombers as they climbed above 500 feet over England. With all the Allied formations heading toward Dunkirk, it was quickly apparent to the German controllers that the target was in northern France. JG 26's I.Gruppe was scrambled from St Omer-Arques at 1017 hours, followed within minutes by all of III./JG 26 from their airfields at Moorseele and Wevelgem in southern Belgium, led by their *Kommandeur*, the redoubtable Major Josef "Pips" Priller, a veteran now of three years' combat on the Western Front. The Würgers set course toward the Channel as the pilots strained for altitude and soon sighted the "Fat Ones," the B-17s and B-24s.

The 93rd's novices in their B-24s were the first to reach Lille, around 1025 hours in a formation depleted by 14 mechanical aborts. There was only light flak. The B-17 groups, minus 16 aborts, were all over the target at 1040 hours. A total of 69 B-17s and B-24s attacked the primary target, with ten others bombing a secondary target. The intercepting German fighters were soon on the scene, with gunners reporting attack by a total of 242 enemy fighters, an overestimate. The fighter pilots were inexperienced in dealing with the American bombers and attacked primarily from the rear, which exposed them to withering defensive fire. The Twelve O'Clock High attack had yet to be devised to counter the lack of forward defensive armament of the B-17 and B-24.

The Germans paid no mind to the P-38s of the 1st Group, which were on their first escort mission and flying at 30,000 feet, or the Spitfires of the 31st and 4th groups, holding formation over the bombers at 28,000 feet.

This was "Pips" Priller's first combat with the American heavy bombers, and he had difficulty comprehending their size. He underestimated the enemy's altitude twice, but eventually positioned the three *Staffeln* correctly and they initiated a mass attack from the rear. Priller bored in and was the first to score when he set a B-17 on fire that dropped out of the formation for his 78th victory (of an eventual 101, all scored on the Western Front).

At 1045 hours, Hauptmann Klaus Mietusch, whose 7.Staffel had overwhelmed the British defenders of Malta six months earlier, firewalled his throttle as his ten Fw-190s closed on the bombers. Mietusch shot down one B-17 while his wingman claimed a second, and a third fell out of formation, smoking and damaged, as the *Staffel* swept through the formation.

Close behind was Oberleutnant Kurt Ruppert, leading 9.Staffel. Ruppert hit one bomber solidly, which fell out of formation, while Leutnant Otto "Stotto" Stammberger, a two-year veteran of the Channel Front who had finally scored his first victory during the Dieppe Raid and a second RAF Spitfire a week earlier, latched onto a B-17. Opening fire at first out of range because he misjudged the target's size, he recalled his engagement:

> I then approached much closer and saw hits on the enemy's left wing. By my third attack, both left engines were burning, and I fired freely at the right outboard engine as the crate spiraled downhill in broad left turns. At about 2,000 meters [6,500 feet], four or five men jumped out; the bomber struck the ground east of Vendeville. I looked up. The sky was empty. I was out of cannon ammunition and slunk home.

The B-17 was his third victory, and the first of five Fortresses he would be credited with shooting down over the next six months.

The bomber gunners claimed 25 German fighters shot down when they returned to their bases. In reality, only Priller's *Gruppe* claimed six bombers – five B-17s and one B-24 – shot down with a B-17 forced out of formation, in their ten-minute engagement. They also claimed one Spitfire. In fact, 315 (Polish) Squadron's 24-year-old Flight Sergeant Marian Kordasiewicz made it back to England in his bullet-riddled Spitfire Mark IX, but was killed attempting to crash-land at RAF Manston.

Mission 14 cost three B-24s and a B-17, with four B-17s seriously damaged; a further 32 B-17s and ten B-24s reported varying degrees of damage, with 31 crew members missing and 13 wounded. The losses from Lille were more than had been experienced in the 13 previous missions. One bomber crewman later wrote home, saying, "Lille was our first real brawl," while another described the mission as "the roughest yet!"

Lille was the first mission in which exaggerated numbers of enemy fighters were claimed by the bomber gunners. The initial claims were 56 destroyed, 26 probably destroyed, and 20 damaged, for a total of 102 enemy aircraft reportedly hit, a remarkable total given that in fact there were only a total of 108 enemy fighters airborne. A London newspaper headline on October 12, 1942 proclaimed: "53 Enemy Planes Bagged in Allied Raid on Lille." In fact, only 7.Staffel's Unteroffizier Viktor Hager had been shot down, with the pilot successfully bailing out. German claims were more realistic. Bomber gunner claims were quickly seen by intelligence officers as "fantasy," but were explainable when as many as 15–20 gunners in different airplanes might shoot at one fighter as it flashed through a formation with each having mere seconds to sight the target and fire. VIII Bomber Command never revised the gunner claims of any mission, on the grounds that accepting the gunners' good-faith beliefs contributed to morale. For the Germans, the initial claims reflected the difficulty the pilots had in dealing with the B-17 and B-24, both of which were tougher than the bombers they had previously been faced with.

The bombing results also reflected the inexperience of the American crews, with accuracy for the raid considered "poor" after bomb damage assessment post-strike photos were examined. With 588 bombs on the target factory in Lille, only nine fell within 1,650 feet of the aiming point. General Eaker had claimed that daylight bombing would be more accurate and lead to fewer civilian casualties, but most bombs hit residences around the Fives-Lille factory, killing 40 French civilians and wounding 90. However, the nine bombs that did fall on the target temporarily put the factory out of operation and damaged equipment. A contributing factor to the poor bombing was the unreported 80–100mph winds at the bombing altitude.

General Eaker wrote to General Arnold that the Lille mission had demonstrated that day bombers "...in strong formation can be

employed effectively and successfully without fighter support." With
the diversion of much of the force to North Africa, it would be six
months before VIII Bomber Command flew a second similarly sized
mission. The Luftwaffe would soon demonstrate that Eaker had been
vastly over-optimistic in his report.

It did not take the Jagdwaffe long to discover that the B-17s and
B-24s were vulnerable to attacks from forward. Crews returning from
the attack on the U-boat pens at St Nazaire on November 23 reported
that the majority of the fighter attacks had come from dead ahead.
JG 2's Oberleutnant Egon Mayer, who led the attacking fighters,
had studied the largely unsuccessful efforts made so far to stop the
American bombers and had determined that they were most vulnerable
to this tactic. The original forward armament of the B-17E and F was
a single .50-caliber machine gun in the extreme nose manned by the
bombardier. Over the course of the past several months, this armament
had been increased by fitting larger windows to either side in the nose
compartment with an additional .50-caliber gun fired from each, but
these weapons could not be brought to bear against fighters attacking
from directly ahead, which were still only defended by the single weapon
that could not be used while the bombardier was busy with his sighting.
The B-24 had similar forward armament.

On November 30, 1942, the men of the 78th Fighter Group arrived
at Goxhill at 0130 hours. While the group awaited the arrival of its
aircraft, Major Peterson was named station commander and promoted
to lieutenant colonel. With pilots anxious to "get on with it," and
knowing they needed to get experience as quickly as possible, "Colonel
Pete" arranged to send pilots to RAF units for "familiarization" after
the Christmas holidays. Captain Charles London, flight commander in
the 83rd Squadron, was sent to Hornchurch. He later reported, "Wing
Commander Bentley wondered what we were supposed to do. We said
he was supposed to teach us to fight the war, so he got us checked out
in Spitfire Mark IXs. I got about three-quarters of an hour in one, and
then he says 'Tomorrow we'll go on a Do.'" The next day the Americans
accompanied the wing on a mission to Calais. London recalled that,
later that day, "We were about to take off on another mission to see
if we could goad the Hun into a reaction, when a teletype came in
stating we were not supposed to fly. This was very embarrassing since
apparently he was just supposed to tell us war stories."

VIII Bomber Command made its only effective attack so far on the German Air Force with a large-scale mission flown against the aircraft repair depot at Romilly-sur-Seine on December 20 that was the deepest penetration of enemy territory yet made. The depot and airfield were 65 miles southeast of Paris, near the Seine, and performed depot-level repair on Luftwaffe aircraft from units in France and the Low Countries. A force of 101 bombers was dispatched, of which 72 bombed the target.

Flying to the target, the force was opposed by all three JG 26 *Gruppen*, reinforced by JG 2, and the air battle became the largest fought to date, turning into an important test of the theory that the bombers could successfully carry out unescorted missions deep in enemy territory. Escort for penetration of French airspace and withdrawal support was provided by eight RAF Fighter Command Spitfire squadrons and the 4th Fighter Group's three squadrons. Diversionary missions involving a total of 89 Spitfires were flown to known German fighter bases, but there was no response to the fighters.

The RAF provided 35 new Spitfire IXs that escorted the bombers as far as Rouen. They turned back at 1150 hours. Minutes later, an estimated 60 Fw-190s from JG 26's first and second groups appeared and made the first attacks. As had happened at St Nazaire, the majority of the attacks came from ahead. The German formations were seen to fly alongside the formation beyond range of the defending gunners till they obtained position two to three miles ahead, at which point they curved in on the formation, attacking at its flight level. The first pass claimed a B-17 from the 91st Group that hit the ground, with a second shot out of formation that lost altitude and came under attack from several Focke-Wulfs that followed and shot it down.

A second group of 50–60 Focke-Wulfs from JG 2 entered the battle at approximately 1205 hours. These fighters made several attacks as the formation neared the target. Bf-109s from JG 1 that had been brought in from Holland joined the battle, with a 30-plane formation diving on the bombers five minutes before they arrived over the target at 1240 hours. One B-17 from the 306th Group was forced out of formation about 1230 hours, crashing five minutes later.

The bombing results were later determined to be reasonably good: hangars, barracks, and aircraft were damaged to varying degrees and the airfield was cratered with 138 bombs.

The flight home saw the Germans make continuous attacks after they had landed and refueled from their first interceptions. The 306th Group lost two B-17s shot down near Paris. The sixth loss finally went down over the Channel, last seen when it dropped out of formation as the smoke from fires aboard increased. Two other B-17s managed to land back at their bases but were so badly shot up that they never flew again. A further 29 returned damaged to varying degrees. Flak had been inaccurate and ineffective throughout the mission, and all losses were due to enemy fighters. The losses exceeded the 5 percent deemed sustainable, and demonstrated that the defenders were quickly learning how to deal with the American bombers whose appearance over the Continent had initially intimidated them four months before.

In post-strike intelligence interrogation of the crews, claims were made that seven enemy fighters were seen to crash, 18 broke up in mid-air, and 27 went down in flames. Total claims included 50 destroyed, 13 probables, and eight damaged. These claims were originally reduced to 30 destroyed and 15–20 damaged. On January 5, 1943, VIII Bomber Command lowered the figure to 21 shot down, 31 probably shot down and seven damaged. The Jagdwaffe only listed two Fw-190s lost and a third damaged. The German records also listed ten fighters damaged in "non-operational" losses.

At the end of December, General Galland issued new instructions for attacking American bomber formations. The preferred method was now an attack from the front in as large a formation as possible. The general stressed that the fighters should attempt to stay together as they broke off their attack above the bomber formation, to allow them to reform for a second attack; however, among German fighter pilots the favorite method of ending an attack was a split-S, pulling out below the formation, usually too far to give time to climb back for a further attack. For the majority of German pilots, one head-on rush into a formation of enormous bombers, with tracers flashing straight at him, and the ever-present likelihood of a head-on collision, was enough.

As missions continued into the new year, the Jagdwaffe's frontal attacks grew in number and soon accounted for most losses. Losses to enemy fighters rose from an average 3.7 percent of the attacking force in November to 8.8 percent in December and 8.7 percent in January. The Germans found that if such frontal attacks were made just before the bombers reached the point of "bombs away," it would most likely spoil the bombardier's aim. Breaking up the bombing run appeared to now be a primary objective of the defending fighters.

Modification for additional nose armament, which had been carried out at English depots and at bomber bases, was now performed at the modification center operated by United Airlines in Cheyenne, Wyoming, before a B-17 was flown on to England. A modified mount for multiple nose guns was developed for the B-17F which improved the field of fire while still allowing sufficient room inside the crowded nose compartment for the bombardier to attend to his primary job. Most bombers in England were equipped with more effective forward fire by late January 1943. The ultimate solution, the adoption of nose turrets for both B-17s and B-24s, did not happen until the appearance of the B-17G and the B-24H beginning in the late summer of 1943.

On January 10, 1943, Major Josef "Pips" Priller became *Geschwaderkommodore* (wing commander) of JG 26, a position he would hold for the next two years. Priller was just 27 years old when he took command. He had first made a name for himself in Werner Mölders' JG 51 during the Battle of Britain, where he was awarded the Knight's Cross in October 1940 at the end of the campaign. He had then transferred to JG 26 where he became *Staffelkapitän* (squadron commander) of 1./JG 26. In early 1942 he had moved up to *Gruppenkommandeur* of II./JG 26. He was, at the time of his promotion to lead the *Geschwader*, the leading *Experte* (German term for "ace," though it was not merely based on how many planes were shot down, but by a judgement of the skill used by the pilot) among the pilots, with 60 victories. He was a notable *bon vivant*, though he took the responsibility of command seriously, and was always concerned with the welfare of his men, both pilots and ground crew; they responded with deep loyalty to his leadership. He would continue his leading role in the air battles of the Western Front until the Jagdwaffe was reduced to near-irrelevance after the losses incurred in *Case Bodenplatte* at the end of the Battle of the Bulge.

Most importantly for the proposed US air campaign, the Casablanca Conference was convened in January to determine Allied strategy in the coming year. Churchill was of the opinion that the Eighth Air Force had not proved its worth, since "not one bomb has fallen on Germany since their arrival." Churchill and Chief of the Air Staff Sir Charles Portal wanted to see the Americans join the RAF in night bombing.

When General Arnold, who attended the conference with President Roosevelt, learned that Churchill had won the president to his position over dinner on the day they arrived, he quickly ordered Eaker, Spaatz, and General Frank Andrews to Casablanca before the conference began on January 13, to defend the daylight bombing campaign. The decisive meeting with Churchill happened on January 20. Eaker's presentation was the most convincing. Churchill later wrote in his memoirs that Eaker's promise to mount a 100-plane mission by February 1, "and as many thereafter as conditions allowed," along with his presentation of the advantages of round-the-clock bombing of Germany, changed his mind. "Considering how much had been staked on this venture by the United States and all they felt about it, I decided to back Eaker and his theme, and I turned around completely and withdrew all my opposition to the daylight bombing by the Fortresses." Eaker later recalled that Churchill merely agreed to allow Eighth Air Force more time to prove its case.

Fortunately, Churchill did not hold Eaker to his promise. On February 2, 1943, VIII Bomber Command's authorized strength rose to six heavy bomber groups with a strength of 210 bombers – 35 front-line and 18 spare per group. However, none of the groups were close to their paper strength. On February 1, there were only 182 B-17s and B-24s total in-theater, including those under repair, and of that total only 98 were ready for combat. VIII Bomber Command had fallen to its lowest combat-ready strength. The force was further marginalized by frightful winter weather conditions, which permitted daylight operations on only a handful of days. Rather than a 100-plane mission by February 1 and "as many as possible thereafter," there were only seven missions flown, two of which failed to reach their targets due to weather; none exceeded 93 bombers.

Shortly after returning to England, Eaker ordered the first mission to bomb a target inside Germany, the U-boat construction yards at Vegesack. Arriving over the target they found it completely cloud-covered. The members of the force then bombed their secondary target, the port of Wilhelmshaven, which was only partially covered by clouds. They were thus still able to drop the first American bombs on German soil. With that, VIII Bomber command had its first major victory.

However, rather than continue bombing targets in Germany, the targets hit over the next several months were still the U-boat bases at

St Nazaire and Lorient; this continued through the spring. Following the first USAAF photo-reconnaissance mission in the ETO on March 28, photo interpreters noted that there was no building still standing undamaged in either Lorient or St Nazaire. On April 1, German submarine commander Admiral Dönitz reported that the two towns had been reduced to uninhabitable rubble and that all support operations for the U-boats had been moved into the massive concrete submarine pens, where they were completely undisturbed by the bombs the Americans dropped. The Allied losses to U-boats in the Battle of the Atlantic continued unabated.

Brand-new P-38Gs arrived at Goxhill during January, but they were not destined to remain long. Having taken one up for a test flight, Captain Harry Dayhuff decided to buzz the field. His first run was successful, so he decided to repeat it, only lower. He kept at it, going lower again on a third pass. By his fourth pass, he was nearly clipping the grass on the field with his propellers and he had gotten closer and closer to the operations shack. When he climbed out after landing, armorer Warren Kellerstadt congratulated his flying and commented that he'd done a very good job of missing the telephone pole right next to the operations shack. Dayhuff went white when he saw the 20-foot pole, which he had not spotted while performing his buzz job.

On January 13, the 56th Group arrived in Britain after a six-day voyage on the *Queen Elizabeth* from New York. It was originally sent to King's Cliffe, a satellite field of RAF Wittering, where the men learned how cold an English winter could be after moving into the new Nissen huts that had been set up for them. Hub Zemke recalled that his first impressions of King's Cliffe were that the airdrome was in a bleak location that overlooked a small river valley to the south and the village of the same name immediately to the west. The field had three short hard surface runways encircled by a paved perimeter track. Civilian workers were still erecting what the British called "utility buildings" and Americans came to know as Nissen huts. The group would be housed at nearby RAF Wittering while the base was still under construction. All were happy to find that Wittering was a prewar RAF base that had steam-heated barracks and was overall much better than King's Cliffe. Zemke's first act was to replace the English cooks and their "English food," which the Americans disliked, with American cooks who provided food that was not what could be found back home, but more to the American palate. Once King's Cliffe was finished and they moved to the base, they quickly found that the stoves in the Nissen huts were terrible. 61st squadron commander Dave Schilling claimed one could be stoked for three days and could still be picked up with bare hands with no fear of harm. Soon, everyone seemed to come down with colds as they got acclimated to the English winter.

When Zemke went in search of transportation, the RAF supplied him with a Wolseley limousine, which he remembered as a big English car that must have been commandeered from the nobility, with separate compartments for the driver and passengers. Deciding it was not a very practical car for his needs, he commandeered a jeep, but kept the Wolseley for use by the group; fueled with 100 octane av gas, the car was even faster than Zemke originally found it and pilots soon put it to use for picking up girls for parties, which resulted in it being named "the Sex Machine." Zemke also made use of it when he had official business to transact at VIII Fighter Command Headquarters and the weather was too poor for him to fly the 100 miles to London, since the vehicle always turned heads when it arrived.

The big Wolseley was a temperamental and cantankerous vehicle. Zemke's driver, Sergeant Curtis Houston, recalled a trip to London that proved troublesome in many ways during the trip home. Driving on the A12 from London to Ipswich, the engine suddenly coughed and died. Houston's guesstimate was carburetor trouble. Zemke found that tapping on the carburetor with a screwdriver caused whatever was sticking inside to become unstuck, and the engine started again without trouble. Zemke hopped in front with Houston and they drove on, only to have the problem repeat itself five miles further on. More tapping brought the engine back to life and they drove on. Just outside Ipswich, they spotted a British Army soldier thumbing a ride. Zemke ordered a stop and offered the man a ride. Surprised to find such a luxury vehicle in the hands of the American Air Force, the private climbed into the luxurious rear cabin and they set off once again. A few miles later the problem raised its head again, but this time Zemke's tapping only revived the engine so long as he continued tapping. The colonel was in no mood to remain at the side of the road awaiting help, so he opened the laterally hinged hood and positioned himself on the long mudguard and continued tapping, which allowed them to drive on without further delays. Curious, the passenger in back opened the window to Houston's driver compartment and inquired, "Who's your mate out there, Sergeant?" "He's my Colonel," Houston replied. The private was silent during the rest of the 25-mile drive while the big Wolseley purred down the road with a full colonel applying a "monkey see, monkey do" solution to the problem as he held onto the mudguard, while his sergeant drove and a private rode in splendor. The incident was a perfect demonstration of the kind of officer Zemke was.

On his first meeting with General Hunter, Zemke learned that the 4th Group had priority on receiving P-47s since they had combat experience. Although General Hunter had a good reputation as a pilot and a war record to back it up, Zemke soon found that while his commander was willing to delegate authority to his staff, he seldom followed up to see how they had dealt with an assignment. Zemke later recalled that as a result, his staff officers became effectively commanders in their own right, which was wrong. Zemke believed Hunter lacked the spark of real leadership and did not understand modern aviation administration and control. Zemke later commented that Hunter's unfitness for his position adversely affected the operations of the fighters through their first crucial year of operations.

Zemke remembered that, as the men grew restless without any chance of flying, one of the officers came up with the idea of simulating formations by using the English bicycles each pilot had been issued. "The spectacle of a dozen men pedaling hard around the perimeter track in echelons of four must have confirmed to the British that we Yanks were crazy."

The 56th finally received its first P-47s on January 24, following re-equipment of the 78th with the P-47 because its P-38s had been sent to North Africa. Zemke's biggest problem was the enthusiasm of his pilots to get back in the cockpit. Because the airplanes had only recently been reassembled, and because theater modifications had been made to them that the pilots would not be used to, he was concerned about flight safety. He remembered later that he called them together and informed them no one would fly the planes till they had been thoroughly inspected and he had signed off. He established a five-pound fine for anyone breaking the rule, which the pilots all took as a challenge. While the mechanics in the 61st Squadron worked on the first of the P-47s, the pilots drew straws as to who the first lucky man would be, and passed the hat. Zemke was surprised when they came into his office and dumped a hatful of coins on his desk, announcing that this contained the five pounds and they were going to fly that afternoon. Zemke later recalled that morale was sky-high when after a few days the first airplanes were ready and the pilots flew them relentlessly over the next week.

Things were different for the 78th. On January 15, Colonel Peterson informed the pilots that they would soon begin escorting missions against the U-boat pens at Lorient and Brest. However, at the same time, the need for P-38 replacements in North Africa meant that airplanes were being sent on arrival in the United Kingdom to the Lockheed facility in Belfast, Northern Ireland, for transfer on to North Africa. The arrival of four P-47C Thunderbolts on January 29 seemed ominous. No one had ever seen a P-47 before and there was great curiosity, particularly when two ferry pilots crashed and died the next day, bringing in more P-47s. Charles London recalled that his first thought on seeing the Thunderbolts was "Thank God we don't have to fly those things!" He soon learned otherwise. These were their airplanes.

Pilots were struck on reading the manual by the dire warnings not to dive vertically above 25,000 feet. On February 6, Captain Herb Ross took one up for a check ride. Climbing to 35,000 feet, he decided to see what the warning was about and pushed over into a steep dive. Speed built rapidly: at 27,000 feet, he experienced tail buffet so intense the stick flailed out of his hands; he was only able to grab the stick as he sped through 20,000 feet, with the controls "set in concrete." Seeing he was at the top of the "yellow arc" of the airspeed indicator and believing his time had come, he stopped trying to work the controls and began to feed in nose-up elevator trim. As he passed through 10,000 feet, suddenly the racket stopped and the nose gradually came up. Leveling off at 5,000 feet and catching his breath, Ross called to ask whether he should land the damaged airplane or bail out. He was told to bring it in to have a look. On arrival, he was still so shaken he had to be helped from the cockpit. A short inspection certified the P-47 "Class 26" as damaged beyond repair: the paint was off the leading edges of all flying surfaces; wing spars had been pulled back and the sheet metal failed at the wing roots; vertical and horizontal stabilizers were pulled back with root failure, and most of the fabric on the elevators was in tatters. Harry Dayhuff recalled, "It was the sickest looking lately-new P-47 one can imagine, having only collided with air." Ross subsequently gained the nickname "Rocket."

On February 7, Colonel Peterson was ordered to attend a meeting at VIII Fighter Command Headquarters. Several hours later he called and ordered all officers to assemble in the briefing room at 1500 hours. When he and the staff entered the room, everyone could see from their faces that the news was not good. Voice shaking, Peterson informed them that all pilots in the group except group headquarters, squadron commanders, and flight commanders of each squadron were to be immediately transferred to North Africa to replace heavy combat losses in the other P-38 groups and they should be ready to depart the next morning. Just as it was about to enter combat as the first long-range fighter escort group of Eighth Air Force, after a year's preparation and training, the 78th Fighter Group was gutted and given a new airplane none of them knew anything about, and pilots none had ever met. They had to start over from scratch; but there would not be another year in which to prepare.

Adolf Galland later wrote of this period in his memoir *The First and the Last* that the hour had struck for the defense of the Reich but that no one wanted to admit that the Germans had lost the initiative in the west, where they were now the defender rather than the attacker. With air supremacy now threatened, it was essential that the fighter force be strengthened since only fighters can achieve air supremacy. "England had given us a practical demonstration of this. It is amazing and shocking that this thought never occurred to either Hitler or Göring."

# 6

# OPPONENTS

Jagdgeschwader 26 "Schlageter" was the German fighter unit best known to its American opponents, who called its members "the Abbeville Boys," identifying them with their main base outside Abbeville in northwestern France. By the end of the war, JG 26 was the leading German fighter group on the Western Front. Manned by experienced aces who had fought since the Battle of Britain when VIII Bomber Command first ventured across the English Channel, they would be a major thorn in the side of the Allied air forces till the last day of the war, even as the experienced pilots were lost in the war of attrition and replaced by partly trained youngsters. On the Western Front, Jagdgeschwadern 2, 1, and 11 were also the primary opponents of the Eighth.

The Abbeville Boys were known for their brightly painted Focke-Wulf Fw-190s, the aircraft known to its pilots as the *Würger* (Butcher Bird). Aviation historian William Green wrote of the fighter:

> No combat aircraft has ever achieved perfection, but at the time of its debut the Fw-190 probably came as near to this elusive goal as any fighter. It was a brilliant design in which weight consciousness and simplicity were keynotes, although they had not been allowed to affect structural strength. But this beautifully proportioned fighter was not merely a pilot's aeroplane – it had been conceived with a careful eye to the problems of both produceability and maintenance in the field.

Grumman test pilot Corky Meyer, who flew a captured Fw-190A-5 in 1944, considered it the most amazing airplane he had ever flown.

Hellcat designer Bob Hall, who also flew the airplane, was so impressed that he designed the F8F Bearcat as a "carrier-based Fw-190."

When VIII Bomber Command began raids into northern France and the Low Countries, and later into central and western Germany, the main route ran through the region defended by JG 26. By the spring of 1943, I and II Gruppen operated the latest versions of the Fw-190A.

At the height of the battles between VIII Fighter Command and the Jagdwaffe, the primary version of the Würger was the Fw-190A-8, which appeared in late 1943 and became the most-produced A-series sub-type. The A-8 sacrificed air combat agility for heavy armament useful in attacking bombers. With additional armor plate installed and other technical changes, the days of the lightweight "dogfighter" that could outmaneuver every Allied fighter were gone; the primary target of this fighter was Allied bombers, not fighters. The 7.62mm machine guns originally mounted in the fuselage ahead of the cockpit were replaced with heavy 13mm MG 131 machine guns for the anti-bomber role. The primary armament was four 20mm MG 151/20 cannon, with some exchanging the outboard MG 151 for an MK 108 30mm cannon. The A-8 was powered by either the standard BMW 801 D-2 or the 801Q, providing 1,800hp. This could be enhanced by the *Erhöhte Notleistung* emergency boost system that raised power to 1,953hp for approximately ten minutes by spraying additional fuel into the fuel/air mix, cooling it, thus allowing higher boost pressures, but at the cost of much higher fuel consumption.

Though the Fw-190A was always the German fighter with the best armament for opposing heavy bombers, it was at a disadvantage against American fighters since the Würger's best altitude performance was at approximately 22–23,000 feet. With the American bombers at 25,000–27,000 feet, the Fw-190-equipped units were at a serious disadvantage if they ran across any opposing P-47s – which were operating at their best altitude.

Thus, the *Jagdgeschwadern* opposing the Americans changed in the summer of 1943 from being solely equipped with Fw-190s in all three *Gruppen* to having two *Gruppen* on the Fw-190 while the third *Gruppe* flew the Messerschmitt Bf-109G, which could fly and fight at altitudes above 30,000 feet. Developed from the *Friedrich* (F)-series airframe, the primary difference of the *Gustav* 109 was the Daimler-Benz DB 605A engine, a development of the DB 601E engine that powered the preceding Bf-109F-4, providing a power increase to 1,455hp. By 1943, this basically clean design began to change with the introduction of the pressurized Bf-109G-5 in which the 7.92mm MG 17 weapons were replaced with 13mm MG 131 machine guns; the G-5 and the unpressurized G-6 – the most-produced Bf-109 sub-type – that quickly followed received the nickname *Beule* (The Bulge) due to the MG 131's much larger breechblock, as well as a bulged fairing on the wings due to use of larger tires. In late 1943, the MG 151 was replaced by a 30mm MK 108 cannon. To increase the anti-bomber firepower, many Bf-109Gs were equipped with a 20mm cannon in an underwing fairing outboard of the main gear well in each wing. These weapons added weight and also contributed increased drag, which adversely affected maneuverability in fighter-vs-fighter combat; 109s so equipped were known as *Kanonenboote* (gunboats). JG 11 *Experte* Heinz Knoke recalled in his memoirs that the Gustav had to be flown in the landing pattern at full power, which he initially found disconcerting.

During the period before American fighter escorts gained the range to accompany the bombers all the way to and from the target, one of the most dangerous opponents the bomber crewmen faced was the twin-engine fighters called *Zerstörer* (Destroyer), the Bf-110G and Me-410 *Hornisse*. The major problem with twin-engine fighters was that, despite the heavy armament and longer range, it would always be at a disadvantage with single-engine fighters due to its size and weight, which limited its maneuverability.

It has become a well-known "fact" that the Bf-110 series was "a compromise in conflicting requirements, resulting in a mediocrity," with a combat record that made it a "humiliating failure." As with many such well-known wartime "facts," there is a kernel of truth in the charge; but looking more closely, that "history" is based on wartime propaganda – both the Germans extolling its virtues, and the RAF claiming that it failed in the Battle of Britain; the result is further proof that if a lie is repeated often enough by a sufficient number of "experts," without it being pointed out as a lie, it becomes "the truth."

The primary design role of the Bf-110 was as a bomber-destroyer, and in this role it was outstandingly successful, from its first interception of 18 RAF Wellingtons off the Heligoland Bight on December 18, 1940, when four of the eight bombers shot down were credited to the Bf-110s of I./ZG 76 (I.Zerstörergeschwader Z6, 1st Group of the 76th Heavy

Fighter Group), to the day battles over Germany in 1943 when the *Zerstörers* hacked down B-17s and B-24s with heavy guns and rockets.

The Bf-110G, which began production in May 1942, was powered by the DB605B-1 engine, providing 1,475 hp for takeoff and *Notleistung* (war emergency) power, and 1,355 hp at 6,000 meters (nearly 20,000 feet). Two belt-fed MG 151s were mounted below the cockpit, and there were four 7.62mm machine guns in the nose. With additional *Rüstsätze* (field modification) sets, the Bf-110G-2 became a very effective, heavily armed bomber-destroyer. R1 was a BK 37 cannon mounted under the fuselage, with the two MG 151s in the lower fuselage removed; one hit by the 37mm shell would explode a B-17 or B-24. R3 replaced the four MG 15s with two MK 108 30mm cannon. R4 was a twin 20mm MG 151 pack under the fuselage, with the internal MG151s retained. The Bf-110G-2/R6 carried two 21cm (8-inch) Werfer-Granate 21 (W.Gr.21) infantry barrage rockets in mortar tubes carried under each outer wing in replacement of the drop tanks; these were developed from the 210mm *Nebelwerfer* artillery rocket. The timed fuse was set for a range of 500–1,200 meters (152–366 feet), to explode in a formation and damage or bring down several bombers, as well as cause the formation to break up. These "rocket guns," as they were called by American crews, were fired beyond the range of the defending guns and were wildly inaccurate, but one hit would tear apart an unlucky bomber. Bf-109Gs and Fw-190As also used the W.Gr.21, carrying one under each wing; since the tubes reduced maneuverability, their use by single-engine fighters was limited, and stopped after the Allied escort fighters gained the ability to cover the deep-penetration raids. So long as the American formations were unescorted, the Bf-110G-2 was deadly. But American fighter pilots considered them "meat on the table." By the late spring of 1944, the Bf-110G was withdrawn from the day fighter role after the units suffered heavy losses.

The Ju-88 bomber, modified as a night fighter, was also used in the *Zerstörer* role, along with the Me-410 *Hornisse* (Hornet). These aircraft too suffered badly once American escort fighters could escort the bombers all the way, and were also withdrawn from the daylight battles in 1944.

So long as the American fighters lacked the range to escort the bombers the whole way to their distant targets and back, by the time of the Regensburg-Schweinfurt raid on August 17, the Luftwaffe was exacting losses among the bombers such that an American crewman on his sixth mission was statistically flying another man's time, since the life expectancy of a bomber crewman by the latter half of 1943 was five missions – with 25 missions required to complete a tour.

The one element of the German defenses that was present on every Allied air force mission, from the first day of the campaign to the last, was flak. "Flak" is a contraction of *Fliegerabwehrkanone*, which translates as "aircraft-defense cannon." For Allied aircrew, "flak" was a generic term for ground-based antiaircraft fire. While a fighter attack might be scary for an instant, when the planes had flashed past, it was over. That was not the case with antiaircraft fire. One B-17 bombardier recalled:

> There was nothing more terrifying than to look up from my bombsight and see the entire sky ahead of us black with flak explosions, with red, orange, and yellow flashes from within that evil cloud, as they put up more. There was no place to go, no place to hide. Every time, I thought to myself, "There's no way we will get through that in one piece." And for too many, they didn't.

The leaders of VIII Bomber Command considered that, while overall losses attributable to flak were small – accounting for approximately 25 percent of USAAF bomber losses in 1942–43 – there was a significant number of bombers damaged by flak and forced out of formation, which were then more easily shot down by fighters. Additionally, flak intimidated the crews and was a major factor in degrading bombing accuracy.

The primary antiaircraft artillery piece used by the Germans was officially known as the 8.8cm Flak 18. The gun could be used against either aircraft or ground targets such as armor or attacking troops. Informally, these guns were universally known as the *Acht-acht* (eight-eight) by Germans and the "eighty-eight" by the Allies. The gun could fire a 9.24-kilogram (20.34-pound) shell to over 49,000 feet. The high muzzle velocity, combined with a high-weight projectile, made the "eighty-eight" the deadliest antiaircraft weapon deployed by any combatant in World War II.

Antiaircraft artillery constituted 29 percent of the German weapons budget and 20 percent of the munitions budget; half of all Luftwaffe personnel were assigned to operate and service the weapons. In 1943 the flak units nearly doubled from 629 heavy batteries in January 1943 to 1,300 in January 1944. By late 1943, there was growing disquiet among senior Nazi leaders regarding the enormous costs associated with the flak force. After the war, Albert Speer acknowledged that the combined Bomber Offensive did constitute a "second front" before the Normandy invasion, and that the personnel and resources devoted to the air defense system – both artillery and aircraft and their associated support systems – diverted enough of Germany's limited military resources to negatively affect the outcome of the battles on both the Eastern and Western fronts.

Overall command of the Luftwaffe was vested in Reichsmarschall Hermann Göring, the last commander of the "Richthofen" Geschwader in World War I and a 22-victory ace, who was one of the long-time leaders of the Nazi Party. Göring's leadership style was once described by General der Flieger Karl Koller thus:

The *Reichsmarschall* delighted in playing one man off against the other, and it gave him malicious pleasure when the two protagonists were at each other's throats. He would stand nearby and make scornful comments to those around him. He often impressed me as being pleased with the disharmony reigning among his most important staff. It seemed that he had no interest in encouraging an atmosphere of smooth cooperation since he was afraid that this would create a united front against himself.

Leader of the German air defenses at the time the American daylight campaign began was General Josef Kammhuber, commander of XII Fliegerkorps (12th Air Corps), who created the air defense control system in 1941 to deal with the British night bombing offensive. His power and influence waned following the disaster of the Hamburg firebombing in July 1943. XII Fliegerkorps became Jagdkorps 1 and Kammhuber's replacement was a man of much lesser ability, General Beppo Schmid. When he was head of Luftwaffe intelligence during the Battle of Britain, Schmid's incompetence led to a complete misunderstanding of the status of the RAF as the battle wore on; he believed that once an RAF airfield was bombed, it was knocked out, and also completely missed the repair system established by Minister of Aircraft Production Lord Beaverbrook, which returned nearly two-thirds of RAF aircraft shot down to service. He was, however, a master at catering to the wishes of his superiors, a necessity for success in the Nazi hierarchy. In this new position, he managed to impress his superiors sufficiently that in December 1944, he was placed in command of Luftwaffenkommando West, responsible for all Luftwaffe units supporting the Western Front, this despite the disaster that 1944 was for the Luftwaffe. Schmid thrived in the chaotic environment created by Göring and was one of the *Reichsmarschall*'s favorites.

Adolf Galland, who commanded JG 26 during the Battle of Britain and was the leading Luftwaffe *Experte* on the Channel Front with 96 victories when he was named *General der Jagdflieger* (General of Fighters) just short of his 30th birthday in November 1941, was capable, competent, charismatic, determined, talented, and had almost no tolerance for the toadies who inhabited the upper reaches of the Nazi government, even being willing to speak back to Hitler in person. He was a constant irritant to Göring due to his championing of the Jagdwaffe. That he survived politically in this position as long as he did was considered miraculous by his fellow fighter commanders.

The system of air defense command and control established in Germany closely mirrored that which Air Marshal Dowding had established for RAF Fighter Command, which was responsible for the British success in the Battle of Britain. The Luftnachrichtendienst (Air Surveillance Service) provided early warning and tracking units. Initially, this consisted of visual-observation posts linked to a *Flugwachekommando*, shortened to *Fluko* (aircraft-reporting center). Between 1939 and 1943, radars and other electronic sensors were added. This sophisticated network was known as the "Kammhuber Line" by the Allies, after its creator, General Josef Kammhuber.

The first line of the system was the Funkaufklärungsdienst (Electronic Intelligence Early Warning Service), which monitored the radio frequencies used by Allied bomber formations as they prepared for a mission, beginning with picking up radio tests by bomber radiomen on their airfield, and then as they took off and assembled over England. This initial data was fed to the *Seeräuber* (Pirate) center at Zeist in the Netherlands, and was then communicated to the relevant fighter and flak command centers. Radio interception was then followed by the long-range search radars positioned along the French and Dutch coasts, which picked up the Allied formations as they crossed the English

Channel or North Sea. This data was communicated to the forward-alert radar centers that used the smaller *Freya* and *Würzburg* radars that tracked the bombers as they entered German-controlled airspace.

Fighter commanders' complaints regarding delays in communicating radar information led to command of the *Luftnachrichten* (air surveillance) regiments being changed from corps headquarters in Zeist to regional *Jagddivision* (fighter division) headquarters. The result was a more responsive though less centralized air-defense system. This culminated in February 1944 with new *Jagddivision* command centers taking responsibility for creation of a common *Luftlagebild* (air-situation report) rather than the previous confusing mix of *Jagdflotte* (fighter fleet) and *Luftgau* (air region) reports. These new fighter sector directors were controlled by the new division command posts, which were now highly sophisticated data-collection and dissemination stations, derisively known as "battle opera houses" by fighter pilots for their choreographed activities. Data from radar stations and other intelligence sources was fed to these posts, where the data was collated and the air-situation report created; the fighter director then used this information to assign missions to the various fighter units under his control.

Airborne fighter direction was conducted by voice radio from the *Jägerleit Gefechtstand* (fighter control center). The main link between the ground-control-intercept system and the airborne fighters was the *Y-Vehrfahren-Kampf* (Y-combat system), known by the codename "Benito." The system's ground stations interacted with a transponder on a fighter through the Morane antenna mounted on the aircraft's lower wing or fuselage, which retransmitted the signal back to the ground, so that the Y-station could track friendly fighters.

The Reichsverteidigung (Defense of the Reich, the German aerial defense force) expanded throughout 1943, though only barely enough to keep pace with the growth of the Allied air forces. Expansion of the single-engine day fighter force came partly from withdrawing units from the Russian and Mediterranean fronts – and partly from increased fighter production and pilot training.

A major difference between the Luftwaffe and the Allied air forces was the matter of combat tours. For a pilot in VIII Fighter Command, a tour was 250 combat hours; this was counted as time over enemy territory, and for most pilots, the nine months to a year it took to amass such a total, flying an average two missions a week, was more than enough. Most were happy to go home and become flight instructors to pass on their hard-earned knowledge. Some few asked for tour extensions of 25 hours; these were usually granted when a pilot was "on a roll" with scoring success. A pilot could volunteer for a second 250-hour tour, which guaranteed him a 30-day leave at home before returning to operations; fewer than one in ten pilots took this option, though the percentage was higher among "aces." This system gave Allied pilots a goal to achieve, while also providing experienced instructors to maintain quality in the training system.

The Luftwaffe combat tour was unlimited – until either a man was wounded so badly he couldn't return to flying duty, or death. A pilot who survived would become very experienced. As the "home team," they fought over their own territory, and when shot down would return to duty. Only one German *Experte*, Addi Glunz, was never shot down during his time in combat, and many were shot down more than once. Flying and fighting took a physical toll as well as the mental and psychological results of combat. Walter Krupinski, who came to JG 26 in the fall of 1944 from three years on the Eastern Front with JG 52 and flew combat from the first day of the war to the last, admitted years after the war that by the time he commanded III./JG 26, "I was shot – no good." He frequently had barely the strength to fly a mission; the duties of group commander, caring for his pilots, ground crews, and other personnel, were very secondary in his priorities. III./JG 26 suffered increased losses in comparison to the records of the other two *Gruppen* because of Krupinski's lack of leadership, despite his demonstrated prowess as a fighter pilot.

The overall leadership of the Luftwaffe, particularly the Jagdwaffe, was not equal to the task. There was no ranking officer corps of experienced aviators. High-ranking commanders lacked contemporary aviation experience, their direct involvement having ended with the German defeat in World War I, and many did not fully grasp the problems of this war. The men who did understand were fighter leaders in their mid- to late-20s, who lacked experience in managing large organizations, and were frequently not promoted in rank upon assuming command of a *Gruppe* or even a *Geschwader* as their Allied counterparts were, which limited their dealings with superiors. Adolf Galland forcefully represented his pilots in his dealings with the upper leadership. However, several years after the war, he admitted he had lacked the knowledge of working in a large bureaucracy that would have given him the skills to deal with policy formation and administration more effectively. Such skill only comes through experience, which comes with age; the Jagdwaffe leadership lacked both, to their detriment.

Göring instituted a policy of promoting leading *Experten* to unit command. The result was that the German fighting force had some excellent front-line leadership, men who commanded the respect of their pilots. Several were truly outstanding, but many proved that the ability to shoot down a large number of the enemy does not necessarily make one a leader.

Attacking the bomber formations was difficult for the German fighter pilots. Initially, German fighters attacked the bomber formation from the rear, which gave the most time for a pilot to aim and fire at a specific target. However, attacking from the rear subjected the attacker to the massed firepower of the formation; both the B-17 and B-24 had their defensive armament positioned to oppose this specific tactic. A standard approach from 1,000 yards astern of the formation, with an overtaking speed of 100 miles per hour, took over 18 seconds to close the distance down to 100 yards, the range at which gunfire had an effect on the target. Probably the majority of valid gunner claims for destroying attacking fighters involved rear attacks.

By the spring of 1943, the standard Luftwaffe strategy for intercepting a bomber force had changed to attacks from ahead, due to the fact the bombers had the least amount of defensive armament facing forward. An attacking fighter unit would fly a parallel course out of range of the defenses. When the force reached a point about three miles ahead, the flights swung 180 degrees to attack the formation from ahead. Initially, such head-on attacks were conducted from the same altitude as the bombers; however, judging range to the target was very difficult. The urge to open fire from too far away and make the breakaway too soon for fear of the collision that loomed in the gunsight was overwhelming.

As they gained experience with the head-on attack, the Germans adopted the "company front" formation; the entire unit spread abreast and attacked from ten degrees above the horizontal. This greatly simplified estimating range, with a constant angle of fire similar to ground strafing. The attack was a single pass through the bomber formation; it became known to the Americans as "Twelve O'Clock High." The major danger was mid-air collision. Walter Krupinski said that just before he would give the order for his pilots to push their throttles forward and initiate their dive, "My entire life would pass before my eyes and I would momentarily wonder how many we might lose to accidental collision."

Second Lieutenant Albert Williamson never forgot his first experience of such an attack. He and his childhood friend had joined the Air Force and trained as pilots together; both were co-pilots in the 91st Bomb Group. On their second missions, each was in an adjoining bomber in the same formation. When the call "Fighters – Twelve O'Clock High!" came over the radio, Williamson glanced out his side window to see an Fw-190 collide nose-to-nose with his friend's bomber. The two airplanes appeared to stop in mid-air. Then the fighter's radial engine broke loose; momentum carried it the length of the B-17 till it fell out the tail. No one got out. The two airplanes, locked together in a death embrace, seemed to float toward the ground below.

Curtis LeMay, commander of 305th Bomb Group, began developing a new defensive formation in collaboration with 1st Bombardment Wing commander General Lawrence Kuter. Originally, each of the four groups in the wing flew its own formation; there was no wing organization and coordination with each other was limited to all being assigned the same target. Initially, individual three-plane "vics" were used, but this formation was too small to provide mutual protection. The "combat box" was developed, with each squadron flying in two three-bomber elements, the different groups flying in line astern. Each was separated from the one following by a distance of approximately 1.5 miles. This resulted in an unwieldy formation that took a long time to get over a target. Kuter pushed for a larger formation for mutual protection, and also a more compact one, to get the bombers over the target faster.

LeMay created a "wing" formation, combining three 18-bomber boxes into one larger mutually defending box formation. Instead of line-astern, the three groups were positioned at high, medium, and low level close to each other. The lead group flew the medium altitude position while the high group was above and to the right with the low group beneath and to the left. Within each group formation, the three squadron formations of six bombers in two "vees" flew in a high, medium, and low position similar to the large formation. The resulting 54-bomber formation occupied a stretch of sky 600 yards long, a mile or so wide, and half a mile deep. Each bomber carried approximately 9,000 rounds of ammunition; the "wing" was defended by 648 .50-caliber machine guns with an effective range of 1,800 feet.

The wing "combat box" provided mutual gunnery coverage, while forcing the flak defense to change altitude settings to fire at each box, as well as the entire wing formation, dispersing and slowing the rate of fire. These formations spent less time over the target and were easier for the fighter escorts to defend. LeMay's concept was gradually accepted through all bomb wings over the course of operations in the spring of 1943.

The new formation, called a *Pulk* (herd) by the Germans, was an unnerving sight for any fighter pilot, be he novice or grizzled veteran. With a combined closing speed of 500 miles per hour in a head-on attack, fighter pilots and defending gunners had only seconds to fire. The Fw-190's four 20mm cannons fired 130 rounds in a three-second burst. It took an average of 20 hits to destroy a B-17 and the average pilot only scored 2 percent hits; thus, 1,000 rounds were fired to score the 20 hits. A head-on high attack gave a clear shot at the bomber's vulnerable oil tanks in the wing between the inboard engines and the fuselage, and the wing fuel tanks between the inboard and outboard engines. Leutnant Franz Stigler recalled one such attack:

> With high speed built up in a dive, my aircraft made a very fleeting target and the more vertical my descent, the more difficult it was for the top turret gunner to get an angle on me. I targeted the pilots, the engines and the wing's oil and fuel tanks. I could get in only one short burst. But I was through the formation before he even saw me.

No matter how experienced a pilot was, attacking an American formation was unnerving. Oberst "Fips" Phillip, *Kommodore* of JG 1, wrote, "Against 20 Russians trying to shoot you down or even 20 Spitfires, it can be exciting, even fun. But curve in towards 40 Fortresses and all your past sins flash before your eyes."

Air warfare in the stratosphere was terrifying to all participants. As the number of missions grew in 1943, some cracked under the strain. Future Secretary of Defense Robert S. McNamara, then a staff officer at VIII Bomber Command, investigated the growing abort rates during the summer of 1943, a phenomenon he suspected was due to pilot cowardice. He recalled that following completion of the report, he was called to a meeting of unit commanders:

> One of the commanders was Curtis LeMay. He was the finest combat commander of any service I came across in the war. But he was extraordinarily belligerent, many thought brutal. He got the report. He issued an order. He said, "I will be in the lead plane on every mission. Any plane that takes off will go over the target, or the crew will be court-martialed." The abort rate dropped overnight. That's the kind of commander he was.

Fighting in the stratosphere over Europe was a nightmare for all concerned.

# VIII FIGHTER COMMAND STRUGGLES TO SURVIVE

As of February 8, 1943, VIII Fighter Command was a shadow of what it was supposed to be. The three fighter groups were now equipped with the P-47, with which only the newly arrived 56th Group was familiar. The 78th and 4th groups were given two months to learn the airplane before commencing operations. The 56th had experience in the airplane, the 4th had experience in combat, and the 78th had neither familiarity with the airplane nor operational experience, and faced the high hurdle of recreating a fighter group. Pressure was on from the highest levels to whip things into shape.

The P-47 in the spring of 1943 was far different from what it would become over the next year. As the only fighter after the P-38 capable of high-altitude operation, its choice was due to *force majeure*; however, it could only fly slightly beyond the European coast from East Anglia. Designed to intercept high-altitude trans-Atlantic bombers, it was no dogfighter; it had the slowest climb rate of any American fighter. The P-47 was defined more by what it couldn't do than what it could. As a result, the fighters were to remain at high altitude and not engage in air combat below 20,000 feet. Unfortunately, an airplane that couldn't fight effectively at every altitude was not much use. The orders were largely forgotten after the first few combats.

The leadership of Arman Peterson, "Colonel Pete," as his men called him, was vital for the 78th's success. Robert Eby recalled:

Colonel Pete put me in charge of bore-sighting the guns. I went to VIII Fighter Command to obtain the ballistic data and it took me three days with the various bureaucracies to find what we needed. I had to go through VIII Fighter Command, RAF Fighter Command, and the English Air Ministry. I drew up alternate combinations of bore-sighting patterns and used the data I cajoled to choose the best ones. Colonel Pete was way ahead of the other groups on this. When they went to the Air Ministry, they were told the Yanks had been given the data once and that was enough. VIII Fighter Command had to come over and get our data. I was very pleased when Colonel Pete told me that when he met at Fighter Command with Colonels Zemke and Chesley Peterson, they accepted our patterns. In the end, all the P-47 groups in the ETO used our material.

Eby also remembered Peterson's struggle to improve the P-47's gunsight. "The American gunsight had a 60-mil ring that was inadequate for our speed, and Colonel Pete loved the Spitfire sight. He tried to get them, but was turned down." Eby scratched a 90mm ring on a reticle, and found a local company that could produce it; pilot performance in gunnery training improved drastically with the new reticles. Peterson did not give up on the Spitfire sights, finally obtaining them in mid-March. Non-magnetic mounts had to be made since the sight was right above the magnetic compass, which was thrown off 20–30 degrees by the standard mount. Peterson's unceasing efforts created a strong bond between him and his men.

On February 16, several American transferees from the RAF and RCAF arrived at Goxhill. Second Lieutenant Harding Zumwalt recalled:

On February 11, 1943, I reported to Goxhill and the 83rd Fighter Squadron. There I saw my first P-47 and it was quite impressive. The Jug weighed twice as much as the Spitfire and appeared large enough to house a couple of waist gunners in the rear. When I first taxied a P-47 it was just like driving a Cadillac, the way it would squat on its gear when you hit the brakes.

VIII Fighter Command made an agreement with the RAF to have US fighter groups occupy RAF fighter stations. At the end of January, the 78th moved to the RAF station at Duxford in Cambridgeshire. Every American ever stationed there remembered the central steam heating. Anyone who spent a night in a Nissen hut knew just how cold an English winter was, and all knew how lucky they were to go to Station Number 357-F – VIII Fighter Command, as Duxford was officially known. The Eagles remained at Debden. Second Lieutenant John T. Godfrey, who joined the 4th in September 1943, recalled Debden:

> The walk to headquarters, occasionally asking directions, was enlightening. There was a base hospital, the Red Cross Club for enlisted men, tennis courts, volleyball courts, armament building, movie house, post exchange, photography shop, enlisted men's barracks, and finally headquarters. The streets and sidewalks were paved and the grass was carefully cut. In back of all this, three huge hangars loomed, and everything was painted with the characteristic camouflage. Fifteen hundred officers and men lived on the base, all slaves to the 48 P-47s sitting around the field.

On February 27, Captain Francis Stanley Gabreski was welcomed to the 56th. Son of Polish immigrants, Gabreski had joined the newly organized Civil Pilot Training program when he was accepted to Notre Dame University in 1938; after six hours in a Taylorcraft his flight instructor advised him to drop out since he "did not have the touch to be a pilot." Despite this Gabreski dropped out in 1940 to join the Air Corps. At Parks Air College, near East St Louis, Illinois, Gabreski showed little talent flying the PT-17 and had to pass an elimination check ride to continue. In basic flight training he began to show more promise in the Vultee BT-13 and completed advanced training at Maxwell Field in the AT-6 Texan. In March 1941, Gabreski earned his wings and commission, and assignment to the 45th Pursuit Squadron of the 15th Pursuit Group at Wheeler Field on Oahu.

On December 7, 1941, Gabreski got airborne in a P-36, but the Japanese had already departed. After Pearl Harbor he applied to be sent to Britain to train with the Polish pilots in the RAF on the grounds that he spoke fluent Polish and would gain valuable experience. The Air Force agreed and he arrived in England in September 1942, promoted to captain and assigned as liaison with VIII Fighter Command Headquarters. He finally managed to fly with the Polish 315 Squadron in January 1943, flying 20 missions and entering combat once, unsuccessfully. When he arrived at King's Cliffe, "Gabby" was the most combat-experienced pilot in the group. Both the 4th and 78th groups declined to bring him into their units, since they had no slot for him. Zemke recalled that when General Hunter asked if he would take Gabreski, he had had a similar reaction; finally Lieutenant Colonel Loren McCollom, 61st Squadron CO, agreed to take him. Gabreski's quick promotion to flight leader was resented by others, and his opinions of the flying abilities of some of his squadron mates, based on his experience with the Poles, didn't help.

While the men of the 56th dealt with cold Nissen huts at King's Cliffe before their move to the RAF base at Horsham St Faith on the outskirts of Norwich in Norfolk on March 5, and bemoaned the lack of flying opportunities, P-47s arrived at Debden in late January; Don Blakeslee's 335th Squadron became the first to convert. While they learned the P-47, the 334th and 336th squadrons continued flying their Spitfire Vbs and Blakeslee's squadron also flew patrols in their Spitfires. On February 19, Blakeslee decided his pilots knew enough to fly 12 P-47s to St Omer. Fortunately, when they found they couldn't communicate by radio due to intense interference – a problem associated with poor electrical shielding of the engines – the enemy paid them no mind. However, some RAF Spitfires mistook them for Fw-190s as they crossed the English coast homebound, and they only escaped by diving away. VIII Fighter Command soon decided to give the P-47 prominent identity markings to avoid such incidents in the future. Orders went out that the P-47 was to be marked with a 24-inch-wide white stripe around the front of the cowling, a 12-inch-wide stripe across the vertical fin and rudder, 18-inch wide stripes on the horizontal stabilizers, and US national insignia twice the regulation size under each wing.

At the end of February, the 334th Squadron began its conversion. After ten days, Chesley Peterson decided to mount the first official P-47 mission. The 14 P-47s from 334th and 335th squadrons that he led to Ostend on March 10 returned frustrated; the Luftwaffe had completely ignored them.

The 336th Squadron flew its final Spitfire mission on March 16. The four pilots who had been flying with the 335th to learn the P-47 became instructors for the squadron's conversion and the 4th was declared fully operational with the Thunderbolt. Missions were flown, but the enemy continued to ignore the Eagles and their P-47s. Don Blakeslee led a Ramrod on April 11 over France but the Abbeville Boys didn't come up. Two days later, one of the group's P-47s was shot down by British antiaircraft gunners when the pilot returned over Dover at low altitude and was mistaken for an Fw-190 on a "tip and run" raid. Overall, most of the former Eagles did not take well to the P-47, which compared badly in their experience to the highly maneuverable Spitfire as regarded handling, and they made no effort to keep their opinions to themselves. The former Spitfire pilots weren't alone in their dislike of the P-47; the remaining pilots in the 78th who had experience in the nimble P-38 also considered the P-47 a clunk when it came to maneuverability. Both groups had strong doubts regarding the Thunderbolt's ability to fight it out with Fw-190s that could fly rings around most Allied types.

Major Cass Hough, an experienced test pilot on VIII Fighter Command staff, was able to fly a P-47 in mock combat with both a captured Fw-190A and a Bf-109G. His results showed that below 15,000 feet both German fighters had all-round better performance than the P-47, particularly with regard to rate of climb. The P-47's performance improved progressively at altitudes above 15,000 feet, until between 25,000 and 30,000 feet its performance bettered its opponents' in all areas but acceleration and rate of climb. At full power, the P-47 was faster than both the 109 and 190, with the advantage rising to 30 miles per hour above 25,000 feet with regard to the Fw-190 and 35 miles per hour at 30,000 feet over the Bf-109G, reflecting the fact that the 190 was supreme below 23,000 feet while the 109 could nearly give as good as it got in terms of performance above that altitude. The German fighters accelerated faster in dives, but the heavy Thunderbolt caught up with them easily and completely out-dived both. Provided it kept its speed above 200 miles per hour, the P-47 was the equal of both German machines in turning ability, though both of them outperformed the American fighter at lower speeds.

On April 8, Zemke got orders to take himself, 62nd Squadron CO Major Dave Schilling, and Captains John McClure and Eugene O'Neill on a mission with 4th's Thunderbolts for a Ramrod to the Pas de Calais that marked the entry of the 56th into combat. On April 13, the 78th Fighter Group sent the 83rd Squadron to fly with the 4th in the early afternoon while the 82nd Squadron flew with the Eagles that evening. Both were high-altitude fighter sweeps taking in the coast from Dunkirk, to Furnes, then St Omer, ending at Calais. Charles London remembered, "The Germans ignored us completely, not even bothering to shoot flak at us." Hub Zemke also took Schilling, McClure, and O'Neill for a second familiarization flight on this mission.

The next afternoon, Zemke led the same four-ship flight, along with four-plane flights from the 61st and 63rd squadrons as they accompanied the 78th on its afternoon Ramrod. During this second mission, 78th Group executive officer Lieutenant Colonel Joe Dickman suffered what was at the time a common P-47 accident, failing to carefully maintain the mixture control as he operated the throttle during the flight. The result was a blown cylinder head over Calais which forced him to bail out two miles offshore. Dislocating his arm when bailing out, he had trouble shucking his parachute and deploying his dingy. Using his hunting knife to free himself, he poked a hole in the dingy; he had to pump to keep it inflated. An RAF Air-Sea Rescue launch was delayed because the crew had to carefully pick their way through the minefield he was in.

On April 15, 1943, Don Blakeslee scored the P-47's first victory when he violated all the rules and dived from 28,000 feet on three Fw-190s flying at 20,000 feet; one tried to out-dive him and he followed it down toward the Channel where he exploded with a long burst from short range at an altitude of 500 feet. When Jim Goodson congratulated him back at Debden for proving the Thunderbolt could out-dive the Focke-Wulf, Blakeslee famously replied, "By God it ought to dive, it certainly won't climb!" Not everyone shared Blakeslee's opinion; Steve Pisanos loved the Thunderbolt, recalling, "I liked the P-47. It was big and powerful and it had eight machine guns. If you put the sight on the other guy and held it there, you had him."

Group flying executive Chesley Peterson, leading the Ramrod, became the second P-47 pilot to score against the Luftwaffe moments later, shooting down his seventh and last enemy fighter. As the Fw-190 caught fire and went down, Peterson turned to re-enter the fight, but the temperamental P-47 he was flying blew a cylinder just at that moment. Peterson dived away from the air battle and managed to nurse his crippled Thunderbolt back across the Channel. Thirty miles short of the English coast, the engine caught fire and Peterson bailed out; his parachute broke his fall only a few seconds before he went into the water. A nearby RAF Walrus heard his Mayday and picked him up after only 15 minutes in the water. While Blakeslee and Peterson scored the P-47's first victories, Bob Boock got Fw-190 number three and Lieutenant Leroy Gover downed number four. Captains McMinn and Anderson were both killed in the fight.

As this happened, Zemke led the 56th on its first solo sweep along the Dutch Coast. It was uneventful, as were the three flown over the following four days. The Ramrod of April 18 saw Bob Johnson fly his first mission with the 61st Squadron.

On April 18, the 78th welcomed the first 18 pilots trained on the P-47 in the United States to Duxford. Among them was a flight instructor who had been fighting for a year to get out of Training Command. First Lieutenant Quince Brown betrayed his Oklahoma origins when he opened his mouth. Second Lieutenant Ernie Russell, would later be Brown's wingman and element leader, remembered:

He could joke and had a little smile, but he was not brash or loud; however, you knew that he meant what he said and, if tested, would tell you what he thought, never loudly, but as matter of fact. He was not prone to jest, but he did have a good sense of humor. Above all he was not a braggart; it just wasn't in his makeup. He was known by all in the squadron as one of the best pilots, though he would never tell you that – like a cowboy, the proof was in the pudding. He had excellent vision – better than mine, and I had 20/10 vision – good peripheral vision that is essential to seeing movements in the sky, and good judgment. All that combined with the fact that he was an excellent shot made him a superb fighter pilot.

Born in 1917, Brown was the fifth of five sons, hence his name. After finishing at the University of Oklahoma, he joined the Air Corps in 1940 at age 23, receiving his wings and commission as a second lieutenant at Kelly Field, Texas, on April 25, 1941. The superb flying ability demonstrated during training resulted in an assignment as an instructor at Randolph Field. When he arrived at Duxford, Brown was older than most pilots and the 1,326 hours in his logbook were bettered in the group only by Colonel Peterson, who had joined the Air Force four months before him. Since he had more P-47 hours than those leading the group, Brown was given a quick promotion to element leader by Gene Roberts when he was assigned to the 84th Squadron.

The 56th finally met the enemy on April 29, when a Ramrod led by Major Dave Schilling was intercepted by Fw-190s from JG 26. The star personality of the group, Schilling was impulsive and subject to taking incautious risks, which he did this time when his radio failed while crossing the Channel; he did not pass lead to a pilot who could communicate with the formation as they took up their patrol along the coast. When they were bounced, Second Lieutenant Winston Garth and Captain John McClure were badly shot up and forced to bail out, then picked up by the Germans. Schilling and his wingman returned to Horsham St Faith with their fighters shot up. Zemke was forced to institute stiffer aerial discipline and end the "buddy-buddy" atmosphere in favor of operational improvement. The result was that the loner commander became more isolated from his pilots, never achieving the popular leadership that Chesley Peterson and later Don Blakeslee won in the 4th or that Colonel Arman Peterson had in the 78th.

Up to April, VIII Bomber Command had only four B-17 and two B-24 groups that could regularly fly missions. Other groups had arrived in England and were training. Thus, it was only in May 1943 that the Eighth Air Force began to command a force commensurate with the responsibilities assigned.

On May 3, VIII Bomber Command leader Lieutenant General Frank Andrews died in the crash of the B-24D "Hot Stuff" in Greenland. The bomber, unofficially recognized as having been the first in VIII Bomber Command to complete 25 missions in late February, was scheduled to be flown back to the United States by its regular pilot, First Lieutenant Richard Shannon, and his crew to participate in a war bond tour. However, just before they were to take off for Iceland, General Andrews and his staff took over the airplane to fly to Washington for the coming Trident Conference. Andrews flew as pilot-in-command. After receiving a weather briefing in Iceland indicating that a storm was brewing over Greenland, he determined to press on. When the bomber flew into snow flurries as it approached Bluie West One airfield in Greenland to refuel, it crashed in the poor visibility, leaving no survivors. In the wake of Andrews' loss, Eaker was promoted to major general and given command. Andrews would be remembered with his name on the main AAF airfield outside Washington, DC.

By May, operational experience recognized the Jagdwaffe as the primary obstacle to expansion of the daylight campaign. German fighter disposition on the Channel Front was unchanged from what it had been in August 1942. Allied estimates that the force had dropped from 270 in August to 215 from diversions to the Eastern and Mediterranean Fronts had resulted in optimistic plans to extend the bombing campaign into Germany itself, but optimism had faded as the enemy defenses seemed to grow ever-stronger. German records had 350 fighters assigned to the Western Front in January and 600 in May; one-quarter of the total Jagdwaffe was located in Germany and the areas of the occupied countries the bombers were forced to overfly. This growing enemy defensive air strength was reflected in growing loss rates for the bombers.

An important milestone was reached in May, when two bomber crews became the first to be officially recognized as having survived their 25-mission tour. On May 13, the B-17F "Hell's Angels" (s/n 41-24577), assigned to the 358th Bomb Squadron of the 303rd Bombardment Group based at RAF Molesworth, returned successfully from its 25th mission. A week later, on May 19, B-17F "Memphis Belle" (s/n 41-24485), assigned to the 324th Bomb Squadron, 91st Bombardment Group based at RAF Bassingbourn, completed its 25th mission.

The event was important to the command because it "proved" to the crews it was possible to survive their tour and return home. The fatal statistics of bomber losses were clear to many: most crews were gone by their fifth mission; statistically, a man flying his sixth mission was "on someone else's time." The operational losses, combined with the great difficulty of obtaining replacements, created a crisis. By February 1, 1943, VIII Bomber Command had received only 20 replacement crews, against 67 lost to combat and "war weariness." In March, things got worse, with 73 crews being listed "war weary" and only eight replacements arriving. By April, the bomb groups were operating at only half of authorized strength, which made the combat losses even harder to bear. This was also a period in the overall war in which the combat needs of the campaigns in the North African, South Pacific, and China-Burma-India Theaters led to the diversion of units intended for the Eighth. All in all, by May 1943, combat crews looked at the statistics of attrition and replacement and saw the likely prospect of a short career.

The two bombers' records of survival were important to VIII Bomber Command, and the command's public relations office had made plans for a major celebration when the event occurred. The Eighth now had an embarrassment of riches, with two bombers and their crews achieving the goal; they also had a public relations nightmare. The plan to celebrate this event included returning the "first" bomber and its crew to the United States; that was, according to the records, "Hell's Angels." Crew and airplane would participate in a national recruiting drive and war bond tour. As such, the B-17 and its crew would represent the Army Air Forces – and specifically VIII Bomber Command – to an American public that was still recovering from the cultural shock of hearing Clark Gable exclaim, "Frankly, my dear, I don't give a damn!" at the end of *Gone With The Wind*. There was a not-insignificant part of that public guaranteed to express moral outrage to their local newspaper editors and their representatives in Washington at the "sacrilege" of a bomber named "Hell's Angels" touring the country as the representative of all the God-fearing "fine American boys" defending the country.

The command looked for some way to change the order of seniority and send home the bomber with the "right" name. Both bombers and their crews had flown their first missions in November. "Memphis Belle" was "senior," having flown her first mission to Brest on November 7, while "Hell's Angels" had bombed St Nazaire on November 17. There was the problem that the crew of "Hell's Angels" had flown all 25 missions in their airplane, while the "Memphis Belle" crew had only flown 21 of their missions in their airplane, with the other four having been flown in other aircraft while the "Belle" had been grounded for repairs. A different crew had actually flown the bomber's 25th mission. Nevertheless, "Memphis Belle" got the nod and pilot Captain Robert Morgan and his crew departed Scotland for the United States on June 8, 1943. After six months being wined and dined across America, Morgan would return to combat on November 5, 1944, as pilot of the B-29 "Dauntless Dottie," lead ship on the first mission to Tokyo since the Doolittle Raid.

"Hell's Angels" remained at Molesworth and the 303rd adopted its name for the group. The bomber flew 48 missions by January 1944, when it was flown back to the United States to tour war factories. While

"Memphis Belle" escaped the scrappers the summer after the war and was eventually displayed at the National Museum of the Air Force at Wright-Patterson Air Force Base, "Hell's Angels" was sold for scrap in August 1945 and likely ended up a part of the aluminum-siding craze in American housing during the 1950s. Thus, "Memphis Belle" is carried in the records as the first bomber to complete 25 missions and return to the United States.

The 78th's first full group 48-plane mission was flown on May 4 to the Brest peninsula; it was logged as an uneventful sweep. Further missions on May 7 and 13 failed to rouse the Luftwaffe.

On May 13, Colonel Zemke, flying his personal P-47, now named *Moy Tovarich* (My Friend) in recognition of his time in the Soviet Union with the Red Air Force, accompanied by a painting of a wheel with a very large hubcap (for "Hub" Zemke), led 34 P-47s to rendezvous with the bombers over St Nicholas for withdrawal support. When the P-47s arrived over Antwerp at 1330 hours, they received a call that the bombers were under attack.

Zemke later remembered that for once, the bright spring day brought excellent visibility. As they crossed the Dutch coast, he saw two Fw-190s at his two o'clock position dive out of sight. He immediately called his flight to follow and executed a 180-degree diving turn to pursue the enemy, but they had disappeared. He suddenly realized that the whole squadron had followed, and ordered them to climb and reform. He then spotted four airplanes a mile to his left and realized they were the enemy. Calling for a turn, he gradually brought his flight in on their tails where he could identify them as Fw-190s; they were in a string formation, unaware of the approaching P-47s.

Zemke, still new at air combat, continually jiggled the throttle and sideslipped so as not to over-run and his flight struggled to keep up with his gyrations. He closed to 500 yards on the enemy number three and opened fire. Missing completely, he nosed down and fired again and there was a flash on the top of the 190's canopy. But again, Zemke's fire was too high and the enemy pilot immediately rolled over into a dive. As he turned in front of Zemke, Zemke gave a last bust and saw flashes along the left wing root and fuselage before the 190 disappeared below him.

He had a newcomer's exhilarating feeling of accomplishment for a moment before he heard a warning that he was about to be attacked.

Breaking left into a climbing turn, he saw four aircraft coming down head-on and as the leader came within range he fired a burst but saw no hits or return fire before he was past and gone. "I looked around and three of my flight were still there, but Bob Johnson was missing."

Back at Horsham St Faith, Zemke learned another flight of the 61st had also engaged the enemy and made claims for probables and damaged. Johnson got separated but flew home alone. Zemke's claim for a "destroyed" was downgraded to a "probable." After the gun camera film was viewed at VIII Fighter Command Headquarters, the claim was further downgraded to a "damaged," with Zemke realizing he had opened fire far out of range for effective gunnery. He made a mental note to get real close next time. Despite another 14 missions in May, the Luftwaffe ignored the "Wolfpack," as the 56th had named themselves.

Five new B-17 groups – the 95th, 96th, 351st, 94th, and 379th – became operational during the second week of May, and the 92nd resumed combat operations after having been used for training since November. Organized into the 4th Bombardment Wing, commanded by Brigadier General Frederick L. Anderson, the groups flew their first mission on May 13. Eaker wrote Arnold, stating that "This date, the 13th of May is a great day for the Eighth Air Force. Our combat crew availability went up in a straight line from 100 to 215. If the groups prove to be superior in combat to the old ones, it will scarcely be a fair fight!" Bomber strength went from 379 to 605.

On May 14, the Luftwaffe introduced the 78th to combat when they escorted 40 B-17s to targets in Belgium. The mission departed Duxford at 1235 hours, and the Thunderbolts arrived over St Nicholas, Belgium to find Fw-190s attacking the bombers. Colonel Peterson led the 82nd and 83rd squadrons in a diving attack, chasing the Germans into the bomber gunners' fire. The 83rd Squadron's CO, Major James J. Stone, scored the group's first victory when he flamed an Fw-190.

Almost simultaneously with Stone, Captain Robert Adamina scored the second victory; unfortunately his wingman, Flight Officer Samuel R. Martinek, was hit by another Fw-190 and had to bail out. Adamina was hit a moment later and also bailed out, to become a prisoner with Martinek. Element leader Captain Elmer F. McTaggart put a solid burst in the victorious Fw-190, then followed it in a dive. Closing rapidly, he hit its wings and rear fuselage with his next bursts. As he passed through 12,000 feet, McTaggart fired again and the Fw-190 burst into flame. Unfortunately, he followed it to low level to observe the crash. As he turned away to head home, McTaggart saw tracers flash past his canopy, fired by another Fw-190. When he attempted to evade the new enemy, he hit a tree and the prop sliced through a telephone line that began to wrap around the fighter. The ruggedness of the Thunderbolt saved him when he hit a second tree; he was able to zoom up to 1,500 feet and bail out. "I was just outside Ath, Belgium, when I jumped. My plane hit in the adjoining field and burned, while five or six Belgians in the grain field below watched me land, but they scattered when I hit the ground."

As he touched down, McTaggart's adventure had only just begun. Shucking his parachute harness, he started to run toward the tree line, but before he could get there, he came across a Belgian peasant who was willing to help. The man led him to an adjoining field and hid him in a line of bushes. He left some food and told McTaggart he would come back after dark. At 2100 hours, he returned and led the American to a farm which was owned by a member of the local Resistance. He stayed through the next day at the farm, but it was apparent from the German search effort that something had to be done quickly. A risky plan was developed: the Resistance man outfitted him as a Basque peasant and gave him forged papers that claimed he was mute. He was given a bicycle and told that the Pyrenees were a several-week journey to the south.

Pedaling along back roads across France, he slept in fields at night. "I'd been a Boy Scout, so I was able to live off the land and taking the back roads allowed me the best chance of avoiding the Germans." He made it to the Pyrenees in 13 days and found the Resistance group he had been told to contact. On June 1, he was taken up into the mountains by a guide to the Spanish border. Crossing into Spain, he stopped at the first village he found and went into the local cantina, where he was able to use the phone and call the number of the American Embassy in Madrid he had been given back in England. Two hours later, the Spanish Guardia Civil arrived and took him to a larger town where he was put in the jail with other Allied escapees.

Most escapees who made it this far had to wait as long as six weeks before the Spanish bureaucracy turned them over to the Allies. However, McTaggart's good luck continued when he found the cell was filled with men who had spent the requisite weeks in purgatory. The next morning, the guards took all and put them in trucks for a three-day trip to Madrid. Once there, they were sent on to Gibraltar, where they arrived on June 11. After a week waiting for a flight to England, they arrived in the United Kingdom on June 21. McTaggart had only been gone five weeks, setting the record for escape, evasion, and return before the invasion. Successful evasion meant he was sent back to the United States. He returned as a squadron commander in the P-38-equipped 370th Fighter Group assigned to the Ninth Air Force after the Normandy invasion.

The same day that McTaggart was shot down, Don Blakeslee shot down a second Fw-190, which – added to the three scored while flying Spitfires with the Canadians – gave him five victories to become an ace, a remarkable achievement for a man who was the first to admit he had to open fire to see where the bullets were going.

Between May 12 and 25, the third wartime US–UK conference was held in Washington, DC to plan future actions. Winston Churchill was still determined to put off a confrontation between the Allies and Germany on the old Western Front until he had exhausted every alternative. In the glow of the Afrika Korps surrender in Tunisia on May 14, he was able to obtain US agreement for an invasion of Sicily that would finally free up the Mediterranean as a shipping route, restoring the Suez Canal as the gateway to the East. The Americans only gave up their push for an invasion of France in 1943 when Churchill was able to convince Roosevelt that a further delay would allow production of more landing craft, as well as give American army units time to train in England for the invasion. At the time, there was only one American division in the United Kingdom. In return for agreeing to a delay, General Marshall convinced the president to get a commitment from the British prime minister that the Normandy invasion would definitely happen in May 1944.

On May 18, the conference approved a new plan for what was now called the Anglo-American Combined Bomber Offensive. The destruction of the Jagdwaffe was given top priority as Operation *Pointblank*, followed by submarine yards and bases, the aircraft industry, ball bearings, and oil. VIII Fighter Command now felt ready to meet the Luftwaffe in combat. Approval was given for sending two VIII Bomber Command B-24 groups and a third destined for the force to Ninth Air Force in North Africa for Operation *Tidalwave*, a special one-time raid on the Romanian oil fields at Ploesti.

These decisions put a time limit on VIII Bomber Command, which had been tasked at the Casablanca Conference in January with establishing air superiority over Western Europe by defeat of the Luftwaffe as a pre-condition for invasion. *Pointblank* approved expansion of the Eighth to 1,750 bombers by January 1944 and 2,700 by the following April. Full equipment of VIII Bomber Command was given priority over all other theaters. As impossible as the situation might have appeared at the time to the crews flying missions and meeting the Jagdwaffe over occupied Europe, they had a year to win the battle.

On May 29, VIII Bomber Command flew its largest mission to date when 279 bombers were sent out, with the three fighter groups sending a total of 131 P-47s for escort. The mission also saw the first use of a possible alternative to the fighters. This was the YB-40, a B-17 variant designed as a long-range "convoy escort aircraft," not a fighter. The concept of a heavy gun platform stationed at weak spots in a bomber formation received strong support from Eaker, and Boeing modified 14 B-17Fs, arming them with a second power-operated turret over the radio compartment, doubling the number of waist guns, and grafting on a remotely controlled two-gun turret under the bombardier's position in the extreme nose. Altogether, the YB-40 carried ten .50-caliber guns in four turrets and the tail position, and four guns in the waist. There was substantial armor plating around the nose, the cockpit, the waist, and the tail, and it carried double the ammunition load of a standard bomber. Fully armed and loaded, it weighed more than a B-17F with a full bomb load. With this excess weight, the YB-40 was unable to climb or keep station with the rest of the B-17s while loaded with bombs, and slowed a returning formation that was now lighter after releasing their bombs. After only a few missions, it was recognized that the YB-40 slowed the formation it was supposed to defend and the additional armor could not withstand direct hits from the 20mm and 30mm cannon carried by German fighters. The YB-40 was quickly deemed a failure and the search for a way for the fighters to provide escort to the target and back continued.

By the end of May, the 56th had joined the 4th and 78th groups mounting 48-plane sweeps and escorts. VIII Fighter Command now felt ready to meet the Luftwaffe.

# THE BATTLE GETS SERIOUS

The 78th's major scrap with the Luftwaffe on May 14 was the announcement that the air war between VIII Fighter Command and their German opponents was now "on." The Germans had taken the measure of the American fighters and taken action on that knowledge. With the increasing American formations, JG 1 was transferred to bases in the Netherlands and Belgium to reinforce JG 26's position in the middle of the American aerial super-highway to Germany and build a "wall" of fighter units from JG 2 on the Cotentin peninsula to JG 11 on the German Bight. JG 1's transfer immediately added 72 Fw-190s and 36 Bf-109Gs to the German order of battle, a 25 percent increase in enemy strength.

The May 14 strike against Kiel saw Heinz Knoke's *Staffel* of JG 1 achieve a milestone in its battle with the Americans. Now that he had proved with himself and his wingman that the tactic of dropping bombs on a formation could wreak havoc with the bombers, the entire *Staffel* was armed with a 250-kilogram bomb on shackles under the fuselage. Knoke later wrote that he attempted a formation attack from 30,000 feet over Holstein, but the bombers below did not hold their course in one direction long enough. He was impressed by the precision by which the Americans bombed the Germania shipyards, describing it as fantastic. Oberfeldwebels Führmann, Fest, and Biermann closed to attack from a lower altitude closer to the bomber formation and each successfully hit a bomber; the explosions disrupted the formations. Knoke dropped his own bomb without success, then attacked a formation of 30 B-17s. He could feel his Gustav take hits, but he hit a bomber in the cockpit. He later described the bomber rearing up, "like a great animal that has been mortally wounded" before it dropped away in steep right-hand spirals until at approximately 3,000 meters (10,000 feet) a wing came off and it crashed near Husum at 1217 hours. This was Knoke's fifth bomber victory since scoring his first in late March, and was one of five brought down by 5.Staffel on this mission, giving the squadron a score of 50 B-17s and B-24s since Eighth Air Force had begun its campaign in February. Knoke was proud to note in his diary that 5.Staffel now had more bomber victories than the *Gruppe* staff flight and 4. and 6.Staffeln combined.

While the 78th was finding the enemy reluctant to engage, the Eagles managed to find enemy fighters willing to do so. On May 14, Second Lieutenant Duane Beeson and his element leader, Captain T.J. Andrews, scored the first two Bf 109s credited to Thunderbolt pilots during a Rodeo mission to Bruges, Belgium. The 334th Squadron's formation was bounced by two Bf-109Gs that shot up Second Lieutenant Bob Boock's P-47 and then dived away. Boock's fighter caught fire before he could get out and he was killed when the plane struck the water below. In the meantime, Andrews and Beeson went after the two 109s, quickly finding themselves pursued by the other two 109s of the enemy formation. Both turned into their pursuers and gave them the full effect of their eight .50-caliber guns, sending them into the Channel. Born in Boise, Idaho – hence all his planes receiving the name "Boise Bee" – Beeson was another Eagle who couldn't qualify for the USAAF due to lack of education, but he trained in the RCAF, passing out of flight training with the comment in his record that he was "... a good average pilot and is slightly overconfident. No outstanding faults." He joined 71 Eagle Squadron on September 5, 1942, just before its transfer to the USAAF. One of the shortest pilots in the group at five foot three inches, he was just short of his 22nd birthday but looked younger than his years. In a unit of strong individualists, he was remembered as "particularly intense" and would make his mark as one of the leading pilots.

The next day, Lieutenant Colonel Peterson was replaced as group flying executive by Major Blakeslee. Peterson had completed 200 missions at this point and moved up to become group executive officer.

Demonstrating that success on one day was no guarantee of success on the next, when the bombers returned to Kiel on May 15,

5.Staffel was not able to fly its usual 12 since several aircraft had been damaged the day before. Knoke reported in his diary after his return from the mission:

> This seems to be one of those days when every blasted thing goes wrong. I lose sight of the Fortress which I have started to shoot up. By this time I simply could not care less. I dive steeply from behind at another Fortress flying at the tail end. At last my firing begins to have some effect. The two left engines begin smoking. The Yank loses height rapidly. Once he is out of the formation, it is all over. I fasten on behind his tail and blaze away with everything I have. Bright flames spread along the belly. All ten members of the crew bail out. The parachutes hang in the sky like washing on some invisible clothesline, while the giant plane goes down trailing a long column of smoke, in a pilotless spin, falling out of control, and finally disintegrating in its descent.

On May 16, following its first serious run-in with the enemy, the 78th engaged formations of more than 100 Fw-190s over Flushing, Belgium, as it escorted the bombers into Germany. With the 82nd Squadron maintaining high top cover, Gene Roberts led the 84th into a fight with 60-plus Fw-190s at 20,000 feet while the low-squadron 83rd climbed to meet 50 others that had attempted unsuccessfully to lead the Americans inland where they could be cut off from returning to England.

The 84th's Flight Officer Charles Brown ran across three 190s and blew up tail-end Charlie, then flamed a second before six others dived on him from above and behind. In a desperate fight for survival, Brown's P-47 blew up under the German fighters' combined fire, wounding him in his foot, leg, and head. Amazingly, he was thrown clear of the wrecked fighter by the explosion and managed to open his parachute. Touching down off Walcheren Island, a German destroyer plucked him from the water. The battle continued above, when Major John D. Irvin scored a third 190 before the combatants separated. Pilots who flew a second Rodeo to Abbeville-St Omer that afternoon were disappointed when the Germans refused to answer the challenge. By May 26, the 78th had added 11 more missions to the records, all of which the Germans chose to ignore, to the dismay and chagrin of the pilots.

On May 17, VIII Bomber Command flew Mission 58 against the U-boat pens at Lorient and Bordeaux. This was a continuation of the anti-submarine campaign that had begun on October 20, 1942. The Germans claimed the pens were impossible to destroy with aerial bombs; their concrete roofs were 20 feet thick. To date, they had proven impervious to the bombs dropped by both RAF Bomber Command and VIII Bomber Command. Even thousand-pounders did nothing but pockmark the structures.

Two formations of bombers struck Lorient: 100 B-17s from the 91st, 92nd, 303rd, 305th, and 306th groups bombed the port facilities and shipping as a diversion for the second group of 59 Flying Fortresses from the 94th, 95th, and 96th groups which bombed the pens themselves. The bombers were intercepted by the Fw-190s of JG 2, the *Geschwader* tasked with defending the Cotentin peninsula and French Atlantic ports. Defending gunners in the first formation claimed 27 fighters shot down, while gunners in the second formation claimed 20.

Things picked up for the 78th at 1015 hours on May 26, when a maroon limousine drove up to the Duxford gate, then proceeded to group headquarters where the unit stood to attention. King George VI and Queen Elizabeth stepped out of the limousine to pay their first visit to an Eighth Air Force base. They were accompanied on their inspection of the base by Eighth Air Force commander Major General Eaker and Fighter Command leader Brigadier General Hunter. Major James Stone's "HL-Z," in which he had scored the 78th Group's first victory, was inspected, with the king climbing into the cockpit while a formation of 72 B-17s passed in review overhead.

Duxford's broad grass field gave an advantage to the group in allowing for launching and assembling quickly. Harding Zumwalt remembered:

Our procedure for departure was to assemble 48 aircraft at the east end of the field. Two flights each – eight aircraft – would line up and take off across the field, followed at 15-second intervals by the remaining flights. Once off the ground, you held your heading for two minutes before executing a 180-degree turn by flights. The one difficult part was that Number Two had to drop down below the flight and move to Number One's left while in that turn. In a minute and a half, all 48 aircraft were forming up on the group leader. With the weather sometimes down to 500 feet, we had to assemble quickly before we went into the clouds, which were often so thick a wingman could barely see his leader, even when tucked in tight. Each flight leader maintained a constant rate of climb until we broke out on top, which sometimes didn't happen till we reached 25,000 feet, but we would be in a reasonable group formation when we popped out.

On June 1, two of Knoke's pilots had a remarkable escape after colliding with each other after Oberfeldwebel Kramer's Gustav took a hit in the tail, falling off and hitting the fighter flown by Oberfeldwebel Biermann. The two 109s, locked together for several seconds, fell nearly a thousand feet before Biermann's plane broke free. Attempting a dead-stick landing at their base, he touched down too fast and overturned. The ground crews were amazed when they approached the mangled fighter to see Biermann open the canopy and climb out unharmed. Shortly after the separation, Kramer had managed to bail out, but he immediately opened his parachute due to the low altitude; his high speed resulted in two of the harness straps breaking, leaving the parachute only half open when he hit the water. Fortunately a rescue launch was nearby and they pulled him out of the water, spitting blood and shocked to have survived.

On June 4, Zemke promoted the 61st's CO, Loren McCollom – whom he considered the best of his squadron commanders – to be flying executive officer for the group. McCollom's replacement as 61st commander was Captain Francis Gabreski. The 56th, which had been "late to the table" since its arrival in England six months earlier, finally got the group's first score on the Rodeo flown on June 12. While over Belgium, 62nd Squadron CO Dave Schilling spotted a squadron of Fw-190s below. Leading his flight down, Schilling was diving so fast that he overshot the enemy fighters. Captain Walter Cook, leading the second flight that dived after Schilling, managed to pull out of his dive onto the tail of the formation and opened fire at one of the trailing Würgers at 300 yards, knocking pieces off the 190's wing before the fighter flipped into an uncontrollable spin and went in with the pilot unable to get out.

The next day, Zemke spotted a formation of Fw-190s 10,000 feet below the group formation. Taking two flights down with him, Zemke pulled onto the formation without being spotted and shot down both Fw-190s of the trailing *Rotte*. Moments later, Bob Johnson shot down the wingman of the other pair in the formation Zemke attacked. On return to Halesworth, Johnson was called to the group commander's office for having left his flight without permission; it was a violation of flight discipline that Zemke would not abide. Johnson offered the defense that he and his element leader had agreed when they first started flying together that whoever saw the enemy first would take lead and attack; the element leader said he had heard nothing from Johnson. The future leading ace narrowly escaped expulsion from the group, with a warning from Zemke that he would not be so lucky if it happened again.

June 7 saw the arrival at "Goat Hill" of the fourth fighter group to be assigned to VIII Fighter Command, when the 353rd Fighter Group, composed of the 350th, 351st, and 352nd Fighter Squadrons, arrived from training in the United States. Originally activated on October 1, 1942, the unit was the second after the 56th to have extensively trained on the P-47 prior to being sent overseas. Among the few experienced pilots in the group was the executive officer, Lieutenant Colonel Glenn E. Duncan, who had been an Air Corps pilot since receiving his wings at Kelly Field on October 5, 1940. P-47s arrived a week later and the group began two months of intensive operational training for the conditions it would meet in the ETO.

Over the rest of the month, the 56th flew mostly Rodeos that were ignored by the enemy and a few close escort missions for B-17s attacking targets within the P-47's limited radius of action. Flying on internal fuel only, the average mission length was 90 minutes, with around 30 minutes of that time spent over enemy-occupied territory. Climbing to 30,000 feet before crossing the enemy coast, combined with the necessity of keeping a high speed in hostile airspace, saw the P-47s consuming their internal 305-gallon fuel load at around 200 gallons an hour. If they engaged the enemy in combat, the R-2800 engines drained the tanks at a rate of nearly 300 gallons an hour. Fortunately such engagements were short and sharp, but pilots nervously watched their fuel gauges as they flew back across the Channel toward home.

At nearly the same time that the 56th was notching its first two scores, the 78th Group – which had flown 14 missions in June, with nine provoking no response from the enemy – ran into 20 Fw-190s near Lumbres, France. The JG 26 pilots were good, and the 78th lost one pilot killed in action (KIA) while another parachuted into captivity; several P-47s landed back at Duxford badly shot up, for no enemy claimed. Eight days later on June 22, the group arrived over Walcheren Island to rendezvous with the bombers and support their withdrawal across the Channel. The B-17s were under fierce attack from Fw-190s, which knocked down three stragglers before they dived away from the approaching American fighters without loss. The 78th finally added to their score two days later, when Bf-109s bounced them between Lille and Ostend during a Rodeo and three pilots divvied up one 109.

On June 22, 4th Fighter Group flying executive officer Major Blakeslee led a Ramrod to Antwerp, though the rendezvous with the bombers was missed due to the cloudy weather. By the time the 4th found the bombers and picked them up, the B-17s were under attack from 20 German fighters. The 335th and 336th squadrons dived on the enemy while the 334th stayed as top cover. In the fight, the pilots claimed three Fw-190s and a Bf-109 shot down. One of each was credited to First Lieutenant Beatie, demonstrating he was fully recovered from his adventure being dunked in the Channel when he was shot up a week earlier. Beatie reported that he and his section spotted four Fw-190s attacking a straggling quartet of B-17s. "I overshot the last '190 and attacked the one in front of him. I saw strikes and a big ball of black smoke as he snapped over and went straight down." Beatie blacked out when he turned sharply away from the Fw-190, but First Lieutenant Paul Ellington saw the enemy fighter hit the water near the Dutch islands of Beveland-Walcheren. Coming to a moment later, Beatie found himself surrounded by ten Bf-109s:

> Three of them went directly in front of me as I pulled over in a tight chandelle. I dove on the last in a line and got in strikes on his cockpit and he started over in a roll and went down. I followed him until he started pulling up. I was very close to him, and was just pushing the firing button when he bailed out.

First Lieutenant Fonzo "Snuffy" Smith shot down another Fw-190, then in turn was chased by two that he outran. First Lieutenant Jim Goodson shot down the third Fw-190 near Hulst for his first victory.

On June 25, Heinz Knoke was badly injured by bomber gunners in one plane when he attacked the B-17 on their plane's wing. He returned to base with a wounded hand and a bit of a scare when it took longer than expected to get back to the coast after the fight. The medics worked on the hand in the base hospital and gave him a room to stay in. Once they were gone, he slipped out and returned to the unit. He changed the bandages on his hand daily, and the *Kommandeur* took the opportunity of his being wounded to give him two weeks' leave back in his home town, Hamelin. After only a week, he returned, unable to relate to his friends who had no understanding of the battle he was fighting daily. On his return, he got his mechanic to create a heavy leather glove he could wear that would protect his hand while allowing him to fly.

Four days later, on June 26, the 4th picked up the B-17s near Dieppe to provide withdrawal support. The bombers appeared along with a swarm of enemy fighters. First Lieutenant Raymond Care and his wingman First Lieutenant Duane Beeson – both flying new P-47D-1s – each scored a Bf-109, with Second Lieutenant Dal Leaf damaging a third. Care reported:

Six Bf-109s came in under us head-on about a mile east of me. I turned and followed them inland. Two of them broke away and turned out to sea. I picked the leading aircraft and fired four or five bursts. I closed to 250 yards and gave two more bursts, which hit the enemy aircraft in the cowling and cockpit. Fire burst out of his engine and the enemy aircraft slid down into the sea.

Beeson knocked down the wingman.

On June 29, the 78th Group refueled at RAF Ford on the coast, so that its pilots could maximize their limited range to penetrate deep enough into northern France to meet the bombers as they came off their attack on Villacoublay airdrome near Paris. The B-17s were under fire from heavy flak and Bf-109s when the Thunderbolts arrived on the scene. Captain Charles London added victories two and three to become the group's top scorer when he chased two 109s through the bomber formation, exploding them within seconds of each other. Flight Officer Peter Pompetti, flying number four in the 83rd Squadron's fourth flight, spotted an Fw-190 below. Radioing a sighting report and failing to receive a response from his flight leader, he split-S-ed onto the enemy fighter, exploding it with his first burst. Back at Duxford, his flight commander called him before the squadron commander for violating flight discipline. When Pompetti asked if his calls were heard, the flight leader responded he had heard them, but that Pompetti had broken formation and left them exposed. Pompetti refused to back down. "Exposed? We were at 30,000 feet!"

Two days later, on July 1, the 78th experienced its blackest day of the war. Although the group was credited with the destruction of four Fw-190s, damaging five others, it became known as "the day 'Pete' didn't come back." Colonel Arman Peterson flying his P-47C "Flagari," callsign "Kingpost Leader," led 32 P-47s from the 83rd and 84th squadrons on a Rodeo to the Dutch coast. Approaching just south of Hoek van Holland at 29,000 feet, Fw-190s were spotted about 5,000 feet below. Peterson led his flight in a diving attack on four while Gene Roberts and his flight took on four others. The battle turned quickly into a dive-and-zoom fight. Peterson missed his intended target and zoomed straight up into the late afternoon sun where his wingman lost him in the glare. With no one covering him, Peterson banked around and dived on the enemy in a second pass, but was in turn hit by an unseen foe. There was no radio call, and no one saw Kingpost Leader plunge into the North Sea off the island of Ouddorp. One moment he was their beloved commander; the next "Colonel Pete" had vanished forever. No other commander would ever be so loved and respected as the 28-year-old Peterson, the man who had brought them together in difficult circumstances the year before, turning a collection of individuals into a fighter group, then led them to England and into combat. Every pilot in the group believed that Peterson knew and liked him personally; everyone knew he would do anything for them to insure their success.

The next day, Bob Hope and Frances Langford brought their United Service Organizations (USO) troupe to Duxford. Hope later remembered, "They were the toughest house I played to in the war."

Over the next week, pilots searched the area off Ouddorp in vain for any sign of their leader. Colonel Pete's callsign "Kingpost" was permanently retired. 83rd Squadron commander Major Jim Stone was made temporary commander with a promotion, taking the callsign "Graywall Leader." Days later, Stone moved down to deputy group commander on the arrival of Lieutenant Colonel Melvin F. McNickle, whose ETO experience had begun with assignment as liaison officer with RAF 601 Squadron in the fall of 1941 following its re-equipment with the Airacobra I, Lend-Lease version of the P-39D; his twin brother commanded the P-39-equipped 350th Fighter Group in North Africa.

Bob Johnson nearly ended his flying career two weeks after scoring his first victory, when the 56th experienced one of its worst days. Group flying executive Lieutenant Colonel Loren McCollom led the mission. After landing at RAF Manston, the most-forward base in England, to refuel, the mission was to meet and bring out the bombers after they hit Villacoublay airdrome. Nearing the rendezvous point at Forges-les-Eaux, they were jumped from above and behind by 16 Fw-190s from II./JG 26. The Germans' first pass scattered the Americans. Johnson, who was sticking to the formation like glue in the aftermath of his run-in with Zemke, was number four in the rearmost flight of the 61st Squadron. His P-47 was badly shot up by an attack that ruptured his hydraulic system with a burst of 20mm cannon fire.

Burned and partially blinded by hydraulic fluid that sprayed in the cockpit, Johnson attempted to bail out, but damage to the canopy prevented him opening it more than about six inches. The Thunderbolt fell into an uncontrolled spin; when he managed to pull out, he found the fire had been blown out. As he headed home at a low altitude, a single Fw-190 spotted him and curved in to attack. With the P-47 badly damaged, Johnson could only take the hits while the enemy pilot made several attacks. As he crossed the Channel coast, the enemy pilot ran out of ammunition.

The German pulled alongside the shot-up Thunderbolt. Johnson recalled the fighter looked beautiful in its gleaming dappled camouflage. Finally, after several minutes spent examining the shot-up P-47, the enemy pilot shook his head and rocked his wings before turning back and leaving Johnson to his fate. The opponent was most likely Major Egon Mayer, *Gruppenkommandeur* of III./JG 2; Mayer reported that he had expended all his cannon ammunition by the time he encountered Johnson, but nevertheless made a claim for the P-47 that was confirmed.

After nursing the smoking P-47 across the Channel, Johnson managed to land at Manston. It took several minutes for the ground crew to remove the canopy, which had been torn up by a 20mm round so that the twisted metal caught on the fuselage and prevented it sliding open. Once out of the cockpit, Johnson tried counting the bullet holes, but gave up after reaching 200 without ever taking a step around his plane.

The German attack on the 56th resulted in four other pilots shot down and killed in the initial attack; two P-47s that managed to get back to Halesworth were damaged beyond repair and five others severely damaged. The "Schlageter" Geschwader pilots were given confirmation for nine Thunderbolts shot down. Johnson returned to combat five days later and recalled the mission as the most harrowing of his career in his memoir *Thunderbolt!*

On July 14, Major Harry Dayhuff led the 78th Group to cover the withdrawal of B-17s attacking Amiens/Glisly airdrome. Over Montreuil, he spotted Fw-190s heading for the bombers and led an attack that turned into a major fight. Second Lieutenant August DeGenero thought he was going to die when he was bounced by two Fw-190s and the right side of his cockpit and instrument panel were shot out while he received splinter wounds in both hands, his ankles, and right knee. He managed to recover, and now "damn mad," dived into another Fw-190 formation; he shot down one from 100 yards, probably destroyed a second, and damaged a third before he ducked into the nearby low clouds and headed for the Channel followed by three vengeful Germans, all while he flew without instruments, controlling the Thunderbolt with his forearms. To make matters more difficult, on the way home he lost his right aileron due to damage and had to fight the damaged rudder and elevators. As he had unstrapped when he thought he would bail out, a crash-landing was out of the question when he found he couldn't hook up his seatbelt. Spotting an English fishing boat, he circled it while he managed to batter open the jammed canopy with his injured hands. Letting go of the controls to jump, the airplane rolled inverted and he fell out, landing in the water near the "Little Old Lady"; her crew saved his life when they managed to pull him out quickly, since he could not unfasten his parachute and was suffering from blood loss. He went home a few weeks later, after being awarded the Distinguished Service Cross.

VIII Technical Command had begun distributing 200-gallon ferry tanks to the three fighter groups, delivering them to the 4th on July 19 and to the 78th two days later. While these unwieldy, unpressurized tanks could not be used above 20,000 feet, the fighters could suck fuel from them as they flew across the Channel before switching to internal fuel, which could add a very useful 50–60 miles' range that allowed the P-47s to reach the Dutch–German border.

Jim Goodson scored his second victory on July 22, shooting down an Fw-190 near Hulst in Belgium while the 4th provided withdrawal cover for the bombers; the victory saw the beginning of his climb to top ace of the 4th.

The final week of July was "Little Blitz Week," the first attempt by VIII Bomber Command to maintain a sustained series of attacks against the German aviation industry. Good weather allowed 14 missions to be flown between July 24 and 30.

The 4th made use of the 200-gallon tanks for the first time on July 25 on a Rodeo to Ghent that saw the Luftwaffe ignore the Thunderbolts. On July 27, the need for the tanks despite the performance loss imposed by their use was made clear when the group was forced to turn back early during an escort mission for B-26s when the "tankless" P-47s ran low on fuel. After this, the tanks were installed on all aircraft.

The next day's Ramrod to Westhoof-Emmerich, which saw the 4th's first penetration of German airspace, demonstrated the value of the tanks. Minutes before making rendezvous, a wing of B-17s over Utrecht was spotted under attack by more than 30 Bf-109s and Fw-190s. The Thunderbolts dived headlong into the enemy fighters, and a big battle developed over the city. In the end, five Bf-109s and four Fw-190s were added to the scoreboard, for the loss of the 336th Squadron's Second Lieutenant Henry Ayres, who was forced to bail out after being shot up by Major Rolf-Günther Hermichen, adjutant of III./JG 26.

Duane Beeson was credited with one of the Bf-109s, reporting:

I saw many strikes, his left wingtip blew off and then there was an explosion just in front of his cockpit, when he lurched violently and went down smoking. While climbing back to rejoin my section, an Fw-190 got on my tail and Lieutenant Care closed up behind me and opened fire. There were many strikes and the pilot baled out.

Captains Carl Miley and Leroy Gover each scored single 109s while group commander Colonel Edward Anderson downed the remaining two Bf-109s for his only victories of the war.

That afternoon, 335th Squadron commander Major Gilbert Halsey showed that every mission was a crapshoot. Flying a Circus to Westhoof-Emmerich, the 16 P-47s ran into the entire III./JG 26, nearly 50 Fw-190s. The Eagles did not spot the enemy until the redoubtable III.Gruppe adjutant, Major Rolf-Günther Hermichen, killed First Lieutenant Frederick Merritt in the first diving pass. The outnumbered

Americans fought for their lives and managed to down five "Schlageter" Geschwader Fw-190s in a desperate fight.

First Lieutenant Aubrey Stanhope spotted three Focke-Wulfs ahead and attacked the one on the right, later reporting:

I was getting hits on his tail and left wing. He side-slipped and went down. I then turned to the one on the left, firing a long burst from 15 degrees deflection to dead astern. I saw strikes on his tail and left wing. Then there was a violent explosion in his left wing where his gun was. There was a huge flash, pieces flew off, and all his wing outboard of his gun came off clean. The plane then tumbled tail over nose and spun down smoking badly.

Second Lieutenant Pierce McKennon saw what he later reported as:

a bomber being clobbered by two Fw-190s. I cut my throttle and dove on one as he broke away and went into a diving turn. He went into a sharp climbing turn to port. I firewalled everything and closed to within about 150 feet and got in a three- or four-second burst. Something flew off his port side and large quantities of white smoke came pouring out. He flicked violently to starboard, and I almost hit him. Passing within just a few feet of him, I saw his engine on fire with long streamers of flame and smoke.

McKennon turned away, having just scored the first of his eventual 11 victories.

Second Lieutenant Ken Smith saw a fighter he mistakenly identified as a P-47 below and throttled back to stay with it, at which point he suddenly saw it was an Fw-190; unknown to him, it was flown by Feldwebel Ernst Christoff of I./JG 26, who had just shot down the B-17F "Lucky Lady II" from the 96th Bomb Group's 388th Squadron. "I opened fire at about 75 yards and immediately saw flashes at the wing root and cockpit area. I broke off as he rolled and went into a spin." Christoff managed to get out, but opened his parachute too soon, snagging it on the horizontal stabilizer as it flashed past; the nine-victory *Experte* was dragged to his death in the crash. The 4th considered themselves lucky to be able to claim five Focke-Wulfs for the loss of Merritt.

The nature of the air battle the Thunderbolts fought changed on July 28, 1943. The seven days of good weather in the last week of July 1943 would be known afterwards as "Little Blitz Week," the first sustained attacks by VIII Bomber Command. The "blitz" now ended with three missions against the Focke-Wulf factories at Oschersleben, Warnemunde and Kassel. They were deep penetration missions beyond the range of escort fighters, and drew maximum opposition from the German defenders.

The sky was clear over the English Channel at mid-day. Fifteen miles west of the Dutch coast, 40 Thunderbolts of the 78th Fighter Group eased their slow climb out of England and leveled off at 23,000 feet to enter enemy air space. Standard Operating Procedure was to enter enemy territory at 29,000 feet, above the flak, which meant switching to the fuselage tank at that point. This time, 84th Fighter Squadron CO Major Gene Roberts was trying something new. He recalled, "We started with the usual 48 fighters – three squadrons of 16 fighters per squadron. However, two pilots reported mechanical problems and had to abort. In each case, I had to dispatch the aborting airplane's entire flight to provide an escort. That left us with 40 fighters by the time we reached Holland." Above Roberts' squadron, the 83rd flew high cover, led by Captain Charles P. London, "Red One," the group's top scorer with three victories. Major Harry Dayhuff led the 82nd in the low position. They stayed at the lower altitude, draining their belly tanks.

The Thunderbolts entered Holland north of Rotterdamn and flew past Nijmegen, where they switched to internal tanks and followed Roberts up to 29,000 feet to enter Germany. He thanked the lucky tail wind they must have found for pushing them so far east since this was the deepest penetration yet made; his decision to delay climbing to penetration altitude as long as possible was proven right.

The bombers targeting the factory at Oschersleben bombed through a cloud deck over the target when a small hole in the nine-tenths cloud cover opened and the lead bombardier was able to recognize a crossroad a few miles from the aiming point. The B-17 crews were thankful the westerly wind allowed them to continue straight on for home. As they came out of the flak field, defending fighters slashed through the formations. Three Fortresses were hit and the sky filled with parachutes. The bombers neared Haltern, where rocket-armed Bf-110G fighters attacked, firing their missiles outside the range of defensive fire.

At that moment, the 78th arrived. Roberts spotted the enemy. "We were outnumbered by at least three-to-one odds but were able to maneuver into attacking position with very little difficulty. The main reason for this success was that the German fighter pilots didn't believe we could possibly show up that far inland and were not expecting to see a defensive force at all."

The Americans took full advantage of German confusion. Reynolds remembered: "There was one B-17 beneath the main formation, and it was pouring smoke and appeared to be in deep trouble. I dove down on the enemy fighters that were attacking the cripple. They broke away and dived for the ground. There wasn't much more we could do to help the crippled B-17. We turned away from the bomber formation, about 1,000 yards out. I discovered on reaching this position that I had only myself and my wingman, Flight Officer Glenn Koontz. We immediately saw enemy aircraft ahead of us and above the formation. I judged that there were over 100 enemy aircraft in the area, as compared with our 40."

"Dead ahead of me was a single Fw-190, at the same level as Koontz and me, about 1,000 to 1,500 yards ahead. He was racing in the same direction as the bombers so he could get ahead of them, swing around in front, and make a head-on pass." Roberts closed to 400 yards and opened fire, hitting the fighter heavily with a 3–5-second burst and it spun down in smoke and flames. He spotted two more and closed so fast he had to pull up and roll in on his second victim to avoid a collision. "I opened fire from dead astern. I observed several strikes and, as before, the enemy fighter billowed smoke and flames, rolled over, and spun down." Amazingly, Roberts and Koontz were still in the middle of the action.

"After the second engagement, we were about two miles ahead of the bombers, about 500 feet above them, and still well out to their starboard side. Koontz was on my right wing. About this time, I observed a 109 on the port side and ahead of the bomber formation. I dropped below the bomber formation, crossed over to the port side, and pulled up behind him, again at full throttle." The 109 turned to attack the bombers head on. Roberts followed – the bombers loomed beyond. "I closed to within 400 or 500 yards and opened fire. He was in a tight turn, and that required deflection shooting. My first two bursts fell away behind him, but I continued to close. I fired my third burst as he straightened out to approach the bombers." The enemy fighter fell over into a spin, trailing smoke and flame. Koontz flamed the wingman Roberts hadn't seen. Gene Roberts had just scored the first triple victory by an VIII Fighter Command pilot. Group top-scorer Charles London caught two Fw-190s; flaming the leader and diving to avoid the wingman, he spotted a Bf-109 and set it afire. With this victory, he was the first VIII Fighter Command ace to score all victories in a P-47.

Quince Brown and wingman Peter Pompetti spotted a flight of four Bf-109s. As he made a high-G turn, five of Brown's eight guns jammed; with only three still working, he hit the 109 on the right in the cockpit, killing the enemy pilot before breaking off to avoid a collision.

Captain Jack Price came across four Fw-190s and flamed the leader. He turned into the enemy element leader and opened fire with his wingman 2nd Lieutenant John Bertrand; each hit a 190 and both went down out of control. Deputy group commander Lt. Colonel James Stone hit a Bf-109 that blew up so close that his wingman flew through the explosion. 82nd squadron commander Dayhuff spotted a Bf-109 attacking the bombers; closing astern, the 109 blew up under his fire.

Suddenly, there were no more enemy fighters.

The battle had been an intense ten minutes. The Thunderbolts broke off while they had gas to return home. The B-17s were soon picked up by the 4th Fighter Group and taken home safe. For a cost of seven P-47s, the 78th was credited with 16 victories. With the eight credited to the 56th and 4th Groups, VIII Fighter Command's total score to date was doubled. The force sent to Oschersleben lost 15 of the 39 that bombed the target; their leaders later said they thought they would be wiped out, had the fighters not intervened when they did.

Among the targets hit in Little Blitz Week was Hamburg, which VIII Bomber Command struck in collaboration with RAF Bomber Command in Operation *Gomorrah*. Hamburg's shipyards produced U-boats, and its oil refineries were crucial for the German war effort. What made this operation different was that it was the first to make widespread use of what the British called "window" and the Americans named "chaff." This was bundles of aluminum strips, cut to the wavelengths of the German radars; as the bundles broke open after they were thrown out of the bombers, the foil strips floated to the ground. While they were in the air, they effectively blinded the German radars, which returned nothing but "snow." This meant that the German night fighters were completely unable to make any interception under radar guidance. While enemy fighters could spot the American bombers in daylight, the lack of radar vectoring meant that the short-ranged German fighters used up crucial gasoline searching for their targets. Both sides had known how this worked conceptually for at least a year before, but neither had been willing to make use of the tactic since its success would inform the other side, which could then use it against the radars of the initiators. British losses at night had grown as the Kammhuber Line became more effective with its *Himmelbett* (heavenly bed) system of radar-guided interceptions, which prompted the Allied decision to finally make use of the new weapon.

By July 1943, both the RAF and USAAF bomber commands in England were at the point of "put up or shut up." They needed a major success. With an extended period of good weather forecast, Hamburg became the target. The bombers would drop incendiaries, aimed at the old medieval heart of the city, where building construction was largely of wood. The USAAF had just received a large supply of the new American-made oil-based incendiaries, which VIII Bomber Command believed was superior to the four-pound magnesium-cased thermite bombs used by the RAF. There would be multiple raids over a period of days to stoke the fires that the earlier raids started. Weather-wise, there had been little rain in previous weeks while the temperatures had been unusually warm. These conditions would allow the bombers to make highly concentrated drops around the intended targets. The dry, warm air would create a vortex and whirling updraft of super-heated air which resulted in a tornado of fire.

Operation *Gomorrah* – named for the biblical city destroyed in a rain of fire and brimstone – began on July 24 and continued for eight days and seven nights. It was the most sustained bombing campaign to date.

The first RAF raid began 57 minutes after midnight on July 24, and lasted for nearly an hour. The 40,000 firemen found their firefighting resources damaged when the telephone exchange caught fire; rubble blocked the movement of fire engines through the city streets. The fires raged out of control and were still burning three days later.

The first USAAF raid arrived over the city at 1640 hours. Although 300 bombers were supposed to participate, problems in assembly in poor weather over England meant that only 90 bombers attacked the Blohm and Voss shipyard and a Daimler-Benz aircraft engine factory;

smoke from the fires made visual bombing difficult and the shipyard was only lightly damaged while a generating station was bombed instead of the factory, which was invisible in the smoke. German flak damaged 78 of the 90 attackers to varying degrees. The smoke was so thick that the planned bombing that night was canceled, with the RAF hitting Essen instead. The raid attempted on the night of July 26 was not considered successful because of thunderstorms and high winds over the North Sea that caused bombers to abort. There was no USAAF raid that day, again due to poor visibility from the smoke of the still-burning fires from the first night.

On the night of July 27, just before midnight, 787 British bombers began dropping incendiaries, with the main aiming points being the dense housing in the working-class neighborhoods of Billwerder, Borgfelde, Hamm, Hammerbrook, Hohenfelde, and Rothenburgsort. The use of blockbuster bombs dropped in the early part of the raid prevented firefighters from getting to the scene quickly. The lack of firefighting and the dry, warm weather let the fires grow quickly, which culminated in a firestorm. The tornado of fire created an inferno, pushing the winds as high as 150 miles per hour and reaching temperatures of 800°C (1,470°F), while the flames reached an altitude of over 1,000 feet. A total of 21 square miles of the city were incinerated. Asphalt streets caught fire, while fuel oil from damaged and destroyed ships, barges, and storage tanks filled the canals and the harbor, which caught fire.

Generalmajor Wilhelm Kehrl, chief of Hamburg's civil defense, reported:

Trees three feet thick were broken off or uprooted, human beings were thrown to the ground or flung alive into the flames by winds that exceeded 150 miles per hour. The panic-stricken citizens had nowhere to turn. Flames drove them from the shelters, but high-explosive bombs sent them scurrying back again. Once inside, they were suffocated by carbon-monoxide poisoning and their bodies reduced to ashes as though they had been placed in a crematorium, which was indeed what each shelter proved to be.

RAF Bomber Command attacked again the next night. The incendiaries merely kept the fires going. Thunderstorms over England led to cancellation of another USAAF raid during the next day, and the British bombers were kept on the ground by the rain that night. The last raid was made by the USAAF and RAF on August 3.

The death toll from Operation *Gomorrah* will never be certain, but by December 1, 1943, the official toll was 31,647 confirmed dead, though only 15,802 were based on actual identification of a body. The number of those who died in cellars and shelters could only be estimated from the quantity of ash on the floors.

The first week after the raid, approximately 1,000,000 survivors were evacuated, since 61 percent of the city's housing stock was destroyed or damaged. The work force was reduced by 10 percent. No subsequent city raid shook the German government the way Hamburg did. Josef Goebbels, who visited the city ten days after the raids, is said to have reported to Hitler on his return to Berlin that more raids like this would force Germany out of the war. Industrial losses were severe: 183 large factories were destroyed of 524 in the city, while 4,118 smaller factories were destroyed of 9,068 total. The losses included severe damage to 580 industrial firms and armaments works. All local transport was completely disrupted and did not return to normal during the rest of the war. Hamburg would be bombed 69 times over the course of the remainder of the war, preventing any real recovery. As late as 1955, the city was still being rebuilt.

In the censored German media, the Hamburg raids were seen as being far worse than the major military reverse that had taken place over the course of July in the Battle of Kursk or the loss of Sicily the same month. An August 9 report by United Press carried an account by a Swiss merchant who had been in the city, stating that "Hamburg's ceaseless, inescapable destruction is on a scale that defies the imagination."

On July 27, Heinz Knoke went flying for the first time since being wounded back in June. He took the unit's Bf-108 "Taifun" hack and flew to Hamburg. What he saw left a strong impression when he wrote in his diary later that he had observed great fires still raging everywhere in what was now a vast area of rubble. An enormous cloud of smoke rose 3,000 feet above the fires, fanning out to a width of ten to 20 miles, slowly drifting eastward to the Baltic Sea. The sky was cloudless and the column of rising smoke stood out starkly against the summer blue. "The horror of the scene makes a deep impression on me. The war is assuming some hideous aspects. I resolve with grim determination to return to operations in spite of my wounded hand."

In the next two years, Hamburg's 35,000 would be joined by the deaths of 25,000 in the fire-bombing of Dresden and the almost-unimaginable loss of 100,000 in one night to a firestorm set by B-29s on March 9, 1945, in Tokyo. But Hamburg shocked the senses because there was nothing before it to compare.

In the aftermath, Adolf Galland advocated a massive fighter production program. In a meeting at Hitler's Wolf's Lair headquarters in East Prussia, even Hermann Göring was finally convinced, stating at the conclusion of the meeting that "The Luftwaffe must now change over to the defense against the west. It should be possible to stop the Allied raids against the Reich by concentrating all forces and their effects on this one aim." He then left the meeting to report their decision to Hitler. An hour later, he returned and walked past them all, wordless, and disappeared into an adjoining room. Galland and Dietrich Peltz, *Inspekteur der Kampfflieger* (Inspector of Bombers), were called in. Göring was at the desk, his head in his hands, a broken man. He finally gathered himself and told them Hitler had absolutely refused to countenance anything he said, stating that the way to counter the Allied bombing was for the Luftwaffe to direct every effort to burning England's cities to the ground.

Incredulous, Galland later wrote that it was difficult to describe how he felt on hearing Göring's words. "Annoyance and revolt were mixed with a failure to understand and a wish to resign. What could I do here now? Should I not have asked to be relieved of my post?" In the end, he and the others remained in hopes that Hitler's decision could be changed. It was not. The decisive moment for German leadership to change course in the light of Allied action passed untaken.

VIII Technical Command had not rested on their non-existent laurels for having found a way to fit the unpressurized ferry tanks on the P-47s. The need was for a tank that was useful at all altitudes, and was hopefully not as aerodynamically inefficient as the bulbous ferry tanks. The technical experts found a way to use the exhaust of the P-47's instrument vacuum pump to pressurize a standard Air Force 75-gallon aluminum drop tank carried on bomb shackles. While the tank held less than half the fuel of the ferry tank, all those 75 gallons were useable, unlike those of the ferry tank; also, the P-47 was more fuel-efficient at high altitude. Thus, a P-47 equipped with the new tank, taking off and climbing to 30,000 feet over the Channel – thus entering German airspace at a "fighting altitude"

– could fly as far into enemy airspace as it could with the larger ferry tanks flying at a far lower altitude; maximum range using all fuel in the tank, with the fighter flying at 25,000 feet or higher, was 340 miles, nearly 100 miles further than with the ferry tank. The major delay in using the tanks was that the P-47Cs had to be modified at a depot with a deeper keel in the lower fuselage between the landing gear, to allow installation of shackles capable of holding the tanks, and a sufficient number of tanks had to be brought to England. The newer P-47Ds that were now arriving at aircraft depots in England already had the keel and the bomb shack attachments installed at the factory. The aluminum tanks had originally been developed as ferry tanks, but were now in use with P-40 and P-39-equipped squadrons in the Pacific, and extending their use to the ETO put a strain on US production of the tanks. Nevertheless, the 4th Group became the first to receive the tanks in early August, followed by the other groups over the remainder of the month.

On August 3, the 353rd Fighter Group was declared operational. Additional P-47s were arriving in sufficient numbers to allow groups to expand their establishment to 72 Thunderbolts each, allowing them to fly two 36-plane escort groups simultaneously. By the end of the month, VIII Fighter Command would effectively increase its strength by 250 percent through this expansion.

With more airplanes in a group, there was a need for more pilots. The 78th Group welcomed a second group of trained P-47 pilots to fill out the ranks on August 5. The men were members of USAAF Class 43-C, all of whom had trained on the P-47 from the time they were designated single-engine fighter pilots. Among them were Second Lieutenants Dick Hewitt and Ernie Russell. Russell was the youngest, having turned 19 on May 19. A policy change made following the outbreak of war allowed an applicant to demonstrate in tests that he had knowledge equivalent to two years of college, thus meeting the educational requirements to enlist as an aviation cadet at age 18; Russell had taken advantage of this the month after he graduated from high school in Mississippi. He later recalled:

We were fortunate to be held off operations for further training at what the group called Clobber College, where we learned things we hadn't been taught back in the States, such as how to fly at very high altitudes, get some real instrument time in actual bad weather, as well as get a good indoctrination on German fighter tactics from guys who had learned to fight the hard way.

Similar groups of pilots from Class 43-C arrived at the other groups over the course of August.

Beginning in August when two more bomb groups were declared operational and able to fill the gap created by the assignment of the command's two B-24 bomb groups to Ninth Air Force in Libya for the Ploesti mission, VIII Bomber Command began bombing targets deeper in Germany. On August 12, the 78th provided escort for a mission to attack the synthetic oil installations at Bochum, Gelsenkirchen, and Recklinghausen. Since the German fighters remained out of range and avoided making attacks while the escorts were present, the group returned to Duxford without incident. Once the Thunderbolts turned away, the Germans hit the bomber formations hard, knocking down 23 and damaging 103 before the 56th Group arrived to cover their final withdrawal. Three days later, the 78th escorted B-17s on a mission to hit Merville, Lille/Vendeville, and Vitry en Artois airdromes in France, during which it claimed three Fw-190s for two losses.

August was shaping up as the month that VIII Bomber Command finally entered battle directly with the Luftwaffe over Germany.

# 9

# AGAINST THE ODDS

August 1943 would mark the one-year anniversary of the entry of the Eighth Air Force into the European Air War. Despite the promise Eaker had made to Churchill at Casablanca that VIII Bomber Command would be committed *en masse* to the bombing of Germany, the first US bombs had not fallen on German soil until nearly six months later. Since then, the command had seen more units added, but there had still not been any major mission flown against the kind of strategic target whose destruction the USAAF "bomber barons" had promised would change the war. The entire USAAF high command was now at the point of "put up or shut up." The Quebec Conference was scheduled for August 17–24, and the topic was whether or not the Normandy invasion would occur on May 1, 1944, or some later date, or whether it would happen at all.

Winston Churchill was still reluctant to commit to a nose-to-nose bare-knuckles battle on the old Western Front, where Britain and its Empire had sacrificed a generation. Britain had defeated Napoleon by striking him where it was difficult for him to respond, on the Spanish peninsula, taking later advantage of his failure in Russia in 1812. Churchill was personally still in favor of such a strategy. He was now pushing for an invasion of "the soft underbelly" through Italy, following the Allied success in Sicily; the Italians were giving every sign of wanting to get out of the war. Churchill argued that giving the enemy a year's "breathing room" between the taking of Sicily and the proposed landing in France would allow them to build up their defenses to a point where the Atlantic Wall that Hitler was planning would indeed keep the Allies out. His argument included the possibility that the Allies might quickly move through Italy following an Italian surrender, and advance through the Ljubljana Gap onto the plains of Hungary, putting the Western Allies into Eastern Europe and blocking an occupation of the east by the Soviets. The failure to date of Eighth Air Force to inflict any serious damage on the German war machine in general and the Luftwaffe in particular as called for in Operation *Pointblank* meant that perhaps the invasion of France would not be possible at all, if combined with the "free pass" to the enemy to build up defenses.

It was now crucial that VIII Bomber Command celebrate its one-year anniversary with a demonstration that it could accomplish what had been promised. The Quebec Conference was scheduled to begin on August 17, the exact one-year anniversary of that first mission by a dozen Flying Fortresses to Rouen. Whatever was going to be done had to be done before that date. What was needed was a target – a "bottleneck" – the destruction of which would maximally damage both the German war machine in general and the Luftwaffe specifically.

Operation *Juggler* was conceived as an attack against the Messerschmitt production facilities at Regensburg in Bavaria and Wiener-Neustadt in Austria. Allied intelligence credited the two factories with producing 48 percent of all single-engine fighters used by the Luftwaffe. The operation was conceived as a coordinated attack by both the Eighth Air Force in England and the Ninth Air Force in Libya; striking simultaneously would leave the defenses at both locations taken by surprise. Regensburg would be struck by VIII Bomber Command while Wiener-Neustadt would be targeted by the Ninth Air Force.

Regensburg would not be VIII Bomber Command's only target. There was a target nearby that was as important if not more so: Schweinfurt.

In 1883, Friedrich Fischer, a mechanic living in Schweinfurt, a medium-sized city in Bavaria, invented the machine that could produce ball bearings on a mass production basis. His son founded the Kugelfischer firm in 1906, which by World War I was the cornerstone of the ball bearing industry. Production had surged after the war. By 1943, the population of the city had grown by 50,000 since 1922. There were now five factories in Schweinfurt, operating 24 hours a day, responsible for the production of approximately two-thirds of all German ball bearings and roller bearings. Demand only grew, with the German aviation industry alone using 2.4 million ball bearings a month.

The British Ministry of Economic Warfare had collected information regarding potential German economic targets since 1939. A hard lesson in the importance of ball bearings had been given during the Battle of Britain when the Luftwaffe bombed one British ball bearing plant, which caused a serious delay in aircraft production. Ball bearings were a "bottleneck." Extensive damage to or destruction of German ball bearing production would destroy the production capability of every factory producing war materiel. When British planners presented ball bearings as a target to the Americans in early 1943, VIII Bomber Command planners immediately saw that destruction of this particular "bottleneck target" by precision daylight attack would shorten the war and truly demonstrate the power of strategic bombing.

Since May, five new B-17 groups had become operational; all now had sufficient experience that a major mission such as this was within the command's capability. VIII Bomber Command could put almost 400 bombers in the air over a target. With the force now available, it would be possible to strike both Schweinfurt and Regensburg simultaneously, thus demonstrating to the conference attendees at Quebec – most prominently Roosevelt and Churchill – that the bombers could disrupt German war industries and strike a serious blow against the Luftwaffe.

The bombers would be operating far beyond their fighter cover. VIII Bomber Command's intelligence section believed that the enemy's single-seat fighters were concentrated in a belt along the coast from Brittany through the Low Countries to North Germany, and that behind that fighter wall the enemy would use their twin-engine fighters – the Bf-110s, Me-410s, and Ju-88s which were believed to be less capable of penetrating the bomber boxes' defenses. Planners determined that they could dilute the defenders by striking both targets closely enough in time that the fighters could not land to refuel and rearm between the two forces. If Wiener-Neustadt was struck simultaneously, the German defenses would be stretched to the breaking point.

Colonel Curtis LeMay's 4th Bombardment Wing would hit Regensburg while the 1st Bombardment Wing, led by Brigadier General Robert B. Williams, would go to Schweinfurt, with the two missions' targets hit close to simultaneously. The Regensburg force would not turn

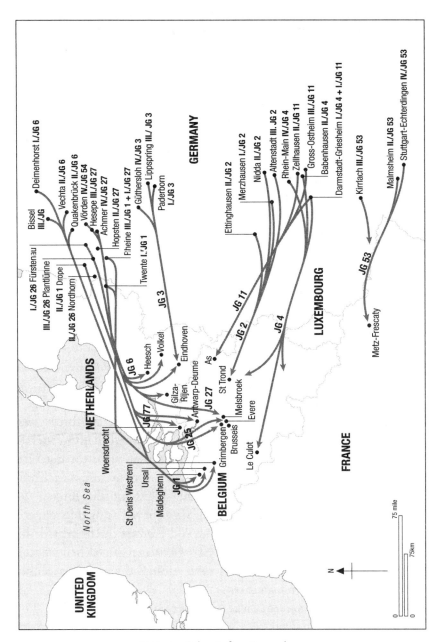

MAP 2: Schweinfurt-Regensburg

147

back and return to England, but would turn south to cross the Alps, landing in North Africa in the first "shuttle mission," with the B-17Fs using "Tokyo Tanks" installed in the bomb bay to provide the necessary range. LeMay's force, arriving first, would face the defenders' initial interception missions, then escape over the Alps. Williams' Schweinfurt armada, arriving shortly after the departure of LeMay's force, would catch the enemy defenders on the ground refueling and rearming, and would thus face the full fury of the Luftwaffe on its return flight to England. Essentially, it came down to LeMay's men fighting their way in while Williams' airmen fought their way out.

All that was needed was good weather. Operation *Juggler* was then set for August 7. Unfortunately, while weather over the Continent was generally good throughout the month, the mission was scheduled and canceled three times because poor weather over England prevented the safe takeoff and assembly of the two forces. Once it was determined that the strike force could not take off early enough to hit targets deep in Germany, missions were flown in mid-morning, after the fog had burned off the airfields in East Anglia and the Midlands, to targets in the Low Countries and northern France. These missions were protected to and from the target by fighters, now that all four operational VIII Fighter Command groups had received additional fighters and pilots that allowed each to fly two missions in a day.

After several postponements it was finally recognized that a simultaneous attack was not possible, and the two air forces were directed to stage their operations separately as weather allowed. The three VIII Bomber Command B-24 groups that were on detached service with the Ninth Air Force for the Ploesti attack, which had happened on August 7, attacked Wiener-Neustadt on August 13. Unfortunately, three understrength bomb groups were not able to create serious damage to the complex, but they did damage the final assembly plant sufficiently that production of Bf-109s was reduced from 270 in July to 184 in August. Repairs were slow enough that production had only recovered to 218 in October.

On August 16, the weather was good enough over England to allow an early takeoff and assembly, but weather over southern Germany was poor. Thus, 170 B-17s were sent to bomb the Renault Factory outside LeBourget Field in Paris. This was the deepest escort mission yet flown, and was made possible by use of the new tanks. The value of complete fighter escort was demonstrated when the Luftwaffe rose in large numbers to protect its main French aircraft repair facility. The 4th provided penetration support inbound, along with the newly operational 353rd Group, which was flying its first combat mission. Target support would be the responsibility of the 56th Group, while the 78th Group flew withdrawal support. A measure of the level of opposition can be seen by the fact that the fighter pilots would claim a total of 18 Fw-190s and Bf-109s shot down over the course of the mission.

The mission would be the most memorable of their tours for group executive officer Don Blakeslee, First Lieutenant Jim Goodson, and his new wingman, Second Lieutenant Bob Wehrman.

The morning of August 16 dawned warm and hazy over England. Pilots were roused at 0600 hours and gradually made their way to the officers' club for breakfast. This was Wehrman's first mission. He remembered breakfasts at Debden:

You could always tell who was flying the mission that day. They were the ones with a plate full of real eggs, any style, bacon or sausage, real bread toast and real butter. The stuff you didn't get any other time – we used to joke it was the condemned man's last meal, but for too many, that wasn't really a joke. A lot of the guys sat there staring at all that food and maybe picking at it, at the most. I was no hero either, but if I thought it was going to be a bad mission, I'd make myself eat because I'd tell myself I didn't know when or where I'd have my next meal.

But there was one guy who never ever had any problem with breakfast. That was Mac McKennon. He'd eat his, look across the table at you and if you weren't eating yours he'd ask if you wanted it, and if you said "no," he'd pull it over and down it. After he'd found every unwanted breakfast within reach and polished them off, you'd think with all that he was going to make one helluva mess in his cockpit the first time he pulled Gs, but he never did. When he was done, he'd push back from the table and go over to this beat-up old upright piano in the corner – you have to remember he was a professional concert pianist before he joined up, and he was really good. He'd turn around and look at everyone with that grin of his, and say, "For those about to die…" And then he'd sit down and play a real mournful version of "The Old Rugged Cross." When he'd get to the end, he'd sit back a minute and look at all the mournful faces, and then he'd launch into the most outrageous boogie-woogie version of that song you could imagine! He never did it twice the same.

You'd look around, and you'd see guys start tapping their toes, drumming their fingers, bobbing their heads, and when he was done all the gloom and doom was gone. He was the best boogie-woogie piano player I ever heard in my whole life, and what he did was the morale boost we all needed. After that you were ready for anything.

Bob Wehrman wasn't one of the "aces" of the 4th, though he would eventually become one of the most respected men in the 336th Squadron and a flight leader. When he was informed in the 1980s that the American Fighter Aces Association had decided to credit him with three victories after reviewing the 4th's records, he campaigned to have that score reduced to one, insisting: "And I'm only about three-quarters certain about that one."

Raised in the Midwest, Bob hadn't had the world's best childhood; he wanted to leave home and do something no one else there would be likely to accomplish, knowing how low people's expectations were of him. A barnstormer had come through town when he was eight, landing on his uncle's farm; he'd gotten a free ride in return for his uncle's permission to use the field. Growing up in the 1930s, he had religiously followed the exploits of air racer Roscoe Turner, listening to the boys' adventure radio show of Turner's exploits.

Turned down for lack of academic credentials by both the Army and Navy when he tried to volunteer for flight training the week after Pearl Harbor, he learned about the Clayton Knight Committee and was accepted, successfully passing basic flight training at Grand Central Air Terminal in Glendale, California, "which introduced me to Southern California, a place I determined I would come back to when the war was over."

After advanced training in Canada, where he was good enough to be commissioned a pilot officer in the RCAF on graduation, Wehrman arrived in England in May 1943. When he discovered what a second lieutenant in the USAAF was paid, and that the USAAF would now take him as a trained pilot, he requested a transfer. "I hadn't really read all that much about the Eagle Squadrons before, but I answered yes when the officer in charge of assignment asked if I would like to serve with them." He arrived at Debden in late June 1943 and went through the group's "Clobber College" over July, to be checked out in the P-47 and instructed in what to expect over Europe:

I managed to impress Jim Goodson when he flew with me for my final check-out in the P-47. When we landed he told me he would take me along as his wingman on my first mission. The way he put it was it would be a milk run, and I should stick to him like glue. As things turned out, that wasn't quite what happened.

After breakfast, the pilots assigned to the mission went to the operations office and then into a briefing by group executive officer Blakeslee, who would lead the mission. "I was in awe of Colonel Don from the first time I saw him in the officers' club the night I arrived. Listening to his briefing, I was sure we'd be okay."

As Blakeslee explained it, the 4th would pick up the bombers near the major German fighter base at Abbeville and stay with them until the Wolfpack showed up just before they got to the target. "It wasn't quite billed as a tour of Paris, see the City of Lights in all its glory from 25,000 feet," Wehrman recalled, "but the general opinion was it would be a whole lot easier than the missions to Germany. Goody told me it would be a good way to get my feet wet without getting hurt."

After a weather briefing in which they were told that there would only be light clouds and haze over France, and an intelligence briefing where they were told the Germans had suffered losses and would likely not be encountered in strength, Blakeslee ended by announcing he would fly with the 336th, with the squadron placed in the low position. Goodson, with his wingman Wehrman, would lead the squadron's second flight.

"It was one of those glorious English summer days," Wehrman recalled. "As we crossed the south coast of England, northern France appeared across the Channel like a map. We crossed into France and I picked out Abbeville and St Omer airfields on my map – I wondered if we'd meet the 'Abbeville Boys.'"

Soon there was a warning call as Fw-190s were spotted in the distance, climbing for an attack. The bombers became distantly visible ahead, and the aggressive Blakeslee determined to hit the JG 26 fighters before they could organize an interception. "I heard Colonel Don call for Goody to cover him, and that's when everything happened."

Blakeslee hit the climbing Focke-Wulfs in a near-vertical dive. Neither he nor Goodson and Wehrman knew that immediately after they peeled off, other German fighters had hit the rest of the group, who were now in a swirling fight. Blakeslee had outdistanced the rest of his flight and was alone by the time he opened fire. Wehrman recalled:

> Goody pushed his throttle through the gate to catch up to Colonel Don. We were going faster than I'd ever flown in a P-47. I saw Colonel Don pull out of his dive right behind four '190s and open fire. He was behind one, but the truth was he wasn't the best shot, and the others broke away and he ended up with all three on his tail and him still chasing the first one. My airplane was shaking, we were diving so fast to catch up to him. All I could think of was to stick like glue the way Goody had said. He started to pull out and we almost didn't make it. I blacked out and when I came to a moment later I was surprised I was still with him.

Goodson called to Blakeslee, "Break Horseback! They're behind you!" Blakeslee broke off his attack, pulling a tight, wings-vertical left turn and streaming contrails from his wingtips in the humid air. The three Würgers followed.

> Colonel Don turned away, but we were under 10,000 feet and the '190 could out-turn a P-47 down there. Goody managed to cut the corner as he followed them and finally got in range of the tail-end German. He opened fire, there was a flash on the fuselage just above the wing and a puff of smoke and then the wing came off! It was the first time I ever saw an airplane shot down. It headed straight down, but he was already after the second one. Colonel Don was calling out he'd been hit and Goody was yelling for him to hang on.

Blakeslee was taking repeated cannon hits in the fuselage and wing of his Thunderbolt from the lead German. All three enemy pilots concentrated on their target and did not see their nemesis approaching low from the rear. Standing on his left wing and using all his strength to haul back on the control stick, blood draining from his head due to

G-force, Goodson managed to bring the third Focke-Wulf into view ahead. "I was turning tighter than I ever had before, I didn't think the P-47 could turn that tight, but I did it," Goodson later recalled. The enemy pilot was engrossed in opening fire on Blakeslee's Thunderbolt ahead as Goodson closed the distance between them. "It seemed to take forever for him to fill the glass, but once he did, I let him have it." He settled on the fighter's tail and opened fire.

Blakeslee was doing everything he could to evade the relentless Fw-190 on his tail, to no avail. His control surfaces were riddled and the big Thunderbolt was not responding well. Goodson remembered:

I radioed "Hang on, Horseback! I'm coming!" and Don replied "Hurry!" The two Focke-Wulfs were darting back and forth as they followed his evasive moves and I followed, I was cutting the corner with each change and it seemed like I was closing on the second enemy fighter. Finally he was in range and I fired. The first burst missed right as he bounced left, then the second missed behind, but the third time I got a good hit just behind the cockpit. I called to Don I got the guy, but he yelled "The hell you've got him – he's got me!"

Goodson hung on, "I fired again and this time pieces came off. Smoke started to pour out his exhaust. I gave him one last burst, and he flicked over to the right and went in. When he exploded on the ground just in front of me, I suddenly realized how low we were."

Blakeslee was in big trouble. His engine had been hit and the big R-2800 was throwing oil out the cooling flaps. He later recalled, "The forward fuselage and the canopy windscreen were covered in oil and it was hard to see straight ahead. I looked in the rear view mirror and that guy was hanging in right behind me." Goodson did everything he could to cut corners as he trailed the German leader, who hung grimly on Blakeslee's tail. Closing, he opened fire and got hits, then fired again. "All of a sudden everything went silent. I was out of ammo, and that guy was still closing on Don."

Goodson sliced to the side, where the German could see him, then turned in on the Focke-Wulf as though entering a gunnery pass. "He suddenly glanced over his shoulder and saw me, I tried closing, hoping he'd break. Finally! He tipped over and banked steep, streaming contrails and he pulled out just over the threes. Now all we had to do was get across the Channel and hope we didn't run across anybody as good as that guy was."

Wehrman remembered, "We finally caught up to Colonel Don. His airplane was a real chewed-up mess. Goody asked if he could make it, and he replied he had to run the engine full throttle just to stay in the air. There was a real chance he could run out of gas that way."

The three Thunderbolts turned back for England. "We attracted inquisitive '190s a few times on the way out, but Goody would turn at them with me, and they'd dive away before either of us could open fire. We didn't chase them, and would just turn back to Colonel Don."

Goodson remembered glancing at his fuel gauges. "I'd been running balls out so long I was close to empty. All we could do was keep on. I knew Don must have been really low, and Bob had to be nearly out too, keeping up with me."

They continued on. Goodson recalled, "We saw a pair that started to turn in on us, but I banked toward them with Bob and they thought better of it. I couldn't tell anyone I was out of ammo, since the Germans were listening to us."

Finally, the P-47s crossed out of France north of Calais. Blakeslee was down to only a few gallons. Goodson remembered, "It seemed to take forever and I had one eye glued on the gas gauge. After what seemed like an hour but was only a few minutes when I glanced at my watch, I could see the white cliffs of Dover." Soon Manston's big grass runway appeared. Wehrman remembered, "Goody fired off a red flare and they cleared us straight in. Colonel Don couldn't see out front to land because of all the oil on his canopy, so Goody flew beside him and led him in."

Fortunately, Manston had the biggest, widest, longest runway in England. Blakeslee touched down and moments later he ran out of gas as he rolled down the runway. Goodson pulled up, came back around, and landed with Wehrman.

Blakeslee was already out of his airplane when Goodson and Wehrman taxied up and shut down. Wehrman remembered:

I was still sort of in a daze from everything, and I sat there in my cockpit after I shut down. Goody got out and went over to check Colonel Don, then he came over and climbed up by me. He told me it was a good show and said "I don't know how you stayed with me!"

to which I replied "Neither do I!" And then he told me that when he hit the third '190, he ran out of ammo. The whole trip back, I was the only one with guns! He couldn't tell me because he knew the Germans were listening to our radios.

For Goodson, Wehrman's cool response, "Hey Goody, the next time you're planning a milk run, be sure to include me," got him the permanent job of wingman. "A guy who can do that on his first mission, he's the one you want with you every time." The two were friends for the rest of their lives.

With the two Focke-Wulfs added to the other two he had claimed in June and July, and the Bf-109 he had claimed in the RAF, James A. Goodson was now an ace and on the way to ultimately leading the 4th's scoring list. While Goodson and Wehrman had been saving Blakeslee, the rest of the group had gotten involved in a big fight with the Focke-Wulfs of JG 26 and returned to Debden with pilots receiving credit for 18 destroyed, the group's best one-day record since entering combat.

Finally, on the night of August 16, the weather forecast showed clearing over England sufficient to allow the bombers to take off and form up, and weather over the targets clear enough for precision bombing. Eaker gave the order: VIII Bomber command Mission Number 84 was a go. It was the anniversary of the first VIII Bomber Command mission, as well as the first day of the Quebec Conference. General Eaker expected to have good news for General Arnold in 24 hours.

Heinz Knoke later recorded in his diary that his pilots were awakened early, and the *Staffel* was told to fly to Rheine in Germany, 120 miles away. Just before they were to take off, they were ordered to fly instead to Gilze-Rijen. They arrived at 1115 hours. Following his success with the air-to-air bombing tactic, Knoke's *Staffel* had been involved in testing the new W.Gr.21 unguided rockets, and they were told that they would use them today against the expected enemy raid.

The Regensburg force was estimated to be airborne for 11 hours. The force would have to take off between 0630 and 0800 hours British Double Summer Time to allow for two hours of climb and assembly, with the bombers reaching North Africa in daylight. LeMay was confident his force would meet that timing, since the crews of the 4th Wing were all qualified for instrument takeoffs; they could fly through whatever clouds might be over England until they broke into clear skies and then assemble. Unfortunately, only LeMay's airmen were so trained.

Dawn on August 17 found England covered in fog, contrary to the forecast. The takeoff time for the Regensburg force was delayed three times as the fog refused to burn off. By 0800 hours, the last possible time for the 4th Wing to take off, the fog had cleared sufficiently over the wing's East Anglia airfields for the B-17s to take off. Despite the fact that attacking both targets close to simultaneously was deemed critical for success, the Regensburg force was ordered to take off while the 1st Wing's airfields in the Midlands remained fogbound. Once airborne, the bombers climbed through 10,000 feet of cloud before breaking into clear air. By the time the fog had sufficiently cleared over the 1st Wing's field, the Regensburg force was making landfall across the Channel over the Netherlands. The Schweinfurt force would have to delay their takeoff until the escorts could return and refuel. The Jagdwaffe would now have more than enough time to land, refuel, and be airborne to meet the second force; the 1st Wing would have to fight their way to the target and then fight their way home. The 1st Wing's bombers did not begin taking off until 1115 hours, a three-hour gap.

The fighters had similar difficulty with the weather. The 56th's Hub Zemke later remembered that when he saw the poor weather that dawn at Halesworth, he doubted that the group could fly the mission because only a few pilots in the group had sufficient instrument experience to take off into the clouds and climb to assembly in clear air. "When I called General Hunter to express my misgivings, he reminded me that this was a maximum effort mission and ended the conversation by saying 'I suggest you better think of going on this mission.' His meaning was clear." At the pre-takeoff briefing, Zemke outlined a new takeoff procedure. After takeoff by element pairs, each pair would make a wide circuit of the field below the cloud base, then commence climbing on a pre-determined heading, holding this until they broke out into the clear, with the element leader flying on instruments and the wingman maintaining visual contact with his leader. As it turned out, the cloud cover was not as thick as expected and the P-47s popped free of the clouds at around 5,000 feet and were able to establish their formation without trouble.

Curtis LeMay flew as co-pilot of the lead bomber. The 4th Wing was composed of seven bomb groups, and 146 B-17s were airborne behind him. Due to his relentless training, the bombers were in tight "provisional combat wing" formations. LeMay's formation consisted of three groups – the 96th, 388th, and 390th – followed in trail by two wing boxes with two groups each in echelon formation; the first box was composed of the 94th and 385th groups, with the 95th and 100th groups forming the second. Unfortunately, the overall length of the formation was too much for effective fighter support. The third wing formation was 15 miles behind the first, almost out of visual range. Two P-47 groups had been assigned for escort, but only one arrived on time at the rendezvous, with the second 15 minutes late, again due to the English weather. The RAF Spitfire escorts were forced to break off as the formation entered Dutch airspace; the P-47s could only stay with the bombers as far as Eupen, 15 minutes further inland after crossing the coast.

Approaching Eupen, the German fighter formations could be seen in the distance, waiting for the American fighters to turn back. The P-47s reversed course and the first Twelve O'Clock High attack hit LeMay's formation three minutes later.

Knoke's *Staffel* was among the attackers. The Messerschmitts had trailed the groups of Fortresses as they headed southwest and kept off to the side while they waited for the moment the Spitfires would turn back for England. Minutes after the Allied fighters turned away, Knoke led his fighters to attack the bombers over Aachen.

As Knoke closed on the formation, he was hit in the left wing before he could open fire and "the left stovepipe" was shot away. With a large hole in the wing and the loss of the weight of the mortar, he was barely able to hold the unbalanced aircraft on an even keel. Fearing that the main spar was damaged, making it possible the wing would come off completely under too great strain, he avoided any sharp maneuvers that would increase G-load and fired his second rocket at the formation. Oberfeldwebels Führmann and Fest each scored direct hits that exploded the B-17s in mid-air. The others fired their rockets without effect. Knoke recalled, "My own rocket also passes through the middle of the formation without hitting anything."

Knoke immediately landed at Bonn, where he taxied to the repair depot and a maintenance inspector confirmed that the main spar in the left wing was broken, which put him out of action for the rest of the day. Fortunately, the Bf-109 had separate left and right wings, and overnight the repair depot fitted an entire new wing.

The battle continued for the next 90 minutes, until the German fighters were forced to break off, low on fuel and ammunition. By then at least 15 bombers – including 13 from the third wing box –had been shot down or fatally damaged. Colonel Bierne Lay, Jr., at the time VIII Bomber Command's official historian, who would later co-author the novel and screenplay *Twelve O'Clock High*, flew as a co-pilot with the 100th Group in a B-17 named "Piccadilly Lady." He later remembered:

After we had been under attack for a solid hour, it appeared our group was faced with annihilation. Seven had been shot down, the sky was still mottled with rising fighters, with the target still 35 minutes away. I doubt if a man in the group visualized the possibility of our getting much further without one hundred percent loss... Near the IP [the initial point for the bomb run] one hour-and-a-half after the first of at least 200 individual fighter attacks, the pressure eased off, although hostiles were nearby.

The Bloody Hundredth lost nine of the 21 B-17s sent on the mission.

The 131 survivors soon saw Regensburg ahead. Visibility was clear and the flak over the target was light. At 1143 hours British Time, LeMay's bombardier called "Bombs away!" and 126 B-17s dropped 299 tons of bombs on the Messerschmitt factories with a high degree of accuracy.

LeMay then led the bombers in a turn south toward the snow-covered Alps in the distance. The move took the defenders by surprise and only a few Bf-110s and Ju-88s were able to attack; they were soon forced to disengage due to low fuel. Two badly damaged B-17s turned away from the formation and headed toward neutral Switzerland and internment. As the formation flew south over the Ligurian Sea past Italy, another badly damaged bomber turned away and crash-landed ashore. Five more ditched into the Mediterranean. The 122 survivors finally arrived at Telergma. The force had lost 24 either in direct combat or as the result of combat damage. Of those that managed to land, 60 had varying degrees of damage. Many would never return to England, left to rot on the airfields in Tunisia because they could not be repaired.

LeMay's force had hit Regensburg as hard as possible, blanketing the entire factory complex with high-explosive and incendiary bombs that damaged all the important buildings in the plant and destroying a number of finished single-engine fighters on the field. However, the machine tools in the factories were largely unharmed because the bombs dropped were not big enough to create blast damage strong enough to affect these large machines. In fact, workers were able to clean up the factory within a week and commence production regardless of the fact the roofs were missing. Despite an immediate 34 percent loss of production, fighter production was quickly restored.

The nine groups of the 1st Bombardment Wing put up a "maximum effort" with four three-group "wing boxes." In addition to the formal group organizations and formations, a third "composite group" was formed of a squadron of spare aircraft from each of the eight groups to make up the formation of four wing boxes. The first task force was formed of the "201st Provisional Combat Bomb Wing" (PCBW) made up of the 91st and 381st groups and the "101st Composite Group"; and the "202nd PCBW" which contained the 351st and 384th groups and the "306th Composite Group." The second task force was formed of the "203rd PCBW" with the 306th, 305th, and 92nd groups; and the "204th PCBW" composed of the 379th and 303rd groups, and the "103rd Composite Group."

The bombers of the 1st Wing were unable to begin taking off until 1130 hours, to allow the escorts to return and refuel. They followed the same route taken by LeMay's bombers. Due to their late start, 11 and 83 groups of the RAF put up 96 Spitfires to escort the B-17s as far as Antwerp, where the P-47s would pick them up to take them as far as Eupen. The force was expected to enter European airspace at an altitude of 23,500–25,000 feet, but on approaching the coast at 1330 hours, the clouds were so thick at that level that the commander of the first task force elected to take the bombers down and cross the coast under the clouds at 17,000 feet.

This time, the German fighter attacks began before the escorts were forced to leave. Over 300 fighters from as far afield as Norway were called in to the battle. The 201st PCBW was subjected to nearly continuous head-on attacks; although the Spitfires claimed eight victories, the fights burned so much gas so fast that they were forced to break off early. Unfortunately, the 78th Group, which was supposed to relieve the Spitfires over Antwerp, arrived eight minutes late due to the adverse weather; the bombers had been left unprotected for seven deadly minutes. The P-47s were immediately engaged by large German formations and were forced to break off after only ten minutes' combat to return with two victory claims.

Finally, at 1436 hours, the bombers turned over Worms; German controllers now knew the target was Schwcinfurt.

Losses in the lead wing were severe. By the time that the bombers were 15 miles from Schweinfurt, fighters had shot down 22 of the 57 B-17s in the formation. General Williams himself took over a machine gun in a cheek blister of the bomber he was in, firing it until the barrel burned out. At 1430 hours, the fighters were instructed by their ground controllers to break off and land at the nearest airfield to rearm and refuel; this was unexpected by the Americans, who had believed the fighters would return to their own bases. There was no "fighter belt" of single-seaters to be penetrated by the formations. Five miles from Schweinfurt, the formation turned on its attack heading. The sky ahead was filled with black clouds and flashing explosions as the enemy antiaircraft guns put an effective flak barrage in front of the attackers; three B-17s went down after being hit over the target.

The 40 surviving B-17s of the lead wing arrived over the target and began unloading their bombs at 1457 hours. The 143 bombers following bombed the five factories over the next 24 minutes. The bombing accuracy of each combat box was increasingly hindered by the heavy smoke from the preceding bomb explosions. A total 424 tons of bombs, including 125 tons of incendiaries, was dropped on Schweinfurt.

Each combat bomb wing reassembled over Meiningen before turning west toward Brussels. Enemy fighters reappeared at 1530 hours, concentrating their attacks on damaged bombers that had fallen out of formation. Among the attackers was Knoke, who had decided to fly again regardless of the damage to his fighter's wing. He gathered the young pilots who had landed at Hangelar airfield outside Bonn for refueling and informed them that he would lead them as an impromptu formation against the bombers as they headed for home.

Knoke led his *Staffel* off in a large, compact group at 1700 hours. The Americans were now homeward bound. He had to handle his plane like a basket of eggs. Climbing to an altitude of 7,000 meters (23,000 feet), they saw the formation of about 250 Fortresses directly ahead. They closed in on them gradually until Knoke was able to send the individual staffel members in to attack one by one.

> I myself remain behind the enemy formation and pick off as my target a lone Fortress flying off to the left and a little below the main body. At a range of 500 feet I open fire in short bursts. The American defenses reply: their tracers come whizzing all round me, uncomfortably near my head. The usual pearl necklaces become thicker and thicker. Once again there is altogether too much of this blasted metal in the air. I am at a grave disadvantage in that I have to fly behind the massed enemy group for several minutes without being able to take evasive action. I keep looking anxiously at my wing with the hole in it. Suddenly my poor plane is literally caught in a hail of fire. There is a smell of burning cordite. The engine still seems to run smoothly, however. I bend double-up behind it. It offers good enough cover. Closing up to within 300 feet, I take aim calmly at my victim. *Woomf*! My fuselage is hit. The sound is more hollow than that made by the engine or wings.

Knoke's fire caught the B-17 on fire as it swerved off to the left and dropped away below the formation. He saw four parachutes mushroom open. Suddenly his fighter was hit several times in succession and badly shaken: "It sounds like a sack of potatoes being emptied over a barrel in which I am sitting." The engine caught fire and the smoke filled his cockpit; he pushed open the side vents, but the smoke only grew more dense. As he broke away from the bomber formation, he saw the Fortress he had set on fire crash in the Eifel mountains below.

Finally he was forced to cut off his engine as oil sprayed from under the cowling. "The flames subside. The fire is out. I pull the emergency release and jettison the canopy. The slipstream rush takes my breath away at first. The wind tugs at my helmet and whips the scarf from my neck. Shall I bail out? My Gustav has been shot full of holes, but it still flies."

Hoping to stretch his glide far enough to get back to Hangelar field, he saw the Rhine ahead and crossed it with the altimeter still reading 4,000 meters (13,100 feet). When the fighter dropped to 3,000 meters (9,800 feet), he tried the engine, hoping to keep the plane airborne. With a clattering bang, the engine started. Not daring to touch the throttle, he climbed back gingerly to 4,000 meters. The engine started to smoke again and smell burnt. Before the engine could catch fire, he switched off again. There was no chance of making Hangelar. As he got lower, he began searching for a likely crash-landing spot. Picking out what looked like a large field, he spiraled down toward it. The ground came rushing up at a terrific speed. He prepared for a belly landing, and once again switched on the ignition. The engine started and he was able to reach the landing field.

> Suddenly the engine begins to grind and clatter to a standstill for the last time. Cut! It has seized. The prop is rigid, held as if by a vise. My plane becomes heavy and unresponsive to the controls. It begins to stall, and the left wing drops. Damn! I push the nose down hard and regain control. Houses flash past below in a nearby village. My airspeed indicator registers 100 kilometers per hour [65 miles per hour]. I almost scrape the tops of some tall trees below. Slowing, I must touch down. My wing tips scrape the treetops and then I smash through two or three wooden fences. The splintering posts and crossbars fly in all directions. Dust and chunks of earth hurtle into the air. I hit the ground, bounce, bracing myself for the crash hard against the safety belt, with feet clamped on the rudder pedals.

The 109 bounced over a dike and came to a crashing stop; he unfastened the safety belt and dragged himself out of the cockpit. "My Gustav looks like an old bucket which has been well kicked around and trampled underfoot. It is a total wreck. There is nothing left intact except the tailwheel."

The 56th Group was able to push 15 miles past Eupen by staying at 20,000 feet to use all the gas in the unpressurized ferry tanks it carried; it then initiated a climb to 23,000 feet to meet the bombers. They surprised the enemy fighters still harrying the bombers when they arrived on the scene at 1630 hours. The Thunderbolts tore into the enemy formations, and in the ensuing fight, First Lieutenant Glen Schiltz and Captain Gerald Johnson each scored three, with Captain Bud Mahurin putting in a claim for two, while the rest of the group claimed 11 more, for a loss of three P-47s.

The 353rd Group, led by the 56th's flying executive Lieutenant Colonel Loren McCollom after losing its group commander, arrived on the scene at 1640 hours, just west of Eupen. Between then and

1700 hours, the 93 P-47s of the two groups and a further 95 RAF Spitfires claimed 21 victories, but eight more B-17s went down to fighter attacks before the lead formation crossed the Dutch coast; three more ditched in the North Sea. The 353rd's performance under McCollom's leadership was such that General Hunter confirmed him as permanent group commander that night; he was replaced as flying executive in the 56th by Dave Schilling, commander of the 62nd Squadron.

Both groups were forced to break off combat west of Antwerp, due to fuel shortage. Zemke – who had shot down a Bf-110 in a formation attacking the bombers – recalled that the group had been in action no more than seven minutes before they were forced to break off and head for Halesworth, carefully monitoring fuel gauges. He wondered how the other groups had fared, and later learned that the 56th had claimed all but two of the enemy fighters claimed by P-47s over the entire mission.

Total losses on the Schweinfurt mission were 36 missing, and nearly 100 with varying degrees of damage. Of the 601 crewmen lost, 102 were killed and 481 became prisoners of war, with 18 missing.

The defending gunners claimed 288 fighters shot down, while fighter escorts claimed another 31 for both missions. The Jagdwaffe units reported 25 fighters destroyed, with 15 pilots parachuting safely. While the German losses were comparatively light, one of the ten pilots killed that day was Major Wilhelm-Ferdinand "Wutz" Galland, *Gruppenkommandeur* of II./JG 26 and an *Experte* credited with 55 victories including eight Fortresses; later judged to have been one of the two victories credited to Bud Mahurin, he was the middle brother of General der Jagdflieger Adolf Galland. The three Galland brothers, Adolf, Wilhelm-Ferdinand, and Paul, had all joined the Luftwaffe before the war and become fighter pilots; Paul, the youngest, had been the first lost when he was shot down during the Luftwaffe fighter-bomber attack against Canterbury on October 31, 1942, one of the last daylight raids over England. "Wutz," who was considered by those who served with both him and his older brother to be Adolf's equal in skill as a fighter pilot and a leader, had become well known to the fighter pilots of both sides during his two years on the Channel Front. Under his leadership II./JG 26 had been judged by Allied intelligence to be the most effective and dangerous of the German fighter units opposing VIII Fighter Command.

Bomb damage assessment photos of Schweinfurt revealed that the two largest factories suffered 80 direct hits and extensive fire damage, but again the bombs were not powerful enough to completely destroy the heavy precision machinery that produced the ball bearings. Even so, and despite the operational fumbles, the raid dealt Schweinfurt a hard blow. German armaments minister Albert Speer later wrote in his memoirs *Inside the Third Reich* that the attack resulted in a 38 percent drop in ball bearing production. Output was so sparse in the weeks following that factories using ball bearings sent men with knapsacks to pick up as many bearings as could be found; there were stocks on hand sufficient only to cover six to eight weeks' production. Speer wrote, "After the raid, we anxiously asked ourselves how soon the enemy would realize that he could paralyze the production of thousands of armament plants merely by destroying five or six relatively small targets." He declared that if three more missions could have been flown to Schweinfurt over the following four weeks, then "the jig would have been up."

General Eaker gave the impression of victory where none existed, writing of Schweinfurt-Regensburg:

> It was a bold and strategic concept, one of the most significant and remarkable air battles of the Second World War... The flight crews demonstrated a determination and courage seldom equaled and never surpassed in warfare... Our bombers could and did press through to their assigned targets... This battle resulted in the recall of many squadrons of German fighters from the Eastern front at a critical time there, in a vain effort to meet the bomber onslaught...

The one part of Eaker's statement that was accurate was that Luftwaffe fighter units were withdrawn from the Eastern Front and returned to Germany. The truth was that VIII Bomber Command was in no position to mount further raids in such operational conditions of enemy air superiority over the target. Because of the losses on August 17 and poor weather over Germany for almost the entire month of September, VIII Bomber Command could only mount a small number of short missions carried out with fighter escort.

There was an unintended result to the raid that would have long-term influence on the air campaign. Although the Luftwaffe had inflicted heavy losses on the Regensburg and Schweinfurt raiders, the writing was on the wall that the Allies were growing stronger and that they would not be set back by the day's events. Fingers were increasingly pointed at the Luftwaffe's chief of staff, Generaloberst Hans Jeschonnek. A World War I pilot, Jeschonnek had hitched his star to Hitler and the Nazis soon after they took power. His slavish devotion to Hitler and Göring had led to quick promotions, with a meteoric rise from *Hauptmann* in 1932 to *Generalmajor* in 1939. His toadying to Göring saw him appointed chief of the Luftwaffe general staff in November 1938 at age 39, following the death of General Walter Wever. With Hitler insisting on a rapid build-up of the Luftwaffe, Jeschonnek canceled Wever's program to develop four-engine strategic bombers in favor of presenting his leaders with a larger force of twin-engine bombers, despite the fact that this would mean the Luftwaffe would lack the capability necessary to defeat Britain. In addition, his policies neglected industrial production, military intelligence, logistics, air defense, and the creation of reserves, in order to please Hitler and Göring, neither of whom had the slightest understanding of what an air force needed to accomplish its goals, and his influence on air force development was almost entirely negative; he was a primary force in the decision not to make production of fighters the overriding priority. As American daylight raids grew in number and intensity in 1943, Göring – facing increasing criticism in light of his prewar assurances that no enemy bombers would appear over Germany – made Jeschonnek his whipping boy, blaming his decisions for the lack of success against the Americans. Following the raids on August 17, Göring excoriated his chief of staff for his failures. That night, RAF Bomber Command carried out the Peenemünde Raid, dealing a serious blow to German rocket development. Informed the next morning of the raid by his adjutant, Jeschonnek went into his room and committed suicide. Although his management of the air force had been faulty, he had been personally popular with the airmen, and his death left a void in the Luftwaffe command at a difficult time, which would not be filled.

# 10

# CARRYING ON

As VIII Bomber Command struggled to meet its commitment under *Pointblank* during the summer and fall of 1943, losses continued to grow. Schweinfurt-Regensburg was a shock to the system. Even for the missions that received full fighter escort support, the lack of fighters was problematic. Over the two months between the Schweinfurt-Regensburg mission and the return mission to Schweinfurt on October 14, there were still only four operational fighter groups, all equipped with short-legged P-47s, and 13 months of combat had confirmed that fighter advocates were right: bombers needed escorts if they were to survive.

VIII Bomber Command did carry on, in spite of the losses. However, there were no further deep-penetration missions while its losses were made good. On August 19, all four fighter groups escorted the bombers to hit Gilze-Rijen and Flushing airdromes in Belgium; the escorts claimed nine destroyed, two probably destroyed, and four damaged for the loss of one Thunderbolt. Zemke recalled that the Germans thought this was another long-range attack and sent up the Luftwaffe as soon as the first bomber crossed the coast. Back at Halesworth the 56th claimed nine destroyed and three damaged; the other three groups only claimed probables. Three weeks earlier, the 56th had been considered the least successful of VIII Fighter Command's groups; now it was in the lead with 28 victories claimed in just two missions. Zemke was gratified that Gerald Johnson had claimed a Bf-109, making him the group's first ace, and was particularly proud that they had sustained no losses in the battle.

Five days later the Thunderbolts escorted another raid on the Villacoublay air depot outside Paris that was unopposed because of the escorts' presence. On August 27, 178 P-47s from all four groups provided penetration, target, and withdrawal support for the first bombing of a V-1 launch site under construction at Watten, France. This time JG 2's Fw-190s rose to defend the target and the escorts claimed eight shot down.

By late August, the 56th Group had found there were benefits to having been moved to the relative isolation of Halesworth. The fact that it was the easternmost of all VIII Fighter Command stations meant the group could maximize its time over the Continent, since the pilots did not have to fly so far to get to the fight or get home. Colonel Zemke remembered that the contractors finally began to make good progress in constructing barracks, allowing the men to move out of the cold tarpaper shacks that were all that was available when they first arrived. He also remembered that there was less trouble over women as when they were near the big towns; the venereal disease rate was nil in August.

Zemke was also glad to learn that General "Monk" Hunter, who he had never thought "had what was needed" to lead VIII Fighter Command, was being replaced by Brigadier General William Kepner, whom Zemke remembered from his days at Langley when he was a fledgling second lieutenant and knew to be an able commander. On the other hand, the 56th's commander was more convinced than ever that the 65th Wing, which was responsible for operational command of the fighter groups, was unduly influenced by the 4th Fighter Group, given that the wing staff was based at Saffron Walden, a small village not far from Debden.

On September 1, Colonel Chesley Peterson, at 23 the youngest "full-bird" colonel in US history, led the 4th on a Rodeo near Formerie as their new commander, after Colonel Anderson was promoted to brigadier general. As with most fighter sweeps, the Focke-Wulfs and Messerschmitts refused to take notice of their presence in the French sky. Things were different two days later, on September 3, when the Eagles escorted the heavies to bomb JG 26's home base at Abbeville. Fw-190s rose to defend the base and the attack was broken up by the 336th Squadron, which failed to score when the Germans dived for the ground after the initial pass.

On September 3, Zemke led the Wolfpack on an escort to bomb airfields in France. Just as they were relieved by the arrival of the 353rd Group, a formation of Fw-190s was spotted and Zemke led the attack. As he closed to attack the element leader of a flight of four, tracers flashed past his wing that he thought came from his wingman opening fire too soon. He closed to 400 yards and fired a long burst, getting no strikes, then fired two more bursts and the 190 caught fire, belching smoke. He skidded after number two, but the enemy were now alerted and broke away. Using the momentum of his dive, he zoomed up to gain altitude, practicing what he preached to the others: strike and recover. Back at Halesworth, he found 20mm holes in his prop; another enemy flight had been followed and had opened up on his flight when they dived to attack.

On September 4, Zemke led three 12-plane squadrons to escort B-17s bombing an airfield near Brussels. Once they were over the target, the clouds forced the Thunderbolts to fly at 23,000 feet, between cloud layers nearly level with the bombers. When the mission leader was unable to find the target in the poor weather, he called off the mission since there was too much chance of dropping the bombs on civilian areas with the poor visibility.

As the bomber formations crossed the coasts, Zemke decided to circle back one more time to cover any stragglers. Visibility was poor and the sun was now low, making it difficult to look to the west. Suddenly he heard an alarmed "Yardstick Lead! Break left!" filling his headphones. Instinctively, he pulled the stick hard over. As he started into the turn, he heard a loud "ping" above the roar of the engine and the instrument panel shattered. With the impetus of fear, he skidded into a dive. A glance at the gauges that were left showed all power was gone. "I couldn't see a pursuer in the mirror, so I eased out of the dive and tried to prime the engine to life. Nothing."

There was nothing to do but bail out. But just as he was about to slide back the canopy, the engine coughed and sputtered and came back to life. Realizing instantly that the turbosupercharger in the rear must have taken a hit, causing the engine to die through insufficient air to the carburetor, he cautiously leveled off, turned out over the coast, and made sure there were no Focke-Wulfs in the vicinity. "Confidence returned and I had no further difficulty getting back to Halesworth." Back on the ground, his diagnosis was proven correct when it was discovered that a 20mm shell had hit the turbo. The P-47 had also taken a 30mm hit, severing a trim control cable in the wing root. No one had seen the 190s dive out of the clouds, and the other two pilots in his flight, Lieutenants Wilfred Van Abel and Walter Hannigan, had both been shot down, with Hannigan killed and Van Abel a prisoner. "The outfit that hit us turned out to be II./JG 26, the same boys we had decimated on August 17."

The fact that VIII Bomber Command was limited in its operations to the radius of action of the short-ranged P-47 was seen by all as preventing the command from fulfilling its reason for existence under *Pointblank*. Eaker had constantly requested replacements for the P-38 units originally assigned to VIII Fighter Command that had been taken away a year before for the North African campaign. Finally, by the end of August, it seemed his requests were about to be answered.

The problem was that there was a high demand for P-38s in all theaters, which could not be met due to the fact that the P-38 was difficult to mass-produce; the original YP-38s had been hand-built, and "produceability" had not been a consideration when Kelly Johnson and his design staff created the airplane, since at the time total production was expected to be limited to only 60 aircraft. The P-38F and G that were the first of the breed considered combat-capable had only started to come off the production lines shortly before those first four groups had deployed to England over the summer and fall of 1942. Every air force command was crying for the fighter; it had proven itself capable of taking on Japanese fighters over New Guinea and the Solomons that were feared by the pilots of P-39s, P-40s, and F-4Fs. A squadron of P-38s had been the only aircraft capable of intercepting and killing Japanese Admiral Yamamoto.

Engine cooling had been a persistent problem with the P-38 from the outset; the problem was due to the fact that the designers had installed the smallest possible radiators to keep the sleek shape, and used pipes in the leading edge of the outer wing to cool the small intercoolers, circulating the air out to the wingtip and back; this had proven insufficient to cool the engines of the P-38F and G, which were heavier and more powerful than the engines used in the first P-38s. The design had been revised in early 1943, to use larger intercooler cores mounted in a "chin" fairing, with larger radiators mounted on the booms; while this was less streamlined and aerodynamically efficient, performance was improved by installing more powerful Allison engines providing 140 percent more power than the engines used in the prototypes. The result was the P-38J: the first P-38 to approach the performance hoped for at the outset. However, the wartime supply chain was not always smooth-functioning; Lockheed's subcontractors were initially unable to supply both production lines with a sufficient quantity of new intercooler cores and radiators. The P-38 was only produced at the Lockheed factory in Burbank, California. P-38 airframes *sans* engines continued to come off the line, and fighters minus intercoolers and radiators now sat on Empire Avenue at the foot of the Lockheed-Burbank airport, stretching across the San Fernando Valley some two miles to where the road passed under the main Pacific coast railroad tracks.

Lockheed's solution to the bottleneck was the creation of the P-38H, a "hybrid" between the earlier P-38F/G series and the more-developed P-38J. Beginning in May 1943, the P-38s parked on Empire Avenue were equipped with the earlier intercoolers and radiators of the P-38F/G, with the new Allison V-1710F-17 engines of the P-38J that provided 1,425hp. At higher boost levels, the air temperature from the intercoolers could increase above limits, with the engine subject to detonation if it was operated at high power for extended periods of time. Thus, the P-38H was limited in performance by the necessity of reduced power settings that did not allow use of the maneuvering flap system which allowed the P-38 to maneuver successfully against more maneuverable single-seat opponents. General Spaatz had said of the P-38, "I'd rather have an airplane that goes like hell and has a few things wrong with it, than one that won't go like hell and has a few things wrong with it." The Air Force now found itself with 601 "unplanned" P-38s, which were used on an interim basis to let Fifth Air Force in New Guinea expand the number of squadrons flying P-38s, while two groups equipped with this model could now be sent to England for VIII Fighter Command, and the 1st, 14th, and 82nd groups in Italy could be reinforced and assigned to the Fifteenth Air Force, the newly organized strategic bombing force that was to take on the bombing campaign against Axis forces in Austria, Czechoslovakia, and Hungary, as well as southern Germany.

The P-38 returned to VIII Fighter Command with the arrival of the 55th Fighter Group on September 4. The 55th Pursuit Group (Interceptor) had been constituted on November 20, 1940, and activated on January 15, 1941. The group was originally equipped with the Republic P-43, the first of Alexander Kartveli's fighter designs to feature turbosupercharging. In May 1942, the unit became the 55th Fighter Group when the Army Air Forces dropped the designation "pursuit."

In late 1942, the group commenced conversion to the Lockheed P-38 Lightning as P-38F and G models became available and was fully equipped by early 1943. As with other groups that had trained on the P-38 earlier, pilot attrition during training was high, due to the compressibility problems associated with the aircraft. Because of this danger, pilots became hesitant to fly the airplane to its limits, a necessity in combat that would hinder the use of the P-38 until the anti-compressibility dive flaps that Lockheed was experimenting with became available in the summer of 1944. Unfortunately, this would adversely affect the P-38's use in VIII Fighter Command. With the availability of the P-38H, beginning in May and June 1943, the unit re-equipped and was designated for operations with VIII Fighter Command.

The 55th was notified in late July that it would be transferring to England. Personnel received two weeks' leave during August while the unit's equipment was prepared for shipment. The 300 officers and 3,000 enlisted men of the group boarded the transport HMS *Orion* and departed New York for England on August 25, arriving in Liverpool on September 4. They were then transported to their operating base at Nuthampstead, near Colchester in East Anglia. The 55th was the first long-range fighter escort group and there was considerable pressure from VIII Fighter Command for it to become operational as quickly as possible since plans were already being drawn up for a second mission to Schweinfurt. However, nothing could happen until its airplanes were delivered.

A week after the 55th arrived in England, the 20th Fighter Group, also operating P-38s, arrived. This group would take even longer to become operational than the 55th, due to the fact that it was second in line to receive the limited number of P-38s that were becoming available in Europe.

On September 6, VIII Bomber Command sent 400 heavy bombers – a new record in numbers as the four B-17 groups that had arrived during the summer became operational – to Stuttgart to bomb the VKF ball bearing factory. The three B-24 groups had returned from the Mediterranean at the end of August, with their losses replaced, and added to the force's numbers. Escort was provided inbound and outbound by 176 P-47s, but the Germans refused to engage while the Thunderbolts were present. Once the escorts left, the Jagdwaffe shot down 45 bombers, 10 percent of the attacking force. The value of full-mission escort was driven home over the next four days when three fully escorted missions to the Low Countries and northern France saw no German response. On September 10 a deep-penetration mission to Anklam-Marienburg resulted in 28 bombers lost, 8 percent of the force, while 30 more were lost the next day over Münster, 13 percent of the attacking force. VIII Bomber Command could not continue in the face of such casualties.

The defenders had reverted to the strategy used during the RAF's "Non-Stop Offensive" in 1941, attacking only when they had the advantage. The 78th's Ernie Russell, who finally flew his first combat mission during this period, remembered:

Generally, when the Germans did respond, it was just a few who checked we intruders from a superior altitude and tactical position, and, if the odds were not to their liking, they would split-S and easily elude us. As we crossed in, the RAF Controller broke through the German static: "Graywall Leader, there are bogies at eleven o'clock, thirty miles, Angels 27." Then, "Graywall – Red Leader: bogies at ten o'clock high." Looking around frantically, I suddenly sighted them. I was fascinated. There were about 12 of the most strikingly beautiful, but lethal, Fw-190s I could imagine, flying parallel to and several thousand feet above us. They must have determined not to engage us as they hung there for a minute or two, then split-S-ed and dove vertically towards the deck; accelerating at a tremendous rate, they were out of sight and range before we could engage them. I had been very fortunate; I had seen enemy fighters on my first combat mission. I would fly nine more missions before I saw another enemy plane.

Additionally, the escort policy limited what opportunities to fight did come along. The escorts were under orders not to attack German formations even when they were spotted forming for attack. An aggressive pilot like Peter Pompetti, who committed the offense of disregarding formation integrity to go after the enemy, could and did find himself removed from operations after repeated offenses. In part, this was due to the belief that the Thunderbolt could not take on German fighters – despite the record over the summer – but also because the number of escorting fighters would not allow greater aggression that drew the escorts away, thus leaving the bombers open to additional attacks, while the fighters could be forced to withdraw early when they used their fuel more rapidly. Zemke, however, had adopted a strategy of placing the group's three squadrons around the bomber formation with the two squadrons to either side separated into two sections at different altitudes, while the third squadron became a freelance, flying above the formation and joining in any fights that developed. He credited this strategy with the group's recent successes. "In written reports and conversations with my superiors I was careful not to elaborate on just how loose our close escort had become, letting results establish the worth of these tactics."

The 55th welcomed its first P-38Hs on September 21. VIII Fighter Command wanted them operational immediately, but the pilots needed the opportunity to learn ETO conditions before they could be committed to combat; within a week, 48 Lightnings were in their revetments at Nuthampstead. Once they began flying over England, two things were immediately apparent: the cockpit heating system was completely inadequate to provide a working environment for the pilot in the cold temperatures at 25,000 feet and higher – altitudes they had not flown at in the States – and the engines seemed more "touchy" than before. Incidents of engine detonation happened during their high-altitude training. The group engineers quickly determined that flying at high cruise power at high altitude for an extended period, then pushing the engines immediately into high power for combat, was practically guaranteed to lead to detonation, which could lead to failure of one or both engines.

The first problem was dealt with by providing pilots with so much increased clothing that it was hard to maneuver the controls once seated in the cockpit. Unfortunately, even this was not enough to overcome the inadequate heating system; one pilot later recalled that his feet were almost warm while his head and hands were painfully cold. The engine problem would never be fully resolved; the fact that the problem did not manifest with P-38Hs flying in the Fifteenth Air Force, despite being used under similar operating conditions, led some to lay blame on the lower-quality British aviation gasoline used by the Eighth, while the air forces in the Mediterranean used US aviation gasoline. This theory was supported by the fact that nearly all other American air units in the United Kingdom had been forced to switch from their US to British sparkplugs, which reduced plug fouling from the lower-quality fuel.

Unfortunately, all this meant that the group was not declared operational in time to fly the Schweinfurt mission.

On September 22, a group of replacement pilots arrived at Debden. Among them were two young pilots who would make names for themselves in the group. John T. Godfrey, the second of three brothers who had been born in Canada to English parents then raised in Woonsocket, Rhode Island, had finally achieved his dream of being a fighter pilot. Following his graduation from high school in June 1941, he tried to get to Canada to join the RCAF, but his mother notified the FBI and he was arrested twice for violation of the Neutrality Act. Finally understanding his determination, his parents agreed to let him go and he joined the RCAF in August, graduating from flight school in October 1942. While in flight training he was told of the death of his older brother Reggie, whose ship was sunk while he was on his way to Britain; he had become obsessed with avenging the brother he had adored. After arriving in England in early 1943, he remained with the RCAF until he transferred to the USAAF in April 1943. He was assigned to the 336th Squadron, where he originally roomed with Bob Wehrman, whose roommate had been shot down the week before. Wehrman had met Godfrey when both were in advanced training with the RAF and described him as being shy at first and a bit standoffish, but "Once you got to know him, he was one of the best. I felt fortunate to become his friend."

Ralph Kidd Hofer had joined the RCAF on a lark. A native of Missouri, Hofer was an outstanding athlete, being especially adept at football and boxing, which he had taken up professionally. Visiting Detroit for a boxing match, he decided to visit Canada. When he crossed the bridge afoot, the immigration officer at the border assumed he was another would-be recruit and sent him to the RCAF recruiting office. Though he had no interest in airplanes or flying, the enthusiasm of the other Americans convinced him to enlist. He had demonstrated real skill during flight training, but shortly after arriving in England he transferred to the USAAF. Once at Debden, Hofer was assigned to the 334th Squadron.

The bombers did not appear again over Germany until September 27, when the target was Emden. By this time, VIII Technical Division had created a new 108-gallon drop tank made of paper rather than aluminum, and British factories had produced enough of them that the P-47s could now carry one each on their belly shackles, extending their range 380 miles into Germany.

With the new tanks, the fighters were able to cover the heavies inbound, over the target and through withdrawal for targets in central-west Germany. The 78th Group sent 45 Thunderbolts led by Harry Dayhuff headed for rendezvous ten miles west of Emden, to provide target cover. Dayhuff led the 83rd Squadron at 27,000 feet, with the 84th at 29,000 feet and the 82nd providing high cover at 32,000 feet. They arrived at the rendezvous to find 30 Bf-109s making rocket-firing passes as two huge fireballs fell away from the formation. The Germans had no expectation of meeting American fighters, and the 78th hit them hard.

Heinz Knoke's rocket firing 5./JG 11 were the first Jagdwaffe pilots to be surprised by the P-47's new capability. The *Staffel* was called to readiness with the rest of II./JG 11 at 1030 hours and the pilots manned their planes at 1045 hours. Takeoff was at 1055 hours, with the fighters vectored to intercept the bombers as they crossed the North Sea coast north of their base at Jever. Knoke later recalled that the day of the battle, the sky was completely overcast. Climbing through the clouds, they broke out at nearly 10,000 feet and saw the Fortresses directly overhead. Climbing on a parallel course, they leveled off at 23,000 feet when Knoke ordered the flight to jettison their auxiliary tanks and they quickly turned in to attack with their rockets. As they got into position, the Fortresses split up into separate groups and constantly altered course, leaving a zigzag pattern of contrails in the blue sky.

Knoke ordered the flight to fire rockets at a range of 2,000 meters (6,500 feet). His two rockets both registered a perfect bull's-eye on a Fortress, which blew up in an enormous solid ball of fire with its entire load of bombs. His second *Rottenführer* (element leader) Wenneckers also scored a direct hit with the bomber going down in flames, while his *Rottenflieger* (wingman), Sergeant Reinhard, hit and damaged another Fortress that swerved away off to the left. Reinhard chased off after the bomber. Just then, Knoke's attention was attracted by the rather peculiar appearance overhead of moisture trails, apparently emanating from very fast aircraft. He thought they could only be other German fighters, though they did not attack the bombers. As he dived again on the formation to attack with his guns:

> Suddenly four single-engine aircraft dive past. They have the white star and broad white stripes as markings. Damn! They are Thunderbolts. I immediately dive down after them. They swing round in a steep spiral to the left, heading for a lone Flying Fortress whose two outside engines have stopped. There is a Messerschmitt on its tail – it is Reinhard. The bloody fool has eyes only for his fat bomber and is unaware of the enemy fighters coming up behind. "Reinhard, Reinhard, wake up! Thunderbolts behind!" Reinhard does not reply but keeps on calmly blazing away at his Fortress. I go flat out after the Thunderbolts. The first of them now opens fire on my wingman. The latter just keeps on firing at his victim.

Knoke had the leading Thunderbolt a perfect target in his sights. A single burst of fire set the P-47 on fire and it spun like a dead leaf. "There is a sudden hammering noise in my crate. I turn round. There is a Thunderbolt hard on my tail, and two others are coming down to join it. I push the stick right forward with both hands, diving for cover in the clouds."

He was too late, as his engine caught fire. Jettisoning the canopy, he pulled off the oxygen mask and unfastened the safety harness; drawing up his legs, he kicked the stick forward, which shot him clear of the aircraft, somersaulting through the air:

> I feel the flying suit whipped against my body by the rush of wind. Slowly I pull the rip cord. The harness cuts in, and I am pulled up with a jerk as the parachute opens. After the terrific drop I seem to be standing on air. I swing gently from side to side. Overhead, the broad, white silk parachute spreads out like a sun awning. The supporting shrouds make a reassuring "whoosh." I quite enjoy the experience. What a marvelous invention the parachute is, to be sure – always provided it opens!
>
> Jever lies off to the north. They must be able to see me from there. If they only knew that this is the commander of the Fifth who is now dangling ignominiously because of having allowed himself to be outmaneuvered by a Thunderbolt. I come down in a field, after dropping the last few feet in a rush.

Time: 1126 hours. Only 31 minutes since I was airborne. Time enough for three aircraft to have been brought down. It is some consolation, however, that the score is two to one in my favor.

Knoke was shot down by either Everett Powell or Jesse Davis of the 78th Group's 83rd Squadron, with the other likely also getting his wingman, Reinhard, when they sent two rocket-carrying Bf-109s spinning down in flames. Lieutenants Harold Stump and Peter Pompetti of the 84th exploded a third 109, with Stump hitting a fourth while Pompetti shot up a Bf-110 that spun down to crash with a dead pilot at the controls. 84th Squadron leader Gene Roberts – with his element leader, Quince Brown – closed on a pair of 109s. Roberts couldn't get position, but Brown set the wingman on fire. The high-cover 82nd Squadron dived into the battle with squadron commander Major Jack Oberhansly setting a Bf-109 on fire and exploding a second.

The five-minute fight broke up the German formations. The Thunderbolts rejoined and stayed with the bombers, beating off later attacks until they were forced to depart 40 miles off the Dutch coast; the fuel-hungry fighters landed at the first fields they came across in England rather than flying on to Duxford. The 78th's claims for nine destroyed and no losses put them on top while the other groups claimed 12 more destroyed for one loss. The mission had demonstrated what was possible when the fighters could close with the Luftwaffe over its own territory. Dayhuff, one of the originals in the group, left the next day for VIII Fighter Command staff, replaced as deputy group commander by top group ace Gene Roberts, while Major Jack Price moved up to take command of the 84th Squadron.

Knoke's diary entry confirmed the P-47s' success:

By evening it is ascertained that among my own pilots Sergeant Dölling has been killed, and Raddatz and Jonny Fest shot down also. Fest is wounded, in hospital at Emden. 4.Staffel has lost two killed and one seriously wounded, while the headquarters flight has lost one. 6.Staffel seems to have got the worst of it. Nine out of its 12 pilots are lost. All of the nine have been killed. The remaining three have been forced to either crash-land or bail out. Not a single one of their aircraft returned. On the credit side, however, we have brought down 12 of the enemy to off-set these heavy casualties. No fewer than six are credited to my lucky Fifth alone. My own score has now risen to 16 bombers. The heavy casualties on our side are to be explained by the fact that nobody had anticipated an encounter with enemy fighters. We were taken completely by surprise.

He ended, "This war has become a merciless affair. Its horrors cannot be escaped."

John T. Godfrey flew on the Emden mission as Shirtblue Purple Eight to second flight element leader Don Gentile. The weather the 4th ran into over Germany was worse than forecast and they were recalled. Cruising at 25,000 feet and heading home on instruments due to the poor visibility, all eyes were on "Mac" McColpin, Shirtblue Purple One, in the lead. After several long minutes of this, Gentile succumbed to vertigo, and quickly went into the "dead man's spiral." While his P-47 "Donnie Boy" spiraled toward the cloud deck below, the inexperienced Godfrey – who had received the standard admonishment "stick to me like glue" before takeoff – followed Gentile's spiraling Thunderbolt. As the airplane entered a spin, Gentile managed to recover his spatial awareness and realized his predicament. He nosed down and broke out of the spin, pulling out just above the cloud deck below. He later recalled that he was amazed to look out and see Godfrey's P-47 off his wing. Now separated from the others, the two flew home together. Back at Debden, Gentile was effusive with his praise of Godfrey for doing something that wouldn't have been expected of an experienced wingman. He asked McColpin to assign Godfrey as his wingman whenever possible. The two would go on to write a remarkable record in the group's annals.

The 56th also benefited from the new tanks, which gave it the ability to surprise the Jagdwaffe. Dave Schilling was leader for this mission. Over the target, a formation of rocket-carrying Bf-110s maneuvering for attack was spotted and the Thunderbolts shot down five for a loss of one P-47, likely shot down by Bf-109s that dived into the fight to protect the Zerstörers.

September continued to demonstrate that fickle weather over England and/or the Continent continued to play havoc with operations. During the month, there were 18 days during which targets in Germany were obscured by 6/10 to 8/10 cloud cover. On 12 other days the weather forecast predicted temporary clearance over the target, but only on two of these days were missions scheduled to German targets completed; on the other ten, the weather closed in too soon after 0800 or 0900 hours. On these days, the weather was better over France, which allowed secondary missions to targets of importance in occupied territory. Overall, VIII Bomber Command was able to complete ten missions during September, as many as had been accomplished during any of the previous months since June. However, most of these were not targets in Germany. Impatience grew both at the Pentagon and at "Pinetree" (the code name for 8th AF HQ) as the coming winter months promised even fewer opportunities to hit the targets that had to be destroyed if *Pointblank* was to succeed.

The bombers returned to Emden on October 2. Again, the 56th was able to put the new tanks to good use. Surprising a group of Fw-190s forming up to attack, Zemke scored his fifth victory to become the Wolfpack's second ace. Dave Schilling, scoreless in 52 missions, was credited with two. Schilling demonstrated that he had "found his shooting eye" two days later on October 4 when the group escorted bombers to Frankfurt, 240 miles inside Germany – a new record for deep penetration by VIII Fighter Command. Catching a gaggle of Bf-110s by surprise, the Thunderbolts knocked down a record 15 Zerstörers, one of which was credited to Schilling. On October 6, Schilling led an escort to Bremen and shot down one of the four enemy fighters claimed by the group. He "made ace" on the October 10 mission to Münster, where he claimed one of the ten Thunderbolts shot down. Dave Schilling had become the third ace in the Wolfpack, in only four missions.

The new capability of the P-47 to provide longer-range escort at high altitude had an unexpected effect on the pilots. Steve Pisanos explained:

We were now regularly flying at 30,000 feet for several hours, and the missions only got longer as Technical Command developed the ability to carry more drop tanks. Our unpressurized oxygen system was unchanged. It was good over 12,000 feet, but over 24,000 feet it wasn't feeding as well as it did lower down, and if anything happened to the system a man could pass out within a matter of a few minutes and not realize anything was happening until he was out; by the time he came to, his airplane was likely in a flat spin or a terminal velocity dive he wasn't going to get out of. After the war, the Air Force declared we had to have a pressurized system for altitudes above 24,000 feet.

But we fought the whole war with an oxygen system that really wasn't giving us everything we needed up there.

As experience grew in the fighter groups, the pilots found ways to express their self-confidence. Dave Schilling – whom Zemke considered the group's leading personality – was a fan of the comic strip "Li'l Abner" which was published in the *Stars and Stripes* newspaper. In September, he had written to the strip's creator, Al Capp, and requested permission to use the strip's characters for nose art in the 62nd Squadron. Capp immediately gave permission, asking that the group set a goal to be met by "Sadie Hawkins Day," a mythological holiday in which any gal was allowed to wed the man of her choice, if she could catch him. After Schilling became an ace in early October, the 56th announced that they would have a group score of 100 by Sadie Hawkins Day, which was November 6, 1943. Unfortunately, Zemke would not be around to discover if the goal was achieved, since he received orders to accompany Curtis LeMay and other officers who were headed back to the United States to present a report on the achievements of the Eighth Air Force; he went on the proviso he could have his command back when the event was completed.

Writing after the war in his memoir *The First and the Last*, General der Jagdflieger Adolf Galland said of the air war in 1943:

Above all, the withdrawal and concentration of the fighter units in Germany came too late. This took effect only when the Thunderbolt escort fighters were operating over Germany with increased range. At the start, the American escorts made tactical mistakes. Instead of operating offensively against our fighter units, they limited themselves to a close direct escort. In doing this, they went through the same negative experience we had done over England; the fighter pilot who is not at all times and at any place offensive loses the initiative of action.

# 11

# MISSION 115 – THE DAY THE LUFTWAFFE WON

In September 1943, British intelligence presented evidence that the Germans had prioritized repairing the damaged ball bearings factories at Schweinfurt, and had purchased massive numbers of ball bearings from Sweden. VIII Bomber Command realized that a second attack on Schweinfurt had to happen. The weather was closing in. Mid-October was the beginning of winter; so far in the war, each winter had been colder with more marginal weather than the one before. The winter of 1943–44 would not disappoint. There was thus a time concern that the mission be flown before the weather closed off the possibility.

In the weeks following Schweinfurt-Regensburg, German fighter groups were recalled from the other theaters of war. The Jagdwaffe had put some 330 fighters in the air on August 17. With the reorganization and transfers, by October 1 it was estimated the German fighter force would number nearly 800 fighters. The defenders had already demonstrated what they were capable of.

With a forecast for five days of clear weather when a ridge of high pressure settled in over central Germany during the second week of October, Eaker launched a multi-mission offensive; VIII Bomber Command flew three maximum-effort missions totaling over 1,000 sorties that came to be called "Black Week" by the aircrews.

The first on October 8 targeted the Bremen-Vegesack area. The mission was memorable to the 4th, when Duane Beeson scored two victories to become the group's first ace to score all victories with the 4th. Steve Pisanos recalled, "The low clouds, fog, and drizzle that had kept us from flying finally broke on October 8. We took 48 P-47s on this mission, refueling at RAF Shipdam. We were escorting 180 B-17s." With Blakeslee leading the group, Jim Clark led the 334th Squadron, with Ralph Hofer flying his first mission as Clark's wingman. The Thunderbolts met the bombers at 1419 hours over Tessel Island off the Dutch coast. Pisanos, Clark's element leader, remembered, "We immediately took up our positions over the well-spread-out bomber formation. Our squadron was assigned to cover the rear group of some 60 B-17s." They had just taken station over the bombers when Clark spotted 30 Bf-109s to the south:

> At first we thought they were after the bombers, but we soon realized we had been duped. Fifteen of them ignored the bombers and went straight for us. Their plan was to break up the escort and open the door for the rest to go after the B-17s. As they got in range, Captain Clark called "Pectin Squadron – break hard. Now!"

Clark and Hofer broke right while Pisanos and his wingman broke left. "This scattered our squadron all over the sky. I couldn't tell who was who – P-47s and '109s were chasing each other, hoping to get a shot." Suddenly, Pisanos saw a Bf-109 below him:

> When I closed in to 300 yards, I tried to place him in my gunsight, but my hands were shaking. I told myself to settle down, then I pulled the trigger. He began to smoke and he turned steeply to the left in a dive. Before he could get away, I gave him another burst and a lot of smoke came out from under his cowling.

At that moment, tracers flashed past Pisanos. He pulled the stick back. When he recovered, the enemy was nowhere to be seen. "The guy had scared the daylights out of me!" As he turned away, he saw another P-47 shoot down a Bf-109 and recognized it was Beeson. "I later learned back at Debden that was his second, which gave him a score of six and made him our leading ace." The two flew home together, but Pisanos was forced to land at Halesworth to get enough gas to get home. His gun camera film confirmed his claim; Pisanos now had a score of four.

During the fight, Hofer followed Clark while he shot down a Bf-109, then spotted another P-47 under attack. Without hesitation, Hofer winged over and shot down Unteroffizier Franz Effenberger of I./JG 3. Unfortunately, he was too late to save the other pilot, who crashed to his death in the Zuider Zee. Back at Debden, Hofer performed a victory roll and on landing told his crew about shooting down the Fw-190. Other pilots were skeptical until that evening, when his gun camera film confirmed the victory. Ralph Hofer had shot down an enemy plane on his first mission and would soon become one of the most memorable characters in a unit full of them, known as the most completely undisciplined pilot in the unit.

The 56th was also in action, flying withdrawal escort. Bob Johnson engaged a "very able" German pilot and shot him down, for his fifth victory, becoming the group's fifth ace. His "very able" enemy was Oberstleutnant Hans Phillip, one of the Jagdwaffe's leading *Experten*, credited with 206 victories in 500 combats going back to his first on September 3, 1939. Following his 203rd victory on March 17, 1943, when he shot down four Soviet fighters, he was awarded the Diamonds to his *Ritterkreuz* (Knight's Cross), promoted to major, and sent to the Western Front as *Geschwaderkommodore* of JG 1, the "front-line" *Jagdgeschwader* on the main route from England to Germany. Phillip's *Stab* (staff) flight was vectored toward the bombers; he shot down a B-17, then spotted the Thunderbolt escorts. His wingman, Feldwebel Hans-Günther Reinhardt, last saw his leader banking toward the bombers just as four P-47s swept down on him in a dive.

Johnson reported spotting one Fw-190 turn toward the bombers. "I was going so fast I only had a chance for a quick shot; the engine caught fire and the plane fell off to the right." Phillip bailed out, but his parachute failed to open. His body was found in a field with the parachute streamed. He was six months past his 26th birthday.

On October 9, the bombers went to Anklam, Marienburg, Danzig, and Gdynia. On October 10, the target was Münster. Over the course of the three missions, the Jagdwaffe and flak had knocked down 88 bombers. Over Münster, the 78th caught 15 Bf-110s and Me-410s, attacking straggling B-17s. Gene Roberts set a Bf-110's engine afire. Rolling to avoid the explosion, he closed behind an Me-410 and opened fire; it exploded, with pieces damaging wingman Glenn Koontz's Thunderbolt. Roberts was now the top ace of VIII Fighter Command with a score of eight. The 216 P-47s escorting the mission claimed 19 enemy fighters destroyed for the loss of one.

After three days of fog, Mission 115, the second strike on Schweinfurt, was set for Thursday, October 14. The dawn revealed weather to which the men of VIII Bomber Command had become accustomed: cold, dreary, and foggy. Captain Wally Hoffman, pilot of the B-17 "Morning Delight" of the 351st Bomb Group, recalled, "When I looked outside at the weather, it was pitch black and very foggy. I thought we can't possibly take off in this weather." Nevertheless, he and the fliers at 16 bases in East Anglia and the Midlands prepared for battle.

Following breakfast, the crews made their ways to their respective pre-mission briefings, where the tensest part came when the briefing officer pulled back the curtain that covered the map of Europe. Wally Hoffman later wrote:

> There is a hushed silence as everyone leans forward looking at the fateful end of the red yarn. "It's Schweinfurt" the major says with a sardonic smile, and gives us time to think. Abruptly a buzz of voices breaks out, and one voice says "Sonofabitch! This is my Last Mission." And it was, as he was one of those who never made it back.

In all the briefings, the group commanders ended the meetings by reading a message from General Eaker:

> This air operation today is the most important air operation yet conducted in this war. The target must be destroyed. It is of vital importance to the enemy. Your friends and comrades, that have been lost and will be lost today, are depending on you. Their sacrifice must not be in vain. Good luck, good shooting, and good bombing.

Mission 115's plan was complex. The 1st Air Division would lead, followed by the 3rd Air Division 30 minutes behind the 1st on a parallel course ten miles to the south. The two Liberator groups of the 2nd Air Division were to fly well to the south of the Fortresses, then rendezvous with them just prior to the bomb run.

First Lieutenant William C. Heller, a B-17 pilot with the 303rd "Hell's Angels" Bomb Group at Molesworth, remembered, "It was misty and raining, and there was some talk that the mission might get scrubbed." At 0900 hours, word was received from an RAF weather reconnaissance Mosquito that the target was clear. At 0930 hours, the fog began to lift over East Anglia. By 0945 hours, the order was given to start engines. The 317 bombers taxied for takeoff at 1000 hours. Almost immediately after takeoff the plan began to fall apart, once again the victim of the English weather.

Once airborne, pilots realized that the forecast was wrong. Instead of breaking out 2,000 feet, most did not find clear air until 6,000 feet; some only broke out at 10,000 feet. Lieutenant Heller recalled, "Visibility was still so bad we couldn't see the end of the runway. But we took off and transitioned to instruments until we broke out into a brilliantly clear sky at 7,000 feet." The excessive cloud cover delayed and in some cases prevented bombers joining their formations.

Most significant was the loss of the entire 2nd Air Division. Only 29 of the 60 B-24s joined up. Failing to contact the others, the air commander aborted the mission to Schweinfurt and flew a diversionary mission to Emden. Only 290 bombers headed for the main target.

The poor weather also disrupted the four escort groups. The 353rd and 56th groups rendezvoused successfully, but the 4th could not rendezvous and returned to base. The 353rd ended up covering the B-24s that went to Emden. The 78th never took off when fog at Duxford failed to clear.

Lieutenant Heller remembered, "We made our way east, in a nice tight formation. Our Spitfire escort left us about mid-channel and the P-47s turned back as we reached western Belgium. From that point, we were on our own." Moments after the Thunderbolts turned for home, the Jagdwaffe mounted ferocious attacks. Fw-190s and Bf-109s made Twelve O'Clock High attacks, while Bf-110s and Me-410s fired rockets into the formations.

The Germans started hitting us immediately and never really let up. My aircraft was an older model without servos to power the controls and my legs got so tired from stepping on the rudder pedals that I had to use my hands to push down on my legs. Just as sure as I'd slip or dive the ship within the formation, shells would burst in a cluster around us, usually in the spot where we had been. There were so many of them that I don't understand how they didn't shoot each other down, or run into each other. Everywhere I looked, there were B-17s on fire, enemy fighters being blown out of the sky, and parachutes. It was particularly horrifying to see parachutes on fire and know those men were falling to their deaths.

Mission commander Colonel Budd J. Peaslee, commander of the 384th Bomb Group, recalled:

The opening play is a line plunge through center. The fighters whip through our formation, for our closing speed exceeds 500 miles per hour. Another group replaces the first, and this is repeated five times, as six formations of Me-109s charge us. I can see fighters on my side, their paths marked in the bright sunlight by fine lines of light-colored smoke as they fire short bursts. It is a coordinated attack; their timing is perfect, their technique masterly.

The 1st Air Division's 306th Bomb Group lost three of its 18 B-17s to mechanical problems shortly after it crossed the Channel. By the time the escorts left at Aachen, two more Fortresses had been shot down. Six of the remaining 13 went down before reaching Schweinfurt, while two others went down after they'd aborted and headed for home. Only seven managed to bomb a target in Schweinfurt and only five returned to their base at Thurleigh.

The 305th Group's losses were the worst. Planned as the low group of the 40th Combat Wing which would lead the attack, it was eight minutes late getting to the assembly point. When the group commander was unable to contact the 40th Wing's lead group, he ordered the bombers to fly to another assembly point where they contacted the 1st Combat Wing, which was also missing its low group. The 305th took position as the low group. Any momentary relief the airmen of the 305th might have felt at not being low group in the lead wing ended when Colonel Peaslee ordered the 1st wing to take the lead because the 40th Wing had no low group.

The 305th's bad luck continued, as the enemy concentrated their attacks on the lead wing's low group. By the time they reached Schweinfurt, 13 of its 16 B-17s were lost. The three survivors managed to bomb the target and return to Chelveston. The other three groups in the 1st Wing formation only lost one aircraft each.

The 3rd Air Division flew to the target relatively unscathed; the 30-minute lag behind the 1st Air Division meant that enemy fighters did not have time to land and refuel. The division also benefited from the course diversion that took the bombers well south of the 1st Division's penetration route and away from the major German airfields. Only 15 B-17s were lost of 140 over the entire mission.

The 91st Bomb Group, first over the target, had an unobstructed view of the five factories. The 3rd Division reached Schweinfurt ten minutes after the 1st Division, to find the entire target area covered by smoke.

The return trip was worse. Many bombers were damaged and had lost engines; these were the fighters' main targets. When the bombers reached Aachen, there were no friendly fighters in sight. The weather had once again intervened; the morning fog that almost caused mission cancellation had persisted and in some cases worsened over East Anglia, closing the airfields that the fighters operated from. Thus, enemy fighters attacked the bombers all the way across the Netherlands and even out into the Channel.

Once across the Channel and over England, the weather confronted the returning crews. Five more bombers were lost when they were unable to find anywhere to land due to the fog and low clouds and were abandoned by their crews, who all bailed out successfully.

Sergeant Piazza stated, "Not until we touched down, taxied to our hardstand and cut engines did we feel a measure of comfort." Captain Hoffman later wrote of the mission after the war, "First it was a feeling of wonder that we were alive and had made it back to good old mother earth in one piece, plus an inner appreciation of being alive which I have to this day."

Somehow, Heller's bomber made it back to the coast, with both pilot and co-pilot manning the controls to deal with the loss of two engines on the same side. The airspeed indicator and artificial horizon were shot out. Back over England, the clouds covered the countryside below. Heller recalled, "When we were down to about 20 minutes' fuel remaining, I saw a small hole in the clouds and we spiraled down and pulled out beneath them. We were able to find the RAF station at Henley outside London and they cleared us for immediate landing." Back on the ground, the ten crewmen were amazed to discover that none had been hit. "Our RAF hosts served us tea and dinner and provided beds for us. I went to bed with a word of thanks to Our Lord for our preservation."

Of the 229 bombers that made it to the target and returned, only 33 were undamaged. A total of 60 B-17s were shot down of 290 that took off. The Luftwaffe admitted losing 100 fighters in the battle, which extended over 800 miles and lasted for three hours and 14 minutes. Among the bomber crews in VIII Bomber Command, October 14, 1943, was thereafter known as "Black Thursday."

Eaker cabled Arnold, detailing the losses and again requesting more bombers and long-range fighters. He concluded: "There is no discouragement here. We are convinced that when the totals are struck yesterday's losses will be far outweighed by the value of the enemy material destroyed." The general was putting on a brave face. While he had not received the final reports, he knew there was little likelihood that the depleted force that had actually bombed Schweinfurt had put the factories out of commission.

In Washington, General Arnold, desperate for a victory in the face of the huge losses incurred, proclaimed at a Pentagon press conference on October 18, "Now we have got Schweinfurt!"

The result of "Second Schweinfurt" did not discredit either daylight precision bombing or the bottleneck targeting strategy. The two strikes had a dramatic effect on ball bearing production; had it been possible to make a sustained effort, the result would have "devastated the German industrial base," in the words of Albert Speer. What Schweinfurt did disprove once and for all was the myth of the "self-defending bomber" when confronted by a determined foe like the pilots of the Jagdwaffe.

# 12

# REINFORCEMENT

During September, rumors abounded among the pilots in the fighter groups regarding things to come. When Chesley Peterson returned to take command of the 4th, he told the pilots that there was a new airplane in the works. Steve Pisanos recalled him saying, "They're coming up with a new fighter that will be far superior to the P-38 and P-47, a kite that can be used for long-range escort." That rumor became reality on September 26, when Pisanos returned from escorting B-17s to Les Andeleys in northern France. "I taxied into the dispersal area only to find a P-51 Mustang with a four-bladed propeller parked on the grass across from my stall." Pisanos was familiar with the Allison-powered RAF Mustang I, having flown one for 40 hours in OTU (Operational Training Units) training and then completed another 40 operational hours with 268 Squadron before transferring to 71 Eagle Squadron. He met the pilot, Captain Jack Miller from VIII Fighter Command staff, who had flown it to Debden in the squadron operations office. "He told me it was equipped with a Merlin engine and that it was on loan to our group for the pilots to fly and evaluate it."

A week later, the Mustang was released for flying. Pisanos recalled, "I was more familiar with the Mustang than anyone else in the group. When Captain Miller saw I had 80 Mustang hours in my logbook, he turned it over to me."

Pisanos found the new airplane to be "everything I hoped it would be." After checking himself out for 15 minutes, "I dropped down on the deck and decided to make a pass over Debden, clocking some 450 miles per hour. As I passed over, I zoomed up and rolled left and right. Then I did a loop, after which I buzzed the runway a few more times."

Everyone was interested in the new fighter. Over the next two weeks Don Blakeslee flew it several times, as did Don Gentile, Jim Goodson, Deacon Hively, and Duane Beeson. All were effusive in their praise of the flying qualities of the new Mustang.

The P-47 was also about to grow a longer set of legs. Republic had heard the requests from VIII Fighter Command to find a way to extend the fighter's range. The P-47D-15-RE, which started coming off the Republic assembly line in September 1943, was equipped with two pylons under the wings outboard of the main gear, plumbed to draw gasoline from drop tanks that could be attached to the pylons. Republic also produced pylon kits that could be used at maintenance depots to modify existing fighters. Once General Kepner learned that the new pylons, each carrying one of the 108-gallon paper tanks, with a third tank carried on the centerline, gave the Thunderbolt a range increased to 600 miles – almost enough to take the fighters over Berlin – he issued orders to VIII Service Command to initiate a top-priority program to modify every P-47 in the command. With P-47s now pouring into England, the existing fighter groups were able to increase their authorized strength from 48 to 96 aircraft, and thus fly A and B group missions of 36 aircraft each. The 78th Group flew the first such "double mission" on November 5, with group commander Stone leading 78A and deputy group commander Roberts leading 78B. VIII Fighter Command had again doubled its strength.

The new pylons also gave the Thunderbolt a new lease on life as a dive bomber. The fighter's repertoire expanded when the 353rd Group was assigned to develop tactics for dive bombing, carrying a 500-pound bomb on each wing pylon. Once proper tactics were developed, the 353rd flew a mission against Artois airdrome on November 25, with the 78th's A group providing escort. Heavy flak claimed the 353rd Group's commander, Lieutenant Colonel Loren McCollom, who was thrown clear when his P-47 exploded in its dive. He was soon captured on the ground. By the time of the Normandy invasion, the P-47 had become the USAAF's premier ground support fighter.

Back in the United States, other groups which would become important in VIII Fighter Command operations were forming and training throughout 1943.

George Preddy had dreamed of being a fighter pilot after falling in love with airplanes and flying when his Greensboro, North Carolina, neighbor Hal Foster took him along for a 30-minute flight in his 1933 Aeronca C-3 from Greensboro to Danville on November 13, 1938, three months before he turned 20. A committed diarist, Preddy wrote in his journal afterwards, "I see now how great the airplane is. That trip was the most wonderful experience I ever had. I must become an aviator!"

Shortly after the new year of 1939 began, Preddy started taking flying lessons from his friend Bill Teague, who owned a 1931 Waco GXE Model 10 biplane; he soloed in a bit over six hours. Teague then suggested they each invest $75 to buy a 1921 Waco Model 4, and they barnstormed it around North Carolina that summer. The next year, having completed two years of college to qualify for admission to the Navy's Aviation Cadet program, Preddy applied but was rejected since he was only five feet four inches tall and did not weigh enough. After two more rejections by the Navy, he enlisted in the Coast Artillery to satisfy the draft while waiting to hear about his application for the Army Aviation Cadet program; just before a transfer to Puerto Rico, he was accepted and sent to basic flight training in April 1941. He excelled with the experience of his 80 hours of barnstorming, and his demonstration of a "shooter's eye" developed in duck and pheasant hunts with his relatives put him on track for assignment to "pursuit aviation" – the fighters he dreamed of flying.

Graduating with his wings and commissioned a second lieutenant the week after Pearl Harbor, Preddy was one of 50 recent flight school graduates assigned to the 49th Pursuit Group; he had 240 hours in his logbook, not counting the barnstorming. In January 1942, the "Forty-Niners" became the first American fighter unit to deploy overseas since Pearl Harbor. Originally assigned to reinforce the Philippines, the group arrived in Australia in February; in March the 49ers became the sole air defense of a continent, assigned to Darwin in the extreme tropical north. The pilots would fly the "Brereton Route" first established to funnel fighters up to Java before its fall. The flight from Brisbane to Darwin was equivalent to flying from Boston to Houston, staying on the coast, with no navigational aids, only a few airports to refuel at, and maps with large portions blank under the legend "Unexplored Territory." Such road maps as existed were found to be more accurate. A veteran explained, "Just follow the line of crashed P-40s; you can't miss it."

Preddy was in the first group to make the flight. Of 25 P-40Es that left Cloncurry airfield outside Brisbane on March 8, 13 arrived safely at Daly Waters airfield outside the abandoned city of Darwin ten days later. Preddy and the other young pilots now had about 15 hours each in the P-40, experience gained on their flights to Darwin. The town had been abandoned after the first Japanese raid on February 19, which had caused a lot of damage. The pilots soon discovered that they were now flying in the equatorial weather system, where storms formed quickly and grew in strength; the tropical Australian "outback" they flew over was dangerous, with several varieties of poisonous snakes and man-eating crocodiles in abundance.

By the end of the month, Preddy was assigned as wingman to First Lieutenant Joe Kruzel, who had been assigned to the squadron after escaping the Philippines and Java ahead of the advancing Japanese. The other wingman in the flight was Second Lieutenant John D. Landers, a Texan who had graduated from flight school two days ahead of Preddy. The element leader was Second Lieutenant Sidney Woods, senior to Preddy and Landers by four weeks in his graduation and commissioning. They were soon known as the "Green Dragon Flight," with each fighter displaying a large green dragon snorting fire that was painted on the cowl.

All four pilots would eventually bring their hard-gained combat experience to VIII Fighter Command, where each would make their mark. But first, they would learn air combat the hard way, taught to them by the experienced pilots of the Imperial Japanese Navy Air Force in their A6M2 Zero fighters, which completely outperformed the P-40E in everything but diving ability. On March 30, the Green Dragons intercepted an incoming Japanese strike. Preddy later wrote in his diary, "We went up about 15 minutes before they arrived to intercept them, and got hit by the Zeros at 11,000 feet. Neither side lost anything, but McComsey had to bail out when he got in a spin. I had a perfect shot at a Zero but missed by not having turned the gun switch on." It was a newcomer's mistake that he never did again.

July 12, 1942, was a slow day at Darwin and flight leader Kruzel scheduled a training flight for the afternoon, led by First Lieutenant John Sauber, who told Preddy that he would execute a simulated attack, for which Preddy would perform the appropriate escape maneuver. Sauber misjudged his separation and the two P-40s collided. Sauber was killed in the crash; badly injured, Preddy managed to bail out and parachute to safety. Evacuated to Brisbane, he spent two months in hospital, then received orders sending him back to the United States. He later wrote of his time at Darwin:

> The Army now finds it was a great mistake to send green pilots just out of flight school into combat. I am thankful I lived through the first stage as I feel I am now a little better prepared having learned from actual experience how to take care of myself up there. There is something to be learned on each combat mission, and I am just a beginner.

After leave at home, he reported to the Fourth Air Force in San Francisco, and managed to wangle getting checked out in both the P-38 and P-47. Preddy finally received orders on February 15, 1943, assigning him to the 34th Fighter Squadron of the 352nd Fighter Group, then based at New Haven, Connecticut. After a transcontinental train ride, he was welcomed by squadron commander First Lieutenant John C. Meyer, who checked him out thoroughly on the squadron's P-47s, then assigned him as a flight leader.

By May 1943, all three squadrons of the 352nd were at Mitchell Field, New York, and the 34th Squadron was now the 487th Fighter Squadron. The early P-47Bs they trained on experienced mechanical problems, and several pilots were killed in accidents as a result. Like every other early P-47 pilot, Preddy had one terrifying experience with compressibility in a dive that taught him to respect the big fighter. In May 1943, group commander Lieutenant Colonel Ramage was relieved because of the accident rate and replaced by Lieutenant Colonel Joe Mason, who rebuilt the group and quickly turned it into a combat-ready organization that First Air Force declared ready to deploy to England on June 14, 1943, two weeks after Preddy was promoted to first lieutenant.

On June 22, the 352nd took the train from its base in Connecticut to Camp Kilmer and went aboard RMS *Queen Mary* on June 30 for the six-day Atlantic crossing that ended in the Firth of Clyde on July 5. Four days later the group arrived at their new station, Bodney, located outside the village of Watton, 90 miles north of London. The pilots were dismayed to find that the only aircraft on the field were a Piper

L-4 Cub and a tired ex-RAF Miles Magister trainer. Five days later, on July 10, the first eight P-47s arrived. Lieutenant Ralph Hamilton remembered that the first Thunderbolt the 487th Squadron received was immediately damaged when a pilot who hadn't flown for a month made a poor landing and banged up the prop. "We soon got another, and George made sure he was the first to take it for a spin before someone else could damage it. He gave us a great buzz job when he came across the field at low altitude and pulled up into a barrel roll."

The group began training to fly in the ETO. Formation flying at high altitude in "finger four" flights was stressed; pilots who had not previously flown for extended periods at those altitudes found that formation flying at 25,000 feet was very different from what they had done in the States down at 12–15,000 feet. The squadron pilots moved into quarters in an English estate, Clermont Hall; Preddy wrote in his diary that "things are quite different fighting here and in Darwin." In late August, squadron and flight leaders went on missions with the veteran 4th and 56th groups, but Preddy was not among those chosen. By the first week of September, the group reported that they had completed all pre-combat training and were ready for assignment. Their first mission came on September 9: patrolling the coast from Southwold to Felixstowe to cover the return of the 56th and 353rd groups from their escort missions.

By late September, the 352nd had flown three Rodeos along the French, Belgian, and Dutch coasts and one shallow-penetration escort, with the Luftwaffe paying them no attention. On September 20, the individual squadrons began sending flights one at a time to "Goat Hill" as Goxhill was now universally known, for gunnery training; Preddy was one of the high-scorers. Their first escort missions involved covering Martin B-26 Marauder medium bombers on missions to Belgium and northern France to attack Luftwaffe airfields. On October 14, the group escorted the B-24s of the 93rd and 392nd groups that failed to fully join up in the bad weather and the 352nd was diverted to a sweep of the Frisian Islands; the poor weather that followed through the rest of October limited flying of all kinds.

James H. Howard returned to the United States in the fall of 1942 after nearly a year in Burma and China – and seven months of combat – with the famed American Volunteer Group (AVG), better known to newspaper readers in the United States as "the Flying Tigers." AVG founder Claire Chennault had offered him the rank of major and command of his own squadron in the newly created 23rd Fighter Group, which replaced the AVG, if he would remain in China. Wracked with the repercussions of a bad case of dengue fever and continuing dysentery, he refused and made his way back to the United States.

President Roosevelt had promised Chennault that the United States would make good use of the experience the Tigers brought home. Hap Arnold wrote Chennault:

> As a concrete example of the world-wide effect of your superior performance of a most difficult duty, I want you to know that I am personally directing an intense effort to enroll in the Army Air Force, all your ex-AVG combat personnel. We are after these lads in order that their skill, experience, and ability which you have instilled in them shall not be lost to the Army Air Forces.

Upon arrival home, Howard, who had been a naval aviator when he resigned his commission to go with the AVG, contacted the Navy to see what they would offer a trained, combat-experienced pilot; their answer was an offer of a commission as lieutenant and an assignment in Training Command. The Army Air Force's offer was the same: a commission as captain – equivalent to a navy lieutenant – and an assignment in Training Command. Still suffering from the aftereffects of the dengue fever he had contracted in Burma, and assured by his local draft board that he had time to consider his options, he traveled to San Diego to visit old flying friends at NAS North Island; when the base commander found out he had come onto the base with his old pass, he was summarily thrown off the base and told not to return. "This soured me on the Navy," he later recalled.

The AAF offer turned into a commission as captain and being trained to fly the P-38, in order to instruct future P-38 pilots at Santa Ana Army Airfield in southern California. The assignment turned out not to be what he had expected. There were three other combat veterans among the instructors, First Lieutenants Jacobs, Miller, and Giess, who had escaped the Philippines after flying P-40s in the 17th Pursuit Squadron. Fortunately, he became friends with fellow instructor Carl Parker Giess, who was given a temporary assignment at Hamilton Army Airfield north of San Francisco in February 1943. A month later, Giess called to tell Howard that the commander of a new P-39 group at the field had offered him the assignment as group operations officer and was also in need of a squadron commander, for which position Giess had nominated Howard. It sounded better than training P-38 pilots who were – justifiably – afraid of their airplanes, and after a phone conversation with the group's executive officer, Major Wallace P. Mace, Howard made the trip north to find out what the offer entailed.

The 354th Fighter Group had been activated at Hamilton on November 15, 1942, under the command of 27-year-old Major Harold Martin, who had joined the Air Corps in 1937 after transferring from the Marines. Martin and Howard hit it off when they met, and Howard accepted Martin's offer to take command of the 356th Fighter Squadron, to replace the previous commander, Captain Charles C. Johnson, who had been killed in a flying accident. Howard later recalled that Martin's youth "belied his maturity and determination – he was unflappable and everyone liked his low-key style of leadership." On joining the 356th, Howard found that Martin had been right when he said that after the death of Captain Johnson, the squadron had "gone downhill." However, after meeting its members, he felt the squadron had potential, "because the men were spirited and eager." Despite his lanky six-foot-two-inch height, Howard managed to cram himself into the P-39's tight cockpit, and found – like many other pilots – that he liked flying the airplane, just not higher than about 10–12,000 feet.

In June 1943, the 354th Group was ordered north to Oregon, with the 353rd and 355th squadrons taking up residence at Portland Army Airfield while the 356th went to Salem Army Airfield, outside the state capital. Howard and Giess were the only combat veterans in the group, as well as the oldest – Giess having just turned 28 while Howard had celebrated turning 30 just before transferring. Howard determined that he would give his squadron as much training based on his combat experience as possible, since he wanted to galvanize the unit into a fighting organization. "I didn't want to dishearten them by harping on the cruel actuality of war, yet what we were about to engage in would not be child's play."

Second Lieutenant Richard E. Turner, one of the recent flight school graduates in the squadron, later recalled that Howard's becoming squadron commander gave the squadron a tremendous boost. The enthusiasm and eagerness kindled under Johnson burned brightly again.

The men recognized Howard's reputation in the AVG and his superior leadership was soon amply demonstrated. Howard initiated a program of training in mutual support tactics as practiced and proven in combat by the Flying Tigers in China. His insistence upon perfection resulted in an aggressive, well-tempered fighting squadron, finely tuned to the anticipated conditions of actual combat. "We came to appreciate his eagerness to impart his knowledge to us. The fact we were as successful as we were when we got to combat was the result of our good luck in having him as our commander."

The pilots trained hard over the summer of 1943 since they had heard a lot about how difficult things were in England and how good the other side was, which galvanized them to work even harder to make the grade. In August, group commander Martin decided to find out just how good a fighter pilot Howard was. Martin told Howard to meet him at 1000 hours, over a bend in the Willamette River near the town of Newburg.

Martin later described the event:

I arrived at the rendezvous point a few minutes early and circled around. After some time, I saw no evidence of another plane, so I opened up on the radio, "Howard, where are you? This is Colonel Martin. I have been circling above our rendezvous point for the past several minutes." And then he came on the radio: "Sir, if you will look to your rear, you will observe me on your tail, where I have been for the past several minutes."

Martin had no doubt of the quality of his new squadron commander.

By the end of September, the 354th had passed its Operational Readiness Inspection by Fourth Air Force and were declared ready for overseas assignment. Howard had hoped they would go to the South Pacific, but on word they would be traveling by train to Camp Kilmer, New Jersey, it was clear the group was headed for England. Everyone knew they would not be flying the P-39 there, and there was much speculation about what fighter would be assigned. They had already heard a lot of stories about the new version of the P-51 Mustang, with the Merlin engine, and there was hope they might get to fly it.

After everyone had received two weeks' leave before departure, the group boarded the train on October 8 for the five-day trip to the east coast. On arrival, they got some opportunity to see New York City, but on October 20 the men were loaded aboard the ferry and crossed to New York harbor where they went aboard the troop transport HMS *Athlone Castle*. After ten days aboard ship, they arrived in Liverpool on November 1. The ship lay at anchor for three fog-bound days waiting for the fog to lift, then finally docked and the 354th went ashore in England. Once ashore, the men were trucked to Greenham Common, where they were issued equipment. The morning of November 11, 1943, the first four P-51B Mustangs were flown in. The 354th would be the first fighter group anywhere to fly North American's new fighter.

On November 13 the group was sent on to its new base at Boxted, near Colchester. At first, it looked as if they would be very comfortable in this English countryside setting. However, shortly after their arrival the rains came, and the whole base became a giant quagmire. The conditions were so bad that it made it difficult to do the work of converting to the Mustang. The Mustangs that arrived had been modified by VIII Technical Command when they arrived in England with an additional gas tank mounted immediately behind the pilot in the fuselage on the Center of Gravity that could carry an extra 90 gallons. When this was filled, pilots discovered that the airplane was slightly tail-heavy, which restricted maneuverability. Operating procedures were modified so that a pilot took off with gas fed from the wing tanks; once airborne he would switch to the cockpit tank to burn off that fuel before reaching enemy territory; when that was empty, he would switch to the drop tanks until either they were empty or the enemy was engaged. The fuselage tank was invaluable, since it provided sufficient range that the P-51 could reach any target in Germany with the combination of fuselage tank, drop tanks, and wing tanks.

When it was announced that a fighter group in the newly established Ninth Air Force, which had recently transferred to England from North Africa to become the USAAF tactical air force in the coming invasion, was the first to receive the P-51, the leadership of the Eighth Air Force was shocked. As Steve Pisanos recalled, "Everyone was paying attention to the P-51. When I was in 268 Squadron, flying Allison-powered Mustangs, those of us with experience in Spitfires talked about how wonderful the airplane would be with a Merlin up front." While US Air Attaché Thomas Hitchcock worked with Rolls-Royce in early 1943 to mate the Merlin and the Mustang, Edgar Schmued and his team at North American also began planning such a powerplant upgrade. Hitchcock's report on the performance of Rolls-Royce's Merlin-powered Mustang X test bed, which gave an 80 miles per hour speed increase and a doubling of effective combat altitude, provided North American with all the evidence it needed to convince the Air Force to support the work. Word of the first flight of the P-51B in Los Angeles spread through the world of Air Force fighter pilots like wildfire. The pilots of the 4th had been unanimous in their verdict that it was the best fighter any had flown after they were given access to one of the first P-51Bs to arrive in England back in October.

VIII Fighter Command's General Kepner immediately protested that a fighter like the Mustang, with a vulnerable liquid-cooled engine and a radiator that only needed one minor-caliber hit to be put out of action, was exactly what was not needed in action over a battlefield in a ground support mission. The Mustang had the range on internal fuel only to fly to targets in western Germany that the P-47 had only been able to reach in the weeks before the Schweinfurt-Regensburg mission, when the fighters were finally equipped with the 108-gallon drop tank. A P-51B carrying two drop tanks could reach Berlin. For VIII Fighter Command, the P-51B was the solution to the problem they had faced since the command first began flying missions. Tests conducted between P-51Bs and captured Bf-109 and Fw-190 fighters demonstrated that the Mustang was competitive with these two fighters in ways the P-47 would never be. Above 25,000 feet, the Mustang was superior to the Fw-190 in all flight regimes, only being out-rolled by the early – lighter – versions of the Würger; it was more maneuverable than the Bf-109 at all altitudes, and its equal in all other aspects of high-altitude performance. Don Blakeslee told Kepner, "The Mustang is a long-range Spitfire!" Both Blakeslee and Chesley Peterson begged VIII Fighter Command to let the 4th be the first VIII Fighter Command group to take the Mustang to war.

No one in England could understand the decision not to send the fighter to the Eighth; the decision had been made in the Pentagon, by officers in Materiel Command who had no knowledge of or dealings with operational realities. The Merlin-powered Mustang was declared a "tactical fighter" because both the RAF and USAAF had decided that the earlier, Allison-powered Mustangs – limited to altitudes below 15,000 feet by their powerplant – would be used in the tactical roles of battlefield reconnaissance, ground strafing, and dive bombing. The decision to send the Mustang to the Ninth Air Force was based on bureaucratic precedent, if it was based on anything.

The first thing VIII Fighter Command did on discovering that the Mustang had been assigned to Ninth Air Force was to "go to the top" and get an agreement that, while the group would remain a part of Ninth Air Force administratively, the unit would operate under the control of VIII Fighter Command until the invasion. When they learned that the 363rd Fighter Group, also assigned to the Ninth Air Force, was second in line to receive Mustangs, VIII Fighter Command put the engines of military bureaucracy into overdrive to insure that the rest of the Mustangs went to the Eighth Air Force as they became available. Additionally, the RAF had received P-51Bs, which were called the Mustang III in that service, and was in process of equipping four veteran Fighter Command squadrons with the new fighter. RAF Chief Sir Charles Portal agreed to send these units to support VIII Fighter Command as soon as they were operationally qualified.

The pilots of the 354th Group were ecstatic to be given the Mustang. The group historian later wrote that after only one day of test hops, "they realized that they had the best airplane of the war to work with." To honor their good fortune, a vote was taken and the 354th adopted the name "Pioneer Mustang Group" on December 13.

Once at Boxted, training to become familiar with their new mount continued while the men moved into their new quarters. On November 15, the 354th celebrated its first anniversary as a unit. On December 1, the pilots were considered proficient enough to fly their first mission in the ETO, a Rodeo fighter sweep over Belgium and the Pas de Calais flown by 24 P-51s led by Don Blakeslee, with group commander Martin – who had been promoted to lieutenant colonel when the group was declared ready for deployment – flying as Blakeslee's wingman. Takeoff was at 1429 hours and they returned 70 minutes later at 1549 hours, with the only excitement having been one flak hit on the plane flown by Lieutenant Lane of the 356th Fighter Squadron. The 354th had established a record, flying its first combat mission only 20 days after its first combat aircraft was assigned to it and 27 days after arriving in England.

The 359th Fighter Group, composed of the 368th, 369th, and 370th Fighter Squadrons, had been created on December 20, 1942, and activated on January 15, 1943, at Westover Field, Massachusetts under the command of Lieutenant Colonel Avelin P. Tacom, Jr., who would lead the unit until November, 1944. His pilots came to call him "Hard Tack," because Colonel Tacom was a believer that air discipline began with discipline on the ground. During his time as commander when the group was in England, there were pilots who said his strict discipline in the air was keeping them from winning the war, since he did not tolerate flights breaking away to chase enemy fighters while he held the group over its assigned bombers. Many others later said that they survived their tours because of his enforcement of air discipline.

Training began in earnest in March 1943 when the group moved to Grenier AAF in New Hampshire, but flight time was limited due to the low number of P-47s available. A move to Republic airfield alongside the factory on Long Island in May saw the group finally fully equipped with brand new P-47Ds fresh off the production lines. In July they returned to Westover Field, where they trained until they passed their Operational Readiness Inspection at the end of September. On October 2, they took a train to Camp Kilmer. On October 7, the group headquarters and the 368th Squadron boarded the USAT *Argentina* while the 369th went to the USAT *Thurston* and the 370th took the former Dutch MV *Sloterdyjk*. The convoy left New York harbor before dawn on October 8 and arrived in Liverpool on October 19.

Over the last part of October, the group was moved to its base at East Wretham, in Norfolk. The base had been constructed by the RAF in the summer of 1940 and used for bombers until the previous summer. The pilots found themselves billeted at the nearby stately Wretham Hall, an English country estate with 75 rooms.

Once their P-47s had all arrived by November 10, the group's senior leaders – Lieutenant Colonel Tacom and Majors William H. Swanson, John Murphy, Albert "Trigger" Tyrrell, and Rockford Gray, as well as 12 captains and lieutenants assigned as flight leaders – were sent on detached service to the 78th Group at Duxford to gain operational experience, while the 352nd Group's Major Luther H. Richmond became the temporary group commander to conduct training on VIII Fighter Command operations for the rest of the group.

The last P-47 group to join VIII Fighter Command in 1943 was the 358th Fighter Group, which had been formed on January 15, 1943, at Westover Field, where its men remained for most of their training before shipping over to England in October 1943. The group flew only 17 missions with VIII Fighter Command from December 1943 to early February 1944, when the unit was transferred to the Ninth Air Force in trade for the P-51-equipped 357th Fighter Group.

Five days after Major Martin had taken command of the brand-new 354th Fighter Group in the fall of 1942, another fighter group was brought into existence at Hamilton Field when Major Loring Stetson read the orders activating the 357th Fighter Group, composed of the 362nd, 363rd, and 364th squadrons. Over the Christmas holiday and the first month of the new year of 1943, the group received men and everything else needed for operations – except for aircraft. In February 1943, the unit went aboard a Union Pacific train for a trip through Donner Pass to Nevada, where they were deposited at the isolated Tonopah Army Airfield, the site of the USAAF's brand-new 3,000,000-acre bombing and gunnery range. It was quickly discovered that Tonopah, which was at an altitude of 6,000 feet in the high desert, was a difficult location from which to operate an airplane that was limited to altitudes below 12,000 feet. Pilots soon learned that mishandling the P-39 could quickly put one into an out-of-control tumble, while coarseness in maneuvering quickly put a pilot into a high-speed stall-spin; the pilot who hesitated in recovery wouldn't make it. Two pilots, including South Pacific combat veteran Captain Varian White, commander of the 364th Squadron, were soon lost, with White losing his engine on takeoff from Burbank Airport and crashing in nearby Studio City on a return to Tonopah from visiting his fiancée.

In early June, 1943, newly promoted Lieutenant Colonel Stetson led the group back to California, where it operated from Hayward Army Air Field in the Bay Area. The group's hard luck continued, with nine pilots killed in training accidents in June and July; two more were lost in August and September.

In the face of these losses, the group was glad to welcome 26-year-old combat veteran Captain Thomas L. Hayes, Jr., who took command of the 364th Fighter Squadron. Hayes had enlisted as an aviation cadet in 1940 and was commissioned a second lieutenant and awarded his pilot wings at Kelly Field, Texas, on February 7, 1941. One of the first pilots sent to Australia in January 1942, he was assigned to the 17th Pursuit Squadron of the 24th Pursuit Group, which was soon sent to Java, where he survived combat with the Japanese Imperial Navy's best until he was shot down and wounded on February 19. After recovering from his wounds in Australia, Hayes went to the 35th Pursuit Group in March; the group took its RAF-rejected P-400 Airacobras to Three Mile 'Drome at Port Moresby in late April 1942. By October, when he received orders back to the States, Hayes had received an advanced course in air combat, flying an outclassed fighter against the Japanese aces of the Tainan Fighter Wing, and been credited with two enemy aircraft destroyed on the ground, for which he received the Silver Star.

One 363rd Squadron pilot took to the P-39 so well that in later years, after he had flown some of the most famous high-performance airplanes in history, Chuck Yeager listed the P-39 as his favorite, "just for the pure enjoyment of flying." Seeing many other pilots succumb to the airplane's ease of spinning while the group was at Tonopah, he remembered:

I took the airplane up and deliberately spun it, to learn to recover quickly. I kept doing that, and pretty soon I could recover from a spin in less than three rotations. I knew I wouldn't be one of those going in while executing other maneuvers. And as it turned out, learning how to get out of dangerous spins eventually saved my life.

Yeager was not one of those young men who had grown up in love with airplanes and the dream of flying them. "The first airplane I ever saw was a barnstormer that landed outside of town. I went out to see it, and the pilot tried to get me to go up with him so he could sell rides to the others, but I told him 'no thanks.' I didn't think there was very much to all of that." In 1940, Yeager enlisted in the Army Air Corps at age 18 after his high school graduation with a plan to become a mechanic and because "there weren't any Air Corps airports in West Virginia. I wanted to see something of the world out there." After graduating from mechanics' training, he was sent to George Army Air Field in the high California desert, where he finally went up for a ride in a B-18. "It was a bumpy day over the desert, and it didn't take me any time at all to lose my lunch, all over my fatigues."

After an additional few months of service, during which time he noted that officers generally received better treatment, Yeager volunteered for flight training and passed the academic background test high enough that he could become a flight officer – a non-commissioned warrant officer – on graduation without the requirement of completing two years in college. During his flight training, it was discovered that Yeager had phenomenal 20/10 distance vision; during gunnery training, "all those years spent hunting ducks with my father paid off," and he was number one in his class for aerial gunnery. "I graduated from training and received orders to the 363rd Squadron of this fighter group that had just formed; I took Christmas leave and then reported to them while they were at Hamilton." Yeager was assigned as wingman to Second Lieutenant Clarence "Bud" Anderson, who had graduated from flight training a month before him; they became immediate friends.

As the 354th Group crossed the country to Camp Kilmer for transit on to England, the squadrons of the 357th were split up for further training, with the 362nd sent to Boise, Idaho, while the 363rd went to Cheyenne, Wyoming, and the 364th to Lincoln, Nebraska, for additional advanced training and familiarization flights with bombers. On October 18, the squadrons were put aboard different trains and met up at Camp Kilmer on October 21; 48 hours later, on October 23, they went aboard the RMS *Queen Mary* with 11,000 other Allied troops, headed for England. The great liner dropped anchor in the Clyde on October 29 and the men of the 357th soon made the acquaintance of the English train system, when they were transported to their base at Raydon Wood in Suffolk. On December 19, a well-worn RAF Allison-powered Mustang II arrived for use in conversion training. In the next ten days, 14 P-51Bs arrived. Chuck Yeager recalled, "It only took me an hour in one to be convinced I was among the most fortunate pilots in the world, that I was assigned to fly this airplane." By January 14, 1944, the 357th had received their full complement of 48 Mustangs.

Air Force bureaucracy again had intended the 357th and their Mustangs for the Ninth Air Force, but this changed in one of the first decisions General Dwight Eisenhower made after his arrival in England as Supreme Commander, Allied Expeditionary Forces (SHAEF). The 357th was transferred to VIII Fighter Command, with IX Tactical Air Command receiving the new P-47-equipped 358th Fighter Group.

# 13

# END OF THE BEGINNING

On October 14, 1943, the Jagdwaffe inflicted a defeat on VIII Bomber Command as decisive as that of RAF Fighter Command over London on September 15, 1940. The 20 percent loss rate was unbearable. On October 15, VIII Bomber Command could not have fielded 50 bombers for a mission. Fortunately, the bad weather now became a friend. Central Germany was covered by thick clouds for the next seven weeks; the bombers could not have flown a deep penetration mission had they possessed the force to do so. For all of November, VIII Bomber Command only struck targets within range of the escorts; the bad weather hid the fact that they could have done no other if the weather had been favorable.

The seven weeks saw a transformation in power. On October 15, the 55th Fighter Group with its P-38s was declared operational and flew a sweep along the French coast. This was the first step on the road to revival. Ten days later, the 20th Fighter Group, which had arrived in England a week after the 55th, was declared operational. There were now 96 fighters capable of covering the bombers over targets in central Germany. Unfortunately, serviceability of the P-38s was low enough that the "senior" 55th Group was forced to commandeer planes and pilots from the 20th to fill out its early missions. It was not until January 1944 that both would have sufficient P-38s to be able to operate individually.

On November 3, VIII Bomber Command sent 539 bombers to Wilhelmshaven, escorted by 333 P-47s from all four groups; the Jagdwaffe stayed clear. Target escort was provided by the 55th Group.

The Jagdwaffe was unaware of the presence of the P-38 groups, and JG 1 received a nasty surprise over Holland when it was hit by P-38s from the 55th, with the 343rd Squadron's Second Lieutenant Bob Buttke scoring the group's first victory, a Bf-109, quickly followed by a second, while his squadron commander, Major Jack Jenkins, claimed an Fw-190. The Lightning pilots claimed six, which JG 1 records would later confirm, though VIII Fighter Command only credited them with three. Overall, the *Geschwadern* reported the loss of 13 fighters – four Fw-190A-6s and nine Bf-109Gs – to the Lightnings and the P-47s of the 4th, 56th, and 78th groups. Eleven B-17 pathfinders equipped with H2X marked the target, the first to be hit by blind bombing.

Steve Pisanos remembered that Don Blakeslee again led the mission as penetration escort. They left Debden at 0945 hours and again flew to Halesworth to refuel before heading across the North Sea. They were cruising at 26,000 feet when they crossed into northern Holland at 1225 hours. Moments later, "We were suddenly bounced from above by a gaggle of '109s. Captain Clark was first to spot them and called the warning just in time for us to drop our tanks and break hard against them." Pisanos turned so tight he blacked out momentarily, and when he came to, he was alone in the middle of a swirling fight. He looked up and saw more enemy fighters diving into the fight. He chased a Bf-109G but the pilot spotted him and dived away. Blakeslee called for everyone to return to base. "As I flew back across the North Sea, I realized the Luftwaffe had suckered us. The attack was meant to make us drop our tanks prematurely and thus prevent our meeting up with the bombers. The bastards had succeeded!" The result was a claim for one Bf-109 for the loss of two pilots. The 56th, 78th, and 353rd groups claimed nine between them while the 55th's P-38s claimed three over the target; and again returned without loss. The bombers had unloaded through the thick clouds by use of H2X. Bomber losses were only seven – four to flak and three to fighters.

On November 5, the 56th, now six victories short of the 100 they had proclaimed they would score by Sadie Hawkins Day on November 6, flew escort to Münster. Dave Schilling was supposed to lead, since Zemke had departed for meetings at VIII Fighter Command prior to the publicity trip to Washington. Zemke, however, learned that the former 56th Group pilots now on fighter command staff had assigned the group to cover the bomb group most likely to be hit by the Luftwaffe; "I flew back to Halesworth and walked into the briefing room just as Dave was about to start. I announced I was taking the mission and he was grounded. I'm sure he spent the next few hours cursing that SOB Zemke."

The group covered the 2nd Air Division, rendezvousing over the Zuider Zee. As the P-47s flew deeper into enemy airspace they encountered small formations of enemy fighters which they drove off. Near the target, someone called in "bandits to the north." It was a formation of around 30 Fw-190s, divided into assault and top cover sections, trying to get ahead of the bombers to make a head-on attack. Zemke took the 63rd Squadron to break up the enemy while Gabreski and the 61st continued to cover the bombers. The Wolfpack maintained the element of surprise and knocked down two on their first pass. Zemke fired on one that exploded when he hit the fuel tank. The flight behind Zemke's claimed three more. Gabreski and the 61st went after the assault group, which were carrying W.Gr.21 rockets limiting their maneuverability. The 61st broke them up before they could fire, knocking down two. In five minutes, the enemy fighters had been completely scattered and no longer threatened the bombers. As a result, only one B-24 was lost. The claims for six victories gave them the 100 they had promised. Zemke authorized an extra allotment of liquor and beer for the officers' club that night to celebrate. As he later recalled, what had been achieved was justification of all that the group had striven for over the past months of training and operations. They had emerged the leading group in England with nearly twice as many victories as the next in line, cubs that had become a seasoned wolfpack. The 56th now had six aces: Gerald Johnson, Bob Johnson, Bud Mahurin, Frank McCauley, Dave Schilling, and Zemke himself.

On November 11, 58 Lightnings from both the 55th and 20th groups and 342 Thunderbolts escorted 237 B-17s to Münster again, though the bombers were forced to abort due to bad weather obscuring the city. The P-47s claimed eight destroyed for the loss of two Thunderbolts. The next day, 45 P-38s and 345 P-47s escorted 262 bombers on a blind-bombing mission to Bremen in which 100 bombers aborted due to bad weather. Ten enemy fighters were claimed destroyed for a loss of seven P-38s and three P-47s. Significantly, the P-38 losses were due to engine failure at high altitude, which would be a continuing problem throughout the winter of 1943–44.

CLEAN SWEEP

On November 13, the 55th Group ran head-on into the problem of operating at high altitude in winter weather with an airplane that was not really suited for the conditions in which it was asked to fight. By the time the pilots reached the target, 48 P-38s had been reduced to 36 with 12 forced to abort en route to the target after suffering engine failures. Only eight of the aborts returned to Nuthampstead, the missing four likely falling victim to enemy fighters who came across the cripples and finished them off.

When the P-47s reached the limit of their endurance and turned back for England, the relatively small force of P-38s was outnumbered by five to one; the enemy converged on the bombers and the Lightnings were badly mauled. Six were shot down when Bf-109s streaked through the formation before they could bring their engines to full power; this inability to push the Allisons from cruise to full power without risking engine failure created difficulties for the P-38s throughout their time in VIII Fighter Command. Of those that returned to Nuthampstead, 16 were damaged to varying degrees. Second Lieutenant Gerald A. Brown – who would become the group's first ace – brought his P-38 back on one engine. When the ground crew examined it, they counted more than 100 bullet holes and five 20mm shell holes, but Brown was unhurt.

Despite the losses and damage suffered, and low claims for enemy fighters shot down, the 55th's P-38s held bomber losses below 5 percent. The Germans were ordered to avoid combat with the escorts if at all possible; the P-38's distinctive shape could be identified at a distance, making it possible for a flight of four Lightnings accompanying a wing of bombers to force the enemy to break off. P-38s tearing up the enemy over New Guinea and Rabaul in the Pacific were doing so at altitudes below 20,000 feet. The war that the Lightning pilots fought over northern Europe was completely different.

The growing ability of VIII Fighter Command was reflected in Heinz Knoke's diary entry on November 16, 1943: "On October 14, November 13 and 15, we are sent into action against formations of heavy bombers over the Rhineland; but no further successes are won by the Flight. Every time, we become involved in dogfights with the escorting Thunderbolts and Lightnings." On November 17, Knoke was introduced to Reichsmarschall Göring as JG 11's leading bomber-killer, credited with having shot down or forced from formation 15 B-17s and B-24s since April. Knoke noted later that Göring made a most peculiar impression, wearing a unique kind of fancy gray uniform with cap and epaulets covered with gold braid. "He had scarlet boots made of doeskin. His bloated, puffy face made him look to me like a sick man. Close up, I am forced to the conclusion that he uses cosmetics. He has a pleasant voice, however, and is extremely cordial to me. I know that he takes genuine interest in the welfare of his air crews." The *Reichsmarschall* was most interested in Knoke's having shot down the first deHavilland Mosquito to fall to a Jagdwaffe pilot a year earlier, taking time to express how much he disliked the airplane and the crews that had once disrupted a major speech he was to give in Berlin.

November 19 saw the weather over northern Europe go from bad to worse. Knoke recorded in his diary that the weather closed in, blanketing Holland and Belgium under a murky overcast and swept by heavy blizzards. "Even before we manage to thaw the chill out of our bones round the stove in the wooden canteen hut, our planes outside are coated with the congealing snow, until they look like petrified monsters out of some fairy tale."

The 55th's Lightnings scored again on November 25 during a mission to bomb the Lille-Hazebrouck airfield in France. The 338th Squadron's Captain Chet Patterson led his flight to the aid of a P-38 under attack by two Fw-190s. Patterson shot down one, while the unfortunate P-38 – flown by Second Lieutenant Manuel Aldecona – collided with the other. Aldecona managed to bail out but his parachute failed to fully deploy. Major Johannes Seifert, *Gruppenkommandeur* of II./JG 26 and a 57-victory *Experte*, never got out of his fighter. The P-38s returned to Nuthampstead with pilots claiming four victories.

On November 26, the 78th A and B groups escorted a mission to Montdidier, where they encountered 30 Fw-190s from JG 26. Jack Price, 84th squadron commander, claimed an Fw-190 and a Bf-109 for victories four and five, making him an ace. Howard Askelson shot down one of three Bf-109s attacking a B-17, while Warren Wessell shot down an Fw-190 when it flew into his fire. The four victories cost two pilots POW and one KIA.

The same day, Bob Johnson looked forward to that day's mission to Bremen. He had finally been elevated from wingman to element leader after becoming the fifth VIII Fighter Command ace back on October 10; today he was to lead the 61st squadron. Unfortunately, he was forced to abort just after takeoff when he discovered a major fuel leak.

To top it off, the mission was one of the best the squadron had flown. Over the target, a formation of rocket-carrying Bf-110s was spotted. Bud Mahurin scored his second triple, bringing his score to 11 as the group's leading ace. Dave Schilling shot down two Fw-190s and Gabreski became the seventh 56th Group ace for shooting down two Bf-110s. A further four Me-410s were also shot down while Ralph Johnson of the 62nd squadron brought down a final pair of '110s. The total claim was 23 victories, three probables and nine damaged, for no losses.

The Bremen mission also saw the 352nd group finally meet the Luftwaffe while providing withdrawal support. Unfortunately, George Preddy experienced engine roughness crossing the Dutch coast and was ordered to abort. He later wrote in his diary, "As luck would have it, my squadron bounced four 109s after I left and three were shot down. Meyer and Dilling got one each, and Bennet and Berkshire shared one. I know my day is coming and I am going to do everything possible to be ready when I do meet the Luftwaffe."

The bad weather almost cost more casualties when Gene Roberts led 78A group on an escort mission canceled by weather on November 28. Lost in the foul weather and unable to see the ground to determine location, he radioed a request for homing to Duxford, receiving a vector heading to the base. When the 36 Thunderbolts finally broke into the clear, they were over the London barrage balloons 50 miles south of Duxford! This was due to unforecast winds aloft from the northwest that blew them off course while flying on instruments. The bad weather in November limited the 78th to 11 missions, claiming six for three losses.

Second Lieutenant James "Slick" Morris of the 20th's 77th squadron, was flying his second mission with the 55th on November 29 as second element leader of a 338th squadron flight. When they came under attack by Bf-109s, Morris went after one, but broke off after hitting it to return to the bombers since they were ordered not to leave the formation. His "damaged" marked the 20th group's first score. Chet Patterson, leading another flight, shot a Bf-109 off another Lightning's tail. The rest of the group got rough treatment, losing seven for claims of three. Over their first month, the 55th lost 17 P-38s in combat and four likely in combat after suffering mechanical failure, while claiming 23.

On November 30, Jack Obherhansly led 78B Group to Aachen. As he closed behind an Fw-190, someone called it out as a P-47. Oberhansly pulled out to the side and, after ensuring it was indeed an Fw-190, rolled back in and exploded it.

On December 1, The 78th celebrated its first year in the ETO escorting bombers to Duren. When the Jagdwaffe intercepted over Aachen, Charles Keppler shot down an Fw-190 and James Wilkinson destroyed a Bf-109. The bombers suffered low losses with the escorts covering them to and from the target.

That day saw the Fourth escort 299 bombers to Solingen. John Godfrey was a spare to replace any aborts. Halfway across the Channel, Bob Wehrman experienced engine roughness; Jim Goodson told him to turn back. Johnny pulled in on Goodson's wing. He now had his own P-47D, Gentile's old "Donnie Boy," and named it "Reggie's Reply," in memory of his beloved older brother whose ship had been sunk by a U-boat in 1941. The cowling carried a portrait of Godfrey's pet spaniel "Lucky" inside a horseshoe he'd paid his crew chief five pounds to paint. The mission marked his first score. He later remembered:

Down below me a lone Fort was headed for home and a Bf-109 was jockeying for position up-sun to it. I dove down on him from up-sun and he never saw me. I closed in on him very fast from astern. I fired at 250 yards. Immediately, red and white sheets of flame enveloped him. I pulled up to watch him go down, but there was nothing left. I'd destroyed my first plane, and undoubtedly killed a man – I trusted that God would understand. I flew, unscathed, through the smithereens of what was a plane and a man, and banking sharply I cleared my tail and watched the clouds hungrily suck the falling debris into their bosom. The wind dispersed the fast-disappearing black cloud, and I flew alone.

George Preddy also experienced his baptism of fire. The 352nd flew withdrawal support. Leading Crown Prince Red Flight of the 487th Squadron, Preddy spotted an enemy fighter ten miles south of Rheydt, Holland. He later reported:

I saw one Me-109 behind the rear box of bombers about 3,000 feet below me. I started a quarter stern attack, and when about 1,000 yards from the enemy aircraft, it started a steep spiral to the left. I followed, closing to 400 yards. As I closed to 200 yards, I fired and saw strikes along the wing root and cockpit. The airplane began smoking and fell out of control at about 7,000 feet. I fired another burst, closing to about 100 yards. After I broke off the attack, the enemy aircraft disintegrated.

Preddy's victory was witnessed by his wingman, Second Lieutenant William T. Whisner, and confirmed by his gun camera film. The 487th was the only squadron to encounter the enemy, submitting claims for three 109s.

Unfortunately, the 55th again suffered serious losses when eight P-38s failed to return. Six were shot down over Solingen by 109s diving out of the sun. An additional two were lost after suffering engine failure while returning to England. This second heavy loss resulted in General Kepner replacing the group commander; however, the problem was not the command, but the airplane – the P-38H was a bad fit with the winter skies over Germany.

The 56th scored another six victories for one loss. Gabreski claimed two Fw-190s to bring his score to seven. Returning pilots reported the enemy pilots were some of the toughest opponents they had fought.

The need of the Mustang for over-the-target support was so great that the 354th Group participated in its first escort mission over Germany on December 5, a record for arrival-to-first mission timing in VIII Fighter Command. The group sent 36 P-51s, again led by Don Blakeslee with group commander Martin flying wing, escorting bombers striking airfields around Bordeaux. The 55th sent 34 P-38s along with the 354th's 36 Mustangs for target cover, though the Luftwaffe failed to come up. On December 11, the 354th suffered its first loss during a mission to Bremen, though no enemy fighters were encountered. The 313 P-47s from the 4th, 56th, 78th, 352nd, and 353rd groups claimed 21 shot down.

The December 11 Emden mission was one of the most hard fought in a year of hard fights; it was Francis "Gabby" Gabreski's best-remembered mission, when he came very close to coming in second place in a two-man shootout with a persistent Bf-109 pilot.

The weather was out of the ordinary, with clear skies over Germany. The weather over England, conversely, was terrible, forcing a takeoff delay until 1100 hours, when fog burned off, leaving a 5,000-foot ceiling over East Anglia. The P-47s took off two at a time, joining into four-plane flights over the nearby North Sea before penetrating the clouds, climbing at 150 miles per hour and 1,000 feet per minute, with wingmen and element leaders glued to the flight leader. After what seemed like forever, the clouds above became lighter as they passed 10,000 feet; they finally popped out into bright sunshine at 11,000 feet. Formations rejoined and the 16 P-47s crossed the Dutch coast at 20,000 feet. Leveling off at 23,000 feet, they rendezvoused with the bombers in completely clear skies.

Moving up the bomber formation, Gabreski spotted other aircraft at the head of the formation and soon identified them as German. Turning the squadron toward the fighters forming up for head-on attacks, he saw a formation of 60 rocket-carrying Bf-110s, Me-410s, and Ju-88s. They were still out of firing range when he led the Thunderbolts in a desperate attempt to break them up before they could fire rockets.

Picking out three Bf-110s, Gabreski closed with his flight, picking "tail-end Charlie" and closing on its tail. At 200 yards, he opened fire; pieces flew off as he concentrated on the right wing root. The right engine billowed smoke as it caught fire. The Bf-110 banked away, then fell off in a final dive. He followed and saw the pilot and gunner bail out, then pulled out, realizing the dive had separated him from his flight.

Looking around for other P-47s, Gabreski saw four radial engine fighters ahead and below. A glance at his gas gauge told him he should be turning back for England. But flying back alone held no attraction and he continued closing. Suddenly, he realized they were Fw-190s! He reduced speed and fell back, hoping they hadn't spotted him. Dropping below their altitude, he turned away and they continued on. He climbed to 27,000 feet to get best fuel consumption, throttled back, and leaned the mixture to get across the North Sea to England.

After several minutes, he checked his fuel – there was a bit over an hour of flying time. Getting home would be close. He spotted a distant shape; it grew in size as it approached and he recognized the Bf-109. Moments later, the airplane turned toward him. He couldn't change power without losing all chance of getting back. The German curved around to attack from the rear. Just before he came in range, Gabreski turned toward him and they passed each other; he turned back to 260 degrees.

The enemy pilot sensed he couldn't engage in combat and made a second pass. Once again, Gabreski turned toward him and the tracers missed. Again he turned west, and the German set up a third pass, taking his time; Gabreski knew he couldn't use the same dodge a third time. As the 109 closed, he tried to climb out of the line of fire but was just too late. The cockpit filled with smoke as a 20mm shell exploded inside, tearing away the right rudder pedal! The engine stuttered.

The enemy fighter flashed past as he fell out of the stall and entered a left spiral that became a spin; he saw a cloud deck below at 11,000 feet and continued spinning, hoping the enemy would take it as the fatal dive. Falling from 25,000 to 11,000 feet seemed to take forever. Halfway there, his opponent recognized the ruse and made another firing pass. Gabreski rammed the stick forward and came out of the spin, diving toward the clouds below. Finally, with the P-47 shaking as it closed on a terminal velocity dive, he disappeared into the clouds.

Gabreski throttled back and recovered, hoping not to mush out of the clouds where his opponent was probably waiting for him. He kept releasing back pressure as he felt himself graying out; as his vision returned he pulled back some more. After nearly blacking out three times he leveled off in the clouds. His eyes were glued to the altimeter, air speed indicator, and ball as he concentrated on staying in the clouds as long as possible. The engine was rough but running, and he had 50 gallons of fuel. Hoping he was near the coast, he slowly climbed, waiting to pop out of the cloud, hoping he could get his position. At 11,000 feet, he sliced up out of the cloud and saw the Dutch coast behind. He was over the North Sea.

A shadow passed over and he looked up – there was the 109! When he saw the pilot set up a pass, he disappeared back into the cloud. Not knowing where he was, he switched to emergency frequency and called "Mayday," hoping for a vector home. The Air-Sea Rescue controller answered after the third call. After being identified, he was told to maintain 260 degrees. Dropping out of the cloud, he was alone between two cloud decks.

Time stood still as he crossed the 100 miles of freezing North Sea. Finally, he saw a line on the horizon that soon became the English coast. Roaring over the beach, he recognized Ipswich below – he was ten miles from Halesworth. Turning south, the airfield was soon in sight. With no other traffic, he made a straight-in approach and dropped onto the runway. A moment later, the engine rumbled to a stop, out of gas. He coasted to the runway's end and turned off, braking to a stop. Smoke curled from under the cowling as he slid the canopy open and dragged himself out; the crash truck and ambulance came to a stop in front of him.

The Emden mission was successful. Escorted all the way, only 17 bombers were lost of the 500 sent. The 56th had arrived just in time to prevent the Zerstörer's rocket attack that would have decimated the formation.

On December 13 the 354th celebrated its first month with the P-51 by sending 36 Mustangs to fly target cover over Kiel, their first trip to Germany. The 355th Squadron's Second Lieutenant "Red" Emerson's Mustang got very badly shot up by flak over the target. Dazed and weakened by loss of blood when a piece of shrapnel cut his neck, Emerson flew back across the North Sea to England and landed without brakes in extremely poor visibility; his fighter looked like a sieve and his parachute harness had been severed by another hunk of shrapnel.

The 354th finally met the enemy in combat during the escort mission to Bremen on December 16 and claimed one Bf-110 shot down by Second Lieutenant Charles F. Gumm of the 355th Squadron. Colonel Martin led this as an all-354th mission. On the way home, the 353rd Squadron's Second Lieutenant Glenn T. Eagleston became the first pilot to survive bailing out after he managed to get across the Channel and almost to the English coast after his Mustang had been damaged by the rear gunner of a Bf-110G that he claimed as a probable. Fortunately for him, he was spotted by the crew of an RAF rescue launch just as he touched down in the icy waters and was plucked aboard after only five minutes of what he later said was, "The coldest I ever was in my life."

A third mission to Bremen on December 20 saw the Pioneer Mustang Group contribute 47 P-51s led by Colonel Martin to an escort force of 26 55th Group P-38s and 418 P-47s from the 4th, 56th, 78th, 352nd, 353rd, and the new 356th, 358th, and 359th groups that had arrived in late October and early November and were flying their first mission; the 546 B-17s and B-24s that made the attack were the largest mission so far. VIII Fighter Command was now twice the strength it had been on Black Thursday, with three long-range groups capable of escorting bombers all the way to the targets.

Over the target, James Howard spotted three Bf-109s, making passes at the bombers. One made the mistake of pulling up under a B-17 as he completed his gunnery pass, which gave Howard the chance to close in on it from four o'clock. While still out of range, he fired a burst to scare his opponent away from the bomber as the pilot positioned for another attack. Pushing his throttle forward, Howard rapidly closed the Bf-109 from dead astern. When it filled his gunsight, he fired a two-second burst and it emitted heavy black smoke. Back at Boxted after their return, his wingman, Lieutenant H.B. Smith, reported that he saw parts fly off the Bf-109 before the engine exploded and that it fell away in an uncontrollable vertical dive. The 354th claimed three victories but suffered its first combat losses when three Mustangs failed to return, including Major Owen Seaman, commander of the 353rd Squadron, who went down over the North Sea after his fighter had been damaged over the target.

On December 22, the group escorted bombers to Osnabrück and Münster, with 28 354th P-51s and 40 P-38s from the 55th Group providing target cover. The P-51 at this point was not reliable, and suffered numerous instances of engine problems forcing a pilot to abort the mission that were later traced to the poor combination of British aviation gasoline and American sparkplugs. On this mission, 20 Mustangs were forced to abort due to rough engines. The 448 P-47s from eight groups claimed 15 destroyed, one probable, and six damaged.

The December 22 mission would be forever recalled by John Godfrey as the one that gave him nightmares for the rest of his life.

The day began at 0745 hours, just sunrise in wartime winter England, when he was awakened by one of the English batmen who served the 4th's pilots and was informed he was on the day's mission. After breakfast, group commander Chesley Peterson briefed at 0900 hours: this time, the target was Münster, 300 miles inside Germany, making it the deepest penetration mission the 4th had flown to date. The group would provide withdrawal cover. Takeoff time was 1245 hours. The weather briefing was low clouds over England, heavy clouds over the North Sea, extensive clouds over most of the Continent, and especially heavy clouds over Münster. The bombers would drop using H2X blind-bombing radar. The intelligence briefer announced that the Luftwaffe now had more fighters stationed in Germany than ever before, and "opposition is assured."

At 1237 hours, Major Selden Edner, the new 336th commander, started his engine; soon the hum of 48 turbocharged R-2800s overwhelmed all other sounds on the airfield. Godfrey, flying Edner's wing as Shirtblue Purple Two, goosed his Thunderbolt from its parking spot as Edner taxied past. At 1243 hours, the squadron braked to a stop on the taxiway behind the 334th and 335th squadrons. Bob Wehrman, who was grounded with a cold, was assistant flagman for the takeoff. He recalled:

> They moved onto the runway two at a time, stood on their brakes and ran up their engines for mag checks. Then they pushed the throttles to takeoff power. When everything sounded right, you waved a black and white checkered flag and they started rolling. The next pair moved into position, and you sent them off when the ones ahead had reached mid-point of the runway. You always had to check nothing had happened on takeoff, because our runway was higher in the middle than it was at either end, and once they passed the midpoint, they were out of sight till they lifted off.

Once off the ground, the pilots sucked up gear and flaps, then banked to the left, circling the field with each pair cutting the turn a little tighter than the ones ahead to speed join-up. By the time formation leader Colonel Peterson had completed two circuits of the airfield, all 48 were in position. They continued climbing and each flight disappeared into the murk. Wingmen kept their eyes glued on their leader, formatting as tight as possible, while they held "best climb." At 1315 hours, 25 minutes after takeoff, they were still in the soup when they crossed the East Anglia coast, unseen below, and continued climbing over the North Sea. Everyone listened intently to their engines; a man had 15 minutes in those waters to get in his life raft before he froze to death, should he go in now.

Finally, as altimeters turned past 15,000 feet, the light inside the cloud grew brighter. The formations continued on up, and the white-nosed fighters suddenly popped into the cold blue sky under a bright sun at nearly 17,000 feet. Each pilot's headphones were filled with the high-pitched whine of German jamming as they continued on up to 22,000 feet and leveled off. A break in the clouds several minutes later revealed the Dutch coast north of the Zuider Zee. The enemy paid them no attention as they flew on toward Germany. Outside the cockpits, the air temperature was 40°F below zero. Steve Pisanos recalled that under these conditions, "Your feet were about melting from the hot air pumped in from the engine, but by the time that air got to the control stick, you hand felt frozen around the grip."

Finally, Münster hove into view. The sky was black with flak bursts. Moments later, Peterson called, "There they are" and the lead bomber formation was sighted. Peterson and the 334th Squadron took up position above the leading bombers, while the 335th Squadron moved to the right around the formation's middle and the 336th took up position to the formation's left rear. Every pilot had his head on the proverbial swivel, searching the skies for enemy fighters.

Godfrey – who would later be known as the pilot in the group with the best vision – glanced down and spotted two shadows racing across the cloud deck. In an instant, he spotted the shadows' source: two Bf-109s! He called them in, but squadron leader Edner couldn't see them. "Follow me! I'll show 'em to you!" Godfrey called. He punched off his drop tank and winged over into a steep dive, failing to notice that no one followed.

He rapidly closed from behind. The 109s gave no sign of having spotted him. His dive turned him away from the bombers' course, taking him further into enemy airspace alone with each second. Closing, he watched the two fighters make their way, only 20–30 feet from the tops. The wingman was higher than the leader, and Godfrey chose him. He was closing so fast he pulled the throttle back almost to idle to cut his overtake speed. It was not enough and he had time for only one burst as he roared past the surprised enemy pilot. The 109 was hit, but not enough to go down. As the enemy pilot turned to latch onto Godfrey's tail, First Lieutenant "Georgia" Wynn from the 334th Squadron, who had heard Godfrey's call and followed him down, pulled onto the Messerschmitt's tail and opened fire. Godfrey rolled onto the tail of the leader before he could react. A solid burst set the engine on fire and smoke billowed from the cowling. An instant later, the canopy flew off and the pilot launched himself into space and pulled his ripcord. The parachute billowed as Godfrey's Thunderbolt flashed past. He was exhilarated at the realization he had scored victory number two.

Suddenly, the Thunderbolt staggered under heavy cannon hits. Godfrey looked in his rearview mirror, and saw a third 109 on his tail, spitting fire from its centerline cannon. Hit again, Godfrey pulled the stick back to his stomach and stomped the right rudder pedal, attempting to flick roll out of the line of fire. Instead, the P-47 flipped tail over nose, tumbling into the clouds below.

Now he was in a life-or-death battle to regain control of the violently spinning fighter. He was thrown around the cockpit despite being strapped in. There was only one option left: bail out. But G-force threw him back into his seat each time he tried to grab the canopy handles to slide it open. Time seemed to slow as his body filled with adrenaline from the terror of dying. In a moment's clarity, Godfrey suddenly thought to grab the throttle and stick and push them both forward. As speed increased, the violent shaking stopped and he was able to execute a successful spin recovery, graying out under the G-force as the P-47 nosed up.

When he glanced at the instrument panel, he saw it had been shot out. There was no altitude indicator and the ball was no longer there in the turn and bank indicator. The airspeed indicator seemed to function and the magnetic compass was still okay. Inside the cloud, he had no idea if he was upright or inverted. Suddenly, the Thunderbolt popped out the bottom of the clouds. Whatever his altitude, the ground was close! He pulled back the throttle then pulled the stick back as far as he could. G-force again greyed him out, then the treetops flashed below as the Thunderbolt streamed thick contrails from its wingtips. Suddenly, he was surrounded by flak explosions.

Flying by instinct, Godfrey pushed the throttle forward and pulled the stick back, climbing desperately for the cloud base. In a moment, he disappeared back into the enfolding grayness. He concentrated on flying carefully, watching the altimeter closely to spot a dive from vertigo as quickly as possible. Suddenly, the airplane seemed to go faster, and then he felt the spin as G-force pinned him in his seat. A moment later, the P-47 again spun out of the clouds in a vertigo-induced dead-man's spiral. He managed to pull out over the treetops again. This time he remained in the clear as he roared on just above the trees. There was a town ahead, then suddenly there was more flak exploding close enough to toss him around. Godfrey turned east, then north, staying low, and left the flak behind; but this wasn't the direction home.

Looking outside, he realized he was now over Holland. A moment later, he suddenly found himself over a Luftwaffe airfield he hadn't seen in the rain! Knowing they would send someone after him, he again took refuge in the clouds, regardless of vertigo. Once inside, he kept climbing. All he could do was watch the altimeter, which kept advancing for several minutes. Then the needle started unwinding and he felt the buildup of G-forces again! For a third time, the P-47 fell out of the clouds in a spin. Desperately, he nosed down to get out of the spin, then pulled the stick back hard, and contrails from the wingtips drew a line that only flattened just above the trees when he blacked out for an instant. Now thoroughly terrified, Godfrey's flying gear was sweat-soaked clear through. He stayed on the deck, heading toward the coast.

Again, flak bursts blossomed around him. There was a line of flak towers ahead and he could see the flashes of gunfire as they opened fire. His fear of being shot overpowered the fear of vertigo and he climbed back into the clouds, reasoning that he only had a few minutes to fly in them to get past the coastal flak belt. Again, he strained to watch the slightest movement of the altimeter, and moments later felt the unmistakable G-force of another vertigo-induced spin.

This time, when he came out, he saw the water of the North Sea below. The prop blast traced a line on the water as he pulled out mere feet above the waves. He steadied the compass and took up a 260-degree heading. The radio was out, wrecked by gunfire, so calling Air-Sea Rescue was impossible. The P-47 droned west, just above the waves of the rainswept North Sea. Godfrey leaned out the mixture till he heard the engine popping, then gave it just enough to keep it steady.

Finally, a smudge on the horizon resolved itself as England, but Godfrey had no idea where he was when he crossed the shoreline. Several minutes later, he came across an airfield he did recognize, Downham Market, west of Norwich, north of the Wash. He lowered flaps and dropped his gear, which thankfully came down and locked, and made a straight-in approach, heedless of any other airplane. He touched down and rolled out, coming to a stop by the small RAF control tower. Switching off the engine, he sat there in the silence a long moment, then slid the canopy open and climbed out. When his feet touched the grass, he was overcome with nausea and was throwing up when an RAF officer arrived a minute later. After downing a tumbler of Irish whiskey to steady his nerves in the tower and sitting still for half an hour, he went back out and looked his Thunderbolt over. There were bullet holes, but nothing serious. He told them he was going home.

Twenty minutes later, never flying above 1,000 feet, Godfrey set down on the Debden runway. In the officers' club later, Colonel Peterson started to reprimand him for leaving the formation, then thought better of it and bought him a drink.

After six days of bad weather that grounded all operations, Ludwigshafen was struck on December 30. The 20th Group finally joined the 55th, with both sending 78 P-38s including four new P-38Js from the 20th, while the 354th sent 41 P-51s to provide target cover. The Mustangs ran into several formations of enemy planes maneuvering to set up attacks and broke them up, with pilots claiming four destroyed. The 483 P-47s claimed another four destroyed. This was the 78th Group's last escort of the year; 78A provided withdrawal support near St Mihiel, where Lieutenant William Julien scored his first victory, a Bf-109 sneaking up on a straggler.

The final escort mission of 1943 was flown on December 31 to Bordeaux-Paris Airport. The two P-38 groups again provided 78 Lightnings, and claimed three enemy fighters destroyed, while the 33 Mustangs claimed two over the target. The P-47s claimed six. The P-38s had problems with the weather; one had an engine explode while the second caught fire over England on the return.

While the main force hit the Paris airport, the 78th flew its first fighter-bomber mission, a dive-bombing attack on Gilze-Rijen airfield. The P-47s carried a 500-pound bomb on each wing pylon. Every pilot returned with a tale of personal terror as they dived into the sea of flak over the field. Ernie Russell flew as wingman to Quince Brown for the first time. He later remembered that "I was never so scared before or after, diving into that flak, but I managed to put the bombs somewhere useful and impressed Quince so much that he asked for me as his regular wingman. That was the best compliment I ever got in the Air Force."

On December 27, 1943, General Arnold sent a New Year's message to the commanders of the Eighth and Fifteenth Air Forces:

Aircraft factories in this country are turning out large quantities of airplanes, engines, and accessories. Our training establishments are operating twenty-four hours per day, seven days per week training crews. We are now furnishing fully all the aircraft and crews to take care of your attrition. It is a conceded fact that OVERLORD and ANVIL [the invasion of Europe] will not be possible unless the

German Air Force is destroyed. Therefore, my personal message to you – this is a MUST – is to destroy the Enemy Air Force wherever you find them, in the air, on the ground and in the factories.

The missions of December had shown that VIII Fighter Command could now provide effective cover to the bombers. Paraphrasing Winston Churchill, it was not the beginning of the end, but it was the end of the beginning.

# 14

# JIMMY DOOLITTLE ARRIVES

The 37 young men attending Southeastern Normal School, Oklahoma's teacher training school in Durant, Oklahoma, answered as one when the United States declared war on Germany in April 1917, all enlisting in the US Army. Among them was Ira Clarence Eaker, then a senior and a week short of turning 21, who was planning to teach science and history in the state to which his hardscrabble family had moved from East Texas when he was five years old. A month short of graduation, he was sent to officer candidate school, and commissioned a second lieutenant of infantry that summer.

Eaker met his destiny shortly after he arrived at Fort Bliss in November 1917. A Curtiss JN-4D landed with engine trouble and Lieutenant Eaker offered to help. Once the cowling was opened, the solution was easily found and Eaker reconnected the sparkplug lead. By chance, the pilot was flying from base to base, hoping to recruit volunteers for flight training with the Signal Corps' Aviation Section. Congratulating Eaker on his mechanical ability, he encouraged the young lieutenant to apply for transfer to the Air Service, and he did just that. Eaker was awarded his pilot's wings at Kelly Field in July 1918 and received an assignment to Rockwell Field near San Diego.

Fate again intervened in early 1919 when Colonel Henry H. "Hap" Arnold returned from combat in France, assigned as the new commanding officer at Rockwell. He was accompanied by another veteran who had flown with him in France, Major Carl A. "Tooey" Spaatz, Arnold's executive officer. A few months later, the command's adjutant was killed in a crash. Lieutenant Eaker had impressed Arnold and he was offered the position. Eaker had found that he liked the Army, but had been on the point of taking his discharge, since he did not see how he could compete professionally with the West Pointers who dominated the officer corps. With Arnold's sponsorship, he soon became one of the Air Service's rising stars.

Still not convinced that his future lay in the Air Service despite his appointment as commander of the 5th Aero Squadron at Mitchel Field on Long Island in 1921, Eaker was ready to submit his papers and leave the Army for law school when fate intervened a third time in the person of Major General Mason M. Patrick, chief of the Air Service, who was forced to land at Mitchel while flying to Boston when his pilot became sick. Eaker volunteered to fly him on to Boston and back to Washington. Impressed by Eaker's flying skill and learning of his plans, Mason offered to sponsor him at Columbia University law school, if he would remain in the Army. Eaker took the offer, though he returned to Washington in 1924 as Patrick's executive assistant, having found the law not to his liking. There, he renewed his contact with Arnold, who was now chief of the Air Service information division.

The two, despite being cautioned by Patrick against risking their careers, became passionate supporters of General Billy Mitchell when he challenged the Army leadership on behalf of the Air Service and airpower. Arnold and Spaatz were among those who did risk their careers to testify for Mitchell at his 1925 court-martial, while Eaker worked behind the scenes; he thus avoided the professional "banishment" that Arnold and Spaatz suffered following Mitchell's conviction. Following Mitchell's dismissal from service, Arnold took on his mantle as leader of the Young Turks in the Air Corps, as the Air Service had been renamed.

Eaker remained in the vicinity of the upper reaches of the Air Corps when General Patrick's assistant and successor as chief, Major General James E. Fechet, retained him as staff pilot and promoted him as Air Corps executive officer in the Office of the Assistant Secretary of War. Eaker was not happy flying a desk, and took every opportunity to get away and fly, continuing the success he had found as leader of the 1925 Pan-American mission in which his planes and crews visited 25 Central and South American nations to demonstrate airpower's long reach. He pioneered aerial refueling in 1929, setting an endurance record of nearly six days in the air as chief pilot along with Spaatz,

56th Fighter Group Formation. (USAF Official)

B-17s on their way to Berlin, March 1944. (USAF Official)

Second Lieutenant Bert Stiles. (USAF Official)

Colonel Donald J.M. Blakeslee briefing the pilots. (USAF Official)

Captain Walker M. "Bud" Mahurin's P-47D. (USAF Official)

Major Robert S. Johnson and Sergeant J.C. Penrod. (USAF Official)

**Above**

Colonel Chesley Peterson
and Captain Oscar Coen.
(USAF Official)

**Left**

Captain Charles E. "Chuck"
Yeager with his P-51D
"Glamorous Glen II."
(USAF Official)

**Below**

Major George Preddy
with his P-51D-5,
"Cripes A Mighty III."
(USAF Official)

Colonel Donald J.M. Blakeslee. (USAF Official)

**Above**

Major Duane Beeson.
(USAF Official)


**Left**

Captain Don S. Gentile
and Sergeant John Ferra.
(USAF Official)

Lieutenant Colonel Francis Stanley Gabreski. (USAF Official)

**Left**

Eisenhower awards
Gentile and Blakeslee
the Distinguished
Flying Cross.
(USAF Official)

**Center**

Captain Don Gentile
and Captain Steve Pisanos.
(USAF Official)

**Below**

Major James A. Goodson.
(USAF Official)

Lieutenant Colonel Dave Schilling's P-47D-25 Thunderbolt "Hairless Joe." (USAF Official)

Damages to First Lieutenant Colonel Robert S. Johnson's P-47C-5 "Half Pint." (USAF Official)

Major Jimmy Stewart. (USAF Official)

Lieutenant Ralph Kidd Hofer. (USAF Official)

First Lieutenant John T. Godfrey (left) and Captain Don S. Gentile (right). (USAF Official)

Colonel John T. Landers (center) in his P-51D, "Big Beautiful Doll." (USAF Official)

Major Walter C. Beckham with his P-47D, "Little Demon." (USAF Official)

Lieutenant Colonel John C. Meyer's P-51D "Petie 3rd." (USAF Official)

P-47M of the 56th Fighter Group. (USAF Official)

Polish pilots with Gabreski. (USAF Official)

P-51D SX-B. (USAF Official)

Damages to
Captain Gentile's
"Shangri-La."
(USAF Official)

P-51B "Snoots Sniper" of the 486th Fighter Squadron. (USAF Official)

"Spokane Chief," the P-47C of Major Gene Roberts. (USAF Official)

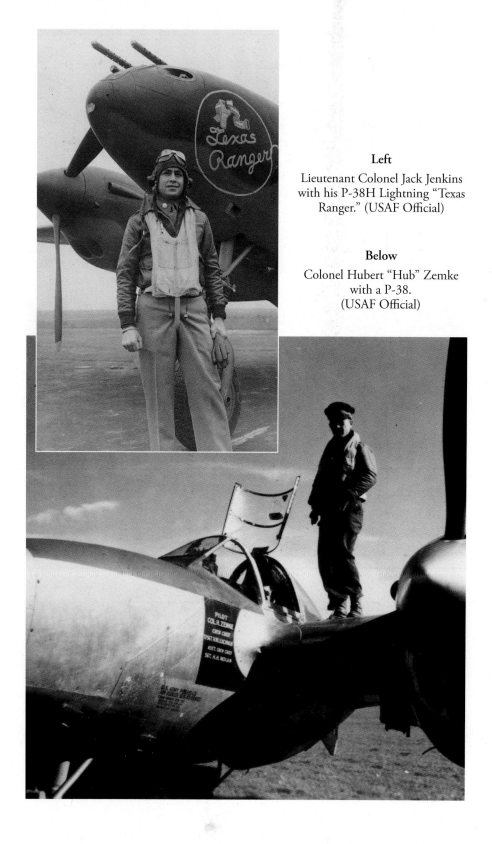

**Left**

Lieutenant Colonel Jack Jenkins with his P-38H Lightning "Texas Ranger." (USAF Official)

**Below**

Colonel Hubert "Hub" Zemke with a P-38. (USAF Official)

First Lieutenant Henry Halverson, and Second Lieutenant Elwood P. Quesada in the Fokker C-2 "Question Mark," which was refueled in flight over Southern California 43 times by a hose from a Douglas DWC "tanker"; this included an appearance at that year's Rose Bowl football game where they overflew the crowded stadium.

In 1931, Eaker obtained a degree in journalism from the University of Southern California, during which time he spent his weekends out at March Field in Riverside, where Arnold was the base commander. After he graduated in 1933, he took command of one of the March-based squadrons; the two also hunted and fished together in the Sierra Nevada. In 1936, he set a record by flying non-stop from New York to Los Angeles entirely on instruments and navigating by the newly built radio beacon system.

When Pearl Harbor was attacked, Lieutenant Colonel Eaker commanded the 20th Pursuit Group at Hamilton Field outside San Francisco. Arnold, chief of the newly designated US Army Air Forces, quickly recalled him to Washington and gave his long-time trusted associate the assignment to organize the American air force in Britain that would take on the Luftwaffe, sending Eaker to London after promoting him to brigadier general and pinning his own brigadier general's stars on his old comrade.

With that history, it was with a heavy heart that Arnold was forced to the conclusion after the Schweinfurt disaster in October 1943 that he must replace one of his oldest and most trusted friends as commander of VIII Bomber Command.

The man Arnold chose to replace Eaker was a friend he had made back when both were members of the "Rockwell bunch" immediately after World War I. Major General James H. Doolittle, former commander of the North Africa-based Twelfth Air Force, now commander of the newly created Fifteenth Air Force, rivaled – and even exceeded – Eaker for setting aviation records and contributing to aviation development. Doolittle had first gained public notice as the first pilot to fly coast-to-coast between sunrise and sunset in September 1922, departing Pablo Beach, Florida at dawn in a deHavilland D.H.4 and flying to Rockwell Field in San Diego, where he landed at dusk; he was awarded the Distinguished Flying Cross for the feat. He was then assigned to the Air Corps Engineering School at McCook Field (later Wright-Patterson). In 1925, he received the first Doctorate in Aeronautical

Engineering at the Massachusetts Institute of Technology (MIT), after completing his MS in Aeronautics there the year before and receiving the Distinguished Flying Cross a second time for research performed for his master's thesis regarding aircraft acceleration. He was then assigned as pilot of the Curtiss R3C-2 racing seaplane, in which he won the Schneider Cup that year with a record speed of 232 miles per hour; for this he was awarded the McKay Trophy the next year. He followed that in 1927 by executing the first successful outside loop, a maneuver previously considered fatal, in which the pilot faces the outside of a loop and experiences negative-G force through the entire maneuver.

Doolittle's most important contributions to the development of aviation involved his work with instrument flight. Working with the Guggenheim Aviation Foundation, he studied the relationships of visual cues and motion senses. In 1929, he was the first pilot to take off, fly, and land an airplane using instruments alone, without any outside view, the result of his work to develop and test the artificial horizon and directional gyroscope. This work resulted in the award of the Harmon Trophy. His other major contribution came after he left active service in the Air Corps in 1930 and became aviation manager for Shell Oil, where he pushed the company to develop 100-octane aviation gasoline and the capability to produce it in large quantity. This was what gave the edge of performance to Allied aircraft over their Axis opponents in World War II.

Doolittle became famous with the youth of America whom he would one day lead in battle when he won the Thompson Trophy in 1932, flying the dangerous Gee Bee racer to a record speed of 252 miles per hour after previously setting a world air speed record for land planes of 294 miles per hour with it. Having won the Bendix Transcontinental Race in 1931, he had now won the top three awards in racing – the Schneider, Bendix, and Thompson trophies. He officially retired at the end of race week in Cleveland with the statement, "I have yet to hear of anyone engaged in this work dying of old age."

While Doolittle was arguably America's most famous flier as the result of these achievements, he became a legend on April 18, 1942, when he led 16 B-25 Mitchell bombers off the aircraft carrier USS *Hornet* to bomb Tokyo, Kobe, Yokohama, Osaka, and Nagoya. Forced to take off earlier – and farther from the target – than originally planned, all the aircraft were lost when they crashed in China, other than one that landed in Siberia and was interned. The next morning, surveying the wreckage of his bomber, Doolittle confided to his co-pilot, Captain Richard E. "Dick" Cole, that he expected a court-martial for failure when they were finally able to get back to the United States.

Instead, Doolittle was awarded the Medal of Honor by President Franklin Roosevelt in a ceremony at the White House that was mobbed by the press. Arnold promoted him directly from lieutenant colonel to brigadier general, and gave him command of the Twelfth Air Force, which would fight in North Africa following the success of Operation *Torch* on November 8, 1942. Even as an air force commander, he continued to fly combat missions to set an example to his men.

A lifelong teetotaler and non-smoker, Doolittle possessed the ability never to forget a face or name, which the author discovered on being introduced to him in 1976, when he immediately remembered the author's father of the same name, whom he had not seen since they met at the National Air Races in 1932. This ability on his part made every man who ever worked for him think he took personal interest in their work; he did keep track of his subordinates, and made certain they were recognized for their work.

There was a major difference between Doolittle and all the other senior USAAF leaders. He had left active, regular service in 1929, becoming a Reservist. He had never taken part in the great battles regarding the future of airpower that Arnold, Spaatz, and Eaker – the disciples of Billy Mitchell and Giulio Douhet, and their advocacy of strategic bombing as the solution to modern warfare – had fought for 20 years. Doolittle, a supreme pragmatist, would use whatever worked, regardless of its position in the hierarchy of True Belief. Eventually, he would come to see the presence of the bombers not as the ultimate purpose of the mission, but rather as "bait" to bring the enemy within range of the fighters in order to destroy him. Had he ever stated such a belief before making the decision to follow the tactic, he would have been branded a heretic by those who now placed him in command. His pragmatism and refusal to do something just because it fit in with a previous belief system would change the nature of the air war.

The problem for Arnold in replacing Eaker was that it had to be done in such a way that there was no hint in public of his being upset with Eaker's performance in England in any way, such an interpretation being deemed "bad for morale."

This was resolved by the reorganization of the Allied air forces in northern Europe and the Mediterranean. The origin of the decision was a memorandum by Spaatz, written to Arnold back on June 24, 1943, in which he pointed out that dividing the strategic bombing force that had been established in England into two, with a strategic force based in Italy after the likely invasion of that country, would allow the campaign to take advantage of better weather when the bombers were grounded by bad weather in England. Additionally, such a division of the force would require the enemy to dilute their defenses against either. Eaker argued against the division of force, but Arnold eventually agreed with Spaatz. The heavy bomber units in the Twelfth Air Force were transferred to the new Fifteenth Air Force in November, initially commanded by Doolittle. This force would be responsible for strategic bombing of southern Germany, Austria, Czechoslovakia, and Hungary from bases in southern Italy.

*Sextant*, the Cairo Conference, held in December 1943, defined changes in the command structure of the Allied air forces to streamline command relationships for the air war and invasion to come, just as the previous Quebec Conference that summer had defined the goals of the air campaign to create the conditions for invasion. The changes first suggested by Spaatz were refined and advocated by General Arnold. At the end of the conference, the following organizational changes were approved:

The Eighth and Fifteenth Air Forces became the United States Strategic Air Forces (USSTAF), commanded by Arnold's closest collaborator, General Spaatz. Doolittle was replaced by Major General Nathan F. Twining as the Fifteenth's commander. Doolittle was then named the new commander of the Eighth Air Force, replacing Eaker. The two strategic air forces were to complement each other and coordinate their missions under the control of Spaatz, who moved his headquarters to London.

The Twelfth Air Force became the tactical air force committed to the campaign in Italy after the Ninth Air Force was transferred from North Africa to England to take the same role in the coming cross-Channel invasion and placed under command of Eaker's old "Question Mark" crewman, Major General Elwood P. Quesada. Ninth Air Force and the RAF's Second Tactical Air Force in Britain were placed under the Allied Expeditionary Air Forces (AEAF), initially commanded by

RAF Air Marshal Trafford Leigh-Mallory, an officer universally disliked and considered by many to be incompetent. When Leigh-Mallory was promoted out of the way to command Air Defense of Great Britain (the former Fighter Command), RAF Air Marshal Sir Arthur Tedder was placed in charge of the Allied air forces committed to the invasion as part of his duties as second-in-command to General Eisenhower, who was named Supreme Commander Allied Expeditionary Forces (SHAEF) at the Cairo Conference.

With British General Sir Harold Alexander now Supreme Commander Mediterranean Theater, it was required that there be an American second-in-command. Eaker was named Commander, Mediterranean Allied Air Forces (MAAF). The North African Air Forces, which included Twelfth Air Force, were combined with the Mediterranean Air Command that oversaw the British Desert Air Force and Balkan Air Forces, and the Free French forces in the Mediterranean, and placed in MAAF, which was also responsible for day-to-day operational control of the Fifteenth Air Force. Arnold notified Eaker of the change in assignment in a curt message dated December 19.

Eaker for his part did not wish to leave his command and made things as personally difficult for Arnold as possible, cabling him, "Believe war interest best served by my retention command Eighth Air Force: Otherwise experience this theater for nearly two years wasted. If I am to be allowed my personal preference having started with the Eighth and seen it for major task in this theater, it would be heartbreaking to leave just before climax." The transfer meant a promotion for Eaker to lieutenant general. Finally, Eisenhower soothed the situation, cabling Eaker, "As you well know, I would be more than delighted to have you with me," ending with "We do not (repeat not) have enough top men to concentrate them in one place."

Realizing there was nothing more to be said, Eaker accepted, but the 25-year relationship between Eaker and Arnold was irrevocably harmed, despite the *New York Times* headline for December 19 blaring "General Eaker Moves Up." Once in his new command, Eaker flourished, directing air support for the Italian campaign and taking a personal role in the shuttle bombing missions from Italy to the USSR that summer. He was in the USSR on June 6, 1944, when he learned that the Luftwaffe had not shown up over the Normandy beaches. He later wrote that the moment was "my greatest personal satisfaction in World War II."

Throughout the Eighth Air Force, New Year's Day brought with it certainty that 1944 would be the war's decisive year, and the most demanding time in their lives. For the whole air force, but particularly VIII Fighter Command, the pressure was on. Defeating the Luftwaffe in the air was the goal without which there could be no successful invasion. The Eighth was still a very long way from achieving that goal. The Jagdwaffe was far from a spent force; aircraft production in Germany had increased monthly while the output of replacement pilots kept pace with losses, though the *Nachwuchs* (new growth), as they were called in the *Geschwadern*, did not have the level of training that had been the standard a year earlier, which had been notably lower than that of those who had fought the Battle of Britain. Nevertheless, the *Jagdflieger* (fighter pilots) were confident that they had the capability to make the Americans pay so heavy a price that their air campaign could be defeated, just as had happened to the German air campaign against England.

Doolittle's arrival as commander of the Eighth Air Force, effective January 6, 1944, sent a wave of shock and surprise through the force. Captain Richard E. "Dick" Hewitt, pilot and maintenance officer of the 84th Fighter Squadron in the 78th Fighter Group, spoke for many when he remembered the news:

> I and every other pilot in the group, and I imagine every other pilot in every other group, had grown up reading about his exploits, and a desire to follow his example had probably been part of the motivation of the overwhelming majority of us to become pilots ourselves. There was nothing he would ask of us that we did not believe he would do first himself, and probably already had.

That said, most – including Hewitt – thought that Eaker had been unfairly treated, to be removed from the command just as the force was finally ready to achieve what it had been created to do.

For the Americans, the key to victory lay in the power of sheer numbers. The call that had been deemed impossible in 1941 for training 50,000 pilots annually had been fulfilled. A new pilot reported to a fighter group with a minimum of 400 hours' training, 150 of that in the fighter type he would fly in combat – his German opposite number reported to his unit with a third of that experience – if he was lucky. The new men filled the veteran groups to bursting, allowing General Kepner to issue orders expanding the decision in the fall of 1943 to divide each fighter group into two; each could now mount two 48-plane missions. New groups arrived each month. VIII Fighter Command now had 12 of the 15 fighter groups planned for the force; the last three would arrive by May. Not only were there numbers, but now those aircraft were capable of providing protection to the bombers all the way to the target and back.

In VIII Fighter Command, two changes in strategy and tactics would have a major effect in the coming battles. The first came soon after Doolittle took command, when he announced a major change in VIII Fighter Command escort policy on January 7, adopting "phased fighter escort," a concept that had been argued at length since the beginning of the air campaign back in May 1943.

Since then, fighter groups had joined with the bombers and stayed with them until they were required to turn back due to low fuel, with each fighter group supporting a particular bomber formation. This tactic failed to maximize the fighters' range, because the escorts ended up flying a further distance than the bombers they were covering; the difference in cruising speeds between fighters and bombers meant the fighters had to weave or fly "S-turns" to remain close to the bombers. As a result, for every mile the bombers flew, the fighters flew half again if not more. This cut the maximum range dramatically when compared with their straight-line range. The early P-47s, which had to break off over the Low Countries due to lack of fuel, actually had the straight-line range to fly well into Germany.

Phased escort involved a group flying directly to a rendezvous point, from where they would cover a particular area as the bomber formations flew through it until another group rendezvoused further en route. Because they were able to fly directly to the rendezvous point, they had more fuel and could take the bombers further. Thus, short-ranged Spitfires escorted the formation across the Channel or North Sea, with P-47s picking them up as they crossed the coast, taking them halfway to a target in Germany, with P-38s relieving the P-47s until the target was in sight, where P-51s would take up the coverage over the target and through initial withdrawal, though both P-38s and P-51s might cover the target if it was not so deep in Germany that only the Mustang could provide cover. The A and B groups meant that a unit could send one group for outbound escort and the second for return. When the leaders of VIII Fighter Command brought their arguments in favor of this to Doolittle, he had no trouble accepting their validity, since he had made that change in the Fifteenth Air Force many months earlier.

While this made sense strategically and tactically, it did not go down well with the bomb groups; crews were comforted by the sight of the "little friends" around their formation, despite the fact that placing the fighters in this position and restricting their ability to take offensive action against enemy fighters actually made the escort less effective. The next change Doolittle authorized was even less popular with the bomber crews.

On January 21, following further discussions with General Kepner, his staff, and fighter group leaders, Doolittle declared that, while the role of protecting the bomber formation should not be minimized, the fighter escorts should be encouraged to "meet the enemy and destroy him, rather than be content to keep him away." Several days earlier, when he had visited Kepner's headquarters, he had noticed a sign that read "The First Duty of the Air Force Fighters is to Bring the Bombers Back Alive!" When he asked Kepner who had made that rule, he was told that it dated to Monk Hunter's command of the fighters. Indeed, the strategy was at first dictated as much by *force majeure* as anything else, since when Hunter led the force, there were only some 175 fighters available in all of VIII Fighter Command at the time of the Schweinfurt-Regensburg mission. But now there were 12 groups, each equipped with 108 fighters, capable of sending two 48-plane escort formations with each mission. Doolittle ordered Kepner to change that rule to "The First Duty of Eighth Air Force Fighters is to Destroy German Fighters!" When Kepner asked if this meant the command was now authorized to "take the offensive," Doolittle replied, "Yes." Pragmatism had just taken a step away from Detailed Procedure.

Fighter group commanders like Hub Zemke and Don Blakeslee had been advocating this change in overall strategy since the previous summer, with Zemke stretching the rules of close escort as far as he could to give the Wolfpack the opportunity to meet the enemy as early as possible. Zemke agreed with experienced fighter leaders like Adolf Galland, who had argued vociferously in 1940 against tying the fighter escorts too closely to the bombers and losing the fighter's best tactic: offensive action to break up the defenders before they could make an attack.

Zemke later wrote of Doolittle's decision:

General Eaker's brief had been that our first objective was to bring the bombers home and our second to shoot down enemy aircraft. Now General Doolittle told us to pursue the enemy when and wherever we could; we were now allowed to follow him down and no longer had to break off attacks. It also meant official recognition of what I had long advocated: getting way out ahead of the force to bounce the enemy fighters before they had a chance to make their attacks.

The result of the change regarding escort policy was that several fighter groups – most notably the Wolfpack and the Eagles, followed by the 352nd who became known as the "Blue-Nosed Bastards of Bodney" from the markings on their new Mustangs once they re-equipped, and the new 357th Group which arrived as the change was made – ran up their scores over the spring months as the daylight offensive finally hit its stride. However, the change was not universally adopted. Some group commanders disagreed with the new strategy and maintained the close escort policy. Prominent among these was Colonel Jim Stone, whose belief in close escort meant that the 78th would not score as highly as the 4th or 56th groups it had served beside from the beginning a year earlier. The 359th Group's Colonel Avelin Tacom, Jr., was another who kept the policy of not allowing his pilots to "go haring off over the countryside" as he put it. This difference between the groups was primarily down to the "aggressiveness" of particular commanding officers.

By May, Zemke had proposed to General Kepner that the "aggressive" commanders like himself, Blakeslee, and those others whose groups were demonstrating the value of the offensive tactics, be replaced in their groups and that they be assigned to the other groups as temporary group commanders for several months, which would allow them to turn those units around by changes in leadership. A few months later, Kepner took Zemke up on the idea and he left the 56th to take command of the 479th Group – the last to join VIII Fighter Command – which had experienced setbacks in its combat operations. Robin Olds, who became the 479th's leading ace, later said that there was a real difference in the group and the way it went about fighting within a matter of weeks following Zemke's arrival.

Choosing to follow a defensive or offensive escort strategy was not the only determinant of a group's success. The escort assignments it received were crucial. A group that was assigned to cover the leading formation was much more likely to run across the opposition than one bringing up the rear. As successful pilots approached completion of their tours, commanders like Zemke and Blakeslee intervened at VIII Fighter Command to have "their guys" assigned to Fighter Command Operations, where assignments were made for each mission. By organizing the individual's transfer from operational unit to staff before their tour expired, they remained in the same overall organization, where their presence could be helpful to their old unit. Unfortunately for the 78th, original pilots Gene Roberts and Harry Dayhuff were not in the operation planning section, but were assigned to tactical development, responsible for bringing new groups up to combat standards. Additionally, its base at Duxford was 50 miles west of the next VIII Fighter Command base in East Anglia, so it could not get assigned to target support cover, where the chance of engaging in combat was the greatest, due to its relative lack of range as compared with the 56th, which was based right on the coast at Halesworth, or the 4th, which was only 30 miles inland at Debden. Thus geographical location and the "politics" of Fighter Command would be a bone of contention between fighter groups for the rest of the war. As Hub Zemke, Don Blakeslee, Joe Mason, and other aggressive leaders demonstrated, taking charge on the ground was at least as important as any leadership in the cockpit.

Doolittle made one other change. If the fighters were to destroy the Luftwaffe, they couldn't allow the enemy to pick when and where the two sides would meet. Ever since 1941, the Jagdwaffe had used a strategy of avoiding combat when conditions were unfavorable and the target was not considered to be so important; thus, most of the time, the only place the fighters could always be found was on their airfields.

Doolittle's new rule was that any group that finished their escort assignment without engaging the enemy, and had sufficient fuel, was to find and hit German airfields on their return. Strafing missions really changed things. A fighter-versus-fighter engagement was a test of skill and ability between the individuals involved. A low-level attack posed the question of whether one could survive the law of probability. German airfields were defended by a multitude of antiaircraft guns, from 88mm high-altitude cannons through 50mm and 37mm medium-altitude weapons to 20mm cannon down low, all throwing up a veritable wall of fire through which a strafing fighter had to fly. The odds were against the attacker, even in an airplane that could take hits and keep going like the Thunderbolt. To counter the reluctance of pilots to engage in strafing, Doolittle ruled that a "ground kill," the successful destruction of an aircraft by strafing, would be credited the same as an air combat victory. No other air force in any theater on either side had such a policy. The result was that more than two-thirds of the German aircraft claimed destroyed between Big Week and D-Day were strafing claims, while 70 percent of fighter losses were the result of such missions.

The 78th Group was the first to follow Doolittle's directive. After chasing Fw-190s to low level during an escort on February 6, 1944, to Troyes, France, 78A Group separated into squadrons and strafed the airfields at Orleans/Bricy, Beaumont, Chartres, and Évreux. They ran into the light flak defending the airfields and lost six shot down. It was quickly discovered that attacking airfields without a plan was a recipe for disaster.

The P-47 got a technical upgrade at this time that would make the fighter more able to carry out such an offensive strategy. The aircraft were in the process of being equipped with a system to inject water into the engine that would increase power by nearly 20 percent for a short period of time – a maximum of ten minutes – which could be used at all altitudes, improving both high-altitude and "on the deck" performance. Additionally, a new Curtiss "paddle blade" prop was fitted to the Thunderbolts that improved climb dramatically, increasing the P-47's rate of climb by 600 feet per minute and allowing the fighter to climb to 30,000 feet in 13 minutes rather than the previous 20 minutes.

Bob Johnson recalled an experience he had shortly after his P-47 was equipped with the new prop. He ran across a British pilot in a Spitfire IX, the most powerful version of the RAF fighter, equipped with a Merlin engine that had a two-stage supercharger. The two flew alongside each other and signaled interest in what the Americans called "hassling," a term used for what would be called in a later war "dissimilar aircraft maneuvering," or simulated dogfighting.

> When we did a straight climb, he had me cold. That airplane could pull away from me like the proverbial homesick angel. But after a few times of having my tail feathers waxed, I managed to get above him and make a dive on him. He pulled up, figuring to out-climb me as he had, but I pulled up in a zoom and rocketed past him! He tried to dive, but I came around and the Jug seemed to literally fall on him, then I zoomed and came around again. So long as I stayed in the vertical plane and used the Jug's incredible dive and the new zoom ability she was now capable of, he couldn't touch me. I knew I would use that on the Germans the next time I ran across one.

Also, by February, every P-47 in VIII Fighter Command had the underwing pylons that allowed them to carry three times as much extra fuel as they had only four months earlier. With the agreement to divert the P-51B from Ninth to Eighth Air Force, plans were already afoot to re-equip four VIII Fighter Command groups immediately with the new fighter. Hub Zemke was surprised when he returned from his stateside tour in late January to find that the 56th Group had been offered the chance to be one of those chosen groups, but had turned down the opportunity. Zemke later wrote that Dave Schilling had done so in his absence, due to the feeling of commitment to the Thunderbolt felt by the pilots who had "tamed the beast." Zemke himself had no such attachment to any type of airplane, and would have gladly accepted the offer because it would have allowed them to chase the enemy anywhere in Germany. On the other hand, Don Blakeslee was calling General Kepner every day to request re-equipment, pointing out how easy it would be since "most of us had flown Spitfires."

In fact, the Mustang was so easy to fly that little thought was given to extensive conversion training before entering combat. When the 352nd Group received its new Mustangs on April 7, 1944, pilot Robert "Punchy" Powell remembered, "We were coming back from a mission and when the field came in sight, we saw all these P-51s parked there." On landing, Powell was informed by his crew chief that he was expected to take one of the Mustangs for an initial flight in 30 minutes. Powell was surprised and initially resisted the idea of not even studying the flight manual:

> But that's what we did. Our engineering officer showed me how to start it, and the next thing I knew, I was at 15,000 feet. To get the feel of it, I did some tight turns, a chandelle in both directions, and a barrel roll. I tested the stall by putting the wheels down, cutting power and bringing the nose up till she stalled. I was surprised by how stable it was. I went back and landed and we flew our first mission in the new planes the next day.

The bombers themselves were different from what they had been during the battles of 1943. The B-17G had entered production at Boeing in late spring of 1943, and at the Lockheed-Vega and Douglas-Long Beach factories over the summer. The first of these had arrived in England in August; by December 1943, only a few of the earlier B-17Fs were left in the bomb groups. The B-17G differed from the earlier sub-types most notably in the installation of a remote-controlled gun turret immediately beneath the bombardier's position, controlled by the bombardier. Fitted with two .50-caliber machine guns, the turret provided a much wider field of fire than did the two-gun armament fitted inside the nose, which could only be fired individually by the bombardier with limited field of fire. The new turret could cover all the sky ahead of the bomber that would be used by enemy fighters in the Twelve O'Clock High attack. Additionally, the two other guns fitted in the nose compartment, which could only be fired to the side with the fitting used by the B-17F, were now housed in "cheek" positions – so named because they bulged out to either side of the nose – that could be aimed much further forward to give a total of four guns defending the nose of the Flying Fortress. The "chin turret" had first appeared on the 12 YB-40 "convoy defenders" that had proven unsuccessful. The turret and cheek guns had also appeared on late-production B-17Fs from Douglas-Long Beach. The B-17G also featured enclosed waist gun positions, protecting the gunners in the rear fuselage from the icy blasts of high-altitude air whipping through the open waist windows on the B-17F.

The B-24 Liberator had also received an armament upgrade. The B-24H sub-type, which entered production in mid-1943, replaced the glazed "green house" nose with an electrically powered manned Emerson A-15 nose turret mounting two .50-caliber machine guns, with the bombardier's position moved to the area immediately beneath the turret. This change had first been created "in the field" at the Townsville air depot in Australia, to modify B-24Ds used in the Southwest Pacific Area. The B-24H was built by Ford Motor Co. at the gigantic Willow Run factory in Detroit, Michigan, at the time the world's largest building. The B-24J, built by Consolidated at their factories in San Diego, California, and Fort Worth, Texas, differed from the B-24H in having a hydraulically powered Consolidated A-6 turret mounted in the nose. On completion of the B-24H contract, Ford's products were similarly equipped B-24Js for the remainder of the war.

Assembling bomb group formations in the cloudy skies over England was difficult and led to much delay in starting a mission, resulting in waste of avgas that could affect the ability to reach a distant target. In February 1944, the B-24-equipped 2nd Air Division began using the old "greenhouse nose" B-24Ds as "Assembly Ships" (or "Formation Ships"). These war-weary aircraft were stripped of armament and armor and equipped with signal lighting, and systems for the quantity discharge of pyrotechnics. They were painted with distinctive group-specific high-contrast multi-color patterns of stripes, checkers, or polka dots which allowed easy recognition by their bombers. The signal lighting arrangements varied from group to group, but were usually white flashing lamps on both sides of the fuselage, arranged to form the group identification letter. Following some accidents involving the accidental discharge of flare guns in the rear fuselage, most of the assembly ships were modified with the pyrotechnic guns fixed to fire through the apertures in the fuselage sides. The airplanes were operated by a skeleton crew of two pilots, navigator, radio operator, and one or two flare discharge operators. They came to be called "Judas goats" by the operational crews, a term loaded with dark imagery of "lambs led to slaughter." When the use of assembly ships led to improved operations in the 2nd Air Division, the B-17-equipped 1st and 3rd Air Divisions adopted the idea, using their cast-off B-17Fs.

With the additional bomb groups that had arrived in the previous four months, Eighth Air Force could now send missions of as many as 700 bombers against targets across Europe, a far cry from January 27, 1943, when 50 B-17s had managed to penetrate Germany for the first time and bomb Wilhelmshaven. By Big Week, they could send 1,000 or more.

Throughout the Combined Bomber Offensive, the weather over Britain and western Europe was unlike any the Americans dealt with elsewhere; it was problematic throughout the year. Summer fog had disrupted the Schweinfurt-Regensburg mission and was a major reason for the losses incurred then. However, the winter weather over England and western Europe presented particular difficulties; on the average, severe storms could be expected every three days between London and Berlin. Jimmy Doolittle dealt with the persistent cloud cover over Germany during January 1944 by directing VIII Bomber Command to use radar-directed blind bombing in order to fly missions at all in the unfavorable conditions.

VIII Bomber Command and Technical Command had gotten involved in intensive development of radar bombing beginning in late 1942 in an effort to reduce the weather-imposed operational limitations in the ETO as much as possible. At this point in its development, existing radar equipment was seen not as a substitute for visual bombing but rather as an alternative that allowed VIII Bomber Command to maintain pressure on the German economy as a whole. When radar bombing missions did begin in the fall of 1943, the missions were restricted to targets that showed up clearly on the radar screen; these were primarily built-up urban areas on coast lines or estuaries, since the distinction between water and land was easy to recognize on the screen. While a large industrial area could be located without difficulty, it was impossible to identify specific factories unless they were either unusually isolated or unusually extensive. The governing philosophy regarding radar-guided bombing was that it was better to bomb low-priority targets frequently, even if it meant less than precision accuracy, than not to bomb at all.

Early plans were based largely on the RAF's experience and British equipment was the first to be used. Of the RAF's radar-equipment, that best suited to VIII Bomber Command's requirements was H2S, a centimetric radar using a beam of transmitted energy to scan the ground below the carrier aircraft, with the reflected signals showing a map-like picture on the indicator screen, with light areas for ground, dark areas for water, and the broad reflecting surfaces of towns and cities showing up as bright areas. The 482nd Bombardment Group was first to use

H2S on September 27, 1943. With first priority for the sets going to RAF Bomber Command, and production pressed to meet those needs, VIII Bomber Command still had only a few sets in October, and the units using them were experiencing difficulty in using the equipment at the high altitudes at which the bombers flew.

The MIT Radiation Laboratory was contracted to develop an improved version of the H2S type. Rather than centimetric wave length, this set used a new and shorter microwave length, which gave a sharper and more accurate ground return. Known as H2X, the sets were placed in production in the summer of 1943; the need for rapid supply resulted in the Radiation Laboratory hand-building 20 sets, which were enough to equip a dozen B-17s with necessary spares. The 12 B-17s, manned by crews partially trained in operating H2X, joined the 482nd Group in October. The crews underwent further training over the remainder of October, and then went operational earlier than intended due to the winter weather being worse than expected. Each H2X B-17, which were distinguished from standard Flying Fortresses by the substitution of the H2X radome in the ball turret position, would lead a combat wing of 60 bombers that would drop on the radar-equipped "pathfinder" leader. The first "practice" mission was flown on November 3; 11 pathfinders – nine using H2X and two with H2S – led 539 bombers to attack the port of Wilhelmshaven. This was primarily due to VIII Bomber Command being familiar with the target, it having been the first German target struck by the command back in January, and the fact that its geographic location, situated on the coast near the estuary of the Weser River, was easily identified by the radar.

Despite poor weather over England, 566 bombers assembled without difficulty, with only 27 aborting; this was the largest mission yet mounted by VIII Bomber Command. The radar worked well and a record load of more than 1,400 tons of bombs was dropped through a solid layer of cloud with sufficient accuracy to damage the aiming point. The 11 pathfinders flew with the seven B-17-equipped combat wings of the 1st and 3rd Air Divisions; the 2nd Division's 117 B-24s were to drop on parachute marker flares; this resulted in considerable error because the interval between combat wings allowed the flares to drift, in addition to their being hard to distinguish from flak explosions.

Unfortunately, while the bombing was effective in terms of hitting the target, the result was less impressive, since the shipyard workshops that were "moderately damaged" were not being used to capacity, and there was no damage to the hulls of under-construction U-boats. But this was not as important as the fact that the yard had been hit through ten-tenths cloud by inexperienced pathfinder crews. The fact that the weather had prevented the Luftwaffe from making any significant interception, with only seven bombers lost and four of those due to flak, was also considered beneficial. The bombers were escorted by eight fighter groups with good results.

This first success encouraged those who believed in radar bombing and converted the doubtful. Using radar, VIII Bomber Command mounted nine more missions in November, all flown in weather that prevented any opportunity for visual bombing. Unfortunately, the accuracy obtained was not repeated in later missions flown in December, though the commanders were satisfied by the greatly accelerated rate of operations that the force achieved through the rest of the winter of 1943–44, serving to meet the insistent demands by General Arnold that VIII Bomber Command go "all out."

The size of the missions mounted was the result of the increase in operating strength in VIII Bomber Command from 20 bomb groups in October 1943 to 30 groups operational by the end of 1943, with double the number of bombers assigned to a group. The November 3 record of 566 bombers sent was broken on November 26 when a force of 633 went out, with that increasing to 710 on December 13 and 722 on December 24.

The supply of H2X sets had not improved by mid-January 1944. Shortly after taking command of USSTAF, Spaatz wrote Arnold, "The most critical need of the Strategic Air Forces is for more Pathfinder aircraft. A few H2X planes now will profit our cause more than several hundred in six months." Further missions were flown to the ports of Bremen, Wilhelmshaven, and Kiel, which were easily identified and allowed the pathfinder crews to gain experience with their gear.

The bombing led by the radar-equipped pathfinders in November and December had been too scattered to result in more than accidental damage to any particular industrial plant or installation targeted. In fact, bombs fell in the assigned target area on only two missions; photo interpretation of bomb damage assessment indicated that only six of 151 combat boxes using radar bombing dropped bombs within one mile of the aiming point; 17 boxes dropped within two miles; and

30 dropped within five miles. At Bremen, the city hit most often in these two months, no bombs fell within two miles of the aiming point; five combat boxes were able to drop within five miles. By the end of 1943, it was clear that radar-directed bombing was unlikely to become sufficiently accurate to replace or even compete with visual bombing. VIII Bomber Command had been involved in the kind of area bombing engaged in by the RAF and deprecated by the USAAF, though the attacks kept pressure on the enemy.

The only way to achieve the accuracy necessary to meet the goals set by *Pointblank* was through visual bombing, and this could not reliably take place before March, leaving too little time to achieve supremacy over the Luftwaffe by the time of the invasion. Thus, when there was any chance of clear weather, missions had to be laid on as a "maximum effort." For now, as VIII Bomber Command intelligence stated in a report, "... the weather continued to be a faithful Nazi collaborator."

# 15

# BLAKESLEE TAKES COMMAND

Symbolic of the major changes coming in VIII Fighter Command, Don Blakeslee took command of the 4th on New Year's Day, replacing Chesley Peterson, who had orders to report to IX Tactical Air Command as Director of Operations; many years later, when asked about this, Peterson said, "If I had had the slightest idea that one-tenth of what was about to happen would happen, they couldn't have dragged me out of Debden with a Sherman tank!" Once he was the leader, Blakeslee told his pilots point-blank what he expected of them:

> The 4th Fighter Group is going to be the top fighter group in the Eighth Air Force. We are here to fight. To those who don't believe me, I would suggest transferring to another group. I'm going to fly the arse off each one of you. Those who keep up with me, good. Those who don't, I don't want them anyway.

Steve Pisanos later recalled, "If anyone had any doubts, it was clear from Colonel Don's statement that the gloves were coming off in 1944."

After leading the January 4 mission, where the weather prevented the group from coming to grips with the enemy, Blakeslee led his second mission as group commander on January 7: withdrawal support to cover bombers returning from Ludwigshafen. The Jagdwaffe rose to the occasion, and he was nearly undone by his own aggressiveness. When 12 Fw-190s dived out of the sun to attack straggling B-17s near Hesdin, Blakeslee turned to attack them but was cut off by a flight of RAF Spitfires; having lost his wingman, he joined Jim Goodson's

Red Section. "I had climbed up back to fourteen thousand feet when I saw more Focke-Wulfs attacking stragglers," Blakeslee later wrote in his combat report. "I dived on these, being covered by Captain Goodson's section, and chased one enemy aircraft down to between two or three thousand feet." Goodson, with newly promoted wingman First Lieutenant Bob Wehrman in tow, followed Blakeslee in line astern. "Other '190s attempted to attack, but usually broke away down through the clouds when I turned into them," Blakeslee reported.

Goodson later reported:

Suddenly I was jumped by three Fw-190s. One made a determined attack, firing at Blakeslee even after I attacked him. When I started getting strikes on him, he broke hard to port, but even though he pulled streamers from his wingtips, I was able to pull my sights through him. He suddenly did two-and-a-half flick rolls and then split-S-ed vertically through some light scud cloud. I followed in a steep wingover, and had to pull out hard to miss some trees as the cloud was lower than I had realized. As I did so, I caught sight of an explosion. Since the '190 had gone through the clouds vertically, I feel sure he could not have pulled out even if he had not been damaged.

Goodson soon joined with Blakeslee and Wehrman, but before he could get close enough, another Fw-190 got on Blakeslee's tail and opened fire. Goodson managed to get on the enemy's tail and fired. "I was relieved to see strikes all over him, and see him peel away and crash in flames on the ground, which was quite close." Jim Goodson had saved Don Blakeslee, but was out of ammunition when a third Fw-190 tried to shoot Blakeslee; Goodson's element leader, First Lieutenant Vermont Garrison, cut off the the enemy fighter and damaged it enough to force the German to break away. This was Blakeslee's second close shave with the enemy where Goodson had saved him.

Blakeslee still wasn't done with fighting that day, despite the damage to his Thunderbolt. When he spotted another Fw-190 going after a straggling Flying Fortress, Blakeslee turned onto the enemy's tail:

The enemy aircraft I was attacking suddenly broke off its turn, straightened out and went into haze. I followed, and as he came out I was dead line astern. I fired a three-to-four-second burst, observing strikes on the enemy aircraft's tail and starboard wing. Pieces came from the cockpit. It then did a half-flick to the right and went in. My radio had been shot out and my aircraft was spraying oil badly.

For the rest of the flight back to England, Blakeslee and Goodson had to depend on Bob Wehrman, who again was the only one with ammunition. The P-47s were again bounced by Bf-109s, which turned away when Goodson and Wehrman turned into them. When they managed to put down at the Manston emergency strip, Blakeslee later counted 71 holes in the tail and rear fuselage of his Thunderbolt.

Following the January 11 mission, in which the 4th was among the groups recalled due to encountering worse weather than originally forecast, the clouds again covered Germany, so heavy that even radar bombing was impossible; the conditions lasted for two weeks while either cloud conditions over Germany made formation flying at high altitude impossible or the weather over the East Anglia and Midlands bases made launching a mission too difficult to carry out.

On January 14, the 4th escorted bombers to strike the under-construction V-1 launch site at Magny Soissons just across the Channel in northern France. Former Eagle Don Gentile was leading Shirtblue Purple Flight of the 336th Squadron, with Johnny Godfrey's best friend, Second Lieutenant Bob Richards, as his wingman and Vermont Garrison as element leader. As the Thunderbolts orbited south of the target at 25,000 feet, a formation of Fw-190s was spotted 3,000 feet below, and Blakeslee ordered the 336th to bounce them. The Thunderbolts fell on the enemy fighters and a swirling dogfight developed. In the course of this, Gentile became separated from Richards and the other element of his flight. Spotting two Fw-190s below flying east to get away from the fight, he dived on them. Pulling in behind, he managed to hit the wingman and set his engine on fire. The leader made a wing-over to escape, diving for the ground below. Gentile went after him, finally putting a fatal burst into the Focke-Wulf's engine as the two fighters roared 50 feet above the trees.

Gentile pulled up to climb back to altitude and rejoin the group, but he spotted two other Fw-190s diving on him. He turned into them to break the attack, and initially both overshot, but they came back around. Gentile managed to get on the wingman's tail and fired a burst but missed; the enemy fighter pulled up and away while the leader pulled around on him, attempting to get on his tail. Gentile pulled the stick into his stomach and slammed it against his right leg as the P-47 stood on a wingtip over the forest, G-force contrails streaming from the wingtips. The two fighters went round and round over the trees; Gentile managed to pull tight enough to get his opponent in his sights, but when he squeezed the trigger, there was no response. He was out of ammo and the enemy pilot was good! The P-47 wasn't supposed to be able to turn with an Fw-190 at low altitude, but Gentile now had no choice. He pushed the throttle into "war emergency power" and the R-2800 screamed as the entire airframe shook, right on the edge of a stall that would spin him into the trees below in an instant. His only option was to stay in the turn till the enemy pilot ran out of ammunition.

"Help! Help! I'm being clobbered!" Gentile screamed over the radio in near panic. He was answered by the imperturbable Carolina drawl of Captain Willard "Milly" Millikan: "Now, if you will tell me your call sign and approximate position we'll send help."

"I'm down here by a railroad track with a '190!" screamed Gentile in reply.

The turning fight continued below as the other pilots of the 4th looked for their comrade. Afraid the German was going to win the battle, Gentile called out to Blakeslee: "Horseback! Horseback! If I don't get back, tell 'em I got two 190s!" He later reported:

I suddenly flicked and just about wiped myself out on the trees. Recovering, I reversed my turn to starboard, and there he was, still inside me and still shooting like hell. I kept on turning and skidding. He slid under and overshot, and I reversed again. We met head-on, and he was still firing. For the next ten minutes we kept reversing turns from head-on attacks, trying to get on each other's tails.

As the Fw-190 began to close the gap, Gentile suddenly leveled his wings and pulled the stick back into his gut, standing the big Thunderbolt on its prop until the shaking told him he was just about to stall out. He was now above the enemy pilot and if he'd had any ammo left, he could have swooped down and finished the fight. His German opponent suddenly flicked over, recovered right above the trees, and fled. Gentile leveled out, breathed a sigh of relief, and climbed back to rejoin the group.

When he bounced down on Debden's runway, he didn't bother to gun the engine before switching off. Gentile sat in the silence, spent and worn, every fiber of his being heavy with weariness. When the intelligence officer jumped on the wing to interrogate him, he didn't answer. The officer later recalled that when he pulled off his leather flying helmet, it was dripping wet with sweat. Gentile finally found the strength to pull himself up and climbed out of the cockpit. "I got two," he said as he jumped off the wing to the ground. The boy who at age eight had seen the movie *Wings* and determined he would be a fighter pilot, who had made up business cards reading "Don Gentile – Ace," had just scored victories four and five. While he was doing that, Bob Richards scored his first victory and lived to celebrate it when Garrison shot the enemy wingman off his tail.

When the winter fog finally lifted over East Anglia after bringing flight operations to a halt for five days, Blakeslee led a Rodeo sweep to the Pas de Calais on January 21. Most of the time, the Luftwaffe studiously ignored such flights, but this time a fight developed when a small force of Fw-190s were caught unaware of the Thunderbolts' presence. Bob Richards recalled:

We were vectored to Beauvais to intercept some bandits in that area. When we got near there, there was nothing to be seen except a little flak. My number one, Lieutenant Kenneth Peterson, was still very keen on the way out, and when I saw him roll his airplane on its side, I looked down also and saw four bogies flying south. Peterson started to go down and I followed. As we got closer I recognized them as Fw-190s.

They didn't see us until we got right on top of them, and Peterson started firing. He overshot, and another '190 came in from 45 or 50 degrees, under-deflecting all the time. Another '190 came in head-on, firing at me. I took a short burst at him. He went over the top of me. I started to pull around to get on his tail when I saw another '190 right in front of me. I had plenty of speed, and I closed in from about a hundred yards, firing all the time. I saw strikes all over him. He pulled up to the right to try to break into me. As he did that I laid off a little deflection above him and I hit him all over the cockpit. It looked as if the cockpit was all ablaze from the strikes. I closed in to about 25 yards and pulled off to the side to watch him go down. He rolled over smoking and headed for the deck out of control.

For the January 29 mission to Frankfurt, the 4th was assigned penetration support. Soon after they left the bombers over Maastricht, Holland, 16 Bf-109s were spotted below. Duane Beeson and the 334th Squadron dived on the enemy fighters. Beeson later reported:

> As our squadron bounced this group of enemy aircraft, I saw six other Me-109s coming in to get on our tails. My wingman Lieutenant Archie Chatterly and I turned into them. One put a hole in my tailplane before we could turn into them, but when the turn was completed I saw Chatterly on a '109's tail.

Chatterly remembered:

> My first strike was on the left wingtip. He straightened out and dived. I hit him with many strikes around the cockpit and other sections of the fuselage. Pieces flew off and the enemy aircraft went out of control and down slowly on its back, with dark smoke trailing behind. I lost sight of it as it floated into the clouds.

In the meantime, the other Bf-109s continued diving. Beeson reported:

> I got on the tail of the nearest one and opened fire. I saw very severe strikes on the fuselage and wing roots, then a large flash somewhere in the cockpit area and the enemy aircraft flicked violently to the right and went down trailing a long stream of grey-black smoke. The last I saw of the '109, he was going straight down through ten-tenths cloud below.

As Beeson pulled out of his dive, he saw a dogfight below him:

> I started down again when I sighted an aircraft off to starboard, also diving. When I closed on him, he turned out to be a yellow-tailed Fw-190 with a belly tank. I was approaching out of the sun and he didn't see me. I fired a burst from out of range, trying to slow him down. No results were seen, so I continued behind him as he went into a cloud at about 3,000 feet and when we came out below I was about 300 yards behind. I opened fire again and saw many incendiary strikes on his fuselage. He dropped his nose at about 200 feet and went in to the deck.

Steve Pisanos spotted 15 Bf-109s below and his flight dived on them:

> I lined up at once and began firing. He went into a dive and I followed
> him down, firing. When we were just above the cloud base, I saw hits
> behind the cockpit. He went out of control and dived straight down
> into the cloud at 3,000 feet. I then started to climb to starboard when
> I saw another '109 below me to my port, flying straight and level. I
> went down and closed on him, opening fire. As he dived into the
> cloud, I saw hits on the cockpit and fuselage, a lot of fire came out
> and he rolled over to the right and went in.

With these two victories, Pisanos was one confirmed kill away from
"making ace."

Altogether, Pisanos got two Bf-109s, while Beeson and Captain
Henry Mills claimed two Fw-190s each. Archie Chatterly got one
Fw-190 as did First Lieutenant Vic France. Unfortunately, the 335th
Squadron's Second Lieutenant Burton Wyman, who had last been seen
chasing a Bf-109 into the undercast with another behind him, failed
to return to Debden, becoming the 4th's first combat fatality of 1944.

The next day, flying a target support mission to Brunswick, the pilots
in the 335th Squadron spotted 12 bogies at 26,000 feet and 15 more
at 12,000 feet. They climbed after the higher group, and the enemy
fighters responded. Second Lieutenant Charles Anderson later reported:

> When we were almost up to them, two '109s dived down between
> my number three and me. When they saw my aircraft, they started
> to climb immediately. I followed them up and fired at the one on
> the left from about 350 yards. He started smoking badly and turned
> away to the left. As there were two, I could not follow the one I had
> fired at for fear the other one would get on my tail. I later saw the
> Bf-109 spinning and burning as it entered a cloud.

On January 31, Captain Raymond Care led the 4th on its first ever
dive-bombing mission to strike Gilze-Rijen airfield in Holland. Two
four-aircraft flights in each squadron flew Thunderbolts carrying a
500-pound bomb on the centerline shackles, while the other two flights
provided cover. The P-47s hit a fuel dump and one of the runways.
While the dive bombers were attacking, the top cover was attacked by

15–20 Bf-109s. First Lieutenant Raymond Clotfelter's 335th Squadron flight dodged four diving enemy fighters:

> I then spotted a Bf-109 coming in at "nine o'clock," and when he started to pull deflection on me, I called a break and immediately flicked over into an aileron turn. I saw three other enemy aircraft off to my right approximately 1,500 yards away. I decided I could catch them, so I pushed everything to the firewall and closed very quickly. When the Me-109s recovered from their dives, I pulled deflection and opened fire. After a short burst, I pushed my nose through again and fired a longer burst. I closed to a hundred yards, seeing strikes all over the cockpit, pieces falling off the tail and a fire. I had to break off to the right, and as I did, I passed within a wing span of the enemy fighter, which dove to earth and exploded.

Captain Mike Sobanski was leading the 336th Squadron's top cover. One Bf-109 made a pass at the flight:

> As he broke away, I saw another Me-109 dive head-on past us, and I followed him down. I gave him a short burst while I was in a seventy-degree dive, observing no strikes. He started pulling up, turning left and I fired a twenty-degree deflection shot. I observed strikes in the wings and near the cockpit. A large puff of white smoke came out after my last burst, and he flicked left, smoking badly. My wingman, First Lieutenant Howard Moulton, saw him go down in flames after he flicked over.

While the top cover was engaged, another group of Bf-109s snuck in behind the P-47s that had just bombed. The Thunderbolt pilots thought they were friendly, and orbited to join up. The 335th's First Lieutenant Paul Ellington later reported, "They turned out all to be Me-109s, about six or eight in number. We engaged them immediately, and three of them dived for the deck." First Lieutenant Kendall "Swede" Carlson shot down a Bf-109, then saw the P-47 flown by the 335th's Second Lieutenant William Rowles with another Bf-109 behind him. "Lieutenant Ellington cut inside of me and took the '109 off the '47's tail." On fire, the enemy fighter crashed on a mud flat. Vermont Garrison and Duane Beeson also claimed a Bf-109 each.

Group executive Lieutenant Colonel Sel Edner led a Ramrod penetration support mission to Emden on February 3 that concluded with the enemy ignoring the Thunderbolts. That changed on February 6, during a penetration target support mission to Romilly, when the Luftwaffe reappeared in force. Some 15–20 enemy fighters continuously attacked the bombers for 40 minutes. The 334th's Flight Officer Ralph Hofer knocked down a Bf-109 while Lieutenants Vermont Garrison and Robert Hobert each destroyed an Fw-190.

Four days later on February 10, escorting bombers to Brunswick, the group battled 25–30 Fw-190s and Bf-109s that made repeated attacks on the bombers between Lingen and Nienburg. Vic France claimed an Fw-190, while "Milly" Millikan, "Red Dog" Norley, and Vermont Garrison claimed Bf-109s with Garrison's claim landing him "ace" status.

On February 14, each of the 4th's three squadrons received a P-51B when the fighters were delivered to Debden. Blakeslee informed the pilots that he expected all to check out in the new fighter between flying combat missions. There would be no down time to permit pilots to transition *en masse*.

# 16

# ONE-MAN AIR FORCE

The 1944 campaign began on January 4 with a radar-bombing mission against Kiel, with Münster as a secondary target. A total of 644 bombers took off, of which 555 were able to bomb the target. Kiel was among several targets the next day; this time, the 215 bombers were able to bomb visually, and inflicted severe damage to the Germania Werft shipyards. On January 7, Ludwigshafen was bombed with radar guidance. The enormous I.G. Farbenindustrie chemical works had been hit on December 30, knocking out the Oppau works, which had halted production after the previous strike and had only resumed production of ammonia two days earlier; no methanol or isobutyl oil was produced for the rest of the month. Once production began again, it would be halted by another radar-bombing attack on February 11 that blocked isobutyl oil production for two weeks and methanol production for five. These chemicals were important to the Luftwaffe in creating MW50, which was used to provide extra engine performance in a fighter powerplant for limited periods.

Heinz Knoke was among the Jagdwaffe pilots who opposed the January 4 mission. He had been granted leave over the Christmas and New Year's holidays to visit his wife and family, but had returned early and was thus able to lead his *Staffel* to oppose the raid. He later wrote in his diary:

At 1002 hours the Squadron takes off for the first mission of 1944. Over Münster we run into fire from our own flak as we attack a strong formation of Fortresses. Closing in to attack one of several separate groups, my aircraft is caught by a direct hit. It immediately becomes tail-heavy. The roar of the engine turns into a high-pitched wail and then into a grating screech, and finally all is silent. One of the flak shells has shot away my propeller, cowling, and the front part of the engine. It is all I can do to hold the aircraft under control.

He was then attacked by a Thunderbolt and hit in the wing, which caught fire. Knoke's wingman Feldwebel Wenneckers turned on the attacker and shot it down.

Knoke had to bail out before the fire reached his cockpit. Jettisoning the canopy and unfastening his harness, he was jerked out of the cockpit by the slipstream. But his seatpack parachute caught on the rear canopy, leaving him with his right leg outside the cockpit while his left was caught inside in the harness straps. The Bf-109G had rolled nearly inverted as it took its final dive toward the ground below:

The terrific force of the slipstream keeps me glued to the back of the fuselage. It whips at my left leg and almost twists it off. I am screaming with pain. It whips at my cheeks and plugs my nostrils. The pressure is such that I can scarcely breathe. The flames are licking across my body. The aircraft begins to flutter, then goes into another spin, practically vertical. I cannot even move my arms in the terrific wind pressure. If I do not somehow get clear of the aircraft it is the end! I have to get clear... get clear... get clear....

The fighter fell 12,000 feet. Finally, with the ground only a few thousand feet below, Knoke was able to hook his right foot around the stick and push it to one side. The fighter rolled, then seemed to stand on its tail while losing speed. No longer pinned by the slipstream, he was able to break free of the cockpit. As he pushed away from the fuselage, he hit his head on the horizontal stabilizer while he tried to pull the D-ring on his parachute. Knocked unconscious, he came to dangling from the open parachute canopy. Breaking through a low cloud layer, he came out a few hundred feet above homes in Münster. When he landed heavily on frozen ground in a garden, he lost consciousness again as the parachute dragged him in the wind.

Coming to again in a hospital, Knoke was told he had a fractured lumber vertebra, a fractured skull with a severe brain concussion, severe bruising of his shoulders and right pelvis, and was temporarily paralyzed on his right side due to displacement of his spine.

The January 5 mission to Kiel saw the 354th Group experience better fortune than they had the day before, when high winds over the North Sea had prevented its timely rendezvous with the bombers. This second mission to Kiel featured slightly better weather when James Howard led the group to provide target support to 245 bombers. The weather became CAVU (Ceiling and Visibility Unlimited) as the force neared Kiel, with the snowy ground below sparkling in the bright sunshine. The Jagdwaffe did not show up until the bombers were turning for home, when some 45–50 Bf-110s and Do-217s appeared.

The 355th Squadron's Second Lieutenant Warren S. "Red" Emerson, who had become separated from his flight, closed alone on six rocket-armed Bf-110s, opening fire on the rearmost 110 from about 200 yards, shattering the canopy while one engine began to smoke heavily. Emerson claimed it as probably destroyed when he saw it going down in an ever-steepening dive, while he turned away and climbed back to 25,000 feet, where he spotted four more Bf-110s and turned to attack. Guns blazing, one of the twin-engine fighters blew up, sending the other three scattering. Minutes later he engaged three more Bf-110s. But this time his Mustang took a hit that damaged the hydraulic lines, while he was struck by a piece of shrapnel that gashed his neck and cut through his parachute harness. At the last moment, he was rescued by the 353rd's Lieutenant Wallace Emmer, who attacked despite being out of ammunition and scattered the enemy fighters.

The 356th's First Lieutenant Richard E. Turner finally got into the thick of things. Flight leader for Starstud Green Flight, he and his wingman, Second Lieutenant Stolzle, and element leader Second Lieutenant Goodnight with wingman Second Lieutenant Miller were directed to cover one of the middle bomber boxes with Starstud Blue Flight. Turner spotted what he later reported was a Do-217 but was almost certainly a Bf-110 that was setting up to the rear of the formation to lob rockets at the bombers. Turner reported:

I tried to come on line astern but overshot the turn, and Lieutenant Goodnight, with his wingman, closed on the enemy. I pulled up and told Lieutenant Stolzle to drop his tanks, after which I spotted another trying to sneak in on the bombers, so I closed in from above and fired at approximately 300 yards, observing strikes on both sides of the fuselage. I continued to close fast and continued firing in bursts of varying lengths. One engine caught fire and started trailing black smoke, and then I observed the right engine blow up in a large flash of flame. The enemy aircraft floundered down in a slow spiral, out of control.

Turner then spotted and fired at another Zerstörer passing overhead, without effect. "I then turned on another which might have been the same as the one just before and followed it down in a twisting turning dive from almost dead astern. I observed strikes but no results. I pulled up in a climbing turn and saw another and started after it." Suddenly he saw tracers fly over his right wing. Glancing back he saw a Bf-110 on his tail instead of his wingman. He pulled the stick back as hard as he could and pulled up into a loop; stalling out while inverted over the Bf-110, which pushed its nose down and dived away. Turner's Mustang fell through the back side of the loop and he was suddenly on the enemy's tail. "I was very close, and fired at zero degrees deflection and saw strikes around the cockpit. Its right engine also caught fire. After I ceased firing I saw the canopy fly off and a round object came into view, which I assumed was the pilot bailing out. I almost collided at this point so I pulled up and away."

The guns in Turner's left wing had jammed, and he was almost out of ammo. Looking around for a P-51 to join with, he saw a single-engine fighter above and climbed to join formation:

Coming up under the single-engined plane, I observed it to be blue-gray instead of dark brown, so I closed to identify it from beneath and behind. I saw the crosses on the fuselage – an Me-109. I tried to line up astern for a shot, but had to be content with 15 degrees deflection to the left with only 20 or 30 rounds coming out, which expended my supply of ammunition.

Fortunately, the enemy pilot split-S-ed down and away and Turner headed home.

Group commander Martin had closed on two Bf-110s which both managed to dive away. He spotted a third and closed to 200 yards. He opened fire and hit the fuselage and the right engine, which caught fire.

Several future group aces got their first victories, including Turner's number four, Lieutenant Tommy "Gnomee" Miller, who shot up two Bf-109s, being later credited with a probable for the first and a definite kill for the second.

With all the Mustangs returning safely to Boxted, the pilots claimed 14 confirmed victories; it was only the group's 12th mission, and its best day so far – an indication of things to come.

The weather over central Germany cleared on January 11, allowing VIII Bomber Command to send 663 B-17s and B-24s to bomb the A.G.O. Fleugzeugwerke A.G. at Oschersleben, which was the main center of Fw-190 production following the destruction of the Marienburg plant in October 1943; the Junkers Fleugzeug und Moterenwerke at Halberstadt, which was producing wings for Ju-88s; and three plants in Brunswick operated by Mühlenbau Industrie A.G. engaged in production of Bf-110s. Such a deep penetration mission – only 90 miles from Berlin – against vitally important aviation targets was expected to bring the Luftwaffe up in numbers.

VIII Fighter Command was able to use 11 groups of P-47s and two groups of P-38s to cover the three different attack formations from the Dutch coast to within 50–70 miles of the target and on the return trip from 100 miles away from the target to the Dutch coast. Six squadrons of RAF Spitfires were detailed to furnish withdrawal escort during the last stage of the route over enemy territory. Only the formation that would strike the Focke-Wulf factory at Oschersleben continued on and would have fighter escort in the target area. This was the assignment of the 354th Group, whose 48 P-51Bs were the only fighters that could cover a target that deep in Germany.

Weather over eastern England made takeoff and assembly difficult. Unfortunately, the en route weather deteriorated so badly that the 3rd Air Division's B-17s and the 2nd Air Division's B-24s were recalled. Several fighter groups found the weather too difficult. The fighters had the worst difficulties; the 4th Group's Steve Pisanos recalled that:

The mission was doomed by bad weather. As we climbed over the North Sea, we could see the forbidding black clouds ahead. Crossing into enemy territory, we were forced to fly through some solid dark clouds, sweating it out for a while until we broke out on top at 33,000 feet. As a result of the weather, our squadron's Green Flight became separated and had to return to base. The other squadrons had similar problems. By the time we had reached the top of the cloud cover, almost half of our group had been forced to turn back. Finally, at 1212 hours, all aircraft were ordered to return to base. Luckily we all got back safely.

By the time the decision to recall was made, the B-17s of the 1st Air Division were 50 miles from the target. The leading combat wing of the 3rd Air Division was so deep in enemy territory when the recall was received that its commander decided to continue on to the primary target. The three remaining 3rd Division wings and all of the 2nd Division Liberators bombed targets of opportunity during their return. Only 238 bombers of the 663rd attacked their primary targets – 139 bombers attacked Oschersleben; 52 bombed Halberstadt; and 47 bombed the M.I.A.G. plant in Brunswick.

With the targets only 60 air miles from Berlin, the Luftwaffe controllers feared that the capital was finally the goal of the American force. The Luftwaffe's reaction demonstrated that the Jagdwaffe had lost none of its ability to exact heavy losses on a deep bomber penetration by daylight since October 14. Indeed, it appeared they had improved their tactics. With the fighters carrying drop tanks, they were able to stay in contact with the bomber formations for extended periods, remaining out of range of the escorts while following the formation until the escorting fighters were forced to return to base or until only a few were left. Dropping their tanks at that point, the enemy pressed home large, coordinated attacks on the unprotected bomber formations. Where the American formation was being flown tight, as was required for mass protection against single-engine fighters, the Bf-110 and Me-410 Zerstörers lobbed rockets into the massed bombers from beyond the defenders' gun range, frequently with deadly effect. Where the defenders' formation spread out, it fell prey to mass attack by single-engine fighters.

The P-51s of the 354th Group rendezvoused with the Oschersleben force to find themselves in the midst of these attacks. James H. Howard, the 356th Squadron leader and most experienced pilot in the group, was leading. He and group commander Colonel Martin had alternated mission lead since the Pioneer Mustangs had been "graduated" by Don Blakeslee. In the five weeks since their first mission, Howard had added two German fighters to his score of six Japanese. The group's existence was still officially "secret" and the P-51B had yet to be publicly revealed. The 354th was referred to in the press as "a newly formed group of the Ninth Air Force with a new long-range fighter plane."

When Howard briefed the mission, he emphasized that pilots were to stick with the group on the way out to rendezvous and not let themselves be enticed into dropping their tanks and going after any German fighters encountered en route. The group climbed to 25,000 feet through a couple of cloud layers and on a course directly to the rendezvous point. Crossing the coast of Holland, it was a clear day, with the sun shining brightly while, below, snow covered the ground. The outside air temperature at altitude was minus 60 degrees Fahrenheit. Over western Germany, Howard spotted a small formation of Bf-109s below, and dispatched Green Flight leader and his wingman to engage them while the rest of the group continued east.

Several minutes later, the Mustangs rendezvoused with the bombers. The bombers were under intense attack by enemy fighters. The Mustangs would have to spread themselves pretty thin to protect that many bombers. Howard first sent the "Fighting Cobras" of the 353rd Squadron to cover the nearest formation, then the "Pugnacious Pups" of the 355th Squadron to cover another. Howard took his 356th Squadron to cover the lead formation.

After he dispatched the flights of the "Red Ass" Squadron (the 356th) Howard suddenly saw a Bf-110 moving up to the rear of the leading bomber group. He maneuvered onto the enemy's tail and waited until his wing span filled the gunsight, opening fire with a four-second burst. The 110 shuddered from the strikes and black and white smoke streamed back, engulfing Howard's P-51. The plane remained level for a moment and then it nosed down. Before it hit the ground, the wings came off and the rest of it tumbled to earth. There was no parachute.

Looking around after the crash of the Zerstörer, Howard saw a Bf-109 taking aim at the bombers. He opened fire on the 109 from about 150 yards and could see flashes from the bullets hitting the fuselage. It spewed smoke and fire and spun down out of control. An instant later, an Fw-190 flew in front of Howard, who pulled up after it in a chandelle. When he was less than a hundred yards behind and ready to open fire, the pilot suddenly jettisoned his canopy and bailed out. Howard wasn't at first aware of what had happened until the pilot's tumbling figure flashed over his cockpit while the 190 nosed over and headed down.

The battle was far from over, as Howard defended the 401st Bomb Group in what is considered one of the most epic fights any American fighter pilot was ever in.

According to the later official account, Howard was up against what was reported as a total of 36 enemy fighters – Bf-109s, Bf-110s, and Fw-190s – that attacked out of the sun. Howard's P-51, now named "Ding Hao!," Chinese for "Very Good!" was the only American fighter in position to oppose the attacking enemy formation. Pushing his throttle "through the firewall," he flew straight at them, attacking first one, then another, as he twisted and turned for several minutes in their midst. His "one-man air force" attack forced the enemy fighters to break away and saved the B-17 formation.

Howard described the fight in his memoir *Roar of the Tiger* somewhat differently:

> Although I never thought I saw thirty-plus enemy fighters at one time, I am in no position to dispute the claims of three hundred pairs of eyes that watched me as I circled the bomb group. I was so busy in my constant pursuit of the enemy fighters, I may not have seen the presence of other enemy aircraft that were out of my visual range... Since I was alone, at first I thought maybe I should filter back to the bombers in the rear, where I could join up with my squadron mates. But the bomber group I was defending seemed to have more than its share of enemy fighters, so I decided to stick around.

After forcing several enemy fighters to break off their attacks, Howard closed on one of the lead 401st B-17s and flew wing with it, throttling back to stay even with it. Suddenly he saw a Bf-110 making a frontal attack on the formation. He turned on it and opened fire. The Bf-110 twisted around several times and ended up on its back. Howard was down to three guns but kept firing until the enemy fighter started smoking and headed down in a steep dive.

The problem of Howard's gun jamming was due to the design of the P-51B, in which the two .50-caliber M2 machine guns were mounted at a 45-degree angle from upright, due to the thinness of the wing. In combat, the G-force could twist the ammunition belt as it curved over to feed into the weapon, jamming the gun. This problem was finally solved by installing electric ammunition feed motors to move the ammunition belts over rollers regardless of the G-forces.

It was not long before Howard spotted a Bf-109 approaching the rear of the formation. From his position in front of the bombers, he pulled up in a loop and came back down in perfect position behind the enemy plane. The enemy pilot spotted Howard and dived, but since he was already in a dive, he was faster. Closing the range he opened fire, to discover he was now down to two guns; his aim was good and he registered strikes on the 109 as the pilot made violent twists and turns to avoid the Mustang. Once the Bf-109 started smoking and its dive steepened, Howard turned back to the bombers, sure his opponent was finished.

Returning to the formation, he spotted another Bf-109 and went after it. He was now down to one working machine gun. He chased that enemy away and returned to the bombers. He had already been with the bombers for nearly 30 minutes, and there were still enemy planes around. With only one gun working, he decided to bluff by making feints in their direction to scare them off.

Howard had to chase away a persistent Ju-88 three times before the enemy dived away for good. After it finally did so, he saw no more enemy planes and decided it was time to set course for England, picking up a couple of stray P-51s as he did.

At Boxted, the pilots were ecstatic. They claimed 18 enemy fighters destroyed, eight probably destroyed, and 16 damaged, with no American losses. Howard recalled, "the bombers had also made mincemeat of their target, but in doing so they had suffered cruelly – fifty-five failed to return." The actual losses for the three formations that bombed targets were 60 missing and presumed shot down by fighters or flak. Howard himself claimed two destroyed, two probables, and two damaged.

Even with the effort by the Pioneer Mustangs, I. and II./JG 26 had been guided to the returning bombers over Belgium. *Gruppenkommandeur* Karl Borris led I./JG 26 in a full *Gruppe*-strength attack against a formation of 19 B-17s west of Nordhorn that lacked escorts. When the slashing German attack was over, eight of the 19 Flying Fortresses had gone down. II./JG 26 found another formation nearby and gunned down three. In the two attacks, defending gunners managed to shoot down four Fw-190s, but the pilots all successfully bailed out.

The men of the 401st Bomb Group spoke to war correspondents when they returned to base about what the anonymous (to them) fighter pilot had done. Major Allison Brooks, who had led the 401st on the mission, stated, "for sheer determination and guts, it was the greatest exhibition I've ever seen. It was a case of one lone American against what seemed like the entire Luftwaffe. He was all over the wing, across and around it. They can't give that boy a big enough award." An article was published in the GI newspaper *Stars and Stripes*, written by Sergeant Andy Rooney, the first time the future famous newsman's name appeared in a byline. At first, it was thought that the 353rd Squadron's Lieutenant Jack Bradley, who claimed two Fw-190s in a ten-second fight, might be the pilot the media was looking for. When Howard's gun camera film was developed and examined at Ninth Air Force headquarters, Howard was given credit for four destroyed and identified as the pilot who had defended the bombers of the 401st single-handedly.

General Spaatz informed Doolittle that it was now time to identify the P-51B to the press, and the Pioneer Mustangs hosted over 100 correspondents on January 16, 1944, for the unveiling of the Mustang and the introduction of Howard, who recalled, "We were taken off the secret list and for the rest of the month there wasn't a day that went by that we weren't invaded by reporters, photographers, and artists trying to cover any willing source of information."

Gladwyn Hill, Associated Press's "Man with the Eighth," remembered the event 40 years later: "Jim Howard was a reporter's dream. He'd been a Flying Tiger, which made him close to legendary, he was good looking so the photographers loved him, and he was older than the average of those kids, so he was better able to handle himself with all the attention." Walter Cronkite, who held a similar assignment with United Press, remembered 50 years later that:

This was the first big press event Eighth Air Force Fighter Command was able to stage. Up to then, the fighter pilots were kids most of us didn't relate to. We couldn't go flying with them, like we could with the bombers, and to tell the truth they hadn't accomplished anything outstandingly newsworthy. They'd obviously been hard at work, but the only thing we ever heard from the bomber crews we knew was how the fighters left just when they were most needed. But with these pilots and that plane, it was obvious the Air Force had solved the problem of being able to stay with them. All my sources in the bomb groups were overjoyed there was now a fighter that could stay with them all the way. Everything heated up the next month, and the fighter pilots became the big story over the spring.

Howard himself remembered, "In general, we enjoyed the press corps visit and the limelight it put us in. For weeks the American press told and retold the story of our exploits – we became national heroes." While he was with the AVG, Howard had only claimed 2.5 aerial victories, though he had also been awarded credit for destroying four others on the ground in the surprise attack made on Moulwein air base; nevertheless, when the press arrived, "Ding Hao" was wearing six Japanese flags in addition to six swastikas for his ETO victories. He was featured in articles in the *Saturday Evening Post* and *Popular Science*, and *True* magazine featured a painting of the battle on its cover with the main feature being Howard's story. The only drawback as Howard saw it was that one reporter had asked if he had been alone during the fight because he had become lost from the rest of the group. "Despite my explanation of how I came to be alone, a story that made that point was printed, and the tale about my being lost came up several times in the following years before it was finally straightened out." Despite the press mistake, upon completion of his combat tour in May, Lieutenant Colonel James O. Howard became the only American fighter pilot in the ETO to be awarded the Medal of Honor, which had been recommended by the crews of the 401st Group who had witnessed his single-handed defense of the bombers over Oschersleben that cold January day.

The January 11 mission had seen VIII Bomber Command suffer the heaviest losses since "Second Schweinfurt" back on October 14. However, this time when 60 bombers were shot down it was not 20 percent of the attacking force; it was 8 percent. This was still higher than the "sustainable" rate of 5 percent or less, but what had been demonstrated was that the newly arrived Mustang-equipped 357th Group needed to be brought operational as quickly as possible, and that the P-47 groups needed to re-equip with the P-51 as soon as the fighters became available, since the 354th had shown what the Mustang could do against the enemy over the target. In addition to the 18 victories claimed by the Pioneer Mustangs, VIII Fighter Command claimed another 13 by the P-47 groups escorting the mission to and from the target.

More important, the bombers had reached and bombed the German fighter factories with good accuracy. The 401st Group that Howard had defended dropped 51 percent of its bombs within 1,000 feet of the aiming point. Two of the groups that hit the Waggum plant near Brunswick dropped, respectively, 73 and 74 percent of their bombs within that 1,000-foot radius. Bomb damage assessment photos showed extensive damage at both plants. At Oschersleben, many buildings were hit directly, while others sustained damage by either bomb bursts or fire. At Waggum almost every major installation received a direct hit.

What bomb damage assessment photos could not show, however, was that in the days after the raids, the workers at the plants returned to the roofless buildings and cleared out the damage, to find that the heavy machine tools that were crucial to production had again escaped destruction because the bombs the Americans dropped were not sufficiently destructive in their explosive force. Despite the cold of winter and the exposure to the elements in the damaged buildings, the work force renewed their production efforts. Within two months, production rates were at some 80 percent of pre-raid levels.

With bad weather over Germany on January 21, VIII Bomber Command launched another strike against the V-1 launch sites under construction in northern France. The weather was so bad over the target that some formations attempting to make clear target identifications through the clouds lost their fighter escorts due to their low fuel state. As the bombers continued to mill about in the murk, I./JG 26's Karl Borris led the *Gruppe* against a 44th Bomb Group B-24 formation that had turned back to England. The 15 Fw-190s made repeated attacks against the Liberators and claimed five. Gunners in the B-24s claimed four German fighters but in fact all returned to their base at Florennes, Belgium. III./JG 26 was not so fortunate, when a *Schwarm* (flight) of four Bf-109G-6s of 12.Staffel was spotted by four P-47s led by the 353rd Group's leading ace, Major Walter Beckham, near St Quentin. The Thunderbolts attacked out of the sun and Beckham sent the number four wingman down in flames as the pilot bailed out. Beckham then turned on the *Rottenführer* in the lead and exploded the enemy fighter for his 14th victory.

The first display of the new, more aggressive VIII Fighter Command fighter escort strategy based on Doolittle's directive took place on January 24. The target was Frankfurt. James Howard was again leading the Pioneer Mustangs. The Jagdwaffe did not come up in force in the poor weather, but the 353rd's second commander, Captain Priser, who had replaced Major Seaman in December when he was lost over the North Sea, was shot down; bailing out successfully, he became a "guest of the Reich" for the rest of the war. Lieutenant Gumm, who had shot down the group's first German fighter, shot down two Bf-109s, while Captain Don Beerbower, and Lieutenants Meserve and Lasko were each credited with a Bf-109 destroyed. Howard led the Red Ass Squadron in a dive on a formation of Bf-110s, but "when I dived, I was blocked by a bunch of eager beavers intent on getting a score." Howard and his wingman returned to cover the bombers.

The 354th was not the only group aggressively chasing the enemy now that it had been let off the leash. The P-47 pilots of the 356th Fighter Group chased a gaggle of 15 German fighters for 65 miles before catching up and downing six of them while one flight chased the eight survivors down to treetop level, where they finished off three more.

In the meantime, after languishing in the hospital for two weeks, Knoke could take it no longer and requested transfer back to the sick quarters on his base at Wünsdorf airfield:

Every morning I was carried out to the dispersal point, where I would spend the day lying in a deck chair wrapped up in heavy blankets. Those must have been the days which caused the hair of our Squadron Medical Officer to turn white. Contrary to his strict orders, I would persist in getting up and trying to walk. At first my paralyzed limbs gave a lot of trouble. Then there was noticeable daily improvement. In time I became accustomed to the never-ending headaches.

Finally, on January 29, the skies cleared sufficiently to allow VIII Bomber Command to send one of the largest forces to date to bomb Frankfurt am Main, known as "the Chicago of Germany," for its importance as a transportation and industrial hub; more than 500 bombers struck the industrial area of the city, led by radar-equipped pathfinders. The mission was one of the first where the fighters operated under Doolittle's new rules allowing them to take the offensive against the enemy. Howard led 40 Mustangs on the mission. Over the target they sighted a number of enemy fighters but were unable to close with them. On the way home a formation of Fw-190s was spotted in the vicinity of Kirchner; the Mustangs fell on them and claimed four kills and two probables without loss.

JG 26's three *Gruppen* caught the bombers as they returned, attacking repeatedly between central Germany and the English Channel. I. and II.Gruppen claimed seven B-17s shot down, another B-17 separated from its formation and a straggler shot down, in addition to two B-24s destroyed and two separated from their formations, as well as a P-47 and a P-38 shot down. The *Geschwader* lost three pilots killed and another wounded.

II./JG 26's 7.Staffel encountered a small group of B-24s, but before they could attack the P-38s of the 20th Fighter Group's 79th Squadron appeared out of the clouds and took on the Fw-190s. One Fw 190 was shot down immediately, while newcomer Gefreiter Alfred Teichmann was caught flying his Fw-190 straight and level by a P-38 that closed his rear to 75 yards and sent him spinning into the clouds below with his fighter engulfed in flames. The next day, 2.Staffel's *Staffelkapitän* Charlie Willius caught a flight from the 79th Squadron and sent two P-38s, including the squadron commander, spinning into the clouds.

On January 29, George Preddy nearly ended his career, when he was bracketed by 88mm flak crossing the Dutch coast returning to England from a mission in which he claimed his third victory, an Fw-190 shot down as it attempted to attack the returning bombers. His wingman, Bill Whisner, who had scored his first victory shooting down Preddy's victim's wingman, later recalled what happened:

I suspect George's radio was unable to receive, though I had heard him call so I knew he could send. We were cruising at about 250 miles per hour at 1,000 feet. As we approached the coast and he took no evasive action before hitting the coastal flak belt, I advised we should get down to low level and increase speed to escape the gunners. When he didn't respond, I told him I was taking evasive action.

Whisner kept Preddy in sight as he dropped down to around 100 feet and increased his speed. "I saw a flak battery that fired a few rounds at me that missed. I looked up and saw four shells explode around

George without effect, then a second barrage went off and he was hit; the airplane started trailing white smoke. I heard him call Marston that he was hit and would likely be going in." Minutes later, Preddy's engine stopped and he started gliding toward the water below. "He went into the undercast. I made a 360 and went down after him. I was just approaching 100 feet and about to pull up when I popped out of the cloud over the Channel in time to see his P-47 hit the water, and then a minute later he touched down in his parachute."

Preddy was able to get into his raft, but the water and air temperature were both about 40 degrees. He only had minutes before he would freeze in his wet clothing. Manston Control told Whisner he was too low to get a fix. "I climbed back on top and circled. They told me the Walrus was ten minutes away." Below, Preddy saw the approaching Walrus. He later recalled that when it touched down, it caught a float on a wave and lost it. "They nearly taxied over me twice, but then I got into the water and they pulled me out." Thoroughly chilled, Preddy was more than grateful to accept the quart bottle of brandy the crew kept for such an occasion. Surviving a crash in the Channel was risky in mid-summer; Preddy had been incredibly lucky that the Walrus had been nearby, having failed to locate another downed flier.

On January 30, the pathfinders led almost as many bombers to strike Brunswick, again bombing through clouds. Howard again led the 354th to provide target cover. Howard later recalled that before the Mustangs reached the bomber formations, he saw Thunderbolts tangling with the German fighters. Off to the left, he spotted a gaggle of Bf-109s, Bf-110s, Fw-190s, and Ju-88s setting up for an attack. He made a wingover and dived with 15 P-51s behind. The surprise attack was so complete that the 110s did not have time to break. Howard fired a long burst at the nearest one; the plane caught fire and spun down. He pulled up, but by that time the rest of them had gotten the news and dived away.

The Mustangs then joined the bombers and took up their escort positions, with Howard and the 356th Squadron at the head of the formation. Specks in the distance soon resolved themselves as 30 Bf-109s. The squadron followed him as Howard dived on them. About half got through and a giant dogfight quickly ensued with the P-51s getting the upper hand. Howard chased a 109, firing at it until it smoked, then turned back to the bombers. He then saw several Fw-190s making passes at a group of B-24s. A couple of the Liberators began smoking. Then the 109s the Mustangs had chased came back and Howard dived on them while they were still in a climb. Approaching Tail-end Charlie, he fired a long burst. He turned over and headed straight down. This was Howard's fifth victory, making him the first P-51B ace (two other pilots "made ace" in the Mediterranean and Southeast Asia, flying an A-36 and a P-51A, respectively, in late 1943).

Richard Turner, newly promoted to captain and flying his P-51B "Short Fuse Sallee," spotted another straggling B-17 being attacked by four Bf-109s. He immediately led his flight in an attack on the enemy, three of which broke for the clouds below while the fourth continued his attack. Turner dropped 30 degrees of flaps to keep from overrunning and opened fire at about 200 yards at zero degrees deflection. He saw that his fire was going underneath the 109, and raised the pip, whereupon the fighter exploded. Turner was so close that he flew through the explosion.

The group claimed five destroyed on the mission, again for no losses. The new year of 1944 had begun well for the newcomers, with the 354th now officially credited with 42 victories for the loss of only three pilots.

That same day, II./JG 11 was ordered to transfer from Wünsdorf back to its previous base at Hilversum in Holland. Knoke managed to force himself into the cockpit of a Bf-109 and took off with the others. As they broke out of the overcast into the sunshine over Holland, they were attacked by a formation of RAF Spitfires. "We are taken completely by surprise, and we cannot put up effective opposition to the Tommies. They drive us off in a wild chase. It is a case of every man for himself. I never once have a chance to fire. We suffer heavy casualties." Knoke's fighter was hit in the engine and he was barely able to make a successful crash-landing a mile short of their destination. Knoke recorded in his diary that 4.Staffel lost five pilots killed, 6.Staffel lost three, and the *Gruppe Stab* (Group Staff) one. Knoke's 5.Staffel lost Feldwebel Nowotny, who had only been posted to the unit three weeks earlier. The survivors were flown back to Wünsdorf in a Ju-52 transport.

On January 31, the 356th Squadron's Second Lieutenant Mo Tyner took a P-51 that had just come out of the shop up for a test flight after having an engine malfunction worked on. Minutes after taking off, those on the ground heard the scream of a Merlin out of control.

Howard recalled looking up just in time to see the P-51's nose break off while the rest of the airframe fell straight into the ground. Examination of the engine revealed that the engine mount bolts had come loose and were missing. A quick inspection showed that almost all the Mustangs had loose engine mount bolts. The group's assistant engineering officer, Lieutenant Konopka, drove all night to the main depot at Burtonwood, where he scrounged the needed bolts. The next day, the ground crews replaced all the bolts on the Mustangs. This was only one of many faults with the early P-51Bs. Howard recalled that the propeller shaft threw oil, which obscured vision through the windshield, and the windshield heating was inadequate, with the result that canopies would suddenly frost over at altitude. The early oxygen tanks weren't large enough to supply oxygen for the long missions they were flying. There were coolant leaks and the sparkplugs got oiled up until they were replaced with English Lucas sparkplugs.

The Wolfpack solidified their claim as the leading group on January 30, when they scored their 200th aerial victory since arriving in England a year earlier. The P-47s claimed 17 enemy aircraft shot down, with Bud Mahurin keeping his status as VIII Fighter Command's leading ace, scoring one to raise his personal score to 15, one more than the 353rd Group's Walter Beckham. Bob Johnson's claim of two tied him with Beckham, while Gabby Gabreski also scored a double to become the third-ranked ace of the command. The same day, the 4th scored their hundredth victory.

On February 3 and 4, maximum efforts of more than 500 bombers in each mission participated in pathfinder attacks against Wilhelmshaven, Emden, and Frankfurt. The size and scale of these radar-bombing missions, with their frequency, was impressive. General Arnold, who had for months been eager to increase both the rate and scale of bombing, was particularly encouraged. But this was not the precision bombing that was necessary to destroy the targets on the *Pointblank* list; they were no substitute for the long-planned campaign against specific factories in the German aircraft industry required to meet the goal of defeating the Luftwaffe. The weather closed in again on February 5. Between then and February 19, VIII Bomber Command flew only three relatively light pathfinder missions to Frankfurt and Brunswick. The raids might have been larger, but the force was still using the same number of radar-equipped planes and trained crews as at the end of

1943. Operations had to be cut to fit the number of pathfinder planes and crews available.

Overall, the January air battles were indecisive for both sides, but the tide was turning in favor of the Americans in the war of attrition. Despite the limited operational opportunities in January, the Jagdwaffe lost 160 irreplaceable pilots and 391 aircraft in battles against VIII Fighter Command, 25 percent of its total strength. JG 26 lost 14 pilots killed in combat and another six when low-time newcomers succumbed in weather-related accidents. II./JG 26 *Gruppenkommandeur* Major Wilhelm Gaeth was shot down and badly wounded on January 14. Losses were such that when 5.Staffel's *Staffelkapitän* Hauptmann Johann Aistleitner was also killed in action on January 14, Oberfeldwebel Adolf "Addi" Glunz was appointed *Staffelführer*, the first non-commissioned officer of JG 26 to hold such a position.

The 357th Fighter Group had started sending pilots to fly missions with the 354th Group after it received all 48 P-51Bs assigned to the 257th Group and the pilots were checked out in them by mid-January. On January 14, group commander Colonel Chickering, with squadron commanders Majors Don Graham and Hubert Egenes, flew with 40 other 354th Group Mustangs led by Major Bickell, escorting 552 bombers to the Pas de Calais area on one of the first missions to bomb launch sites being built for the V-1 cruise missile. The weather closed in and it was not till January 24 that Captains Joseph Giltner, Joseph Broadhead, Ed Hiro, and John Storch were able to fly the mission that James Howard led, escorting the bombers to Frankfurt. Near Antwerp, Giltner's flight was bounced by Fw-190s. He managed to get on the tail of an Fw-190 and send it down on fire, but the wingman claimed him moments later, making him both the 357th's first pilot to score a victory and the first group loss.

Finally, on February 1, 1944, the trade between Eighth and Ninth Air Forces was official, and the 357th became the first VIII Fighter Command Mustang-equipped group, while the P-47-equipped 358th Group went to IX Tactical Air Command. The two groups also exchanged bases, with the 357th moving to Station F-373, located between the villages of Leiston, Saxmundham, and Theberton. Although the base was officially named Leiston, Nazi propaganda broadcaster "Lord Haw-Haw" chose the name of a village further from the field than the others, using it to name the new group "the Yoxford Boys" during an evening radio program. As an impudent reply to the Nazis, the 357th soon adopted this as its group name.

Even with the heavy losses incurred on January 11, VIII Bomber Command losses were 2.5 percent, well in the "sustainable" range. While VIII Bomber and Fighter Commands had nearly tripled in size since Black Thursday, the Jagdwaffe was starving for new pilots, and veterans like Knoke pushed themselves to return to operations when they should have continued under medical care for their wounds.

Spaatz and Doolittle assured Arnold that they only needed one week of clear weather to turn the tables on the enemy.

# 17

# BIG WEEK

At the outset of February, 1944, General "Hap" Arnold wrote his old friend and comrade, General Carl Spaatz, regarding his concerns about the way in which the Combined Bomber Offensive was being handled, worried that RAF Bomber Command might overshadow the USAAF effort. He concluded:

> Already, the spectacular effectiveness of their devastation of cities has placed their contribution in the popular mind at so high a plane that I am having the greatest difficulty in keeping your achievement in its proper role, not only in publications, but unfortunately in military and naval circles, and in fact, with the President himself.

After a year, VIII Bomber Command had not achieved the goals set with the approval of Operation *Pointblank* in the previous summer, or those agreed to at the recent Cairo Conference. The Soviets were calling loudly for the opening of the long-delayed Second Front. To put it bluntly, as Jimmy Doolittle recalled Spaatz saying, it was "time to fish or cut bait." Doolittle sent a public message to the men he commanded: "During the next few months it is mandatory that we secure complete air superiority over the German Air Force in this Theater... we must adopt every expedient to improve the effectiveness of the Air Force."

The plans for Operation *Argument* were first developed in November 1943. The goal was destruction of the German aviation industry, accomplished through a series of closely spaced attacks against the aircraft factories. Such a blow over a short period would prevent the enemy from having the ability to repair the factories one at a time, stretching repair capacity beyond its limits. The operation was not immediately possible due to the continuing bad winter weather. In the meantime, new bomb groups became operational, while VIII Fighter Command re-equipped the P-47 groups with new aircraft that had extended range; most importantly, by the time the weather finally broke in February 1944, there were two operational P-51 Mustang groups that could cover the bombers over the most distant targets.

In the meantime, the fighter groups discovered the hard way that following Doolittle's new directive to attack German airfields came with a cost.

On February 8, James Howard and group commander Martin agreed that if there was no major Luftwaffe response to the coming mission, on the return flight they would look for a German airfield to strafe. As it turned out, they experienced their worst losses when they did so. Lurking German fighters hit the Mustangs as they approached the target; Lieutenant Jack Turk was shot down and killed. Two other group pilots failed to return; no one knew what happened to them. Howard later described the light flak defending the airfield as "horrific."

On February 10, the 354th got its revenge during a mission to Brunswick that resulted in claims for eight destroyed and 18 damaged, for loss of two pilots. Colonel Martin claimed his fourth victory in a twisting dogfight with a Bf-109 that ended when it caught fire and the pilot immediately bailed out.

The next day, First Lieutenant James "Slick" Morris from the 20th Group's 77th Squadron, who had shot down four Bf-110s on February 8, was leading the squadron's Blue Flight when Bf-109s attacked Yellow Flight. Morris led his flight to the rescue, closing on a Bf-109 that was on the tail of "Yellow Four." "I opened up at a 60-degree deflection, mostly hoping to scare the Jerry off Yellow Four." The concentrated fire of four .50-caliber machine guns and a 20mm cannon caught the enemy fighter in its engine; smoke and flames leaped from beneath the cowling and the airplane fell off into a spin and disappeared into the undercast. With this victory, Morris became the first P-38 ace in the ETO. The victory came at a high cost, though; eight P-38s failed to return to King's Cliffe, in return for claims of three destroyed.

Hub Zemke learned the danger of airfield strafing on February 11. Returning from the Frankfurt mission, Zemke spotted a large airfield in northern France and decided it would be the group's first airfield strafing. Zemke led the 61st Squadron, followed by the 62nd while the 63rd flew high cover. He dropped down to low level some distance from the target in hopes that the antiaircraft gunners had not spotted the fighters. The four lead P-47s raced across the French countryside at 340 miles per hour, just above the treetops. Before they knew it, they were over the field. Zemke saw several 109s in a hangar. He lifted his nose and hosed the aircraft. In an instant, he was over and past the target. He fired a final burst and the Thunderbolts were past the field. All the Thunderbolts returned successfully to Halesworth, but Zemke had seen enough to know that hitting the Luftwaffe on its home bases was going to be a task few, if any, would relish.

A few weeks later Zemke circulated a strategy that became the "bible" for strafing airfields. Airfields spotted were put on a list for future action, rather than subjected to an immediate strike. With full information about the locality, a group approached at low level, dropping to treetop level several miles from the field, flying line abreast so that everyone was over the target simultaneously to divert the flak gunners; it made one pass only, then stayed low for another five miles before pulling up to be certain it was out of flak range. When a target was too juicy to pass on first sight, the rule was to fly past as though it was unspotted, drop down to the deck 20 miles away, and return for a single pass. Any other method was certain to increase casualties.

Operation *Argument*'s goal was achieving air superiority by striking targets the Jagdwaffe couldn't ignore. *Argument* was not primarily a bombing campaign. As important as the factories were, the bombers were sent to attract fighters; the purpose was to kill fighters in the factory or the sky, and their pilots. On January 19, three frustrating months of bad weather ended; the USSTAF weather section became aware of two extensive high pressure areas, one in the Baltic and one just west of Ireland, which would give good weather over central Europe and the home bases. If the one over the Baltic moved across Europe as anticipated, it would leave clear skies or, at worst, scattered clouds in its wake. The weather observers of Eighth and Ninth Air Forces shared USSTAF's confidence. The first mission was laid on for the next day. The resulting battles became known as "Big Week."

The force assembled on January 20 was the largest in the history of the American strategic forces. Sixteen wings of heavy bombers flew the mission – 1,003 B-17s and B-24s – of which 941 were credited with the mission. Both VIII Fighter Command and IX Tactical Air Command provided fighter escort: 13 P-47, two P-38, and two P-51 groups. Additionally, RAF Fighter Command provided 16 squadrons – 12 flying Spitfire IXs and four Mustang IIIs.

The targets were the aircraft production factories in the Brunswick-Leipzig region, only 80 miles south of Berlin. As the formations entered Germany, the clouds cleared as the forecasters had said. The 56th Group's Thunderbolts, with 150-gallon belly tanks for the first time, led the way; the new tanks allowed them to penetrate 400 miles. "Gabby" Gabreski, leading A group, later remembered that the enemy failed to show up until the Thunderbolts were over Dummer Lake, where they would break off. Suddenly, he spotted 30 Bf-110 night fighters – identifiable by the radar "horns" on their noses – a thousand feet below and dived on them, followed by the squadron. The night fighter crews had no experience fighting in daylight and paid the price. In ten minutes, all but one were damaged or destroyed. The pilots claimed eight destroyed, one probable, and ten damaged back at Halesworth. The records of III./ZG 76, the unit they hit, listed 18 losses and the rest damaged.

The B group, led by Dave Schilling, was 23 minutes behind. They spotted a gaggle of Bf-109s attempting to form up to attack. In a wild fight B group claimed six destroyed, one probable, and eight damaged. The 62nd's Captain Leroy Schreiber claimed three of the 109s.

The 354th, led by James Howard following Colonel Martin's loss, provided target cover, along with the new 357th. The Mustangs flew over 1,100 miles round-trip, the longest mission yet. Howard later remembered that they converged on the bomber stream on time, just short of the turn onto the Initial Point (IP). Suddenly enemy fighters appeared from everywhere and he called for the Mustangs to drop tanks. There were more than 50 Fw-190s below, which scattered when they saw the P-51s diving on them. When Howard pulled up from the attack, he could see four going down in smoke; two of the pilots were seen to bail out. Howard went after a 190; as "Ding Hao" passed through 15,000 feet, Howard's wingman called out two enemy fighters on their tail. Howard immediately pulled up and partially blacked out as he did, but plane and pilot held together. As he circled, the enemy must have gone after another target, for his pursuers were nowhere to be seen.

Don Beerbower, leading the 356th's Blue Flight, spotted a *Schwarm* of Bf-109s 1,500 feet below. They dived onto the enemy fighters:

> I closed the formation leader and fired a four-second burst from dead astern at 200 yards. He started smoking and exploded just as I turned left to avoid a collision. I broke into his wingman just as he rolled over in a split-S. I fired a two-second burst from a hundred yards at a 25 degree deflection and saw strikes along the wing root and cockpit as he started smoking and went down.

Beerbower lost his wingman, so he joined another flight. Spotting two Bf-110s, the Mustangs missed them in their first pass, but one made a slow right turn that put him in front of Beerbower:

> I crossed over and attacked from his left and above. I fired several long bursts and hit his left engine, which exploded, throwing the aircraft up on its right wing. I pulled my fire into the cockpit, and he came apart in an explosion. I flew through the pieces of airplane as the main part flipped over on its back. I pulled up and saw two chutes open, then I joined with another P-51 and we flew home.

The 4th covered withdrawal. Steve Pisanos reported, "We intercepted a gaggle of enemy fighters about to attack the bombers and destroyed four, while only losing one of our own."

First Lieutenant Pierce McKennon and wingman Second Lieutenant Bernard McGrattan spotted a gaggle of Bf-109s, Fw-190s, and Bf-110s attacking with rockets. Both overshot them, but McKennon managed to tack onto the tail of an Fw-190 and opened fire. "I was going to give him another burst when the '190 half-rolled and the pilot bailed out."

The 335th's First Lieutenants Paul Ellington and Clemens Fiedler scored a Bf-110 each; First Lieutenant Paul Riley and Second Lieutenant Richard Reed shared a third Zerstörer. Moments later, Reed was shot down and killed by a pair of Fw-190s near Aachen.

Five minutes later, Duane Beeson sighted two Fw-190s below the bombers. "They were about 5,000 feet directly below, and as we circled around to come in on their tails, they both began to go around in a circle, and we ended up with Green Section coming at them straight down from above." As Beeson finally got behind them, another Thunderbolt caused them to dive away:

> The other P-47 was nearer than me, and closing fast, so I waited for him to get the second one so I might take the leader. He overshot and they whipped around in a starboard turn, so I closed in on number two, who began to climb just as his leader dived for the cloud. I opened fire and got good strikes around his fuselage and on his wings. As I overshot him, he pulled straight up and jettisoned his cockpit hood, then bailed out.

Henry Mills saw a Thunderbolt chasing an Fw-190:

> The P-47 started to overshoot and broke to the right. I closed in, firing from astern and above. He pulled up ahead of me and I pulled through deflection so that he was under my nose and opened fire, firing until I was less than 50 yards from him. I broke at the last instant to keep from ramming him. He pulled off slowly to my left, smoking slightly, and the pilot bailed out in front of Captain Care, who was following me.

Mills was now an ace.

The mission marked the first time that the 357th Group met the enemy. They were led again by Don Blakeslee. Light snow was falling when they took off, but the weather cleared by the time they crossed the Channel. Their assignment was target support for the 1st Division over Leipzig. Thy claimed their first victories when several Bf-109s jumped Lieutenant Calvert Williams' 362nd Squadron flight. One overshot and Williams immediately opened fire, sending it down trailing black smoke. The 363rd's Donald Ross tangled with another pair of Bf-109s and shot down the wingman, but was so close behind that when it exploded, he was forced to fly through the explosion; his radiator was damaged by debris sucked into the belly intake. His Merlin quickly overheated and Ross was forced to bail out.

Flight leader Bud Anderson of the 363rd was fighting the cold in his cockpit when he spotted an Fw-190 4,000 feet below. He dived and came out 300 yards behind; the enemy pilot evaded with a split-S. Anderson followed. "I was determined I would go wherever he went, do whatever he did. I wanted a victory." Suddenly, he felt an unexpected blast of cold air and looked up to see that the "coffin lid" was lifting, separating from the side piece as the canopy latch started to fail. It got worse as he went through 11,000 feet at nearly 500 miles per hour. Prudence finally won out; he pulled the throttle back, then nosed up into a climb and rejoined the group. Years later, he said, "Thinking about it afterwards, I realized I had come close to doing something unforgivably dumb."

During the battles over Leipzig and Brunswick, 21 of the 941 bombers were shot down, while the escorts lost four. They claimed 61 enemy fighters shot down; Luftwaffe records admitted loss of 53 Bf-109s and Fw-190s, and 25 Bf-110s. Only 362 German defensive sorties were flown, less than half the number expected.

First Lieutenant Grant Turley, from the 78th's 84th Squadron, had scored his first two victories in December, then added two more on February 11. He wrote his parents to tell them he had scored his fifth on this day's mission:

Bad weather all week, no flying till today. Eight Fw-190s were encountered over Belgium. Yours truly got one bringing his total to five. Well, I'm an ace now. It is a thrill and yet not nearly as much as I thought it would be. Sometimes I wish that we didn't have them outnumbered so badly. But in war you can't let your feelings get the upper hand. After all, it is he or you!

VIII Bomber Command leaders had been prepared for the loss of 200 bombers. The results were more than they had expected in their wildest dreams; reports indicated that four assembly plants in Leipzig had been hit hard. The fighters scored an even more one-sided victory than was claimed. Spaatz was euphoric as report after report was received listing one or two – or more frequently no – losses; in the end, the losses were 2.8 percent. Spaatz was described as "on the crest of the highest wave he had ever ridden," in the memory of one staffer.

With a forecast for more marginal – though flyable – weather, teletyped orders went out at 0100 hours on February 21. This time, it was factories in Brunswick and Braunschweig; crews groaned when told they would return to Brunswick a second time in as many days. Dawn revealed that the weather over England was much better than before; there was no difficulty assembling.

Unfortunately, the weather over Germany was not as good. Thus, bombing results at Brunswick were not what was hoped for. Due to the bad weather, the 762 bombers followed the H2X-equipped pathfinders; the city was hit by area bombing. Losses were again lower than expected, only 16 lost and seven written off after returning damaged.

The fighters performed above expectations. Colonel Henry Spicer, who had replaced Colonel Chickering as commander of the 357th on February 17, led them to Braunschweig. Bud Anderson was not on the flight schedule, but his brand new P-51B-5, which had received the name "Old Crow," was flown by First Lieutenant Alfred Boyle. Shortly after they entered Holland, a gaggle of Bf-109s was spotted trying to attack. Boyle's flight went after them and he got on the tail of one in a wild dive. Closing to 50 yards astern, Boyle opened fire; the 109 disintegrated, but pieces of debris damaged his propeller and he followed squadron mate Ross into captivity after bailing out of the tumbling Mustang. When Anderson learned that his new airplane had been lost, he pretended to be upset but later wrote, "By now I was getting pretty good at blocking out unpleasant distractions. I was developing a thick hide."

The 56th were again the top scorers, claiming 12 destroyed. Two were the first claims of an eventual ten by Squadron Leader Michael Gladych during his unofficial service with the group. Gladych, who graduated from the Polish Air Force Academy the day that World War II began, escaped Poland and claimed 17 victories with the RAF. Removed from operations following his second tour, he contacted Gabreski, whom he knew from Gabreski's time with 302 Squadron; he unofficially joined the squadron, assigned to organize combat flight training for new pilots. Five Poles eventually arrived at Halesworth over the spring of 1944, welcomed by Zemke, who valued their experience and insured that they were not listed among group personnel.

That night, the forecast was again favorable for visual bombing the next day. The high pressure ridge was moving south, opening up Regensburg and Schweinfurt. Thought was given to attacking the Erkner ball bearing factory near Berlin, but spreading the force that much would disperse the force. The weather was good over Italy; Fifteenth

Air Force would strike Regensburg. VIII Bomber Command, which had just been renamed the Eighth Air Force, would bomb Schweinfurt, Gotha, Bernburg, Oschersleben, Aschersleben, and Halberstadt.

The missions did not go as well as before. Bad weather over 3rd Air Division's bases made it impossible to assemble, with several mid-air collisions as they struggled through heavy clouds. Curtis LeMay was forced to order the Schweinfurt force to abandon the mission. Second Division's B-24s – assigned to strike Gotha – ran into poor weather that left them strung out crossing the Channel; unable to re-organize, the mission was recalled. Thus, only the five 1st Division wings continued into Germany. Their targets were Oschersleben, Halberstadt, Bernburg, and Aschersleben. Unfortunately, Oschersleben – the most important – had a thick cloud layer; they were forced to find targets of opportunity. Poor weather over Halberstadt forced another search for targets of opportunity. Only 99 of the 466 bombers sent out bombed their primary target; only 255 bombed any target. Better weather over Bavaria and Austria allowed the Fifteenth's 183 B-17s and B-24s to strike Regensburg, with 118 hitting the Messerschmitt factory at Obertraubling.

Bombing results were very uneven, though the 34 B-17s attacking the Aschersleben Motor Works that assembled Ju-88s caused a 50 percent production loss over the next two months. The Bernburg factory saw 70–80 percent destruction of the assembly buildings.

German fighter tactics changed. Rather than concentrating in the target area and the later stages of the flight toward the target, the *Jagdgruppen* attacked as the bombers crossed into the Low Countries, when their cover was reduced or not yet present. Of 430 bombers, 41 were lost. Splitting formations to seek targets of opportunity spread the escorts too thin to give cover. Regardless, the escorts claimed 60 destroyed for a loss of 11. The Fifteenth lost 14 shot down over Regensburg.

While I./JG 26 made no claims in two missions and III.Gruppe claimed only one P-47, II./JG 26 flew missions as the bombers crossed into Belgium and on their return. Oberfeldwebel "Addi" Glunz, the only *Experte* never shot down during his years on the Western Front, led 5.Staffel and had his best day ever. On the first mission, Glunz claimed two B-17s shot down and a third separated from formation, while the rest of II.Gruppe claimed two more B-17s for the loss of one pilot. On the return, Glunz claimed two more B-17s shot down and a P-47 destroyed.

Feldwebel Peter Crump of 6.Staffel experienced his most difficult day in two years on the Western Front with JG 26. On the first mission, he attempted to attack the bombers unsuccessfully, unable to penetrate the escorts. Landing at Duisburg to refuel from a drum using a hand pump, he flew to Düsseldorf where the *Gruppe* had been ordered to reassemble. Once there, he found that only his *Staffelkapitän*, Hauptmann Horst Sternberg, and a young *Nachwuchs* from 5.Staffel, Unteroffizier Paul Gross, were present from the *Gruppe*. The dozen Bf-109s and Fw-190s from different *Gruppen* were ordered to fly to Venlo in Holland to reinforce JG 11 and JG 1. Before takeoff, Sternberg ordered Crump and Gross to stay with him, regardless.

Arriving over Venlo, the 12 fighters joined another mixed force of 40 fighters that had just taken off. When the homeward-bound bombers were spotted, the group leader turned to attack. Crump was astonished to see Sternberg turn away and head toward a badly damaged B-17 trailing smoke, straggling below the others. Crump looked up and saw 12 P-47s diving on them!

The 4th provided withdrawal support on this mission; the 48 Thunderbolts were about to rendezvous when 335th Squadron commander Major George Carpenter spotted Sternberg's threesome just as several parachutes blossomed when the crew began abandoning the B-17. Carpenter flew past Crump, who fired a burst that raked the Thunderbolt but did no damage, as Carpenter opened fire on Sternberg from 300 yards. He attempted to evade, but Carpenter stayed with the darting Fw-190, continuing to fire as pieces flew off Sternberg's fighter. At 500 feet, he pulled up and watched the Fw-190 hit the ground and explode.

Poor Unteroffizer Gross, with barely enough training to keep his fighter straight and level, found himself under fire from Captain Raymond Care. He could only make gentle turns, but they were enough that Care pulled off and came around again. Closing from 50 to 30 yards, Care set the Fw-190 on fire. Gross was seen to bail out, but he bled to death from his wounds before reaching the ground.

Crump executed a split-S and dived for his life as four Thunderbolts from Green Flight chased him to the deck, but were unable to close into firing range and eventually gave up. His problems weren't over;

three P-47s from the 78th's 83rd Squadron spotted him and took up the chase. Unhit, Crump tried to out-climb them, but their new paddle props put them on him quickly; he turned as tight as possible as the P-47 opened fire. Crump later recalled: "Suddenly my stick was ripped from my hands and a rush of flames shot past my face. So this is what it is like to be shot down! With a single motion, I threw off the canopy, drew up my legs and jumped out."

Crump immediately pulled his D-ring as soon as he cleared the tail. "Apart from tearing ligaments in my right leg when I contacted the frozen bare ground – it was winter after all – and a minor flesh wound, I had survived the disaster in good health." He lost consciousness and came to in a farmer's home 30 minutes later. "I was in Germany, about 24 kilometers [15 miles] north of Aachen." The farmer told him that three German fighters had crashed near the village, as well as two B-17s that barely missed several homes. The authorities arrived and took Crump to investigate. "My plane dug a deep crater in the embankment of a small stream. When I was taken to the others, my fears were confirmed – they were the other two members of my flight, both dead."

Major Jack Oberhansly led 78A group to Cologne, where they found the bombers under attack by 40 Bf-109s and Fw-190s. The Germans spotted the Thunderbolts and broke off, diving for the ground; the Thunderbolts followed in a fight that went from 22,000 feet to the deck. Oberhansly shot down a Bf-109 while Lieutenant Alvin Jucheim blew up a second. Captain Kenneth Dougherty chased four to the deck. Having lost his wingman, he discovered that another four had latched onto his tail. Jinking to avoid his pursuers, he fired at the lead pair and set the wingman on fire. With the 109s behind getting closer, Dougherty pushed his throttle to "war emergency" and pulled away as he climbed to rejoin the others. Back at Duxford, he praised the new water injection system and paddle blade prop.

Leaving Germany, Oberhansly spotted a damaged Fw-190 approaching Gilze-Rijen airdrome. He quickly attacked and exploded it just as the pilot lowered his gear on final approach. Spotting two Fw-190s that turned after the P-47s, he and his wingman stayed low, roaring across the Zuider Zee. As the pursuers closed, Oberhansly told his wingman they would turn and fight on his signal. Just as he was about to call the break, the sky was lit by an explosion when the two pursuers collided as they maneuvered to take on the Americans.

Harry Dayhuff, at the head of 78B group, caught 25 Fw-190s west of Dummer Lake trying to form up. The Thunderbolts tore into them and scored seven for no losses. Returning from this mission, Pete Pompetti and his wingman strafed an airdrome near St Wendel, hitting two Bf-109s. Pompetti then saw a group of German officers near a staff car and kicked his rudder to strafe them. "They ran into the fields on both sides of the road, and due to my closeness to the ground I do not know whether I hit them."

The 56th caught enemy fighters in the vicinity of Dummer Lake, which the Wolfpack now considered the "Happy Hunting Ground." The 61st Squadron claimed 17 destroyed without loss. These victories gave the squadron a score of 100 shot down in eight months since its first credited victory back in June 1943.

Heinz Knoke, who had still not recovered completely from his January injuries, led the five surviving pilots of his *Staffel* in combat that afternoon. He later wrote:

Today the bomber stream happened to pass directly over my old home town, Hamelin. By a strange chance I go into action directly over the familiar hills and mountains just west of town. Accompanied by Corporal Krüger, who was posted to the *Staffel* only two days ago, I attack a Fortress in a formation of about 30 heavy bombers. In a frontal attack, I place my first salvo directly in the cockpit. I come in again, this time diving down upon my victim from above the tail until a collision is imminent. The Fortress tries weaving out of my line of fire and swerves sharply round to the left. Yet my shells continue to plaster the left wing and left side of the fuselage. Flames come belching out of the tail. I pull in close beneath the monster fuselage and continue blasting away with all I have in the magazines.

Then the crew bail out. The fuselage is a blazing torch. It makes a wide sweep round to the left and begins to go down, its passage marked by a long trail of black smoke. Hamelin is directly below. The blazing Fortress dives ever more steeply, and soon it is in a vertical spin. It crashes in a pasture beside the river at the south end of my old home town. A tower of flame spurts high into the air. The pasture directly across the river was the one from which as a boy I had taken off for my first flight during that air display so long ago.

At that moment a second aircraft comes hurtling down out of the sky. It crashes in a lumber yard at the south end of Hamelin, on the premises of the Kaminski wagon-manufacturing and repair workshops. It was my wingman, the young Corporal. This was his first mission. I swoop low over the flaming wreckage, but he was killed instantly. In a wide sweep I fly low over the rooftops of my old rat-hole. The streets are deserted. All the good citizens of Hamelin are no doubt sitting timidly in their cellars and shelters.

While the American escorts submitted claims for January 22 of 60 destroyed, the Jagdwaffe admitted to the loss of 48 Fw-190s and Bf-109s, and 16 Bf-110s and Me-410s.

The weather report that night predicted cloudy skies over Germany; Eighth Air Force stood down for a day. Doolittle welcomed the break, since his crews had made three successive "maximum effort" missions. That night, the weathermen spotted another high-pressure ridge moving across Germany and promised weather good enough for visual bombing. The target would be Schweinfurt, site of so much death and destruction for VIII Bomber Command on August 17 and October 14, 1943.

The 1st Air Division's five combat wings went to Schweinfurt, while the 2nd Division's B-24s hit Gotha, where the Gothaer Waggonfabrik A.G. produced Me-410s. LeMay's 3rd Division was sent against aircraft component factories and assembly plants in northeastern Germany and Poland at Tutow, Kreising, and Posen, where Fw-190s were produced. The Fifteenth sent bombers to Steyr, Austria. The targets in north Germany and Poland were beyond the reach of even P-51s, which meant they would strike unescorted. Visions of 1943-level losses were mitigated by plans to have the other strikes occur when the northern force lost its escorts, in hopes that enemy controllers would not be able to divert defending fighters against this mission. As it worked out, poor weather over north Germany and Poland kept enemy fighters away, but also contributed to bombing results that were less than what planners had hoped for.

While the northern force did not meet strong aerial opposition, the 1st and 2nd Air Divisions striking Schweinfurt and Gotha and the 87 B-17s that flew to Steyr experienced attacks by formations of four to six single-engine fighters, twin-engine aircraft firing rockets at long range, and aerial bombs. At Steyr, the rear formation was hit hard; all ten bombers were shot down while the whole force lost 17 in total, despite excellent withdrawal support by 146 P-47s and P-38s. The B-24s attacking Gotha had almost continuous fighter cover; despite this, they suffered persistent, concentrated attacks, particularly over the target, resulting in loss of 33 of the 239. Losses were considerably less with the Schweinfurt force, only 11 failing to return. The escorts claimed 37 enemy fighters against a loss of ten; the intensity of the battle is shown by the claims of 108 destroyed by bomber gunners.

Among the escorts for this mission was First Lieutenant Lindol Graham from the 20th Group, who caught two Bf-110s of a gaggle closing on the bombers and shot them down to become the second Lightning ace in the ETO. The 20th did better on this mission than it had on February 12, returning to King's Cliffe with claims for five Fw-190s and a Bf-109 in addition to Graham's pair of Zerstörers, for a loss of only one.

While the Americans dropped 54.3 tons of high-explosives and incendiaries on the Schweinfurt ball bearings factories, that night RAF Bomber Command sent 734 Lancasters and Halifaxes – guided by fires left burning from the American attack – in two waves 20 minutes apart, dropping over twice as much high explosive as had the Americans. The combined attack was the heaviest directed against Schweinfurt, but the October 14 mission inflicted more damage. It was not that the bombing was inaccurate; during the daylight raid three of the four factories were hit hard. However, since Black Thursday Vereinigte Kugellager Fabriken A.G. had moved 549 heavy machine tools to new locations, removing 27 percent of its total in the Schweinfurt plants.

Gotha, now more important strategically than Schweinfurt, saw very effective bombing. Over 400 high-explosive and incendiary bombs heavily damaged the factory buildings. The half of the plant dedicated to aircraft assembly was totally destroyed, although machine tools again received slight damage. Recovery was rapid; by late April, the factory was again at full capacity.

The 357th flew target cover for Gotha. As it rendezvoused near Koblenz, the 364th Squadron's Captain John Medieros and his wingman, future ace Second Lieutenant Richard "Pete" Peterson, spotted a gaggle of Bf-109s below and split-S-ed onto their tails. Medieros tagged onto one and later reported:

The enemy aircraft tried skidding and small turns to evade us, but to no avail. When he quit skidding I gave him a burst and observed strikes on the left wing root. The next burst was short and the third short burst hit him square on the tail. I had to pull up to avoid running into the debris.

Peterson reported that as Medieros pulled away, "The airplane blew up in a ball of red fire and smoke."

Colonel Spicer and his wingman Henry Beal spotted two Bf-109s, but the enemy saw them coming and dived away. Moments later, Spicer saw a Ju-88 and gave chase, later reporting:

He went down fast, losing altitude in a steep spiral. At about 3,000 feet I turned tight inside of him and he obligingly straightened out, allowing me to do the same, so I closed and opened fire at about 600 yards in an attempt to discourage the rear gunner. I kept firing until he burst into flames.

Spicer started to overrun the Ju-88 so he banked out to the side as the enemy fighter came apart. Beal later reported seeing two men jump and their 'chutes open. "The ship continued straight ahead, diving at an angle of about 40 degrees until contact with Mother Earth was made, which caused the usual splendid spectacle of smoke and flame."

Spicer then spotted a Bf-110:

He showed a little sense and tried not to turn, so I was forced to resort to deflection shooting, opening up and spraying him up and down, round and across. Fortunately, the left engine blew up and burst into flames. As I overran him, still indicating 500 miles an hour, the pilot dumped the canopy and started to get out. He was dressed in brown and had streaming yellow hair, the handsome devil. No 'chute was seen, but the aircraft descended impolitely into the center of the town of Erfurt, causing rather understandable confusion as it blew up and burned merrily.

The 56th escorted the bombers on their inbound leg to Schweinfurt. Zemke later recalled that the lead B-17s called that they were under attack before the group made rendezvous over Holland. Arriving over the bombers, Zemke spotted a flight of Fw-190s below at 18,000 feet and led his flight in a dive onto the enemy fighters' tail. As he closed, he suddenly found himself under fire from the wingman of the Fw-190 he had chosen as a target; fortunately his wingman, Lieutenant Archie Robey, clobbered him. As he closed on the enemy's tail, his gunsight suddenly failed and he immediately switched to the ring and bead back-up. The 190 made a split-S to evade and Zemke followed. When he found himself over the trees at very low altitude, he decided that having fired over 360 rounds and having hit nothing with the back-up sight, it was prudent to break off and try again another day. Zemke was surprised on return to Halesworth to discover several 20mm cannon shell holes in his flaps and elevator. "This was the fourth time Mrs. Zemke's son little Hubert had returned with evidence that someone was trying hard to eliminate him."

The A and B groups bounced several gaggles and returned to Halesworth with claims for nine destroyed, but also had to report the loss of Second Lieutenant Wilbur Kelley, who had followed his element leader Captain Fred Christiansen in a strafing attack on an airfield they spotted, and was taken down by flak. Kelley was the group's first loss in a dozen missions.

February 24 saw JG 26 score the *Geschwader*'s 2,000th victory since September 1939. It was also the day of the group's worst losses during Operation *Argument*. All three *Gruppen* were heavily engaged against the bombers inbound and outbound. The rendezvous airfield for pilots after their initial attacks was Rheine. Only 11 JG 26 fighters were among those that showed up, but the *Gruppenkommandeur* of I.Gruppe, Karl Borris, took command of the "Schlageter" survivors. As he and his wingman taxied for takeoff after refueling, two P-47s suddenly appeared. Their slashing low-level strafing attack caught Borris' wingman, but Borris was able to get off the ground under fire and soon caught up with the strafers, shooting down one of them north of the airfield.

The others quickly took off and joined Borris, who soon spotted a formation of B-24s near Wetzlar. Oberleutnant Walter Matoni of 5.Staffel went after "tail-end Charlie" of the formation while 3.Staffel's Oberfeldwebel Hackman and 7.Staffel's Leutnant Waldi Radener attacked the two bombers just ahead of Matoni's target. Matoni's fire set the bomber afire in the fuselage and it crashed near Rastorf, followed by the crash of the one attacked by Radener, north of Wetzlar. Charlie Willius and Oberleutnant Willi Hartig also brought down Liberators.

Radener made an attack on a second Liberator, but quickly ran out of ammunition. At this moment, the 357th Group P-51s arrived and he was jumped by a Mustang. All he could do was try to out-turn his opponent until the American's fuel state forced him to break off to return home. The tail chase continued for seven minutes with Radener shouting over the radio for someone to come and take care of the Mustang. Suddenly, the P-51's engine began spewing clouds of white smoke. The pilot immediately broke out of his turn and set course to the west. Radener caught up and took position off his opponent's wing. Suddenly, the Mustang rolled over and the pilot took to his parachute. Radener, who had been flying through the whole fight with the red light flashing his low fuel state, immediately turned away and landed back at Rheine.

That night when the group's claims were examined, Matoni's claim for his 13th victory was judged to be the "Schlageter" Geschwader's 2,000th claimed victory.

Despite JG 26's limited success, the Jagdwaffe reported the loss of 39 Fw-190s and Bf-109s, and 14 Bf-110s, 16 percent of the total 336 sorties flown that day. Eighth Air Force reported the loss of 44 B-17s and B-24s, a loss rate of 5.4 percent, and only ten fighters. Among the victorious Americans was the 20th Group's Lieutenant Morris, who shot down one of the Bf-110s over Schweinfurt for his sixth victory, making him the leading Lightning ace in VIII Fighter Command.

What was distressing about this particular mission was the loss of 13 B-24s from the 445th Group over Schweinfurt and on the return when they ran into JG 26. That night when the telex came through announcing the weather forecast was for CAVU skies over Germany and England and the final mission of Big Week was "go," squadron commander Major James Stewart – who had given up Hollywood stardom and fought the system to be treated like any other aviator – learned he would lead the 445th the next day. Several times that night after retiring to his quarters, Stewart woke up, unable to sleep. He went to the window and pulled aside the blackout curtain, staring out at the dark countryside surrounding the base at Tibenham in the Midlands. "My thoughts raced ahead to the morning, all the things I had to do, all the plans I must remember for an emergency. How could I have a clear mind if I was saturated with fear?" When daylight came, "maximum effort" for the 445th meant 17 B-24s, all the airplanes capable of flight, would fly the mission to bomb Nuremberg. At the morning briefing, the crews were told that they must do everything to conserve fuel. The Liberators carried fuel for ten hours of flight – going to Nuremberg and back would take nine and a half hours. "Do not lower the ball turret unless absolutely necessary," they were ordered.

The final mission of Operation *Argument* saw Regensburg hit again, this time by 290 B-17s of the 3rd Air Division – more than the entire Eighth Air Force had sent in August. The Fifteenth also sent 180 B-24 bombers against the Messerschmitt factories in the city. In the end, both forces took their worst casualties of the *Argument* campaign, with 21 B-17s and 14 B-24s failing to return, 25 percent of the total attacking force.

The losses at Regensburg meant that the bombers met fewer defenders over Nuremberg, Stuttgart, and Augsburg.

The 4th flew penetration escort. When they rendezvoused over Holland, enemy fighters were already mounting large attacks in accordance with the new tactic of hitting the bombers before they had full fighter protection. The 336th immediately went after five Fw-190s making a head-on pass on a B-17. Vermont Garrison attacked one of the Fw-190s, but overshot when the enemy fighter turned away.

I whipped around on his tail again. His engine was smoking badly now. I did not catch him the second time until he was down on the deck at about a hundred feet. I closed up and started shooting, getting good strikes, and I set his engine on fire. We were right down just above the ground. I hit him several times at close range. I overshot again as his engine was gone and he was slowing down. I slowed down and got behind him, gave him a few short bursts and he went straight into the ground. A wing came off and the engine hit about a hundred yards from the rest of the airplane.

Don Gentile and wingman First Lieutenant Glenn Herter went after two Fw-190s that Herter had spotted 10,000 feet below. Herter later reported they were hard to identify because their camouflage blended in with the background. The two enemy pilots were unaware of the P-47s diving on them until they opened fire. Herter went after the wingman:

He was flying straight and level, and apparently did not see me. I held my fire until I reached approximately 125 yards, then opened fire in one long burst. I immediately observed hits from the port wing root to the cockpit. On being hit, the enemy aircraft did a violent flick and the pilot shot out of the aircraft with his 'chute streaming behind him. The Fw-190 continued straight down into the ground, trailing smoke.

While Herter took care of the wingman, Gentile went after the leader, recalling:

I closed to about 400 yards for my first burst. I opened fire again at about 300 yards, observing many strikes and large and small pieces coming off the '190. My whole aircraft was covered with oil, and my wingman was hit by pieces of the enemy aircraft in the cowling and the prop. When I last saw the '190, he was close to the ground going almost straight down. He had definitely had it.

When the pilots arrived back at Debden, they found that 25 more Mustangs had been delivered; with the others that had been delivered two or three at a time over the past ten days, there were now 48 P-51s. The fortunes of the 4th Fighter Group were about to be transformed.

Jimmy Stewart's Liberator took an 88mm hit in the nose over Nuremberg, with the shell passing through the airplane and exiting just in front of the cockpit. Stewart maintained course, and the formation was able to bomb accurately. When he landed back at Tibenham, the bomber's nose broke off when the nosewheel touched ground, and the rest of the plane swung violently around, coming to a stop a complete wreck. The crew climbed out and discovered that everyone was safe. One remembered later that Stewart surveyed the wreckage and commented, "Well, anything you can walk away from can't be all that bad."

Zemke later recalled that a sign that Operation *Argument* had the desired result was the fact that when the 56th Group escorted bombers headed again to Brunswick on February 25, for the first time since the group had entered combat, the Luftwaffe made no attempt to intercept the bombers. Indeed, the Jagdwaffe had been forced to change tactics once again. The new aggressiveness of the American escorts made it impossible for a *Gruppe* to form up and make a mass attack on the bombers. Instead, small formations of no more than *Staffel* strength attempted to find their way through the escort screen and were frequently rebuffed with losses. Most western-based *Jagdgeschwadern* adopted "hit and run" tactics with no more than a four-fighter *Schwarm* attacking. These pinprick attacks were nearly inconsequential when compared to the *Gruppe* and even *Geschwader*-strength Twelve O'Clock High attacks made only three weeks earlier.

While the 56th came up dry, the 357th's Mustangs managed to claim three over Regensburg. Rendezvousing with the bombers as they approached the city, Captain Joseph Broadhead spotted a Bf-109 2,000 feet above the bombers, below the fighters. Broadhead and his wingman, Second Lieutenant Thomas Beemer, went after the enemy fighter. They followed the 109 as its pilot dived toward the bombers. Second Lieutenant Gilbert O'Brien, who watched the incident, recalled, "Broadhead and Beemer followed him into the formation. Then I saw Beemer's ship start smoking. I saw him make three 360-degree gliding turns as every turret on the B-17s was smoking and winking."

Hit by the defensive fire from the bombers, Beemer had to bail out, but his parachute failed to open properly and he fell several thousand feet to earth. Amazingly, his fall was broken by a clump of trees, and the badly injured pilot survived to be taken prisoner by the Germans; he was repatriated several months later due to the injuries he had suffered.

Broadhead finally managed to overhaul the enemy fighter, but the pilot spotted him and banked left to evade:

I closed fast to within 50 yards and observed strikes on his engine and right wing. He reversed direction and split-S-ed to the right. He then pulled out at 15,000 feet, rolled twice to the left and began a shallow dive. I continued to fire and hit him repeatedly. As soon as he began his dive the aircraft started disintegrating. Cowling, canopy and various pieces flew off

All three *Gruppen* of JG 26 saw action on the 25th, as the bomber stream passed over the *Geschwader*'s bases coming and going. II. and III./JG 26 were able to fly missions against the bombers inbound and outbound. III.Gruppe's Bf-109s were particularly successful, penetrating the escort screen on both missions. *Gruppenkommandeur* Klaus Mietusch shot down a B-17 in each of two missions, while all three *Staffelkapitänen* also scored a B-17 each. II./JG 26 pilots scored four B-17s, two in each mission, though they also lost two experienced pilots shot down by the escorts.

The mission against Regensburg saw the German defenders concentrate on the Fifteenth's bombers rather than on those from the Eighth. The result was a 20 percent loss rate for the Italy-based bombers with 33 shot down, while the Eighth lost only 31 of the total force of 738 credited with sorties; the fact that this force flew in a single well-protected stream contributed to the low loss rate. The likely reason for the German concentration on the Fifteenth was the fact that the force's P-38 and P-47 escorts did not have the range to cover the bombers all the way to the target.

Despite the losses, the results at Regensburg were particularly good. The Messerschmitt factories there were the heart of Bf-109 production. The raids by the Fifteenth on February 22 and 25 resulted in heavy damage to the Obertraubling factory with scarcely any buildings escaping damage, while many were completely destroyed. Aircraft production was reduced from 435 planes per month in January 1944 to 135 per month in March; the Regensburg factories did not recover to scheduled production levels until June 1944. The Messerschmitt plant at Augsburg lost 30 buildings destroyed and production was reduced by 35 percent. However, even though 30 percent of machine tools were damaged, the plant was back in full production by early April.

That night, snow began falling over the airfields in England and the cities of Germany. The weather stopped nearly all air operations for the next six days.

The 3,300 sorties launched by Eighth Air Force during Big Week dropped nearly 10,000 tons of high explosive on their targets, as much in a week as the command had dropped in its entire first year. USSTAF leaders had been prepared to accept the loss of 200 bombers in a single day; the actual loss was 137 over all six days, a loss rate of just under 5 percent. Of 2,548 fighter sorties by VIII Fighter command and 712 from Fifteenth Air Force, total losses were 28. In addition to the daylight raids, RAF Bomber Command raided Leipzig, Stuttgart, Schweinfurt, Steyr, and Augsburg, with 2,351 sorties dropping 9,198 tons of bombs for a loss of 157 bombers. The RAF loss rate of 6.6 percent was actually higher than the daylight loss rate.

Working from aerial photographs of the targets, which showed a roof blown off but not what damage had happened inside the factory, Allied intelligence initially believed that the strikes had been more effective than events would later demonstrate. The German aircraft industry had not been destroyed. In the wake of Big Week, responsibility for aircraft production was removed from the Reichsluftfahrtministerium (Air Ministry) and handed to Reichsminister Albert Speer, who was able to organize a decentralized industry that was not so vulnerable to attack, with assembly lines established in forests and salt caverns. This came at the cost of lowering production standards as the skilled workforce was diluted with slave laborers who had no reason to put forth any extra effort beyond that enforced; after the war, several German fighters recovered from crashes contained evidence of industrial sabotage as the reason for their loss. Additionally, the dispersal program left the industry vulnerable to any disruption in transportation; when Allied bombers went after the German transportation system and trains became targets for strafing fighters, this cut back production, despite the ability of Speer's deputy Otto Saur to organize this decentralized system so well that the high point of German aircraft production was not reached until September 1944. Moreover, most of the aircraft produced from the summer of 1944 on never flew, because there was no aviation gasoline for them. And those that did fly had pilots in the cockpit who were increasingly less capable than their predecessors.

In fact, the great victory of Big Week was not to be found in German production records, but rather in Jagdwaffe loss records. A total of 225 pilots were killed and 141 wounded. These men were irreplaceable. Their number might be replaced, but their skill and experience were forever gone. For example, JG 26 lost 15 pilots killed in action; among the dead were three of the 12 *Staffelkapitänen*. The "Schlageter" Geschwader would never fight as well after Big Week as it had before.

After Big Week, Eighth Air Force bombing missions were no longer scheduled and routes selected to avoid enemy defenses. Instead, it became deliberate policy to use the bombers as "bait" to force the Jagdwaffe into combat, where they could be shot down by the increasingly capable VIII Fighter Command groups. Fighters were no longer seen in defensive terms but rather as the offensive force most capable of maintaining the air superiority that had so irrevocably passed to the Allies during Big Week.

# 18

# "I KNEW THE JIG WAS UP"

Allegedly, after the war, when he was questioned by American interrogators at the Nuremberg War Crimes Trial, Reichsmarschall Hermann Göring said, "When I saw Mustangs over Berlin, I knew the jig was up." Whether he said that to his interrogators or anyone else is open to question, but the fact that American fighters did show up over Berlin, the capital of Nazi Germany on March 6, 1944, was proof that the only question remaining was how long World War II would last. The winners were already known.

Berlin had been listed as an especially suitable target for the strategic bombing forces in USSTAF's original assignment of priorities issued in January. The purpose of attacking Berlin was not just to destroy the several important industries that were located within the city and its area, or to shake the enemy's morale. The desire now was to goad the Luftwaffe into coming up to defend a target, so that the defenders could become the targets of the fighters escorting the bombers, inflicting losses of pilots as well as aircraft. If there was a target the Germans could not ignore regardless, Allied planners believed it was Berlin. The tactic had been used in the multiple missions to Brunswick and Frankfurt, but they had resulted in less than full-scale opposition. Believing they had inflicted major damage on the aviation industry, the planners' goal now was to create higher attrition in the existing Luftwaffe.

The decision to strike Berlin was a result of confidence in the capability of long-range fighter escorts to take the bombers to distant, well-defended targets. Since January, the range of the P-51 had been extended. Without external tanks its range of 475 miles was close to the P-47's maximum escort range using two 108-gallon wing tanks. The P-51 with two 75-gallon tanks had an escort range of 650 miles, and with two 108-gallon tanks that range was 850 miles; no target in Germany was out of range now. The only holdup was a bottleneck in the supply of P-51s as both Eighth and Fifteenth Air Forces demanded them. This was despite the fact that the airplane was plagued by serious problems with its engine, propeller, wing tanks, cooling system, guns, and radio.

By March 1, VIII Fighter Command had a second unit equipped with Mustangs, as the 4th Fighter Group became fully operational, flying its first Mustang mission on February 28. The 334th's Major Jim Clark led 35 P-51s escorting bombers sent to attack V-1 launch ramps near Boulogne-Compiègne. There were now some 150 P-51s available to the 354th, 357th, and 4th groups. The airplanes were still not fully reliable as the "bugs" were worked out and changes made on the production line. Back in the United States, North American opened a second production line for the fighter in their Dallas, Texas, factory in addition to those coming off the line in Los Angeles. Over the course of the next two months, five more P-47-equipped groups would re-equip with the airplane, and over the summer the P-38 would depart VIII Fighter Command as those groups followed. By the end of 1944, only the 56th Group would cling to their P-47s. The upward fortunes of Eighth Air Force in the crucial year of 1944 mirrored the upward line in the number of Mustangs available.

The 4th was blooded with the Mustang on March 2 when Lieutenant Colonel Edner led a target withdrawal support mission to Frankfurt. Six Bf-109s attacked the Mustangs over the Rhine town of St Goar in a head-on attack, followed by ten Fw-190s. First Lieutenant "Georgia" Wynn scored the 4th's first Mustang victory, later reporting:

I saw five Me-109s positioning at 11 o'clock to the bombers. I positioned myself astern the last enemy aircraft. I started firing and closed to 50 yards. The aircraft took slight evasive action and dived for a cloud as I observed strikes. I fired very long bursts and kicked the rudder. Glycol started streaming from the enemy aircraft. I followed him through, and I saw the enemy aircraft pull back up.

I gave him another long burst and observed strikes on the fuselage. I circled under the cloud base, and soon the enemy aircraft came down, followed by the pilot and 'chute.

The 336th's First Lieutenant Glenn Herter scored number two when he shot down one of the Fw-190s.

As it happened, the weather that had closed in at the conclusion of Big Week did not open up all that much through the month of March. It took three tries to get the maximum force over Berlin.

On March 3, the first Berlin mission was launched, but the bombers ran into steadily worsening weather over the North Sea, with the cloud tops exceeding 28,000 feet over the Jutland peninsula, making formation flying nearly impossible when combined with the dense contrails at formation altitude. While the majority of the bomb groups turned back, a few managed to bomb Wilhelmshaven and other coastal targets of opportunity with the guidance of H2X. Blakeslee led a target support mission to Berlin that ended up engaging no fewer than 60 Fw-190s and Bf-110s near Wittenberg, in which pilots claimed five destroyed but lost Vermont Garrison after he shot down an Fw-190 and a Bf-110 probable when he was hit by flak on the way home, while Philip "Pappy" Dunn ran out of gas after chasing an He-111; both bailed out to become POWs. Glenn Herter was killed when he was unable to get out of his Mustang when it was shot down by an Fw-190.

Don Gentile and Johnny Godfrey, flying as leader and wingman for the mission, came out the victors in the first of the fights that would see them become famous over the next month. Gentile recalled that he and Godfrey were never able to join up with the rest of the 336th Squadron in the poor weather:

After being on course for a couple of hours, still no one joined us, so we decided to continue on alone. When we were approximately a hundred miles from the target, the weather seemed to clear up. In the distance, I spotted approximately 50 Do-217s in formation climbing for altitude, and above them were about a hundred Fw-190s. They were getting ready to attack the bombers head-on. I called Johnny and asked him if he wanted to go ahead and attack knowing there were no other friendly fighters in this area. As usual, he said "You're the boss."

With Gentile in the lead, the two P-51s attacked the Do-217s in an attempt to disrupt the formation.

I began firing at "tail-end Charlie" and they started diving for the deck. About this time Johnny started screaming that the '190s were coming down on us. The Dorniers were cross-firing on us at the same time. I had one smoking badly when I had to break away due to the others coming in on us. Johnny and I met them head-on, going through the formation. From then on all hell broke loose. Airplanes were going up and down and every which way. I thought this was it. In the midst of twisting and turning, I managed to get on a 190 who overshot me, and was lucky enough to get him. Johnny started to scream that 50 more were coming in at six o'clock, so I started to aileron roll for the deck.

At this time I noticed one on my tail, blazing away, and Johnny screaming for me to break. I broke so hard that my airplane started doing snap-rolls – when I got it under control the '190 was slightly ahead and above, with me on his tail diving and twisting. This lasted a good ten minutes. I managed to get his aircraft on fire and noticed he had had it, so I broke away.

Both pilots were out of ammunition:

We had to dive for the clouds with them on our tail, skidding at the same time. By the grace of God we reached the cloud bank, and after flying on instruments for a while, we let down through the bottom of the cloud deck. During the combat I lost my maps, so I didn't know my position, and Johnny didn't know either, so we took the general direction home.

They landed at Hurn airfield, in Dorset, landing practically on fumes.

March 4 saw 29 B-17s of one of 14 combat wings get through the weather and bomb the Berlin suburb Klein Machnow, but the rest of the force once more either had to turn back or bomb targets of opportunity in the Ruhr. Steve Pisanos later remembered, "Eight Mustangs from our squadron and almost an equal number from the other two squadrons had to abort for various mechanical problems."

Eight pilots from the 335th and 336th squadrons failed to hear Blakeslee announce that the group was turning back since the bombers were aborting. Gentile and Godfrey were among those who did not hear the recall and the eight fighters ended up in the vicinity of Berlin with 14 B-17s that had also failed to hear their recall order. Gentile later reported that they ran across some 60 Bf-109s, Bf-110s, and Fw-190s. The eight P-51s shot down an equal number of the enemy, but four Eagles were also shot down.

The 335th's Second Lieutenant Hugh Ward chased one of the Bf-109s that dived through the formation, later remembering:

> I opened fire as he started a slow turn to the left. I observed strikes on his wing root. He realized the situation and flicked over, and he dove straight down with me on his tail. I gave him a three-second burst with good strikes. He continued straight down, heading for heavy clouds as I began to overrun him. I pulled back on the throttle and gave him another blast. I got a heavy concentration of strikes all over his cockpit and engine covering. I kept firing as the Me-109 started to come apart. I attempted to back off but was too late. A large section of the enemy aircraft smashed my canopy and windscreen, and it must have sheared off most of my tail section. My airplane began to snap viciously, end-over-end, and my right wing snapped off. I was stunned momentarily, but I managed to jettison my canopy. I pulled my harness release, which threw me out of the cockpit. I delayed opening my 'chute because of the speed, and I fell through the cloud layer. I opened my 'chute just in time. I landed in the suburbs of Berlin and was captured by civilians.

The 334th's First Lieutenant Nicholas "Cowboy" Megura chased after a Bf-109 on Ward's tail. He later reported, "At 18,000 feet, the Bf-109's wing came off at the root and disintegrated. The canopy and tail came off as I dodged past. Pieces carried away my antenna and hit my stabilizer." Megura's airplane was frozen in a compressibility dive from which he only recovered by using trim to bring up the nose as he backed off the throttle:

> The only evasive action taken by the enemy aircraft immediately in front of me throughout this action was a weave to right or left. I barrel rolled and positioned myself a thousand feet above and to the side of him. This engagement brought us down to 2,000 feet. Just as

I was about to fire, the enemy pilot pulled up sharply to 3,000 feet, jettisoned his canopy and bailed out. The enemy aircraft crashed and burned.

Down on the deck, Megura cleared his tail and spotted a grass airfield. He strafed it, setting fire to a Ju-52, then spotted a train and shot up the locomotive. Realizing he was out of ammunition, "I set course for home."

Back at Debden, Gentile reported, "By rights, the Jerries should have shot down all of us, but they failed because they flew poorly and couldn't shoot straight." This mission, combined with their report of their battle with the Do-217s the day before, began a controversy within the 4th about Don Gentile and Johnny Godfrey that would still divide the survivors 40 years later. As Jim Clark explained it, "They kept getting off on their own, and Godfrey would confirm Gentile's claims and vice-versa when they got back. Nobody else was ever around when those fights happened." Jim Goodson said, "They were both good pilots and excellent shots, and we were coming up against opponents who seemed to be less capable every mission, so they certainly had the opportunity and the ability. Some of the others got jealous, especially when the press arrived and they became the news."

The Mustang's "gremlins" claimed First Lieutenant Paul Ellington when his Merlin engine failed while he was crossing Holland on his way home, forcing him to bail out to become a POW. Johnny Godfrey later wrote that his life was "forever changed" when his best friend Bob Richards, with whom he had gone through training in Canada and England and come to the 4th, was killed when he crashed near the advanced base at Framlingham after being damaged over Berlin by a Bf-109. Richards' saxophone playing as the only officer member of the 4th's swing band had made him popular with everyone in the group.

The 354th managed to arrive over Berlin at half-strength due to aborts, led by James Howard. Lieutenants Bob Shoup and Frank O'Connor from the 356th shared a Bf-109 destroyed before the group was forced by weather to turn back. Gremlins were responsible for two pilots failing to return, one of whom was killed attempting to ditch his Mustang in the North Sea 25 miles east of the Suffolk coast.

The weather over central Germany was worse on March 5. With a good weather forecast over France, Blakeslee led the group on a mission to escort B-24s of the 2nd Division attacking airfields around Bordeaux. Halfway there, Blakeslee's engine started acting up and he was forced to abort. Duane Beeson took over the lead. Steve Pisanos, who was flying element lead for Blakeslee's White Section, would consider this day the most memorable of his time in the 4th. Over the course of the flight to Bordeaux, Pisanos later recalled that "From the 16 aircraft of our squadron that took off, we were reduced to six. The whole group was reduced from 48 to 30 by the time we rendezvoused with the 200 bombers north of Cognac."

The six 334th Squadron P-51s stayed with the 48 bombers that attacked Bordeaux while the rest turned off to hit airfields around Limoges. Pisanos spotted specks in the distance that turned into ten Bf-109s and "about six" Fw-190s. The Germans dived on the Mustangs and Pisanos ended up with one on his tail. "I broke sharply right, so tight I blacked out momentarily. I recovered and barely avoided putting my plane in a high-speed stall." The Bf-109 pilot overshot and now Pisanos was on his tail. "He made a wide left turn that allowed me to cut the corner and close the distance. When I was 200 yards away, I pressed the trigger. He flipped over and exploded in flame, and pieces of the airplane flew around me. I watched the fireball fall to earth."

Pisanos joined up with Beeson, whose Mustang had been damaged in the attack. They set course to return home, but minutes later Pisanos spotted a pair of Bf-109s flying toward them. Beeson called the break and banked left while Pisanos banked right:

His bullets missed me and he overshot, making a shallow turn. I started my chase. I caught up with him but he spotted me and pulled into a tight turn. I followed and opened fire with a deflection shot. Black smoke poured from under his cowling, then flames engulfed the engine and spread along the fuselage. The pilot didn't get out as the plane went straight in.

Pisanos spotted Captain Deacon Hively and they joined up. Again they came across a *Schwarm* of four Bf-109s. Hively dived on the first pair while Pisanos went after the second. Dropping below, he zoomed up and hit the wingman solidly. "The airplane rolled over and went straight down." The leader tried to split-S and escape, but Pisanos followed. "I used deflection again and hit him in the engine. He emitted smoke and dropped into the clouds below."

Now alone, Pisanos knew it was time to head home:

> I had reached 22,000 feet over Le Mans, when my engine began cutting in and out. I held on until I had reached the outskirts of Le Havre and could see the Channel beyond. The engine got rougher, and I flew directly over the city, heading for the water beyond. Just then, my engine began cutting out and then the bastards below cut loose with some of the heaviest flak I had ever seen.

Knowing he couldn't make it across the Channel, Pisanos turned away "to put some distance between me and Le Havre before I bailed out."

> At 2,000 feet, south of Le Havre, I trimmed my plane for level flight, unfastened my harness. I opened the canopy and as I tried to get out, I felt something holding me in. I looked down and saw the dingy cord was wrapped around the seat. I tried to cut the cord but I couldn't, and the plane started diving toward the ground.

Standing on the wing of his P-51, he reached inside and grabbed the stick. "I was about a hundred feet above the ground and headed for a barn. I managed to pull back on the stick enough to go over the barn, but that killed my speed and I crashed into the field beyond."

Knocked unconscious when the Mustang first hit the ground, Pisanos came to in the middle of the field with his airplane burning at the far end. "My shoulder was sore as hell, but I heard the Germans coming into the field by my plane. I managed to get up, and crawl through the fence into some trees beyond." He hid in the bushes while the enemy soldiers hunted for him. After an hour, things were quiet. "I got out of the bushes and started walking down the road when suddenly I came across a French farmer with a hay wagon. When he saw me, he motioned to get in the wagon. He covered me with hay and I passed out again from the pain." Steve Pisanos was now embarked on a six-month odyssey with the French Resistance that would read like an adventure novel, ending with his participation in the liberation of Paris in August, before he returned to Debden.

The 357th Group also participated in the Bordeaux mission, with the assignment of withdrawal support. Like the 4th, the group experienced several aborts, and by the time the Mustangs hooked up with the bombers its numbers had been reduced to fewer than 30. Among the pilots whose airplanes held together to arrive over the French city was Flight Officer Chuck Yeager of the 363rd Squadron. This was his eighth mission; on his seventh the day before, he had shot down a Bf-109 before the group aborted the attempted Berlin mission. Yeager's P-51B carried the name "Glamorous Glen" in honor of his then girlfriend and future wife, Glennis Faye Dickhouse, whom he had met while the group was training in Northern California. The group had just rendezvoused with the bombers 50 miles east of Bordeaux, when the 363rd was surprised by three JG 2 Fw-190s that swept through their formation. Almost before he knew the enemy was there, "Glamorous Glen" staggered under several 20mm hits. The engine caught fire and the Mustang fell from the formation. Yeager later remembered, "I got hit real good and immediately knew I was going down." He managed to open the "coffin" canopy and unfasten his harness as flames licked through the firewall from the engine into the cockpit. "My airplane began to snap and roll as it headed for the ground. I managed at almost the last minute to fight my way out of the cockpit. I was afraid I'd get strafed by the ones who shot me down, so I held off pulling the D-ring till I was as low as I dared." Yeager swung four times before he went into the trees below.

He was more fortunate than Steve Pisanos. His wounds came from clawing his way out of the cockpit and his feet and hands were bleeding; he also had a hole in his right calf, from a glancing hit by the enemy. "I was cold and scared, but I knew how to hunt and trap and live off the land, so I was pretty confident if they didn't get me now that I might get away."

Minutes later, he looked out of the bushes he was hiding in and saw a woodcutter with an ax. He jumped the man, thinking to get the ax as a weapon, but the man spoke enough English to say he was with the Resistance. Yeager relented; the man told him to stay in hiding and he would return. An hour later, he returned with an older man who spoke better English. They took him to a small hotel, where the imperious woman who owned it questioned him and decided he was not a German agent, due to his thick West Virginia accent. The next day, he was handed over to a group of Maquis guerillas. They told him he would stay with them until the snow melted in the Pyrenees, then they would get him into Spain.

Yeager was not the 357th's only loss that day. Group commander Colonel Russell Spicer was hit by flak and forced to bail out. Unlike Yeager, he was quickly captured and became a POW.

The next day, March 6, 1944, was one of the most important in the history of the Eighth Air Force. Captain Robert S. Johnson, now the second-highest ranked Wolfpack ace, later recalled the mission he flew that day as his most memorable, worthy of the name on the Thunderbolt he flew: "All Hell." This time, rather than playing the would-be victim of his encounter with Egon Mayer back in July 1943, he would lead the 56th's B group with the callsign "Keyworth Red Leader." It was a big advance for the pilot who had flunked gunnery in training and been designated for bomber service, then publicly shamed by his group leader for "over-aggressiveness" in the group's early missions. March 6 was the day the Eighth Air Force finally appeared over the Nazi capital in strength, in what was the biggest air battle of the war to date. The 730 bombers that took off from England were covered by 800 fighters.

The 660 bombers that would eventually make successful attacks of the 800 that took off that morning were assigned to bomb the Erkner ball bearing plant; the Bosch electrical equipment plant; and the Daimler-Benz Moteren GmbH at Genshagen, 20 miles south of the capital, producing the DB 605 that powered the Bf-109s, Bf-110s, and Me-410s. Pathfinders accompanied the force in case of overcast. The mission would see a total of 1,626.2 tons of bombs, both high-explosive and incendiary, fall on Hitler's capital.

Hub Zemke led the A group when it took off from Halesworth at 1013 hours. Johnson led the B group off at 1032 hours. The skies over eastern England were clearer than they had been since the middle of Big Week. The 56th's assignment was to take the bombers into Germany as far as the vicinity of Dummer Lake, the group's "Happy Hunting Ground," where they would hand off to the three P-51 groups – the 4th, 354th, and 357th. Johnson later remembered that the Dutch coast was covered by a light haze but the sky at 27,000 feet over Walcheren Island was cloudless.

Zemke remembered that his group made landfall over Egmont and the rendezvous was made with the bomber stream over Lingen at 1128 hours. "We passed one formation after another of the Big Friends. So far, the enemy had not shown his hand. Several minutes later, 'Tackline,' our fighter wing ground control, gave me the coded warning that a large formation of enemy aircraft was somewhere ahead to our north."

Johnson's B group had to contend with P-47s from the Ninth Air Force's 358th Group, which flew through the formation twice to the consternation of the Wolfpack pilots. Several minutes after the second fly-through at 1140 hours, just after Captain Mike Quirk led eight 63rd Squadron P-47s to bounce enemy fighters below, Dummer Lake appeared in the distance and Johnson spotted bogies approaching from the side. As they drew closer, he again recognized them as radial-engine fighters. One of his pilots commented over the radio, "Those same guys..." Johnson agreed they must be the same P-47s and replied "Watch these monkeys ahead." An instant later, he realized the "monkeys" weren't flying P-47s – they were Fw-190s! "Hell! They're Focke-Wulfs!" he called as the group showered the sky when they dropped their 150-gallon belly tanks and turned toward the enemy.

At nearly the same time, Zemke's group got a radioed warning from the 61st Squadron's Jim Stewart that they were engaging 75–100 enemy aircraft. Zemke called to the 63rd Squadron he was leading, "Yardstick here – Postgate Squadron – follow me!" The P-47s surged forward as pilots increased their throttles. "We cut through the air with the tense commands of men in combat coming over the radio. All eyes scanned the horizon for sight of combats. After five minutes the radio calls ceased. We finally saw parachutes and burning aircraft further to the west; we had arrived too late."

Bob Johnson winged over as the Fw-190s and Me-109s flashed past, heading for the lead box of bombers; they were too close for the eight Thunderbolts to break up the attack. The enemy ignored the P-47s as they aimed at the B-17s. Johnson pulled in on their tails, close enough behind to be indistinguishable to the defending gunners in the bombers. As he closed, he glanced to either side and spotted other gaggles of 30–40 enemy fighters attacking! Red tracers from the bombers reached out and flashed past his canopy. He saw the white trails of rockets flash through the formation and one bomber exploded when it was hit. The bombers grew closer, larger, and then they were through the formation!

He tacked onto the four Fw-190s ahead; out the corner of his eye he saw parachutes blossom in the sky. Just as he closed into range, the enemy spotted him and broke left and right by pairs. He followed to the right and took the wingman under fire. Tracers went into the engine and the propeller seemed to slow; pieces flew back, one clanged against his fighter. Suddenly the Focke-Wulf's canopy flashed past and then the enemy pilot came out of the cockpit. Johnson roared past him as his parachute deployed.

Zemke caught up with a lone Fw-190 diving on the formation and lining up to attack one of the trailing B-17s. Zemke gave the engine water injection but couldn't catch the enemy before he opened fire on the bomber. As he banked left Zemke cut across onto his tail and gave him a quick burst; the engine caught fire and he had to make a quick evasive maneuver to get past and avoid hitting the 190. As he glanced back, he saw the fighter going down trailing flame and smoke.

Johnson looked back at his wingman and realized that an Fw-190 was closing on him. Having never lost a wingman, he banked toward the Fw-190 and the enemy pilot dived away. There were some 30 bombers falling from the formation and the sky was filled with parachutes. He looked up and saw four other Fw-190s strafing men in parachutes. His wingman followed close as he pulled his nose up and turned "All Hell" toward the enemy. Out of range, he fired a burst to distract them from strafing the parachutists. The enemy leader banked over toward him, followed by his wingman. The two Fw-190s and the pair of Thunderbolts converged on each other, then the Germans broke away to the right. Johnson winged over on their tails. The heavy P-47 quickly caught up with them, the air speed indicator pushing past 450 miles per hour. The wingman turned away to the right but the two Thunderbolts stayed with the leader. The ground was coming up quickly as Johnson pulled into position dead behind his opponent. Suddenly he saw the exhaust smoke disappear as the enemy pilot pulled back his throttle to make the P-47 overshoot and stood on his right wingtip. Johnson pulled back his throttle but still gained on the enemy. He opened fire from 100 feet as he banked away from the impending collision and turned tight, G-force pushing him in his seat; the opponent dived away. He turned again onto the Fw-190's tail and fired another burst. He had to pull out of the dive or go in himself. As he banked away, he saw the other fighter explode on the ground below.

Johnson spotted another Fw-190 coming in on his wingman and drove the enemy off by turning toward him. It was time to climb back up and rejoin the group. Running into another group of Fw-190s attacking a straggling B-17, he again followed the enemy down but had to break off when another pair came to their rescue. Fortunately, the enemy was as ready to break away as he was and as they headed east, he and his wingman leveled off at 5,000 feet and set their throttles for best economy as they pointed their noses west to return to Halesworth. On the way, they picked up a damaged B-17 and escorted it to the coast.

Zemke's group had also come to the limits of its gas after breaking up the two attacks. When both groups returned to Halesworth, claims were submitted for a total of ten destroyed, with Zemke and Johnson responsible for four of that number.

The P-51s picked up the escort over Dummer Lake to take the bombers to Berlin. The 357th managed to arrive with 33 P-51s after suffering 15 aborts for various mechanical problems. Captain William R. "O'Bee" O'Brien, a flight leader in the 363rd Squadron, remembered it as the group's first "Big Day."

> While the group had performed well during the "Big Week," it had not had a "Big Day," which was when a group tallied 20 or more victories. In truth, our losses had been severe, involving the loss of group, squadron, and flight leaders. In fact the previous day, we lost our group commander, Colonel Russ Spicer. All things considered, we were not yet setting the world on fire.

Shortly after takeoff, on March 6, new group commander Lieutenant Colonel Donald Graham had to abort; since he was leading the 363rd, his departure left O'Brien in the lead.

> It could and probably would have been worse for me if Major Tommy Hayes, who led the 364th Squadron, had not assumed command and led the group. Weather at takeoff was good. The penetration was flown over low scattered clouds which prevented me and other leaders from being able to navigate with precision. In fact, I hadn't seen a recognizable landmark since the Zuider Zee, in Holland. By now the under-cast had increased in cloud density to about eight-tenths solid. It was time for the rendezvous with the bombers when

Tommy Hayes broke radio silence to ask me, "Where is Berlin?" This was the first, and only time, I was ever consulted during an ongoing mission. I told Tommy, "I think Berlin is behind us." Tommy said we would hold course for two more minutes. We did just that, then we made a one-eighty which had us flying into the Berlin target area from the East. And guess what? There 20–30 miles away was a wonderful sight, the VIII Bomber stream. About this same time, we had more company, in the form of forty-plus enemy aircraft on a convergent course with the bombers and us.

The Mustangs broke by squadrons toward the enemy aircraft. "The Me-110 that I latched on to was easy pickings, which was OK with me. I got him burning in his left engine and we were in a very steep diving right turn, when my machine guns started jamming." O'Brien found himself almost in a compressibility dive as the Bf-110 headed for the deck. "I pulled up, rolled a bit and watched the enemy crash into a large structure resembling a factory. You never saw such a fine explosion! It was plainly visible above 20,000."

O'Brien tested his guns and found they were all jammed. He immediately turned and set course for England. "When I had climbed to about 20,000 feet, I saw a P-51 approaching me from about four o'clock and identified it as a 'Yoxford' Mustang. The pilot identified himself as Leroy Ruder. I told him to hang on and I'd get us back to England."

Minutes later, Ruder called out a bogey approaching from two o'clock. "I told Leroy to take the enemy aircraft. He did and I had a first-class seat to watch him destroy the Me-110. We made it back to base in good shape. I never did tell Leroy that my guns were not working. I guess he just went on thinking that old O'Bee was a real nice guy."

Hayes, who had come to the 357th after fighting the Japanese over Java in 1942, then scoring two victories flying P-400s over New Guinea, remembered the long flight from England, two hours and 12 minutes flying in haze, between two layers of clouds, leading without visual navigation. "The calls started coming in, 'Where the hell are we?' 'I bet we overshot the target.' 'Geez, we must be over Russia!'" Major Hayes quickly silenced this by tersely ordering radio silence.

B-17s from the 1st Division suddenly emerged from a cloud bank to the left, seven miles in front of the Yoxford Boys. Hayes then spotted Major

Hans Kogler's seven Bf-110Gs from ZG 1, followed by 41 Me-410Bs of ZG 76 and 72 Bf-109Gs. The 33 Mustangs burst out of the haze and scattered the German fighters all over the sky. Hayes turned into four Bf-109s. The leader broke into a right-hand turn with Hayes in pursuit, circling, climbing, and descending. Suddenly, his adversary went into a steep dive. Hayes followed but lost it in a smoke cloud at 15,000 feet.

All of a sudden, Hayes saw a line of 500-pound bombs dropping past his right wing. He looked up, shocked to see B-17s above with their bomb bays open. He flipped his Mustang over and dived parallel; pulling out at 500 feet he turned west. Climbing rapidly, he stumbled into his original flight at 15,000 feet. They turned and picked up the B-24s and remained with the Liberators until new escorts arrived.

During their return home, Hayes spotted a Bf-109 flying the opposite direction over Uelzen, Germany. He winged over and closed to 200 yards before opening fire. Hits sparkled all over the opponent's cockpit area and it dived straight and exploded into a ball of fire, for Hayes' third victory in the ETO.

Back at Leiston, O'Brien remembered, "We had shot down over 20 German aircraft, without loss of a single plane in the fight. This was the group's first 'Big Day.'"

The Me-410s of ZG 76 and Bf-110s of ZG 26 shot down eight B-17s over Berlin on March 6; they lost 16 to the Mustangs of the 357th and 4th groups. The Me-410s were removed from daylight operations by the end of the month after losing 26 of 43 fighters that took off on March 16, 1944, to defend Augsburg while only ten returned undamaged; this was despite the fact that they were Hitler's favorite bomber-destroyers.

In a wild fight over Berlin, the 4th claimed 15 destroyed, with Blakeslee downing an Me-410, Megura two Bf-110s, McKennon and Alex Rafalovich a Bf-109 each, and McGrattan a Bf-110 claimed as a "Ju-88." Lieutenants Anderson and Dye claimed a Do-217 apiece (these were likely Bf-110s) and another Bf-110 went to Flight Officer Lloyd Waterman while Moulton and Van Epps shared a Bf-110. Losses included Lieutenants Manning and Whalen killed, while Lieutenant Messenger bailed out as did Major Henry Mills when he suffered engine trouble west of Brandenburg, with both made POWs.

The Pioneer Mustangs of the 354th did not encounter the big gaggles that the 4th, 56th, and 357th groups engaged, though its pilots claimed seven destroyed.

The 78th escorted the bombers as they withdrew from Berlin. Colonel Stone led 78A to a rendezvous with the 1st Division B-17s southwest of Dummer Lake; the 36 P-47s provided escort as far as Celle, where they handed over to 78B without having made contact. Five minutes after the handover, 25 Fw-190s hit 83rd Squadron, flying high cover. Focke-Wulfs and Thunderbolts engaged in vicious combat that ranged from 24,000 feet to 4,000 feet near Steinhuder Lake. Grant Turley, who had "made ace" a month earlier, shot down one of two Fw-190s his flight went after, then the P-47s chased three Fw-190s to the deck, where Turley got into a turning fight with one while a second got on his tail. Dick Hewitt saw Turley score his seventh victory, but success was short-lived as the wingman closed the gap and pulled enough deflection to put a burst into the R-2800. As he spun in, Turley was unable to bail out and was killed in the explosion; he had just turned 21 two days earlier.

The newly arrived 364th Fighter Group, based at Honington, became the third P-38 group declared operational just in time to fly its first mission on March 5. On March 6, Major John Lowell, commanding the 384th Fighter Squadron, claimed two Bf-109s destroyed west of Hannover, though one was reduced to a probable due to faulty gun camera film. Lowell had been a project officer on the P-38 at Wright-Patterson before getting an assignment to the 364th before they were shipped overseas.

The March 6 mission to Berlin saw the turning point in the Eighth Air Force's battle against the Luftwaffe, with the largest air battle in the European air war. Till now, the control of European skies had been exercised by the Jagdwaffe day fighter force based in France, Belgium, and Germany. The Americans lost 69 heavy bombers shot down over Berlin, more than Black Thursday at Schweinfurt. The "Bloody Hundredth," the 100th Bomb Group, lived up to their name; a gap in fighter coverage gave the defenders three uninterrupted minutes to attack the B-17s, with 15 falling out of the sky when Thunderbolts dived to the rescue too late. Eleven Mustangs were lost in the wild fights over the city. However, the situation was very different from that of five months earlier. The Mustangs accounted for 35 German fighters over Berlin, while the Germans lost an additional 29 to the rest of the escorts. The worst loss was the 25 irreplaceable experienced pilots.

The United Press report written by Walter Cronkite that day began, "A 15-mile long parade of American bombers thundered across the heart of Berlin for 30 minutes today and set great fires in the stricken Nazi capital after smashing through a huge German fighter screen." The *New York Times* reported that at least 600,000 men and women on both sides were engaged in the battle. This included 12,000 Allied airmen, 1,000 Luftwaffe pilots, 50,000 Allied and 25,000 German ground crewmen, and more than 500,000 Germans manning the flak defenses across the Low Countries and Germany. A day later, Swedish reporters wrote that "Large sections of the capital's industrial suburbs were still burning and were without light, power, gas, or telephone service."

Weather on March 7 prevented operations from England, but the Americans returned to Berlin on March 8 with 623 bombers escorted by 725 fighters; 37 bombers and 18 fighters were lost. Among the pilots claiming victories was the 364th's Major Lowell, who was credited with two over Berlin, with credit for an Fw-190 and a Ju-52 claimed when his squadron strafed an airfield that it came across on the way home; he became the first pilot credited as an "ace" with both air and ground "kills" under Doolittle's new policy. The 4th claimed 16 more shot down for the loss of Lieutenant Colonel Edner. The Eagles' main competition, the 56th, had their best day ever for both A and B groups which were led by Dave Schilling and Gabby Gabreski, respectively, despite the fact that the fight started with the Luftwaffe surprising the P-47s and shooting down three from A and one from B group. On return to Halesworth, total claims were 27, nearly one-third of all claims over Berlin that day; Bud Mahurin's victories made him the first VIII Fighter Command ace to reach a score of 20. Luftwaffe actual losses were 42, with three killed, 26 missing, and nine wounded, fewer than American claims but still terrible, since these could not be made good. On the third mission, flown on March 11, the defenders did not show up. The Eighth Air Force replaced their bomber losses by mid-month. The Luftwaffe never replaced its crucial losses.

Following the March 11 mission, the weather, which had been particularly nasty with snow flurries and biting east winds, took a turn for the worse; towering and extensive cloud hung over northwest Europe and restricted the few bombers sent out on radar-guided attacks. In fact, all the missions flown for the rest of March and most of April were primarily radar-guided blind bombing, in which the Eighth engaged in area bombing just like RAF Bomber Command. The precision destruction of German industry was no longer the bombers' purpose; they were sent to attract the Luftwaffe into the eager arms of the American fighter pilots.

Adolf Galland later wrote of the period:

The combined Anglo-American air offensive grew constantly in extent and intensity. Devastating nightly area bombing was complemented by daylight precision raids against our bottleneck industries. The British and American governments were determined to see the plan through which they had devised together. They had prepared and started it with a terrific expenditure of energy and power. Now it was running.

# 19

# THE BATTLE OF GERMANY

On March 15, the Wolfpack escorted bombers to Brunswick and once again found Dummer Lake the "Happy Hunting Ground." Fierce engagements gave them a score of 24 destroyed for the loss of one. Bob Johnson was credited with three, which gave him a total of 22 and put him past Mahurin for leading ace of both the group and VIII Fighter Command. Zemke recalled in retrospect that they did not know it at the time, but the late February to mid-March period of 1944 was to be the heyday as far as air fighting went. From then on, the Luftwaffe grew more difficult to encounter.

The mission flown against Berlin on March 18 saw the 700 bombers subjected to all-out attacks by the defenders; it was the first time that the total of claims for German fighters destroyed or probable was more than 100, which indicated the ferocity of the battle. But only 15 bombers were lost. The 20th Group unfortunately lost P-38 ace Lindol Graham when he followed the Bf-110 that became his sixth and final victory as it dived toward the ground. The German pilot managed to crash-land in an open field, but Graham – following at extreme low level – clipped the ground with his wingtip when he turned away and the P-38 cartwheeled into the trees where it exploded.

Over Strasbourg on March 16, the 78th's Quince Brown got into an extended fight that his element leader, newly promoted First Lieutenant Ernie Russell, would remember as his most memorable. "Our time with the bombers had been uneventful – just a lot of tricky crossover turns, rubbernecking, looking for bogeys and disappointed that the Jerries didn't turn up. I'm sure the fact there were no Jerries didn't bother the crews on the big friends half as much as it did us." Only a few minutes after the formation had turned west to head home, Brown pulled alongside Russell and pointed down. He and his wingman, Second Lieutenant Ross Orr, followed as Brown and his wingman, Second Lieutenant W.N. Smith, went looking for "targets of opportunity."

The foursome was near St Dizier airdrome, a major fighter base southwest of Paris. The Thunderbolts were indicating over 450 miles per hour as Brown started to pull out of the dive, 100 feet above the hillsides. The airfield was soon in sight; several enemy fighters were in the landing pattern as they returned from the air battle. The P-47s flashed over the runway approach at over 400 miles per hour; Brown hit one Bf-109 in the landing pattern – it caught fire and went in, exploding beneath the attackers. Russell suddenly found himself 250 yards behind another 109 that had just turned to final approach:

As the '109 filled my gunsight, I pulled the bright dot in the middle of the glowing ring along his line of flight for a deflection shot of about 30 degrees and squeezed off a burst. Immediately, APIs [armor-piercing incendiary bullets] from my guns lit up the grey engine cowling from the prop to the cockpit. My closure rate was so great I passed over him a fraction of a second later.

Russell and Orr followed Brown and Smith as they dived toward the south end of the runway, with the four fighters lining up abreast:

We made a sharp diving turn and lined up on the runway. I was several hundred feet east of Quince, who was lined up on the runway. A Ju-88 was just about to take off in front of him, while I spotted a Bf-110 on a taxiway just to the right of the strip, presenting me with a head-on shot. I centered needle and ball and waited till he was about 400 yards away, then opened fire. I heard my guns over the roar of my engine at full throttle. Almost instantly, the front of the 110 lit up with the flashes of API rounds. I fired until I was less than 200 yards distant, at which point it seemed judicious to pull up.

Brown's Ju-88 exploded and the four P-47s joined up so low that Russell was afraid he might hit the ground if he banked too tight, and they roared away from the scene of destruction. "We had taken the base by surprise, for there was no antiaircraft fire. However, we strongly suspected we had stirred up a hornet's nest." They stayed low till the field was out of sight before Brown turned northwest and started climbing to altitude.

An instant later, Russell spotted a mixed group of Bf-109s and Fw-190s diving on them as they popped out of the haze. Yelling "Break Right!" he slammed his throttle into war emergency power and turned right as hard as he could to meet the attacker head-on:

> He had the advantage of speed, altitude, and position; my luck was he wasn't behind me, and was presented with a tricky firing angle. He missed and flashed past. From experience, I was confident I could out-climb and out-turn him, but more important I could turn on a dime at the top of a near-vertical climb and give back change; we called that maneuver a "stall turn." My chief advantage was that the Jug happened to have the fastest aileron roll of any fighter, even at low speed. The maneuver was fairly simple: in a vertical climb at full power, just before I stalled, I would roll and smoothly apply rudder in the direction I wanted to go, nurse the stick back to get the nose down, and then accelerate. I could almost fly back down the air corridor I had ascended.

Russell was surprised when he looked over his shoulder to see the Bf-109 doing the same.

> I waited for him to be forced into a turn; he committed to a right turn as I had hoped. I was right at the stall and I rolled left to meet him head-on. I looked opposite and he was just completing his turn as I pulled out ahead of him. We passed again without firing and I yanked back straight up again. I watched over my shoulder; he was forced to match my climb or run. Up we went. I waited and watched him opposite me and significantly lower. Finally he committed to a left turn. I turned opposite and beat him out. Now it was my turn as I maneuvered into position 45 degrees off his tail. He rolled into a steep left turn trying to out-turn me, but I was only 150 yards behind him. Like lining up quail, I pulled my sight through him, sensed my lead and pulled the trigger. I gave him a two-second burst that hit his cowling. My next burst quickly dwindled into "pop – pop" as seven

of my eight guns jammed! He was less than 50 yards away; to avoid over-running him I pulled up steep and rolled down on him, but he was out of the fight. I had to worry about the others that were still after us, but my gun camera film later confirmed he was on fire. As I rolled out to meet the next ones, we were suddenly alone in the sky.

Russell was glad to head for home as he joined Brown. Moments later, they were bounced again. As they broke right, the enemy fighters dived away straight down. "Why they decided not to take us on I'll never know. Quince was low on ammunition and I only had one gun working, so I wasn't unhappy to see them go." As they winged homeward over the Channel, Russell suddenly realized that his RAF-issue helmet was soaked through with sweat.

While Russell had engaged in his turning fight, Brown had managed to shoot down a Bf-109 and an Fw-190, putting his score at ten, and making him the group's third "double ace." II./JG 26, the Luftwaffe unit they fought, reported three Bf-109s shot down over the field in addition to the Ju-88 and Bf-110 by strafing, and loss of two Bf-109s and an Fw-190 in the following engagement. VIII Fighter Command eventually confirmed Brown's claim of four destroyed and credited one destroyed and one probable for Russell, as well as one for his wingman, Orr. Writing of the fight 50 years later, Russell called it "The most exciting day of my combat life." Brown was awarded the Silver Star for his achievement. With water injection and the paddle prop, the P-47 was a far different fighter than it had been a year earlier.

Ernie Russell was two months short of his 20th birthday when he experienced his "most exciting day." It was considerably different from the "most memorable" experience of Unteroffizier Heinz Gehrke, also 19, which happened that same day. Gehrke had reported as a replacement to III./JG 26's 11.Staffel three days earlier, with 147 hours in his logbook, including 34 in the Bf-109G; today he was assigned as a *Rottenflieger* when the *Gruppe* took off from Lille-Vendeville to rendezvous with II./JG 26 at Reims for a mission against the returning bombers that Brown and Russell had escorted. Gehrke later recalled the event: "I was very excited. Wherever I looked, the sky was full of airplanes. I was very reassured. When we landed at Reims, I overheard from the other pilots that they were glad they had landed in one piece. I then realized all the airplanes I had thought were ours were the enemy!"

The *Gruppe* soon took off to intercept the bombers. Gehrke felt reassured when told the bombers had no escorts:

My job was very simple, to stay with *Feldwebel* Laub. Soon the bombers were in sight. Our *Staffel* made an attack on a group of Liberators on the far right edge of the formation. I was the last. Suddenly, I was behind one that fell from the formation! After I made three attacks, the bomber dropped away. I looked for my *Staffel*, but they were gone. I then saw several fighters circling in the distance. Believing they were my unit, I approached, but they turned out to be Thunderbolts! Four of them came after me. I stood my bird on its head and dropped away. The Thunderbolts filled my crate full of lead but I dove on. Suddenly, my machine leveled off and would not respond to the controls. More hits registered. I jettisoned the canopy, unbuckled and jumped out. Thank God the 'chute opened and soon I was sitting on the ground, more a wretched heap than hero. I could only move with difficulty due to a severe back pain – I then realized I had struck my aircraft's tail when I bailed out.

Gehrke was ultimately credited with the final destruction of his B-24 and survived the following year of combat.

That same day, newly promoted "full bird" Colonel Blakeslee led the 4th to Munich. The troublesome P-51s had been grounded March 13–15 so that mechanics could go over the fighters and try to correct the myriad of problems. Bob Wehrman recalled, "I loved the P-51 from the first minute I flew one, but the first two months we had them, we had nothing but trouble. You never knew if you were going to fly an entire mission or not." Shortly after the Mustangs rendezvoused with the bombers, seven Bf-110s were spotted attempting to attack the bombers from behind. Kidd Hofer, who was flying as Major Jim Clark's wingman, recalled Clark's attack on one of the Zerstörers:

As Major Clark closed, he discovered his guns wouldn't fire, and he told me to take over. I attacked two Me-110s that jettisoned their rockets and dove for the clouds. I followed one – the rear gunner was firing all the time, and hit my prop. I fired and saw strikes, followed by explosions as it nosed down from three hundred feet and crashed.

Another formation of 20 Bf-110s was engaged, and six more went down. Archie Chatterly reported, "I engaged an Me-110 and saw strikes around the cockpit cover and fuselage. It tumbled straight down as if the pilot had been hit." The group returned to Debden with Goodson, Carpenter, Fred Glover, and "Swede" Carlson each claiming two apiece, while Hofer, Chatterly, Kenneth Smith, Bernard McGrattan, and Johnny Godfrey claimed one each.

Two days later, the 4th went back to Munich on a withdrawal support mission. Just after rendezvous, eight Bf-109s were sighted 5,000 feet below, just above the bombers; four flights of Mustangs went after them. Duane Beeson later reported:

> As we started down on the enemy fighters, they were darting in and out of the clouds. I closed on one, and my second burst must have hit his belly tank, because the whole aircraft immediately blew up in my face and I was unable to avoid it. I had to fly through it, and I felt pieces strike my aircraft before I could break clear. I could feel the heat in my cockpit, and I immediately checked my instruments. I looked down and saw what was left of it going down, covered in flame.

Blakeslee, flying with Don Gentile as his wingman, also engaged these fighters. "As we approached, the eight enemy aircraft split, with four diving line abreast, so we followed them to the deck." Blakeslee, a notoriously bad shot, closed to 50 yards before he opened fire on the enemy element leader. "Captain Gentile took number four. When I finally closed on the number three aircraft, I saw strikes all along the tail, fuselage, cockpit and engine. The cockpit hood fell off, the engine started to smoke and burn and the left undercarriage fell down. I did not see him go in, but Captain Gentile saw him hit the ground."

Ralph Hofer reported opening fire on a Bf-109. "I saw strikes and an explosion as pieces flew off and black smoke poured out of the falling enemy aircraft which went into the clouds but popped out again as the canopy came off. The pilot bailed out." With this, Hofer was the only pilot in the ETO to become an ace while still a flight officer. When he went after two other 109s, his prop ran away. Setting course for nearby Switzerland, he had started to unstrap to bail out when his prop returned to normal. "I decided that with a little luck I could make it home. I landed at Manston with just six gallons of gas."

A week after experiencing "the most exhilarating day of my combat life," Ernie Russell did all he could do to keep up with his flight leader when Quince Brown gained victory number 11 on March 23 in a difficult fight with an Fw-190 that he chased through a hole in the clouds over western Germany. Pulling out low over the forested hills, the German was able to pull ahead when Brown's water injection system failed, and outmaneuvered him over the trees. Brown hung on grimly until he nearly rammed his opponent in a skid. Firing as he closed on the fighter, the Fw-190 exploded so violently that Brown was forced to perform a violent wingover at 500 feet to avoid the debris, barely missing the trees with his wingtip on the pullout. The flight spotted two badly damaged B-17s as they headed home and escorted them to England.

The 352nd Group had an extended conversion from the P-47 to the P-51, due to delays in getting the North American fighter to England. The 486th Squadron, first to receive Mustangs, had eight in the unit when it flew its first mission on March 8 with two flights of P-47s and two flying the Mustangs. During the mission, 487th Squadron's Captain Virgil Meroney, the group's leading ace, scored his eighth victory when he shot down 60-victory *Experte* Klaus Mietusch, III./ JG 26 *Gruppenkommandeur*, whom he caught attacking a B-17. Mietusch bailed out of his burning Bf-109 at low altitude and was severely injured, badly enough to put him in the hospital for two weeks.

On March 22, the Wolfpack finally made it to Berlin. They failed to draw any aerial opposition and on the way home both A and B groups shot up trains and canal shipping. Four P-47s of the 61st failed to return. As Zemke later wrote, "What the Luftwaffe pilots could now rarely achieve, the flak gunner did with a vengeance."

March 27 saw the loss of Bud Mahurin on an escort mission to southern France when he and his flight ran across a Do-217 bomber near Chartres. When Mahurin went after the bomber, the rear gunner put a burst of fire into the Thunderbolt's R-2800 that set it on fire. As the Dornier went down, Mahurin bailed out and was last seen by the others running into the woods. He would connect with the Resistance and remain at large until Patton's Third Army liberated the area in late July, at which time he made his way back to Halesworth to be sent home for being a successful evader.

At the end of March, 78A and B groups were sent on a strafing mission over the Low Countries. One 82nd Squadron flight sank several barges that it ran across on the Rhine while another spotted four trains east of Wesel and shot up the locomotives, leaving them in clouds of steam. Since the Berlin missions, strafing missions had taken equal importance to escort missions in VIII Fighter Command; the 78th's group victory board was expanded to include a new column for ground targets destroyed in addition to aerial victories. The group's score for March was 21 missions flown and 12 air and nine ground victories for the loss of nine pilots in combat – with only Grant Turley having fallen in aerial combat, while two others returned wounded.

These would be the highest monthly claims by the 78th for the rest of 1944. By the end of March, VIII Fighter Command had credited claims by the fighter groups for 406 German fighters destroyed in the air and 100 strafing claims over the month. As a result, General Galland withdrew the *Jagdgeschwadern* deeper into Germany to provide some respite from the American fighter attacks. The result was that the P-47 groups would score less frequently in April and May, with the nearest German fighter field now 350 miles distant.

The aircraft of VIII Fighter Command began taking on the plumage of victory at the beginning of April. Back in February, the 56th had repainted the white identity bands on their cowlings in traditional prewar Air Corps squadron colors – red for the 61st, yellow for the 62nd, and blue for the 63rd – to aid in-air identification. At the beginning of March after they began flying Mustangs, the 4th painted their white noses red. As other groups requested authorization to follow the examples of the leaders, VIII Fighter Command realized that with the increase in fighter groups, individual group formations needed new ways of quick identification to avoid friendly fire incidents and a system was developed and promulgated; the command also saw such painting contributing to unit morale and *esprit de corps*. The noses of all fighters in a group would be the same. With this, the 56th adopted red for its P-47s just as the 4th had for its P-51s, painting their rudders in the traditional squadron colors. The 359th Group adopted standard Air Force medium green, while the 352nd painted the Mustangs they re-equipped with a medium blue that was mixed in batches and resulted in the Mustangs having noses that ranged from sky blue to almost royal blue. The 353rd adopted yellow and black diamonds while the 355th Group determined it could leave its noses white. The 20th Group painted the spinners and cowl fronts of its P-38s yellow while the 55th painted them white; previously the P-38 had no identification markings, since its shape was so distinctive. The 78th's Thunderbolts adopted black and white checkerboard cowlings. The checkerboard was applied after painting the entire cowling white, after which the squares were marked off by tracing the outline of a metal square and a ground crew painter with a steady hand filled in the black area by brush. With all markings done freehand, no two were exactly the same.

Now that the Allies had established the basis of air superiority with their victories over Berlin, without which the invasion could not happen, the spring of 1944 leading up to that Day of Days was spent consolidating the initial victory.

In the weeks after the three Berlin missions, morale plummeted among the bomb groups as men who had been taught that they were fighting a superior war to that of other air forces, with their concentration on daylight precision bombing, were sent on mission after mission where all the bombardiers toggled their bomb releases on signal from the radar-equipped pathfinders, rather than on specific targets. The growing knowledge that their leaders were sending them on missions where it was hoped they would provoke response from the Luftwaffe, so that their escorts could engage the enemy in battle, added to a spreading belief among the crews that the campaign had no clear purpose or plan. Army surveys showed that aircrew morale remained higher than that of infantrymen, but so many missions, in bad weather or good, with the bombers turned into bait, worked on men's minds. Navigator John Miller of the Bloody Hundredth recalled after the war that "Twice our co-pilot went nuts and tried to crash us into the sea. The crew fought him off the controls and we aborted. After the second time he didn't return to our crew. He wasn't a coward; he just couldn't go back to Berlin."

Binge drinking became a problem in both fighter and bomber groups as the rate of operations increased. Bob Wehrman remembered, "There were more than a few times I was still drunk that morning from the night before. You'd go out to 'check my plane' and the crew chief would help you into the cockpit and turn on pure oxygen. It could take as long as 20 minutes for 'the cure' to happen, but it always did." Ground officers concerned with the problem lacked the moral authority to call a flier for drinking when the man could look them in the eye and ask where they were "yesterday, when I was over Berlin." Heinz Knoke also mentioned increased wild drinking among the pilots of his *Staffel* and others, with the young Germans also resorting to "the cure" the next morning, flying and fighting with hangovers. Both Knoke and Wehrman remembered pilots they knew flying drunk.

At the end of March, a replacement crew flew their B-17 to Bassingbourn, with orders to join the 401st Bomb Squadron of the 91st Bomb Group. Their co-pilot, who freely admitted that he was "not among the best," was a 23-year-old drop-out from Colorado College, where he had been a fraternity brother to the crew's pilot, First Lieutenant Sam Newton. Second Lieutenant Bert Stiles aspired to a career as a writer, and the *Saturday Evening Post* had published four of his short stories about life as a forest ranger in Colorado's Estes Park, with a few others picked up by *Liberty* and *The American* magazines; he wrote of the two of them, "Neither of us did very much except play around at school before we went to the cadets." The crew had been assembled in the Second Air Force combat pool at Salt Lake City. Stiles recalled joining up with Newton: "It was the purest luck we ran across each other in Salt Lake City." The rest of the crew had also been put together there. First Lieutenants bombardier Donald Bird and navigator Grant Benson were 24 and 22, respectively; flight engineer Technical Sergeant William Lewis was 20; radio operator Technical Sergeant Edwin Ross was 23; waist gunners Staff Sergeants Gilbert Spaugh and Edwin Crone were 21 and 24; tail gunner Staff Sergeant Ed Sharpe was 21; the crew's "old man" was ball turret gunner Staff Sergeant Gordon Beach, 34, who was from Denver as was Stiles. Fraternity-brother Newton later said of Stiles, "He should have been a war correspondent; he would have been another Ernie Pyle." Stiles wrote that the day after their arrival, it was announced that since losses were now lower, the tour was increased from 25 to 30 missions. "Five more opportunities for the law of chance to catch up to us." By the end of May, the tour was increased to 35 missions.

At around the same time Bert Stiles arrived at Bassingbourn, Major Jimmy Stewart was relieved as commander of the 445th Group's 703rd Squadron and moved ten miles from Tibenham to Old Buckenham, where he reported to Colonel Ramsay D. Potts, Jr., as group operations officer. Potts, a veteran of the "Tidal Wave" Ploesti mission, had been assigned to command the 453rd Bomb Group, which had suffered staggering casualties since arriving in England six months earlier; Potts and Stewart were replacements for the first CO and group operations officer, who had both been shot down over Berlin. Potts recalled, "Our job was to revive the group." Though Stewart could have stopped flying missions due to his new assignment, he continued flying. Gunner John Robinson remembered, "He skipped all the milk runs. High command didn't like that." Intelligence officer Captain Starr Smith recalled that Potts and Stewart were everywhere, checking every detail, seldom leaving the base. Their inspiring, hands-on leadership improved formation discipline and target proficiency, which led to lower losses. "He was just like his characters in the movies," Potts said of Stewart. "He had tremendous rapport with the men, that humorous way he had of settling them down in some pretty stressful situations."

The German defenders, operating under orders to avoid the escorts and concentrate their attacks on the bombers, were accused by Göring of cowardice – he called it "*Jägerschreck*," fear of fighters – due to their failure to force their way through the escorts to attack the bombers despite the fact that the escorts were now going after the defenders, allowing little opportunity to get in among the bombers. This resulted in fast-rising claims by the American pilots in the latter half of March and on into April, as the Luftwaffe hemorrhaged experienced pilots, with many of the new replacements being lost during their first few missions in which their lack of experience meant they were unlikely even to know that the American who shot them down was anywhere near.

On April 8, the 20th Group, now led by Lieutenant Colonel Harold Rau, who brought a different attitude to his leadership of the group with his open enthusiasm for the airplane they flew – unlike the previous group commander, who had made no bones of disliking the P-38 – led the Lightnings on an afternoon free sweep after the morning fog that prevented them flying the scheduled escort mission lifted from King's Cliffe. Spotting an airfield north of Salzwedel with several parked enemy aircraft, the Lightnings made four passes over the field once they discovered that it was only lightly defended with flak. The P-38s stuck around long enough for defending fighters to be called in, and seven Bf-109s dived on the Lightnings. Spotting one enemy fighter on the tail of his element leader's wingman, Rau shot the 109 down for his fifth victory, but the airplane crashed into the P-38 it was attacking after he hit it, and both crashed. "Slick" Morris added three "ground" victories to his previous score of six in the air, to increase his status as leading P-38 ace. Between April 8 and the group's re-equipping with the P-51 in June, only one other P-38 pilot would score a fifth victory to "make ace."

George Preddy, who hadn't scored since January, recorded his first victories in the P-51 on April 11. He had named his P-51B "Cripes A'Mighty II," following the name of his P-47. The group flew penetration support to Berlin, since the 328th Squadron was still flying P-47s. Again, the Luftwaffe failed to show up and the "Blue-Nosed Bastards" found a German airfield on the way home. Preddy later reported:

> After being relieved of bomber escort, the group made a strafing attack on an airdrome containing 30-plus medium and heavy bombers. On my first pass, I fired at a He-111 on the edge of the field and noticed strikes and a burst of flame. I turned after passing the field and fired at another He-111 but saw no results. As I departed, I saw many large fires from burning aircraft.

Preddy's gun camera did not record his second pass, resulting in him only being credited with the first Heinkel bomber he strafed. Two days later, returning from what he called "another unproductive escort" (i.e. there was no air combat) the group discovered an airfield used for training. Preddy led Blue Flight of the 486th Squadron on a run across the field and later claimed a Bücker Bü-133 *Jungmeister* trainer biplane destroyed.

Following the strafing successes by 78th, 4th, and 20th groups during early April, VIII Fighter Command mounted a multi-group strafing mission to central Germany on April 12; unfortunately, despite a more optimistic forecast, the weather turned out to be terrible. In return for 58 strafing victories, the groups paid with the loss of 33 fighters. Still, the mission was deemed a success that resulted in 616 fighters going out two days later on another mass strafing mission; this returned claims for 40 aircraft destroyed and another 29 damaged on airfields across northern France and Holland, with a further 18 destroyed in air combat.

As the tide changed for the fighter pilots and their scores against the enemy increased, the Air Force made much of "competitions" between leading pilots, calling them "ace races." In February 1944, the 353rd Group's leading ace, Major Walter Beckham, and the 56th's leading ace, Bud Mahurin, were promoted as being "neck and neck" for top honors as leading ace of VIII Fighter Command. Forty years later, Mahurin said of the stories at the time:

> It was a way for the Air Force to get the interest of all the reporters getting drunk in England waiting for the invasion to happen. Given the nature of air combat, the total unpredictability, there is no way anyone could be in a race with anyone else. You took your chances and grabbed your opportunities where you found them, and if you were good enough that day in that fight, you came home with a score. The only people who saw it as a race didn't know what the hell they were talking about.

Asked about Eighth Air Force publicity stunts, Walter Cronkite, who spent three years as United Press's "Man With the Eighth," observed:

> The Air Force, in my experience, was always the most overtly political of the services. They had an agenda that started at the top and to which every commander was committed, to become a separate service, and they saw their achievements in the war as their best argument. They had a public relations officer with every unit, and they never let an opportunity pass to make sure "the Air Force story" made it into the press.

Gladwyn Hill, who was Cronkite's opposite number for the Associated Press, recalled:

> There were a helluva lot of reporters sitting around the bars in London waiting for the big show to happen, and their editors back home were asking for stories. The Air Force could entice some of the more adventuresome, like me and Walter – for which it was our job – to go on a mission in a bomber; I did three myself. But there was no way for a kibitzer to go along with the fighter boys. So the Air Force public relations folks – they were headed up in London by the former head of publicity at Warner Brothers, as I recall – were always looking for a story they could push to get the reporters out to the airfields. An "ace race" was something even the guys who knew nothing about airplanes could understand and write about.

Hub Zemke remembered that as the 56th consolidated its position as the leading American fighter outfit in Europe, it brought them considerable publicity which, in his view was unwanted. "As a nation we Americans are awfully vain, we have to shout about our successes and wave the flag. We must have heroes to worship. In World War II, the fighter pilot was one of the main recipients of this kind of adoration." The Air Force command placed little restriction on the release of pilots' names by the press and groups were identified by the commander's name. The official *Stars and Stripes* newspaper made frequent mention of "the Zemke group" and published a daily box score of fighter aces and their victories as if it was some sort of sporting event.

Zemke correctly believed that VIII Fighter command leaders thought the publicity encouraged competition between fighter groups and made the pilots more aggressive, which annoyed him "because it reduced the bloody business we were engaged in to the level of a ball game." Both Zemke and Blakeslee were vociferous in their opposition to this kind of publicity, because both saw in their groups that it made some pilots take unnecessary risks in pursuit of getting their names in the papers back home. As Blakeslee put it years later, "We could do without the unnecessary pressure imposed by a continual stream of press people to our base who were little more than glorified sports reporters."

With the air battle against the Luftwaffe now becoming increasingly successful, group and individual scores soared, and VIII Fighter Command's press office made the most of the opportunity this presented. At the outset of the war, Eddie Rickenbacker, America's World War I "ace of aces" with a score of 26, had publicly offered a bottle of expensive bourbon whiskey to the first pilot who equaled or bettered his score. So far, he had given away two such awards: Marine Joe Foss had scored 26 victories in the desperate fighting over Guadalcanal in the fall of 1942 and come home to a victor's welcome. At the moment, Air Force Major Richard Ira Bong, a P-38 pilot in New Guinea who had scored 27 victories, was making a war bond publicity tour back home. But to the publicists in London, Europe was the main theater. It was certainly the location with the most reporters, coupled with air bases that were not hacked out of jungles on distant islands. In the days following the three Berlin raids, Air Force publicists started asking, "Who will be the first to beat Rickenbacker's score?"

The pilot most likely to do that was the Wolfpack's Robert S. Johnson, who came out of the Berlin battles the leading VIII Fighter Command ace with 22, only four away from Rickenbacker's score. Forty years later, he recalled, "We had the good fortune that Halesworth was out in the middle of nowhere, with no amenities that would interest someone to leave London to come sample, and Colonel Zemke wasn't very welcoming to the ones who did show up, so we were able to get on with the war."

The Eagles, however, were at Debden, a base not that far from London, which did "offer the amenities" to those who showed up. Ever since the days of the Eagle Squadrons, the unit had been the subject of publicity. Don Blakeslee, who had refused to become a part of the Eagles until he had no other choice if he wished to keep flying on operations, had deplored the unit as "publicity seekers" then, and he disliked the idea now. Blakeslee was so "GI" that he never had a name or a score painted on any of his airplanes. While other pilots studiously worked to get their uniform hats to the proper crushed "100-mission" look, his hats and uniforms were always "regulation"; in contrast, Don Gentile was a leading proponent of this "look." As Bob Wehrman put it, "Colonel Don was all business, all the time, and he didn't have time for anyone who wasn't."

At the time, Duane Beeson of the 334th Squadron and Don Gentile of the 336th were the new "neck and neck" contenders for high scoring. Additionally, Gentile and Godfrey flew together more often. They had devised what would be called 15 years later the "loose deuce" fighting formation when the US Navy "invented" it in the late 1950s. Rather than the rigid formation in which the leader is the shooter and the wingman's duty is to keep the enemy off the leader's tail (frequently by becoming the substitute target), which the Air Force would maintain through the Vietnam War, Gentile and Godfrey operated on "whoever sees them first takes them, the other follows," as Godfrey explained in his memoir *The Look of Eagles*. They frequently got separated from the other element of the flight, and returned to Debden with one confirming the other's claims.

Unlike most fighter groups, the 4th had a real newspaperman running its public relations office. Grover C. Hall's family owned and published the *Montgomery Advertiser* in Montgomery, Alabama. Hall had worked as a reporter on the paper for seven years prior to joining

333

the USAAF after Pearl Harbor. He ran his office professionally, finding experienced photographers and getting them transferred to the unit, which resulted in the 4th being possibly the best-photographed fighter unit in England. He later regretted having written a press release on March 9, extolling Gentile's three victories over Berlin the previous day, that had mentioned Beeson as his nearest competitor in the group. Gladwyn Hill later recalled, "He ended up feeling he had created his own monster, since that press release got picked up by headquarters and pushed to the correspondents."

VIII Fighter Command also had their own reasons for pushing Gentile and Godfrey as a "team," despite their unorthodox fighting methods, because Godfrey could be used as a "model" for all the young pilots newly arrived who might never get beyond the position of "wingman." Hill also observed, "It didn't hurt that Gentile was handsome enough to be a movie star and Godfrey looked like the all-American kid next door. They were a public relations officer's dream."

Godfrey came to rebel against the publicity campaign when he realized he was being presented as something he wasn't. Writing later, he said, "The truth was, we weren't leader and wingman; most everything that was put out about us wasn't true. We didn't really fly together all the time as they made out we did." Gentile, on the other hand, welcomed the publicity and accommodated himself to the campaign. Godfrey later wrote that Gentile confided to him that he intended to use the publicity after the war to give himself the opportunity for business advancement, the way he perceived that Rickenbacker had done. Gentile had charisma and was willing to say things in ways he knew reporters would pick up and use, such as describing an aerial battle being "like a football game." For others in the group, saying such things publicly was tantamount to heresy.

Being publicized as having enough victories to be in the running for Rickenbacker's record also got pushback from other air force commands, since VIII Air Force was the only one that gave formal recognition to "ground kills"; seven of Gentile's victories were from strafing claims. Several of the other groups within VIII Fighter Command differentiated aerial victories from strafing claims, to the point of pilots using different symbols to separate the two on their airplanes.

There had always been a certain degree of tension between Blakeslee and Gentile dating back to the group's formation. Speaking of it 40 years later, Bob Wehrman attributed it to the times in which the two had grown up:

> Don Blakeslee came from Fairport, Ohio, which his ancestors had helped found after the American Revolution. Don Gentile was the first-generation son of Italian immigrants, and this was in the days of a lot of animosity towards people with an Italian background. The two of them came from different worlds that didn't get along, and it showed in their actions toward each other. Gentile had no patience with that. He was ready to fight anytime somebody was stupid enough to crack an "Italian joke" in his vicinity.

Blakeslee, for his part, had always recognized that air warfare was not an individual event, but rather a "team sport." He had no difficulty getting rid of pilots who did not subscribe to being part of a team. Jim Goodson recalled that Blakeslee often said that individual scores didn't matter, that "It's what we achieve as a group that matters." Goodson also recalled that Blakeslee's attitude resulted in his being dressed down by General Kepner who told his most aggressive commander that there was a "bigger team" he needed to be part of if he wanted to have a career in the Air Force after the war.

Duane Beeson was the polar opposite of Gentile. "Bee was actually shy until he got to know you," Goodson recalled. He had adopted the "all business" attitude propounded by Blakeslee, which made him less interesting to reporters than Gentile. "The guys who were Bee's friends took his side," Wehrman explained, "and they proceeded to question the claims Don and Johnny made and said they didn't play by the same rules everyone else did."

Into all of this came Lee Carson, International News Service's leading reporter and at the time the highest-paid reporter in America. Gladwyn Hill said of her, "She was that era's equivalent of Barbara Walters, and she operated with the full support of her boss, William Randoph Hearst. It was advisable not to get in her way."

Reporters became a constant presence at Debden and mobbed the pilots on their return from a mission. Lee Carson decided that "the Gentile Story" was hers, and a serious competition broke out when Ira Wolfert, who had gained fame as a war correspondent covering the Battle of Guadalcanal, showed up looking to write about Gentile.

Carson went so far as to enlist the support of senior officers in VIII Fighter Command's press office in her effort to get Gentile to sign an "exclusive" with her. This only became more intense after Beeson was shot down on a strafing mission on April 5 and became a POW, leaving Gentile the "winner" by default. Three days later, Gentile returned from a mission to Berlin with claims for three Bf-109s that took his score past the magic 26. To settle the controversy over ground kills, Gladwyn Hill remembered that Grover Hall wrote a release, saying "Let them make of this what they will," which became the basis of his report for Associated Press:

> Capt. Don S. Gentile's claim of five planes destroyed on the ground on April 5 was confirmed today while he was blasting three more Nazi planes out of the sky to run his bag to 30, and the Piqua, Ohio, Mustang pilot became the first American ace of this war formally recognized as having broken Capt. Eddie Rickenbacker's World War record... The confirmation brought his official total to 27 of which seven were destroyed on the ground and 20 in the air.

On April 11, General Eisenhower visited Debden to award Blakeslee and Gentile with Distinguished Flying Crosses. Pinning on Gentile's, the general was heard by nearby reporters to say "You're quite the one-man air force," which was picked up and only heightened the publicity craze.

Gentile's tour was coming to an end and it was decided to make his final mission a major publicity event. Hall later wrote that by this time, "Don Gentile, master of the Hun over Germany, felt like the fox in a foxhunt." Over Berlin on April 13, Gentile spotted three Bf-109s and dived on them; they didn't see him and a triple score would have been easy. Just as he was about to pull the trigger, he heard another pilot call for help and banked away, searching for the squadron mate. Goodson later said, "Those three kills would have solved his problem, and for those who say Don Gentile was only ever out for himself, I will point to his action as proof to the contrary."

Returning to Debden, Gentile knew the cameras were running and the reporters were present. Dropping rapidly from high altitude, he made a low pass over the main runway at Debden. Suddenly, those on the ground realized he was much lower, as the Mustang approached the high point in the runway that blocked full view from either end. As

Grover Hall later described it, "The airplane hit, then bounced, spraying parts over the crowd before it hit again and plowed the distance of the runway, coming to a stop a total wreck."

Don Blakeslee had one ironclad rule that was never set aside: "He who prangs his kite goes home," meaning that any pilot who was involved in an accident due to violation of flying discipline was automatically out of the group. Gentile was hustled into the ambulance before Blakeslee could arrive at the scene. Reporters heard him say, "He is out! He is gone! Now!" The leading ace of the Eighth Air Force, the man who had beaten Eddie Rickenbacker, was to go home in disgrace? General Kepner intervened with General Doolittle, and it was determined that Gentile had crashed because of damage his airplane had received in combat that he was unaware of, and that he would go home to the war bond tour as planned. When the decision was announced, a reporter asked Blakeslee his reaction, to which the colonel replied, "You people have just destroyed one good man!" Don Blakeslee never spoke to a reporter again in the 20 years he spent in the Air Force.

Three weeks later, Johnny Godfrey, who had just tied Gentile's score, was taken off operations and sent back to the United States to accompany Gentile on a tour of USAAF training fields, where he would be presented to young pilots, who would never be more than wingmen in the year remaining of World War II, as "the best wingman in the air force."

On April 19, Bert Stiles' crew flew their first mission; he later wrote, "The squadron was short on crews or we would have had some more practice missions." The night before, Stiles had been awakened in his barracks when a drunken co-pilot from another crew broke into his room and was forcibly pacified by his navigator and bombardier; the bombardier returned and told Stiles, "He won't last much longer. He's seen too many guys go down." Stiles lay awake most of the rest of the night. "I wasn't scared. I was just wondering what I was doing here at all. All I knew of war I got through books and movies and magazine articles, and listening to a few big wheels who came through the schools to give us the low down. It wasn't in my blood; it was all in my mind."

Being junior, they flew an old B-17 still painted in camouflage, "The Keystone Mama." During form-up, another wing flew through their formation. "Bird yelled over the interphone, 'Here they come!'

I ducked and he said 'I don't wanna die this way.' Nobody got it head-on, but nobody missed by far." As he recalled, they missed the target, dropping on the formation leader. "It was a fighter park, they'd told us before." Two planes went down. "One was the Fort the drunk co-pilot was in."

The Wolfpack moved from Halesworth to take over the 354th's home at Boxted during the last week in April, when the Pioneer Mustangs moved to a temporary landing ground in the south of England as they prepared for the invasion. Hub Zemke was glad because the move put the Wolfpack closer to the fight.

While VIII Fighter Command had indeed decimated the Luftwaffe's *Experten*, there was one leading pilot who managed despite all to rise to prominence during the air battles over Germany. Major Heinz "Pritzl" Bär, whose combat record began in the Polish campaign and the Battle of Britain, where he had first distinguished himself as an enlisted pilot, returned to the Channel Front at the end of 1943, a leading ace both on the Eastern Front and in North Africa and Sicily, where he led Jagdgeschwader 77. When Göring blamed the leaders of the Jagdwaffe for failing to stop the Western Allies in Europe and the Mediterranean in a meeting held in the *Reichsmarschall*'s Karinhall lair in December, Bär – a leader of what was called "the Revolt of the *Kommodores*" – rose in opposition, accusing Göring to his face of failed leadership. His attitude of forthright honesty in an organization whose high command was so thoroughly corrupt put him in personal danger. Oberstleutnant Walter Oesau, the new *Kommodore* of JG 1, managed to get him away from Göring's vengeance by taking him as a *Staffelkapitän* in II./JG 1 at Woensdrecht, the only officer of his rank with such an assignment. A grateful Bär willingly supported his inexperienced *Gruppenkommandeur*. With JG 1 directly in the path of the growing American offensive, he soon became a "Fortress specialist." On March 15, now credited with 14 B-17 and B-24 victories, he was "rehabilitated" and appointed *Gruppenkommandeur* of II./JG 1. On April 22, a lone B-24 was sighted northwest of the field. Despite having just landed from battle, Bär sprinted to his reserve Fw-190 and took off with his wingman, Oberfeldwebel Leo Schumacher. Fifteen minutes later, the Liberator became his 200th victory – 101 of which were scored against the RAF and USAAF. In May, Galland promoted him *Kommodore* of Jagdgeschwader 3. Göring managed to find it in himself to privately apologize to Bär, perhaps the only time the *Reichsmarschall* ever did such a thing.

Unteroffizier Heinz Gehrke's experience was much more representative of the average Jagdwaffe pilot. He participated in his first Twelve O'Clock High attack on the bombers on April 24. He later recalled the mission:

> Staiger gave the order over the radio – we attack from the front and reassemble afterward at altitude so-and-so. My heart dropped into my boots. Never before had I attacked heavy bombers from the front, but my *Staffel* comrades were around me and it would be all right. How can I describe the sensations of such an attack, straight through the enemy formation? It literally took my breath away. We went hell-for-leather, thrown about like leaves in the wind by the prop wash. I was so nervous I forgot everything. I just flew straight ahead, firing. Everything happened lightning-quick, and I suddenly found myself alone.

Gehrke caught up with another Bf-109; they then spotted a single B-17 below them. "We attacked and I had the good fortune to hit its right inboard engine with my cannon. The right wing broke out in flames and the aircraft went into a spin and crashed." When the two went back to their base to refuel and rearm, Gehrke landed first. "Just as I landed, my comrade was shot down. Several Mustangs appeared just behind us. Not only did they shoot down my companion, but proceeded to strafe the field. It was with weak knees, pounding heart, and increased blood pressure that I realized I had just escaped being shot down myself."

Over the month of April, Luftflotte Reich (Air Fleet Reich), the main Luftwaffe defense organization covering central Germany, lost 38 percent of its fighter pilots; Luftflotte 3, which controlled the Western Front *Geschwadern* JG 2, JG 26, JG 1, and JG 11, experienced 24 percent pilot losses. The casualty rate was ruinous, and even the accelerated pilot training program could not replace these numbers; the entire Luftwaffe lost 489 pilots while only 396 completed training and were assigned to operational units. II./JG 26, which had an authorized strength of 36 Fw-190s, had only 15 at the end of April. The month saw Eighth Air Force record its heaviest bomber losses of the war, with

409 B-17s and B-24s shot down by flak or fighters. These losses were made good and saw increases in planes and personnel beyond the losses by the end of May.

On April 1, Dwight Eisenhower assumed control of Eighth Air Force, its operations now dedicated to supporting the coming invasion. VIII Fighter Command's P-38s, P-47s, and P-51s reigned supreme in the skies of Europe. *Pointblank*'s goal of air supremacy was achieved.

# 20

# LIBERATING EUROPE

Once SHAEF assumed operational control of all air forces in England, Air Marshal Tedder, second-in-command of the invasion force to General Eisenhower, directed Eighth Air Force to concentrate its missions against the rail transportation system in Germany, Holland, Belgium, and France in the weeks leading up to D-Day.

The problem for all fighter-bombers was accuracy. Individual attacks resulted in bombs spread all over, sometimes not even close to the desired target. Once equipped with P-47s that could carry a 1,000-pound bomb under each wing, the 56th Group had experimented in November 1943 with a squadron of P-47s so armed being led by a "master bomber" B-24, with the fighters salvoing their bombs when the bombardier in the B-24 dropped his; this was little different from the "bomb on leader" being used for the heavy bombers and had the value of using fighters that could defend themselves after dropping their ordnance if necessary.

The P-38 Lightning could carry the same bomb load as a medium bomber, since it was capable of lifting a bomb as large as 2,000 pounds under each inner wing in place of the drop tanks. While this maximum capability was only possible over a short range, the airplane could also carry a maximum-size bomb under one wing and a drop tank under the other, giving sufficient range to make attacks on the transport system in northern France. Even a 1,000-pound bomb made an impression on the enemy; carrying one such bomb and a drop tank, the P-38 had range sufficient to fly into the Low Countries.

With the Wolfpack's experiment in guided formation bombing proven successful, VIII Technical Command and Lockheed Air Services created a "master bomber" Lightning, modifying a P-38J in which the gun armament in the central nacelle was replaced by a bombardier with a Norden sight, sighting through a blown plexiglass nose. The design was the work of the redoubtable Colonel Cass Hough, assisted by Colonel Don Ostrander, an expert in armament and ordnance. This conversion was more versatile than using a bomber that was less maneuverable with fighters in close formation. Also, an enemy would not necessarily recognize a formation of bomb-carrying P-38s as a threat to a ground target until they dropped their loads.

The first mission using what was called the "Droop Snoot" Lightning to guide a bombing mission was performed by the 55th Fighter Group on April 10. Two squadrons were sent to bomb St Dizier airfield from 20,000 feet, with each P-38 carrying one 1,000-pound bomb and a drop tank. The enemy airfield was obscured by cloud when the group arrived, so group commander Colonel Jack Jenkins chose to attack Coulommiers airfield which was nearby and clear. The 28 bombs were dropped in a good pattern, and Jenkins then led the third squadron that had escorted the "bombers" down to strafe the field. When his canopy fogged over at lower altitude, Jenkins cleared it by rolling down a side window, then made a second pass; the defending gunners had the range and set one of his engines on fire. Jenkins managed a successful belly landing, and was taken prisoner.

The 20th Group, using the second modified Droop Snoot, was sent to make a simultaneous attack on Florennes airfield, but it was also covered by cloud and there was no suitable alternative. Frustrated, the pilots ditched their bombs in the Channel on return. That afternoon, the group flew a second mission with the Droop Snoot, to Gutersloh airfield, across the border in western Germany. The Lightnings put 25 1,000-pound bombs right on the airport hangars; explosions revealed the presence of aircraft within.

General Eisenhower put the stamp of approval on the Droop Snoot on April 11 when he went for a flight in the 55th's airplane after the awards ceremony held at Debden. The idea was a success and more Droop Snoots were modified. Each Lightning group in both Eighth and Ninth Air Forces was equipped with one. Since the airplane had no armament, its presence in the formation was disguised by having the noses of the normal fighters highly polished, with a white stripe immediately to the rear, so that in sunlight all the noses "glinted" and the one with plexiglass was invisible to an enemy pilot. The Droop Snoots also flew as "master bombers" for P-47 units during the run-up to the invasion and afterwards over the summer. Using fighter-bombers as medium-altitude "level bombers" saved the B-26 Marauders and A-20 Havocs from attacking heavily defended targets. On April 20, the 55th Group's attack was blocked by poor weather and the bombs again ended up in the Channel. The 20th was able to bomb the Fw-190 repair facility at Tours but the poor weather gave inconclusive results. The two groups went out on more missions over the last ten days of the month, but were only partially successful due to the cloudy weather. The experts at Lankford Lodge began work on a radar-equipped Droop Snoot that could give the fighters a blind-bombing capability, but this did not arrive until fall.

In April, General Doolittle decided to standardize VIII Fighter Command on the Mustang, re-equipping the groups equipped with P-47s and P-38s as P-51s were delivered and became available. Priority was given to re-equipping the Lightning groups, due to the airplane's poor record in the command. The P-38H and the early P-38Js that arrived in early 1944 suffered from poor heating in the cold winter skies, though the J-model had more reliable engines due to possessing better radiators for cooling. The problem of compressibility that had plagued the Lightning from the first days that it equipped fighter groups continued, and it was believed that the pilots were not flying their airplanes to the maximum possible due to fear of getting into a compressibility situation. Lockheed had attempted to change the men's minds back in March, when test pilot Tony LeVier was sent on a four-month tour of the ETO groups. LeVier went to each base, gave a talk to the pilots about proper procedures with the airplane, then gave a practical demonstration of what the airplane was safely capable of. As he recalled when interviewed many years later:

Those boys only had the minimum training to operate the airplane, and they knew there was a lot about it they didn't know. Unfortunately, the P-38 had the highest loss rate of any fighter in training, so they had already lost friends to accidents that came from not having full control of the operation. No wonder they were afraid of it!

After his lecture, LeVier would fly a new Lightning named "Snafuperman," which had been modified to full P-38J-25-LO specifications. "I performed all the fighter maneuvers common wisdom there held were suicidal. I had told them the proper entry speeds, and other technical details, to fly these maneuvers safely, and then there I was doing it." While the result of LeVier's visit was an infusion of confidence for the pilots, the P-38's technical problems persisted and the decision to phase the fighter out of VIII Fighter Command remained.

Lockheed worked hard to find a way to control the compressibility problem, and found a solution in the use of electrically actuated dive recovery flaps just outboard of the engines on the centerline of the lower wing. These flaps disrupted the airflow, slowing the airplane. The flaps were installed on the production line for the final 210 P-38J-25-LO models. Additionally, Lockheed manufactured 200 retrofit modification kits to be installed "in the field" on the P-38J-10-LO and J-20-LO Lightnings already in Europe. The need was considered so great that the entire production run of the kits was loaded on a C-54 to be flown direct to England. Unfortunately, the transport was shot down over the Bay of Biscay by an RAF Beaufighter whose pilot mistook it for a Luftwaffe Fw-200 Condor.

When the P-38s were assigned to fighter-bombing for the invasion, it meant they were operating at altitudes under 20,000 feet, similar to the conditions found in the Pacific. Suddenly, the airplane performed better. Regardless, the 20th Group began to transition to the P-51 after the invasion. Major Jack Ilfrey, who had become the first P-38 ace flying with the 1st Fighter Group in North Africa the year before, joined the 20th at the end of April as the new commander of the 79th Squadron. Commencing operations in May, he had engaged enemy fighters twice, flying a new P-38J, and been victorious. In one fight, he had collided with the enemy fighter, which crumpled three feet of the outboard end of his right wing. Despite this, he was able to nurse the Lightning home. He later recalled, "By then, I had pretty much convinced the boys that the P-38 was a good bird, but the high command didn't want to listen."

On April 8, when the 4th's score was 405.5, Don Blakeslee set a goal of 500 destroyed by May 1, a good indication of how fast the air war was now moving, since the 4th only had a score of 100 over 18 months of combat at the end of January. The Eagles outdid their leader's challenge, with credits for 207 destroyed in the air and on the ground by April 30, for a total score of 503, passing their long-time rivals the Wolfpack to become the top-scoring fighter group in the Eighth Air Force. Following an epic party on the base on the night of April 30, the group was still able to provide escort on May 1 to Saarbrücken. John Godfrey, now promoted to flight leader in his own right, no longer in Gentile's shadow, led his flight after a gaggle of 12 Bf-109s that he spotted below. He chased one to low altitude where he hit the engine solidly and the pilot bailed out to give him his 14th aerial victory. Ralph Hofer scored his tenth victory when the enemy pilot bailed out so close ahead of him that "I could see his uniform and his black boots in the sun." Two other pilots also scored off this group of enemy fighters. The 4th failed to score again for a week.

The May 8 mission, with the bombers going to both Berlin and Brunswick, saw the 352nd Group fly its first all-Mustang escort mission as the Blue Nosers finally appeared over Berlin. The Jagdwaffe responded with over 200 fighters taking to the air. The group's patrol area was soon the scene of dogfights from 30,000 feet to street-level with the action hot and heavy for nearly an hour.

Over Brunswick, the 487th Squadron's Second Lieutenant Carl Luksic gained the distinction of being the first VIII Fighter Command "ace in a day." His encounter report provides an accurate description of the action:

While Lieutenant Bob O'Nan was chasing this Bf-109 I saw on my left five or six FW-190s which I immediately turned into. I put down ten degrees of flaps and started queuing up on one of the '190s. I fired very short bursts from about 300 yards, 15 degrees deflection and observed many strikes on the canopy and fuselage. He immediately pulled up and rolled over and the pilot bailed out, his airplane going straight in from fifteen hundred feet. At this time in this vicinity there were three 'chutes – one from the enemy aircraft that I had shot down and one from the enemy aircraft that Lieutenant O'Nan had shot down, but I do not know where the third one came from.

I then broke away from one shooting at me and got onto another '190's tail and fired short bursts, but did not see any hits. However, the pilot evidently spun out as he went straight into the ground from eight hundred feet or so and blew up. I was then joined by two P-47s but lost them, and finally joined up with two from our own group,

Captain Cutler [from the 486th Squadron] and his wingman. He started down over Brunswick to strafe a 'drome, but observing so much ground fire and flak I pulled up and away and lost them. I then saw another airplane which I thought to be a P-51. I closed on it to about thirty yards and identified it as a '109. I gave a short burst, but don't know if there were any strikes, and I found myself riding his wing as I was at full throttle. He was about two hundred feet off the deck, and when he looked at me he pulled up, jettisoned his canopy and bailed out. I went down and took a picture of the airplane, which had crashed into a small wood, and right onto a small fire.

I started to climb back up when I was rejoined by my wingman, Lieutenant O'Nan, and Red Leader, Captain Davis. We started back towards the bombers when off to our left at nine o'clock low we observed about twenty-plus in close formation going down through the clouds. The three of us immediately turned into the attack and came down on them through the clouds. I found myself directly astern of a '190, with a '109 flying his wing in close formation. I was evidently unseen as I got in a very successful burst at the '109 and observed numerous hits on his wings, fuselage, and tail. He was at about eight hundred feet, and after catching fire he went straight down into the ground.

I immediately kicked a little right rudder and got in another successful burst at the '190 and observed numerous hits on its left wing, engine and canopy. The '190 went into a tight spiral and crashed into the deck from a thousand feet. At this point there were about fifteen or more enemy aircraft in the vicinity and they started aggressive tactics, and since I was alone, and they were making head-on passes at me, I had to take violent evasive action. I evaded into the clouds.

Following close behind Luksic were 487th Squadron commander Lieutenant Colonel John C. Meyer and Lieutenants John Thornell and Clayton Davis, who claimed three each. The group returned to Bodney with total claims of 27 destroyed, their best day ever. The day's action earned the "Bodney Blue Nosers" their first Distinguished Unit Citation, while Luksic, Meyer, Thornell, and Davis were awarded the Distinguished Service Cross.

The question of who was the top ace of the ETO, and the pilot who matched Eddie Rickenbacker's score, was also settled on May 8. Bob

Johnson had brought his score to 25 – all aerial victories – in mid-April and gotten a 25-hour extension to his tour. The mission to Berlin saw the Wolfpack return with claims of five shot down, including two by Johnson, giving him an uncontested score of 27; this was later changed to 28 when an earlier "probable" was upgraded – all in the air and all either Bf-109s or Fw-190s. The pilot who had flunked gunnery in flight training, who had nearly been expelled from the group at the outset of their battle with the Luftwaffe for lack of aerial discipline, who had told his father at age ten that he was going to be an Army pilot, the best Army pilot, went back to the United States as the best Army pilot.

While the Blue Nosers scored over Berlin, VIII Fighter Command Mustangs were ranging farther and farther afield. That same day, the 4th escorted bombers to Brux, Czechoslovakia, nearly 800 miles from Debden. JG 27's Bf-109s provided opposition, but the P-51s came out on top with five pilots – including Jim Goodson – submitting claims for five destroyed. The next day, the group flew east of Berlin to pick up bombers returning from a strike on Poznan, Poland over the Oder River.

After the May 8 mission, Hub Zemke presented his ideas for adopting the fighter tactic that was later known as "the Zemke Fan" to General Kepner. Zemke's plan was to confuse enemy ground controllers who were following the US fighters over Germany by breaking up the large group or squadron formations into individual four-plane flights. As he explained, this would allow greater coverage of the sector of sky that the group was responsible for covering, with a better chance of sighting enemy aircraft. The plan was that the group would fly to the sector it was assigned for bomber coverage, then break up into individual flights that fanned out into a 180-degree arc. "If we went in well in advance of the bombers, we stood a good chance of picking up some of the Luftwaffe units assembling for a mass attack and breaking them up." Kepner liked the idea and the Wolfpack put it into practice with their next mission on May 12, which resulted in claims for 18 destroyed for a loss of three. By June, all the fighter groups in VIII Fighter Command were using the Zemke Fan and enemy fighters had even more difficulty attacking the bombers.

While the Eagles flew to Poland, the 352nd again went to Berlin on May 13 where the Blue Nosers got involved in a massive battle with intercepting enemy fighters. Nearing Tribsees-Demmin, huge formations of Bf-109s and Fw-190s were spotted forming up to attack the bombers. First blood was drawn by the 328th Squadron's Captain

John Coleman and his element leader, First Lieutenant Francis Horne, who each scored two. Group commander Colonel Joe Mason led the 486th Squadron into a force estimated as "100-plus." The squadron broke into individual flights, with the Mustangs attempting to break up the enemy formation. Mason, leading White Flight, swept through enemy fighters that turned away, and he later reported:

> I saw strikes on the wing of one Me-109. Upon coming out on the far side, I lost the rest of my flight. As I pulled up in a climbing turn and looked down at the large formation of bandits, I saw two Me-109s spinning down, one with about two-thirds of its wing gone. This collision was forced by my flight flying through the large formation of bandits at about a 90-degree angle. I am not certain as to whether the '109 I damaged was one of the two I later saw going down.
>
> My wingman broke away and down when we started through, and my second element pulled up and came in on the rear of the bandits. They did not see the collision. I then rolled back and down, chasing 20 Fw-190s and Me-109s which had split off from the bunch and were diving for the clouds. I closed on an Fw-190 and after a few short bursts, set him on fire. The first burst knocked his left flap off. He was taking evasive action in the clouds, and just before entering one, smoke, flame, and debris came back over my ship and we both went into the cloud. I then pulled up to keep from running into him in the cloud, and came out on top. My ship was covered with oil from the '190.

Mason claimed two Bf-109s and one Fw-190 destroyed and one Bf-109 damaged. The three victories made him an ace, though the other three flight members believed that the two Bf-109s their commander claimed, which had collided as a result of the entire flight sweeping through the enemy formation, should have been shared equally. The dissenters were quiet when the group commander celebrated his new status that night in the officers' club.

George Preddy, leading the 487th Squadron, joined the fight shortly after Mason scored his victories. Spotting 30 Bf-109s below, Preddy led the squadron's bounce on them and personally downed two; with these he became an ace with a tally of 5.333 aerial victories. While Preddy scored, Lieutenant Nutter closed in when the remaining Bf-109s tried to flee and sent another down on fire. "Ace in a day" Carl Luksic and his wingman Lieutenant Glennon Moran spotted a Ju-88 attacking a B-17. Both attacked and the Junkers crash-landed in a ploughed field. When it did not catch fire, Luksic strafed it and set it afire. The 352nd's score of 16 destroyed made it the top-scoring VIII Fighter Command group for the day. Colonel Joe Mason was awarded a Distinguished Service Cross. The Jagdwaffe reported 58 losses, three fewer than the day before.

The result of the success that the fighter groups had achieved in April and early May saw morale in the bomber groups begin to recover as the crews realized they were flying missions with fewer casualties, due to the offensive fighter escort tactics. Losses would get progressively lower for the rest of the war, but May 1944 was the time when those who climbed into the bombers began to believe they had a chance to make it home, even when Doolittle increased the tour to 35 missions that summer.

Even so, life and death in the battles that happened in the stratosphere over Europe was ugly. The 401st Squadron returned from the Berlin mission on May 8 with one casualty – a waist gunner who was hit by shrapnel from a flak burst. Bert Stiles and the squadron flight surgeon entered the bomber to deal with the dead man. Stiles later wrote about the experience:

> The waist gunner wore a flak suit and a flak helmet, but they didn't help much. One chunk of shrapnel hit low on his forehead and clipped the top of his head off. Part of his brains sprayed around as far forward as the door into the radio room. The rest of them spilled out when the body crumpled up. The flak suit protected his heart and lungs all right, but both legs were blown off, and hung with the body, because the flying suit was tucked into electric shoes. Nobody else on the plane was hurt. I climbed in and put my hand in a gob of blood and brains that had splattered back that way. I took one look at the body and climbed out again, careful where I put my hands. I felt no nausea, just a sense of shock, just a kind of deadness inside.

Range for P-51s would increase as the Mustang-equipped groups saw their aircraft modified to allow them to carry two 108-gallon paper tanks, rather than the metal 75-gallon tanks they had been using. The modification took several days for each group and was carried out a group at a time over mid-May; the 4th was the first to do this between May 14 and 18. Now able to take their Mustangs to places where no American fighter had been seen before, or to stay longer for the fight over targets like Berlin, the 4th continued amassing victories.

On May 21, as part of the transportation program that SHAEF planners had developed to disrupt German rail transportation, VIII Fighter Command and IX Tactical Air Command flew what was called "Chattanooga Day" (named for the popular song, "Chattanooga Choo-Choo"), with 552 Mustangs, Lightnings, and Thunderbolts turned loose over central and western Germany, and northern France and Belgium to attack the railroads. The groups came back with claims for 225 locomotives attacked, with 91 considered destroyed. Strafing ground targets had not been limited to railroads, since the pilots also claimed 102 aircraft destroyed on airfields, with a further 76 damaged. The 361st Fighter Group, led by Philippines and Guadalcanal veteran Colonel Thomas J.J. Christian, great-grandson of Confederate general Stonewall Jackson, made its first appearance flying P-51s after transferring from P-47s and submitted claims for wrecking 23 locomotives.

The P-38 groups demonstrated the power of a concentrated armament of four .50-caliber machine guns and a 20mm cannon, with the 55th Group destroying 23 locomotives and leaving another 15 bullet-riddled; 16 of the trains that its pilots attacked were left in flames. The group's First Lieutenant Peter Dempsey proved that a Lightning could survive serious tail damage when he tried to fly under a high-tension wire that suddenly appeared in his path as he flew away from a strafing run that resulted in two Bf-109s going up in flames. He snapped the cable, which sheared off the upper part of his port fin while a two-foot section of wire jammed his right rudder. He managed to get home, changing power settings between his engines to effect any turns.

Chattanooga Day was the pre-invasion high point of railroad attacks that had begun back in February and saw over 900 locomotives destroyed over four months.

Berlin was attacked again on May 24. Jim Goodson, leading the 4th, spotted 40-plus enemy fighters near Hamburg gathering for an attack on the bomber stream. When the Mustangs hit the formation, they soon came across several gaggles of Fw-190s nearby, which Ralph Hofer later reported. When they returned to Debden, the pilots claimed another eight destroyed.

The next day, Goodson again led the group, this time an escort to bomb the rail yards in Chaumont-Sarreguentines in northern France. He later reported, "We saw fighters and immediately went to investigate." The opponents were from JG 26, with 20 Fw-190s from II.Gruppe, covered by 30 Bf-109s from III.Gruppe. "We split them up, but due to the fact that we were outnumbered 50 to eight, we were not able to destroy any. My wingman and I ended up alone on the deck." As he climbed to rejoin the group, Goodson spotted 24 Bf-109s and Fw-190s flying in close formation of six "vics" of four each, in line astern.

> I told my wingman we would try to sneak up behind and knock off the last section and then run away in the haze. As we were closing on the last section, all the Huns broke, and a lengthy dogfight ensued, with the Fw-190s showing amazing fighting ability and aggressiveness. It was only after the most violent maneuvering and excessive use of throttle and flaps that I was able to get good strikes on the most persistent '190. He pulled up and bailed out.

Goodson's 14th aerial victory turned out to be his last.

With the fighters of IX Tactical Air Command striking every target they could find in northern France and Belgium, and fighter groups from VIII Fighter Command strafing targets during their returns from every escort mission, while the A-20 Havocs and B-26 Marauders of the IX Tactical Air Command and VIII Bomber Command's B-17s and B-24s hit every rail target in the region, the German Army in northwestern France was cut off from its supply bases. The strikes on airfields forced the defending fighters to pull back deeper into France and Germany. The week before the invasion, the commander of the German Seventh Army, tasked with defending Normandy, called the roads in the army's area of operations *Jabo Rennstrecki* (fighter-bomber racecourses).

After the F-5 photo-reconnaissance Lightnings from the 13th and 27th Photo Reconnaissance Squadrons of the Eighth's 7th Photo Reconnaissance Group were replaced in the bomb damage assessment role by reverse-Lend-Lease Spitfires with superior high-altitude performance after Big Week, the Lightnings began photographing northwest Europe to create invasion maps. To mask the actual invasion location, they flew missions from Blankenberge to Dunkirk, and from Le Touquet to S. Vaast de la Hague – almost the entire Channel Coast – and flew three missions elsewhere for every one flown over Normandy and the Cherbourg peninsula.

On May 26, Major Hubert "Chili" Childress, commander of the 27th Photo Reconnaissance Squadron, flew one of the most important, yet hair-raising missions that any photo pilot flew in the ETO:

> SHAEF wanted pictures of all the Loire River bridges, so they knew how they were made, because they wanted to blow them up to keep the German forces south of the Loire from crossing into northern France after the invasion. That meant going in at low level. We decided that we should fly the mission at a maximum altitude of 50 feet to stay below the treeline in our approaches to the bridges. In fact, I flew most of the mission at an altitude of 30 to 40 feet.

There were a total of 64 bridges to photograph. Knowing the importance and danger of the mission, Childress assigned himself the flight.

The F-5 did not have a forward-facing camera, which meant that Childress would be forced to make his photo runs parallel to the bridges. "I had to fly straight and level, at a maximum speed of 320 miles per hour, a minimum of 200 yards from the bridge, to get the pictures." The mission parameters put him at the optimum distance to be taken down by defending flak. A second P-38 from the 13th Squadron was detailed to follow Childress. "He was there to take over after I got shot down. I figured I might make it for four bridges before that happened." Since the Germans would be surprised at the first bridge but fully warned and prepared as the F-5 flew on, it was deemed so dangerous that – like Childress – the 13th Photo Reconnaissance Squadron's CO assigned himself, unwilling to risk the life of any other pilot.

The mission was the first flown by the 7th Photo Reconnaissance Group to receive fighter escort. "We had 16 P-38s from the 55th Fighter Group that met us over Cherbourg. Four flew with me to provide flak suppression, four were with the other F-5, and the other eight were there to keep any German fighters that showed up off our backs."

Staying low and flying fast, Childress was only exposed to flak during the few seconds he was directly over the bridges. By varying the direction of approach, he was able to maintain the element of surprise over the first 50 bridges. "I took hits, nothing serious, though every time I went past a bridge and saw all that flak coming up I figured I was taking a year off my life."

Things came to an end at Tours. The four bridges inside the town forced Childress to head back and forth between them while staying directly over the city:

> This meant they could shoot at us continuously. The second and third bridges were so close together that when I was photographing one, I was directly above another. I got hit over the third bridge. I felt a thump, but everything seemed to continue working, so I got pictures of the last bridge and then we were out of there.

Flying to the next bridge, the escort leader spotted a trail of smoke from Childress' left engine and warned him over the radio:

> I looked over and sure enough, the cowling had a few holes in it and smoke was pouring out of the turbo. I feathered the prop and called to Major Smith that he'd have to get the rest of the bridges. I started climbing for altitude to get above the light flak, and managed to get up to 10,000 feet by the time we got to the Channel.

Back at Mount Farm (the base for the 7th Photo Group), Childress performed an overhead 360 to the left, into the dead engine:

> I'd always been told never to turn a Lightning into the dead engine, but the airplane was running so well no one on the ground even realized I was only on one engine. I landed, but then I couldn't turn left off the runway, so they had to come out and tow me back in. The airplane had enough holes in it that it didn't fly again for about ten days.

Eighth Air Force had no difficulty awarding Major Childress a Distinguished Flying Cross for the daring mission. During the week following Childress' mission, Allied fighter-bombers destroyed all the Loire bridges, cutting off Normandy and Brittany from the rest of France. To keep the enemy confused, all the bridges in the Pas de Calais region were also destroyed, as well as the Seine bridges north of Paris.

The Luftwaffe had fewer aircraft available on the Channel coast at the end of May than had been available at the time of the Dieppe Raid. JG 2, which had been assigned to the Cherbourg peninsula since 1941, was closest to the Normandy beaches. I./JG 2 had only recently returned from the fighting at Anzio. The Bf-109-equipped II./JG 2 was at Creil outside Paris, while III./JG 2's Fw-190s were in the process of transferring to Fontenay-le-Comte north of La Rochelle.

With a forecast for stormy weather during the first week in June that seemed to preclude any likelihood of invasion, JG 26 *Kommodore* Oberst Josef "Pips" Priller felt safe giving some pilots time off. II.Gruppe left for Mont de Marsan near Biarritz for a week's leave on June 1. The other two *Gruppen* were ordered to move inland on June 5, with I.Gruppe moving to Reims and III.Gruppe to Nancy. Their ground echelons were still on the road when dawn came on June 6.

Bob Wehrman remembered:

June 6, 1944, really was the longest day. We had Double-Daylight Savings Time in England, which meant dawn came around 0300 hours. None of us had slept much that night. The sky was filled for hours with the drone of aircraft. I spotted bombers heading toward invasion targets and C-47s carrying what I later learned were the British and American paratroops.

At Duxford, 78th Group ground crewman Warren Kellerstadt recalled:

They didn't tell us when D-Day was going to be, but the night before we could smell something in the wind. They closed up the base tight and wouldn't let anyone on or off and right after supper on June 5, they ordered black and white stripes painted around the wings and fuselages of the planes. We armorers were kept busy all night lugging bombs from the dump out to the dispersal area to stack next to the planes. I worked till midnight, then had guard from 0200 hours. All night long the bombers went out, first the RAF, then ours. They all had their navigation lights on because there were so many of them they had to worry about collisions, and the sky looked like a Christmas tree, full of red and green lights.

The 78th cranked engines at 0320 hours for the first D-Day mission. Rain poured and visibility was so bad that pilot Richard Holly remembered that when Colonel Gray's first section took off, "He just barely cleared the end of the runway before he was out of sight." When his flight lined up for magneto check Holly instructed the other three pilots to set their gyros on his and follow him. "It was the only instrument takeoff I made in the war and also the only one I made with water injection all the way because we were so heavy."

Nearly every pilot who flew on D-Day remembered that the biggest problem faced was avoiding mid-air collisions with other units, there were so many Allied aircraft airborne. The 78th's Thunderbolts found themselves flying in and out of rain showers across the Channel. As they flew through one storm, they encountered a formation of Lancasters and barely avoided disaster. Holly remembered, "I did not see anything on the ground through the clouds, but the red glow below the clouds told us it was Omaha Beach. As it got daylight the red glow went away but we knew from the smoke and haze there was still plenty going on down there."

A formation of Ninth Air Force B-26 Marauders was caught over Pointe du Hoc just after dawn during the initial phase of the invasion by 20 JG 2 Fw-190s as the Marauders bombed the beaches prior to the landing of the Army Rangers tasked with spiking the guns on the cliff top. The German fighters made one pass and then turned back to their base as masses of Allied fighters appeared overhead. This would be the biggest battle fought by the Luftwaffe on D-Day.

"Pips" Priller learned the invasion was on when he was awakened by the phone in his Lille command post. It was from 5.Jagddivision, ordering him to move his headquarters immediately to Poix, closer to the anticipated invasion site on the Pas de Calais. The dawn skies were a leaden grey at 0800 hours as Priller and his longtime wingman, Unteroffizier Heinz Wodarczyk, mounted their Fw-190A-8s and prepared to take off for a reconnaissance of the invasion beaches. With Wodarczyk sticking close, Priller headed west at an altitude of 325 feet. East of Abbeville, he looked up and saw several large formations of Spitfires flying through the broken cloud base. Near Le Havre, he climbed into the cloud bank hanging at 650 feet and turned northwest.

Moments later, the two fighters broke out of the clouds, just south of the British invasion beach code-named Sword. Priller only had a moment to stare out to sea at the largest naval force ever assembled in history. He could see wakes of the inbound invasion barges as they approached the beaches for as far as he could see in the hazy weather. With a shouted "Good luck!" to Wodarczyk, Priller winged over into a dive as his airspeed indicator climbed above 400 miles per hour. Dropping to an altitude of 50 feet, the two roared toward Sword Beach, where British troops dived for cover while ships offshore opened up with a barrage of antiaircraft fire so loud that those on the ground had trouble hearing Priller and Wodarczyk open fire as they flashed overhead, unscathed by the fleet's fire.

In a moment, the only appearance by the Luftwaffe over the Normandy beaches on D-Day was over. Priller and Wodarczyk zoomed back into the cloud bank and disappeared, having just flown the best-known mission in the entire history of JG 26, due to its later inclusion in Cornelius Ryan's book *The Longest Day* and the movie made from it.

The 78th flew three missions over the course of the day. Using both A and B groups, planes were landing and taking off at Duxford all day long. Eight-plane attacks were made on targets inland. The 83rd Squadron bombed a railroad bridge 40 miles west of Paris, while the 84th Squadron hit the Alençon marshaling yard and blew up a nearby ammunition dump. Armorer Kellerstadt remembered, "All that day they were dive bombing and strafing everything that moved. When they returned from a mission, we hopped on the planes, rearmed and bombed them, and cleaned as many of the guns as we had time for before they took off again."

Colonel Gray was leading the 83rd Squadron on the third mission of the day. As the Thunderbolts approached the Mayenne rail marshaling yard, eight Fw-190s were spotted, flying low on the deck. Gray sent two flights after them. Lieutenant Peter Caulfield singled out one and got into a Lufbery, circling his opponent. He pulled 90-degrees deflection and fired; the Fw-190 snap-rolled, spun, pulled out, turned, hooked a wing on the ground, and exploded on impact. Colonel Gray and his wingman Vincent Massa pursued two Fw-190s and caught up to them using water-injection. Gray opened fire on tail-end Charlie until its canopy came off and the engine quit. He overshot his opponent, and Massa pulled behind it to give the *coup de grâce*.

The group's final mission of "the Longest Day" was flown at 1800 hours. Thirty-two P-47s patrolled the area from Chaillone to

Coulonche. Two flights from the 84th strafed a train pulling fuel tank cars that exploded so violently that debris hit the attackers. Wallace Hailey had to abandon WZ-F over the Channel and was quickly rescued by ASR; two other damaged Thunderbolts managed to land safely at the RAF Coastal Command airfield at Ford.

Back in the United States, where he heard President Roosevelt's broadcast announcing the invasion, Ernie Russell – who had returned home at the conclusion of his tour ten days earlier – remembered, "I was filled with a great sense of relief that I was not there for what I knew was a tough fight, and at the same time a crazy wish that I had extended my tour long enough to see it."

That night, after flying two missions during the day, Bert Stiles wrote in his journal, "the only thing that matters is to win, win in a way so there is never another one."

Operation *Pointblank* had succeeded. The Allied air forces now had air superiority over western Europe. The five-month campaign had cost the Eighth 2,600 bombers and 980 fighters lost, with 18,400 casualties including 10,000 dead.

# 21

# THE BATTLE OF NORMANDY

JG 26's I. and III.Gruppen flew the majority of the 172 Luftwaffe sorties in the invasion sector on June 6. It was a drop in the bucket compared to the 14,000 sorties flown that day by the Allied air forces. By the end of the day, II.Gruppe arrived after flying across France in time to fly a mission over Normandy in the last light of day, during which they caught the 4th's Mustangs strafing enemy positions and shot down four P-51Bs in the first pass for no losses. For most of the next eight weeks, I.Gruppe and III./JG 54 operated from Cormeilles and Boissy le Bois, while II.Gruppe was based at Guyancourt outside Paris, and III.Gruppe at Villacoublay Nord and Sud in the Paris region.

By the evening of June 7, there were only six *Jagdgeschwadern* left in Germany, while 17 had flown into northwestern France to oppose the invasion. Had these units been at full strength, this would have been over 1,000 fighters, a force that might have had an impact on the battle. Unfortunately, with the losses suffered over Germany in the preceding months and the disorganization of the move from Germany to France, only 289 fighters were listed as operational at sundown of the second day of the invasion. On their arrival in France, the *Jagdflieger* discovered that nearly all the Luftwaffe's airfields in France had been too badly damaged by American bombing during the previous three months to sustain operations; they would be forced to fly and fight from improvised airfields that were so far from the battlefield they would have less than 30 minutes' combat time over Normandy. Due to the inability of 5.Jagddivision to exercise control of the newly arrived units in the form of planning and direction of operations, most fighter missions flown during the Normandy battle were *freie Jagd* uncontrolled independent fighter sweeps, an ineffective use of the limited resources. Over the course of the next two months, what was left of the flower of the Jagdwaffe would die in the Norman sky, outnumbered by odds of 100:1 and outflown by better-trained and more experienced Allied pilots. Even with the fighter force growing to 1,000 by the end of June, it was a case of "too little, too late."

The day's action saw Priller score his 97th and 98th victories, a P-47 and P-51, respectively. The hard-pressed pilots of I. and II.Gruppen scored eight for two losses. The next day, Priller led 11 Fw-190s of I.Gruppe on a strafing mission against the invasion beaches; their "score" was the "destruction" of 15 crashed gliders.

Among the other units fed into the Normandy killing ground was 2.Staffel of JG 54, which was brought directly from the Eastern Front to join III./JG 54, which had been serving in the Reich since 1942. One of the leading pilots in the unit was Leutnant Hans Dortenmann, a former infantry officer who had transferred to the Luftwaffe in 1942 and joined the *Staffel* a year previously, after graduation from flight school. On February 6, 1944, he scored his first victory by ramming a Lavochkin La-5. By the time he arrived with the rest of 2.Staffel to join III./JG 54 in Germany on the evening of June 6 after flying across Poland and east Germany that day, Dortenmann had 15 victories. III./JG 54 flew to France the next morning, where it became a "fourth *Gruppe*" with JG 26. Three days later, on June 10, Dortenmann scored his first Normandy victory, a P-47, and a P-38 the next day.

On June 8, 130 Bf-109s and Fw-190s were spotted. Allied fighters claimed 46 shot down, of which 31 were claimed by VIII Fighter Command units, with the Thunderbolts of the 56th and 353rd groups the top scorers, claiming seven and five destroyed, respectively. In return, the fighter groups lost 24, primarily to flak while flying ground support. The weather, which became progressively more stormy, cut into air operations over the beaches. The weather became progressively worse overnight, and on June 9 the only VIII Fighter Command mission was a single-squadron escort by the Yoxford Boys for an F-5 mission.

The day saw III./JG 2 lose its *Kommandeur*, Hauptmann Herbert Huppetz, in a dogfight with Thunderbolts. Major Josef "Sepp" Wurmheller, who had scored seven victories over Dieppe, replaced him in command. Wurmheller would last only 15 days with the *Gruppe* before he was shot down and killed in a fight with P-51s near Alençon on June 22.

The weather cleared on June 10, a day that saw the 78th suffer its worst losses since entering combat the year before. Two P-47s were hit by flak and went down during the first attack of the day near Le Touquet, while a third crash-landed near Duxford on return. Forty P-47s from the 83rd and 84th squadrons went out on a dive-bombing attack southwest of Argentan, led by original group member Major Harold Stump, who was flying his first mission of a second tour. When Stump and three other Thunderbolts of the first flight pulled up after dropping their bombs, they were attacked by 20 Bf-109s later reported to be wearing D-Day stripes and fake British insignia; this would have been impossible for a German unit to have accomplished with the limited time and resources available. Stump, Major William Hunt, and Second Lieutenant Daniel Loyd were shot down and killed.

The airspace below the low cloud deck and the ground became a storm of wildly maneuvering aircraft. Lieutenant Dorian Ledington salvoed his bombs just as a Bf-109 flew past; he fired into its wing root and the pilot bailed out. Luther Abel pulled off the target after he dropped his bombs and fired on a distant Bf-109 that caught fire and the pilot bailed out. Robert McIntosh shot down an Fw-190, but was in turn shot down by a Bf-109 moments later, bailing out to become a POW.

The 83rd's Franklin Pursell ran into 15 Fw-190s and got one while Robert Ealey out-climbed a Bf-109 and shot it down while a squadron mate shot down the Bf-109 on his tail. In a close-in combat, Donald McLeod hit one Bf-109 that exploded in front of him; as he turned away another flew in front of him and he fired at it – it went straight in. Moments later, when he spotted three 109s pursuing a P-47 and turned to give help, he was hit by flak and forced to bail out. He was lucky to avoid the Germans on the ground and met up with two members of the Resistance; three days later, he walked the ground below where the battle had happened and found the body of his friend Vincent Massa who had also been shot down and killed in the fight.

While the 78th's pilots fought for their lives, the Blue Nosers' 328th Squadron, led by Captain John Thornell, came across 40 bomb-carrying Bf-109s flying low toward the beachhead at 300 feet. When the German pilots spotted the Mustangs as they turned in to attack, they salvoed their bombs and split up, but not before Thornell got two of them for his 17th and 18th victories.

Throughout the battles over Normandy, the cloudy skies and rain would give cover to fighters of both sides, with units that chanced on each other becoming involved in sharp, vicious fights. On June 11, the P-38s that had been restricted to flying patrols over the invasion fleet on the (mistaken) assumption that their distinctive shape would be recognized by Allied gunners aboard the ships, who thus would not fire on them, were released from this duty; as it turned out, many gunners on the ships opened fire at any airplane they saw, regardless of distinctive shape or black and white D-Day stripes. The 55th Group flew a mission to Compiègne, where they hunted trains, trucks, and anything moving.

As they turned for home, their controller informed them of aerial activity around Beauvais. When the Lightnings showed up over the airfield JG 26 called home, 4.Staffel Fw-190s led by Priller appeared out of the four-tenths cloud cover overhead and ambushed them. Leutnant Gerd Wiegand, who claimed two P-38s shot down in the fight, later wrote in his diary that the *Staffel* had taken off at 1430 hours with orders to patrol and attack Allied fighters attacking transportation. Spotting ten Lightnings over the airfield, Priller led the *Staffel* in a full-throttle climb to get above the American fighters. Priller immediately hit one P-38 that went down for his 99th victory. One flight dived away to the right and Wiegand followed them with his wingman. He caught up with them and shot down number four. However, the flight leader turned on him and the two fighters attacked head-on. The American's fire hit Wiegand's Fw-190 and exploded it when the oil tank was hit. Wiegand was thrown from the cockpit and came to hanging under his parachute with a useless right leg and six P-38s circling him. When he hit the ground just under two miles from the airfield, he collapsed on his right side to discover his thigh was shattered.

While Wiegand claimed the second P-38, in fact his opponent had shot him down with a 70-degree deflection shot and Wiegand's fire had passed close over his canopy but struck nothing. Although the JG 26 pilots claimed four Lightnings, the only ones lost were the two shot down by Priller and Wiegand. This battle and others in June would mark the high point of the Lightning's career in VIII Fighter Command as all four groups were re-equipped with P-51s between late June and early September.

Meanwhile, the 4th's Ralph Hofer made history as the first Allied fighter to land at the advanced strip near Grandcamp in Normandy after his oil system was damaged by small-arms fire during a strafing pass near Vire. When he returned to Debden the next day, he brought a German helmet and canteen and a German-language version of *Mein Kampf* that he had bartered from the GIs near the front, which only added to his "screwball" reputation.

On June 12, Priller led what passed for all JG 26 in France – the 32 Fw-190s of II./JG 26 and III./JG 54, and 16 Bf-109s from III./JG 26 – on an early morning sweep northwest of Caen. Once airborne, he received orders to attack heavy bombers heading inland. Finding a formation of B-17s, he led II./JG 26 in an attack to no effect. Recovering from that, he spotted a formation of B-24 Liberators in the distance and turned toward them.

The 492nd Bomb Group's formation had almost no warning as JG 26 flew through them. Priller opened fire on the B-24 in the outboard position of the first vee and hit it in the cockpit and the two left engines. The bomber fell away from the formation with three engines afire. It turned for the beach, trying to make Allied territory before crashing. Two engines were dead and a third was aflame. Just as the third engine failed, the navigator reported they were over Allied territory and bailed out. The pilot held the bomber in the air for another few minutes until the fourth engine quit, at which time the rest bailed out. The navigator had gone too soon; he was picked up by German troops and became a POW, while the rest of the crew landed safely behind Allied lines. In a cruel twist of fate, the navigator survived the war because of his mistake, while the others were killed three weeks later in a crash back at their base.

The B-24 was Priller's 100th victory, all scored on the Western Front in the Battle of France, the Battle of Britain, the Channel Front, and the American daylight offensive. While his men congratulated him on landing, he was more interested in the letter informing him that his first child would be born in a week. Priller's record of five years' continuous combat service on the toughest front of the war by the time he left JG 26 in early 1945 to become *Inspekteur der Jagdflieger* (Inspector of Day Fighters in the West) was unequaled by any other pilot.

June 12 saw 200 German aircraft spotted over the invasion battleground, the largest number yet and a sign that the recently arrived units from Germany had gotten themselves organized. The 353rd's Thunderbolts were caught while dive bombing by a *Gruppe* of Bf-109s that the Americans described as "experienced and aggressive" when the survivors got back to Raydon. Although the American fliers had chased off the Germans, they paid for it with their highest losses since D-Day, with eight P-47s failing to return. The group sought revenge that afternoon with the assistance of the Wolfpack. The 353rd fighters attacked Dreux/Évreux airfield, which was now home to the Bf-109s of I./JG 3, and ran into 20 Bf-109s that headed toward Paris where they were joined by another 40. The 56th had arranged to arrive over the target 20 minutes after the 353rd made its attack to provide reinforcement if any air action developed. By the time the Wolfpack fighters joined the battle, the 353rd's pilots had already shot down nine and damaged three, to which the 56th added five more destroyed for no American losses.

Both the Mustang and Thunderbolt groups were now receiving newer and more capable versions of the two fighters. In both cases, the P-51D-5 and the P-47D-25 could be distinguished from their predecessors by large clear-vision plexiglass "bubble" canopies with the fuselage cut down behind the cockpits to give pilots enhanced visibility to the rear, where they were most vulnerable to attack. The P-51D also upped the armament from four to six .50-caliber machine guns, with these mounted vertically rather than slanted as was the case with the P-51B. This resolved the gun-jamming problem the earlier Mustangs had experienced. At first, these newer models were given to squadron and flight leaders, but by late August the earlier "razorback" fighters had been largely replaced, though some hardy early versions were still in use as late as early 1945.

The American pilots also received a piece of personal gear that gave them a real advantage over their opponents. The G-suit fit around the waist and over the thighs. The suit was plugged into the vacuum system, and under increased G-loads during air combat the suit tightened around the thigh and waist, preventing blood from pooling in the lower extremities and preventing the pilot blacking out while maneuvering. Ninth Air Force had been aggressive in obtaining the G-suits and all the P-47 groups in IX Tactical Air Command were using it by D-Day.

VIII Fighter Command first began getting the equipment shortly after D-Day and all groups had the gear by mid-summer. Bob Wehrman recalled, "We had just gotten the K-14 'no missum' gyro gunsight in July, and then we got the new G-suit. Between the two pieces of gear and the new P-51Ds, we could out-fly the enemy under just about all conditions." In April, the 4th had tried using the British G-suit, which used water, but it had been discarded for being uncomfortable. As Wehrman described it, "You didn't even notice you had the new suit till it started squeezing your legs and you didn't black out as before."

On June 13, the still-lucky *Nachwuchs*, Unteroffizier Hans Gehrke, became separated from his flight when III./JG 26 escorted other Bf-109s that attacked the British sector of the Normandy beachhead with W.Gr.21 rocket mortars. Low on fuel, Gehrke was diverting to Orleans in hopes that he could find gas when he spotted a cloud of dust ahead. As he flew closer, he saw 12 P-47s strafing ground targets. He later recalled, "I turned and flew balls-out at minimum altitude. They came after me, ignoring the fact I was flying two to three meters [six and a half to ten feet] above the ground, pulling up for each hedgerow and tree." The Thunderbolts, which were from the 78th Group, took turns shooting at the fleeing Messerschmitt. "As I pulled up to avoid a power line, my crate cracked open. My engine was hit, and began to smoke heavily. I climbed out. My parachute opened and I found myself sitting stupefied on the ground." The Bf-109 crashed into a farmhouse and set it on fire. Gehrke couldn't move, due to shell splinters in his legs; he was soon surrounded by a group of Frenchmen armed with sticks and scythes, who wanted to know if he was the one who had burned down the farmhouse. Before the situation could go from bad to worse, Gehrke was rescued by the timely arrival of a truck full of soldiers who picked him up and delivered him to a field hospital, where his wounds were tended to. Ten days later he returned to Villacoublay Sud. "They were glad to have another pilot back on duty; we had suffered a number of pilot casualties in my absence."

The Luftwaffe bases around Paris were targeted by bombers from both VIII Bomber Command and IX Tactical Air Command. On June 14, III./JG 26 *Kommandeur* Major Klaus Mietusch led 18 Bf-109s to attack B-17s headed for Le Bourget. The bombers were escorted by the 55th Group. Mietusch led the dive on the P-38s and shot down one. Two more Lightnings exploded as the Messerschmitts flashed through the formation, heading for the bombers. Unteroffizier Erhard Tippe of 11.Staffel got one of the P-38s, but quickly found four others on his tail. He headed for a cloud, but just before he reached its safety, the engine failed as coolant sprayed from a hit. He later recalled, "When I left the cloud, my pursuers were nowhere to be seen. I landed my good old Yellow-13 on its belly in a field outside Paris. We had scored seven victories, a great success, but had lost seven. It had again been 18 against 120, the same odds we faced daily."

On June 16, the 357th's Lieutenant Colonel Tom Hayes used an old trick that he had learned while flying P-39s in New Guinea to attack a rail yard. The group only had 108-gallon paper tanks available, which provided far more fuel than they would need for the mission to the St Pierre marshaling yard outside Paris. He instructed the pilots to drop their tanks, which were about three-quarters full, on the rail yard in their first pass. Then they returned and set the tanks ablaze with gunfire. There were four large explosions and the target was on fire when the Mustangs departed.

Word got around among the groups about the 357th's success with using drop tanks as "incendiaries" for strafing. The 20th and 55th groups were now engaged in regular Droop Snoot bombing missions against heavily defended transportation targets where the fighters could save the B-26s and A-20s from missions that could be "high-casualty" for the slower bombers. The Lightnings attempted to use Hayes' tactic of dropping partially full drop tanks, but the 160-gallon tanks they carried tumbled when dropped from their position inboard of the engines due to airflow between the booms and the central pod, with the result that the tanks ended up falling nowhere near the desired target. The 55th experimented with attaching the tailfins for 2,000-pound bombs to their drop tanks. Tests over Bradwell Bay, dropping on the Droop Snoot leader, revealed that doing so at 5,000 feet and an indicated airspeed of 210 miles per hour would put the tanks where they were aimed. This was finally attempted on July 14 against a V-1 warhead dump with "satisfactory" results.

It was around this time that pilots like Dick Hewitt of the 78th's 82nd Squadron, who had completed their first tours and volunteered for a second, returned from their 30-day leave back home. The example of Major Stump, killed on his first mission of his second tour, was faced by many of the "retreads"; several who had survived 200-hour tours in 1943–44 went missing on their first few missions after their return. This reflected the very different combat that they now engaged in. Out-flying an enemy by piloting skill had little to do with survival at low level where flak was a constant concern.

George Preddy, who had destroyed an Fw-190 and shared an Me-410 with his wingman on June 20 during the first mission to Merseburg (nicknamed "Mercilessburg"), scored again the next day, destroying one of two Bf-109s shot down by the 487th Squadron on a second mission to hit the Leuna synthetic oil plant outside "Mercilessburg." With the majority of the Jagdwaffe in France, there was a very limited defensive response, despite the importance of this target.

In a conference of fighter leaders on June 20, III./JG 26 *Kommandeur* Major Klaus Mietusch and III./JG 54 leader Hauptmann Robert "Bazi" Weiss had stated that losses were so bad, and the replacement pilots so inexperienced, that the units should only operate in *Gruppe* strength due to the shortage of experienced leaders. Events two days later demonstrated how right they were.

On June 22, III./JG 26 took off in full strength from Villacoublay airfield, tasked with patrolling for Allied fighter-bombers near Cherbourg. As they passed southwest of Caen, Leutnant Petyer Rescher, *Staffelkapitän* of 11.Staffel, attempted to lead the *Staffel* in a bounce of four 356th Group P-47s that he had spotted. The Americans spotted the eight Bf-109s and broke into them while their cover flight dived on the German fighters from above. Reischer was able to out-fly the P-47 that went after him, split-S-ing so low he nearly crashed. With the American pulling out of the maneuver, Reischer had to crash-land due to damage moments later. The rest of the *Staffel* fought for their lives, with two pilots shot down and killed while a third was able to bail out safely. One P-47 was shot down in the fight. In the meantime, the other two III./JG 26 *Staffeln* got into fights with P-47s from IX Technical Air Command's 368th Group, with one pilot killed and three successful bailouts. At the end of the day, III./JG 26 was left with only three experienced leaders – Kommandeur Mietusch, 10.Staffel's Oberleutnant Paul Schauder, and Reischer.

The Fw-190 pilots of I. and II.Gruppen fared much better than the Bf-109 pilots of III.Gruppe in the Normandy battles. Many surviving Fw-190 pilots said after the war that they believed the fighter could outrun any Allied opponent at very low altitude, regardless of any performance figures. Even the heavy Fw-190A-8 still had remarkable ability to out-roll every fighter it came up against, while the fighter's heavy armament of four 20mm cannon and two 13mm machine guns meant that any pilot who could hold an opponent in his gunsight long enough to open fire was certain to heavily damage if not destroy that fighter. Over the course of the Normandy battles, the two Fw-190 units maintained a 2:1 victory-loss ratio.

The 78th had been heavily involved in air support for the invasion over the month of June, flying multiple missions almost every day in marginal weather. By month's end, the group had flown 45 missions, during which it claimed 20 aerial victories, one ground victory, and 13 locomotives, for a loss of 16 pilots killed and one evader, the heaviest monthly loss yet experienced. The 83rd Squadron flew 639 sorties with 14 aborts including eight failing to take off successfully with their heavy loads. They fired 78,000 rounds and dropped 79 tons of bombs; the pilots averaged 78 flying hours each, also a new record.

At the end of June, the Jagdwaffe had lost 230 pilots killed and 88 wounded, with 551 aircraft shot down in combat over France and a further 65 destroyed on the ground. For this cost, they claimed 526 Allied aircraft shot down including 203 P-47 fighter-bombers. On July 1, Captain Wally Starck led 352nd Group's 328th Squadron on a mission to strafe suspected V-1 launch sites, but the squadron became involved in a battle between the 78th Group and 20 Bf-109s and Fw-190s over St Quentin. The 78A group mission had been dogged by bad luck from the mission's beginning, when two P-47s had collided during a mass takeoff on Duxford's wide grass runway and exploded. The P-47s were 12,000 feet over St Quentin when Lieutenant James Stallings spotted five Bf-109s diving on the Thunderbolts; bombs tumbled from their wings at his warning. Stallings managed to avoid the attackers by throwing his P-47 into a violent spin; when he recovered at 3,000 feet, he found he had no elevator trim. "I'd taken two 20mm cannon shells in my tail surface and was darn lucky my controls weren't completely gone. I had to keep a lot of forward pressure on the stick to fly straight and level."

Starck led the Mustangs into the fight and immediately became involved in a turning fight with a pair of Bf-109s that dived for the deck when they couldn't turn inside him. He followed, opening fire on the wingman at a distance of 100 yards. The fighter burst into flames and the pilot bailed out, narrowly missing Starck's wingman, Lieutenant Sheldon Heyer's P-51. Starck closed on the leader and succeeded in damaging the Messerschmitt before losing it in the clouds. Two other Bf-109s were also damaged, belonging to Lieutenants Cyrus Greer of the 487th and the 328th's "Punchy" Powell. This was the last fight the Blue Nosers would engage in during July, despite flying eight more missions between July 4 and 12.

The Wolfpack managed to celebrate Independence Day, July 4, by rousing the enemy fighters during a dive-bombing mission to Conches airfield. Forty Bf-109s were spotted. The Thunderbolts got rid of their bombs and went after the enemy in dogfights that ranged from 10,000 feet to just over the trees. The Thunderbolt pilots returned to Boxted with claims for 20 destroyed and 12 damaged, with all claims verified by gun camera film. The victories gave the 56th a score of 503. The next day, the group was among 139 Mustangs and 89 Thunderbolts sent out to welcome the B-17s and the 4th Group, which were returning from Italy after their shuttle mission to the USSR. The Wolfpack P-47s found enemy fighters over Évreux and Lieutenant Colonel Gabreski scored his final aerial victory, putting him past squadron mate Bob Johnson with 28 victories to become the leading ETO ace.

The danger of "friendly fire" was ever present over the battlefield with units of different air forces engaged with each other. On July 5, Jack Miller of the 78th's 83rd Squadron was returning to England after having to abort due to failing oil pressure. Nursing the P-47 over the Bay of Seine, several RAF Spitfires suddenly appeared and shot up the Thunderbolt in the mistaken belief it was an Fw-190, despite the prominent ID stripes. Miller bailed out and was picked up by an Allied beach patrol.

By July 17, Unteroffizier Gehrke was considered experienced enough to be assigned as *Rottenflieger* to Gruppenkommandeur Mietusch. He had been credited two days before with shooting down an RAF Lancaster during the first Bomber Command daylight raid. Returning to Villacoublay from a patrol, Gehrke spotted distant dots, but when he warned Mietusch, his commander kept flying straight and level. The dots quickly resolved themselves as RAF Spitfires and a dogfight developed in which Mietusch was shot down. Gehrke returned, dreading being blamed for Mietusch's loss, but his good fortune continued when it turned out that Oberst Hannes Trautloft, *Inspekteur der Jagdflieger West*, had arrived for a visit and overheard the radio calls leading to the fight. He absolved Gehrke of responsibility for Mietusch, who returned two days later, having bailed out and been forced to make his way back amidst the chaos of the Seventh Army's retreat.

As losses mounted in this low-level battle, some of the new pilots who arrived proved different from the veterans they replaced. 78th Group Crew chief Sergeant James Tudor remembered:

> Some young pilots coming into the unit gave us mechanics a fit. While flying your plane on a mission, they would get as far as the Channel when all of a sudden the engine would begin to act up, so back to base they came. The write-up in the Form One was familiar: "Engine runs excessively rough," or "Prop surges at a given altitude." Some of these guys we hated to draw once we got to know them, because you could predict an abort with a high degree of accuracy. Some overcame it after a few trips, others never did.

On July 25, the 78th put up a maximum-effort mission to Saint-Lô. Following the bombing of the German front lines by over 700 B-17s and B-24s in Operation *Cobra*, the group joined the 56th and 353rd groups, bombing and strafing the blasted German positions. While some US troops had been killed by bombs dropped "short," the bombing had shattered the Wehrmacht's resistance and the US Seventh Army pushed through the survivors and opened a front 15 miles deep. General George S. Patton Jr.'s newly arrived Third Army raced through the gap and into Brittany, beginning the advance across France that would see them stopped by lack of gasoline just short of the Siegfried Line in early September. With the breakout at Saint-Lô, the Battle of Normandy was over and the liberation of France began.

When Unteroffizier Walter Stumpf reported to II./JG 26 at Rheinselen, he had 180 hours total in his logbook, including 20 hours in the Fw-190. He later recalled, "It took me less than a day with the *Gruppe* to learn that the average replacement pilot lasted three missions. None of the veterans would talk to me." Over the course of a week, II./JG 26 grew from 30 to 78 pilots, all similar to Stumpf in experience. Over the course of another week, the *Gruppe* flew formation and simulated combat flights. Stumpf recalled that "the experienced pilots talked flying all the time and we new boys sat and listened intently. The best advice I got was that the Americans didn't shoot us in our parachutes and I should free fall for 200 meters [650 feet] before opening my 'chute; I would have a good chance of survival doing that."

On August 15, Stumpf had survived the transfer from Rheinselen back to Guyancourt. He didn't recognize the field he had trained at only four months earlier:

> We landed on a dirt strip next to the flying field. I landed and managed not to run into the plane next to me. A ground crewman who was standing in a patch of woods waved to me. I taxied in and shut down. I was then told no one was allowed to taxi into the woods; the airplanes were to be pushed in tail-first so they could get out. The flight was no fun at all. I was totally confused about everything. All of our aircraft were being covered with tree limbs. Spitfires and Mustangs had already passed over, but didn't spot us. A bus came and collected us. There were observers on the fenders, to spot the enemy's airplanes. They had a fearsome superiority and there was hardly a moment in which none could be seen or heard.

At about the same time Second Lieutenant Frank Oiler arrived at Duxford, assigned to the 82nd Squadron. His logbook recorded 600 total hours, including 150 in the P-47. He later remembered that even with operations flown at the high rate they were that summer, new pilots were given as much time to learn what they needed to survive as possible. Over his first two weeks, he flew only local flights:

> It took some getting used to the English weather, which was a far cry from what we had experienced in the States. At the end of that time, I had doubled the number of instrument flight hours in my logbook and felt comfortable lifting off the airfield to disappear into a cloud within a minute, sticking with my leader until we broke out on top.

August 11 saw Hub Zemke leave the 56th Group he had formed. The 479th Fighter Group – the last to join VIII Fighter Command in May – had just lost its commander, Colonel Kyle Riddle, the day before, shot down on a strafing run. Major General "Butch" Griswold, who had replaced General Kepner as head of VIII Fighter Command earlier when Kepner was promoted to command the 2nd Air Division, asked Zemke if Dave Schilling could take command. When Zemke asked him, Schilling stated clearly that he wanted nothing to do with the P-38, the fighter the 479th was flying. Zemke, who knew his tour was nearly up and was not interested in the staff job he knew was coming, told Griswold he would take over the new group. An era ended the next day when he turned over command of the Wolfpack to Schilling and left for Wattisham to take command of the 479th.

After three missions flown in whatever plane was available, Frank Oiler was assigned an older P-47D "razorback" when its regular pilot moved up to one of the new "bubbletop" P-47s. Oiler's choice of personal insignia, a large colorful bee with stinger, and the name "Eileen" made both this airplane and his later P-47D among the most memorable Thunderbolts in the 78th.

Tragedy could strike even when no operational flying was involved. On July 19, a 401st Bomb Group B-17 flew over to Duxford for a visit around 1330 hours. The B-17 pilot's friends gathered others and 13 group members climbed aboard for some fun. Once airborne, the B-17 proceeded to perform a "beat-up" of the airfield. Turning for a second run, the pilot brought the big bomber down less than 50 feet above the grass runway and headed toward the hangars. Just too late, he pulled up to go over the 84th's hangar and hit the beacon on top. The left wing outboard of the engines was ripped away, taking half the left stabilizer with it. The B-17 rolled over as the wing fell on the officers' club roof, then soared over the baseball field as the players ran off in all directions, finally hitting the roof of the 83rd Squadron's enlisted men's barracks. Full of fuel, it exploded, destroying a major section of the two-story brick building. Sergeant Ernest Taylor was killed and two others who got out were badly burned. All aboard the bomber perished. Chaplain Zink became the first chaplain in the Eighth to win the Soldier's Medal for his heroism, rescuing victims in the barracks fire. The next day, Doolittle made low-level buzzing a court-martial offense.

The low-level air combat over Normandy cemented in pilots' minds how lucky they were to fly the virtually indestructible Thunderbolt. 78th Group crew chief Sergeant James Aicardi remembered a P-47 that returned alone, "flying kind of crazy." The pilot taxied it to its revetment, with the whole airplane vibrating. "We thought the engine would shake loose it was shaking so much." When the propeller swung to a stop, it was discovered that two prop tips were bent back 90 degrees, telephone cable was wrapped around the prop shaft, small tree branches and leaves were jammed down the cowling scoop, and there were dents in the cowling and leading edge of the wing; the pilot had flown through a tree and a telephone line during a strafing run. "How he got that thing back with that out of track prop was a miracle."

At the end of July, JG 26 reported a score of 30 Allied aircraft shot down during the month, for a loss of 20 pilots, including two *Staffelkapitänen*. II./JG 26 had been withdrawn to Rheinselen in Germany, while III./JG 26 remained at Villacoublay and I./JG 26 retreated from Chaumont to Rambouillet. Hauptmann Emil "Bully" Lang, an Eastern Front *Experte* with a score of 150 with JG 54 on the Northern Front who had been awarded the Oak Leaves to the *Ritterkreuz* for his skill, became *Gruppenkommandeur* of II./JG 26 three days before the move.

On August 2, the 78th's 82nd Squadron lost its second commanding officer within two weeks when Captain Charles Clark fell victim to the flak to become a POW. He was replaced by newcomer Major Joseph Myers. About the same time that Myers took command, Second Lieutenant Wayne Coleman arrived at Duxford, having completed pilot training back in the States the week after D-Day, and was assigned to the squadron. Coleman later remembered, "They were able to give me and the other five newcomers six days of concentrated advanced flying training so we understood what we were doing, and then we were turned loose as wingmen. By the end of August, I had added nearly 70 flying hours to my logbook, and felt considerably more experienced."

On August 12, the 78th went after the transportation system again. The 82nd Squadron destroyed five locomotives at Fournières while the 83rd Squadron destroyed two more locomotives and blew up 35 oil tank cars. The 84th topped the others when they strafed a 20-car ammunition train and set off an explosion that completely destroyed the rail yard at Breuil.

The group returned to escort duty on August 15, shepherding one of the first RAF Bomber Command daylight missions to hit Deelen airdrome southeast of Amsterdam. Sadly, seven Lancasters and Halifaxes were lost to 88mm flak. Coleman remembered, "the Brits didn't have any experience with daylight operations, and they flew like they did at night, which was a big loose formation. It took them a long time to bomb the target, and that gave the gunners down below time to get their aim."

The biggest strafing day of the invasion campaign came on August 19. The 83rd Squadron's Captain Charles Peal discovered an airfield at Château Salines that had 30 He-111s and Ju-52s under camouflage netting. The squadron left 14 blazing after their run. Lieutenants Harold Beck and wingman Wilbur Grimes hit a roundhouse full of locomotives at Conflans, then found another airfield where they left two Ju-88s and a Bf-109 destroyed. That afternoon 78A group flew a group strafing mission against marshaling yards at St Menehould, Tagnon, Fagnières Suippe, and Épernay, where a train with 50 oil tank cars was destroyed. At the end of the day, the group claimed 18 aircraft burned on the ground and ten locomotives destroyed for the loss of Lieutenant Louis Dicks to the ever present light flak.

On August 27, 78B group found the marshaling yard at Metz that they were sent to attack full of trains and put two bombs into the midst of them that set off a sympathetic explosion of ammunition and fuel which demolished the rail yard and everything in it. The smoke column ascended to 10,000 feet and could be seen across much of northern France.

On the evening of August 28, Major Myers was leading a flight of 82nd Squadron at 11,000 feet, with newly arrived Second Lieutenant Wayne Coleman as his wingman, and First Lieutenant Fred Bolgert as element leader with his wingman Second Lieutenant Manfred Croy, returning to Duxford from a strafing mission to Termonde, near Brussels. Near the Belgian village of Haaltert, Myers happened to glance down at the early evening shadows and caught sight of a twin-engine aircraft that he thought at first was a B-26 Marauder, flying low over the fields. Quickly realizing that no B-26 could fly that fast, he radioed Bolgert to follow with Croy as he dived to investigate, leaving Coleman as top cover.

The stranger was so fast, Myers had to throttle up into war emergency power and engage water injection. The airspeed indicator was registering 450 miles per hour in a 45-degree dive when he finally overhauled what he recognized as an Me-262 jet fighter. The first of these mysterious planes had only been spotted by an VIII Fighter Command pilot in late July. This particular Me-262 – 9K+GL of KG 51 – was one of the first "bomber" versions, known as the *Sturm Vogel* (Stormy Petrel). Leutnant Rony Lauer was transferring it from the unit's base at Juvincourt to Chiévres. At takeoff, the nose gear had failed to retract completely, which prevented him from flying at maximum speed and was why he was at such a low altitude, hoping not to be spotted.

Coleman watched from above as Myers opened fire and missed. "With tracers flying around him, the German was so low that he just put it on the ground wheels-up in this open field. I saw the pilot get out and run for the trees, but then the three Thunderbolts made strafing runs. I told Major Myers I was certain they had killed him," Coleman recalled. Lauer had landed just outside the village cemetery and had been able to hide among the trees when the Thunderbolts came around and strafed his airplane. Later that night, he was picked up by Wehrmacht troops and returned to KG 51. In October, he was wounded in a fight with Thunderbolts of the 356th Fighter Group and later was shot up while trying to bomb the Remagen bridge in March 1945. Myers' victory made him the first Allied pilot to shoot down the new German jet. Quince Brown was later identified as the pilot who made this first German jet kill, but Coleman and Bolgert – the two surviving members of the flight – as well as the official group records, confirm that Myers was the victorious pilot.

On August 28, top 78th ace Quince Brown returned from his 30-day leave and took command of 84th Squadron with a promotion to major. The pace of missions was such that by September 6, Brown was already on his fifth mission of his second tour, leading 78A group to strafe Vogelsund airdrome, near Schleiden, Germany. Fellow second-tour veteran Captain Dick Hewitt led the 82nd Squadron as high cover for the mission. He later recalled:

> I was flying top cover at only 8,000 feet with my four flights and had a good view of what happened when they hit the target. After one pass, Major Brown chose to abandon the attack after being hit. He pulled away from the airdrome with the rest of the group behind him and headed towards Schleiden. He must have figured that he might find a locomotive or two, since Schleiden was a rail center. Once we were over the town, it was evident from the tell-tale smoke in the rail yard that we had found a good target. Major Brown turned toward the smoke and started a pass. Suddenly, the sky was full of 20mm

and 37mm tracers all aimed at Brown's flight as a flak car embedded
in the train immediately started firing. When he started his pullout,
I heard him call that he'd taken an engine hit and was bailing out.
I saw his 'chute billow as it opened, but it was only a moment later
that he hit the ground. Civilians from the nearby train and farmers
in the nearby field surrounded him almost immediately, giving him
no chance to escape into a nearby woods.

At that point, other flak positions in the town opened up and the
Thunderbolts turned for home.

Brown was popular and admired by everyone, and the group was
hard-hit by the loss of its leading ace. After the war, there were reports
that Brown had been shot by a German civilian, who was later executed
in 1947 for the crime. In fact, the story of the death of Quince Brown,
the leading ace of the 78th Fighter Group, is very different. In 2003,
Dick Hewitt was called by Mr. Frank Guth of Schleiden, Germany,
who was researching a book about the war as it had happened in the
city. Hewitt told him the story recounted above, after which Guth told
him what had really happened, as recounted by his aunt, who was nine
at the time.

The civilians who surrounded Brown in the field brought him into
Schleiden, planning to turn him over to the Luftwaffe detachment
as a POW. Before this could happen, two Waffen-SS troopers took
Brown from the civilians. To the horror of all, one of the troopers then
pulled his pistol and shot Brown in the head in the middle of the town
square. After the war, townspeople reported the crime to the American
occupation authorities; the two SS men were identified and tried as war
criminals in 1947 for shooting a surrendered prisoner. They were found
guilty and hanged.

The day before Brown's loss, Major Robert Eby, who had first joined
the group the month after the 78th was formed back in February 1942,
and had most recently been the group operations officer, completed
his tour. Promoted to lieutenant colonel, Eby was transferred to 3rd
Air Division Headquarters as Director of Fighter Operations. At last,
the 78th had a "friend at court" who would have a voice in their future
combat assignments.

The liberation of northern France was over by early September,
following the liberation of Paris on August 25. Steve Pisanos, who had

remained with the Resistance since crashing in France back on March 5, remembered the liberation:

> Over the two weeks before the Germans were chased out, my friends in the Resistance had been terrified they would put up a fight for the city and leave it like Stalingrad. In fact, there was some attempt by the Germans to destroy things. They set out to rig the Seine bridges with explosives, but the Resistance went out every night and removed the explosives. They would leave all the wires and the boxes the explosives were in, so the Germans wouldn't realize what had been done.

With the city restored, Pisanos was able to turn himself in to the American army and returned to Debden. "I got back to Debden and three days later I was on my way back to America. I got there just in time to be best man for Don Gentile's wedding."

The Luftwaffe had been reduced to impotence during the battle for France. I. and II.Gruppen of JG 1 and all three *Gruppen* of JG 11, all of which were dedicated anti-bomber units, had been transferred to France, where they lost a combined 100 pilots killed and 200 Fw-190s destroyed in the air and on the ground over the three months of combat. In comparison, III./JG 1, which had been transferred to the Eastern Front and fought there over the summer, suffered the loss of one pilot killed.

Unteroffizier Hans Kukla, who joined II./JG 26 in late August, would never forget his first combat mission. Six of his *Staffeln* took off with the rest of the *Gruppe* for a ground-strafing mission. Kukla was "tail-end Charlie" and charged with looking out for the enemy. The Fw-190s were escorted by III.Gruppe Bf-109s. They attacked some tanks and turned for home. Suddenly, Kukla realized the Bf-109s behind him were P-51s!

> I was the first to be hit. My plane took strikes in the engine and immediately burst into flames. I pulled the nose up and bailed out. My parachute opened at 20 meters [65 feet] and I landed in the garden of a farm. The farmer's wife told me I was in no man's land. I gave her my parachute and started walking north.

Kukla had received facial burns and other injuries in his bailout that put him in a hospital until October. He later learned that the other three members of his *Schwarm* had been shot down and killed.

II./JG 26 had gotten out of Normandy on August 20 still relatively fresh, having only been back at the front for six days. As such, it was assigned to cover the retreat of the other Jagdwaffe units, all shattered to varying degrees, over the ten days at the end of the month. On September 3, "Bully" Lang was killed in a battle with P-51s from the 55th Group's 338th Squadron over St Trond, Belgium. First Lieutenant Darrel Kramer, who shot him down, later reported:

> I closed on him very rapidly because he was not going very fast. I was closing fast and he was turning toward me. As I got within range I was 75 degrees off. I only fired a short burst and he went out of sight below my nose because of the lead I was pulling. I broke up, then hard right. I then saw the Fw-190 upside-down in a steep dive. It hit so hard it generated shock waves along the ground. It skidded a few yards then blew up in a fireball.

During two months of combat over Normandy, Lang had added 25 victories to his total for a final score on both fronts of 184. He was among five JG 26 *Jagdflieger* lost that day. Lang had been known for never having been hit by the enemy in combat, and his loss left the *Gruppe* in shock.

Of a thousand fighters that had arrived in France by the end of June, fewer than 200 returned to Germany in September.

# 22

# OIL: THE KNOCKOUT PUNCH

Once SHAEF took control of the Eighth in the lead-up to the invasion, General Spaatz fought to gain Eisenhower's support for the Strategic Air Forces undertaking the one "strategic bombing" campaign that really could knock Germany out of the war: the destruction of the Axis oil industry.

Germany and her allies had nowhere near the access to oil supplies that the Allies did. The Germans had been forced to create a synthetic oil industry in the 1930s in anticipation of going to war, and the Nazis considered their alliance with Romania to be their major diplomatic coup, since it gave them access to and control of the oilfields around Ploesti, the only source of oil in Europe. Ploesti's oilfields were the source of 30 percent of the Axis oil supply. The major thrust of the assault on the Soviet Union had been on the southern front, where anticipated success at Stalingrad would have allowed access to the oilfields of Baku.

The Allies had long been aware of the Nazi Achilles' heel. One of the first missions flown by American heavy bombers had been the abortive attempt by Colonel Henry Halvorsen's HALPRO force, the first B-24s assigned to the Ninth Air Force in 1942, to bomb Ploesti. The force had not been strong enough to inflict any lasting damage. With the Axis forces driven from North Africa after May 1943, Ploesti again became a target. Operation *Tidal Wave*, flown on August 1, 1943, with the two VIII Bomber Command B-24 groups and three B-24 groups of the Ninth Air Force, was one of the epic operations of the war, with 173 bombers making a low-level daylight raid on the refineries around

Ploesti. Again, due to operational mishaps, a knockout blow was impossible. Of the 171 bombers that hit the targets, only 88 returned to their Libyan bases, 55 of which were damaged to varying degrees. Five Medals of Honor – the most for any air mission ever – were awarded to crewmen. While damage was estimated at 40 percent of the targets, most damage was repaired within weeks, with the net output of fuel greater than before the raid since several of the refineries had been previously operating below maximum capacity.

One of the first targets set for the Fifteenth Air Force on its formation was Ploesti. General Spaatz's USSTAF planners estimated they could drop German gasoline production by 50 percent with 15 raids against Ploesti by the Fifteenth Air Force and ten against the German synthetic oil industry by the Eighth. Ploesti and the German synthetic oil industry was the only lifeline the Wehrmacht had to maintaining the ability to fight a mechanized war. British planners in the Ministry of Economic Warfare had long pleaded to no avail with Bomber Command's Sir Arthur Harris to attack these targets, with Harris dismissing such a plan as a "panacea" that would divert him from his campaign to destroy German cities. Spaatz argued to Eisenhower before SHAEF took control of the Eighth that destroying the Panzers' gasoline supply was a far greater blow against the enemy than destroying easily repaired railroad marshaling yards. Knowing he could not get SHAEF's focus away from the transportation plan, Spaatz pointed out that an aerial offensive against oil would only need half of Eighth Air Force's bombers; the rest could be employed against the rail system. Unfortunately, the Air Force's history of over-promising on the decisive results of striking "strategic" targets and the failure of the ball bearing campaign the previous fall, worked against Spaatz, even with the full support of General Arnold in Washington.

Churchill, who was concerned that killing large numbers of French and Belgian civilians living near the rail yards would create political problems both during the war and in its aftermath, favored the oil campaign. However, in a meeting at SHAEF Headquarters on March 25, Eisenhower pressed VIII Bomber Command's General Frederick Anderson about the likelihood of success for a campaign against oil, with Anderson forced to confess that the Air Force "could not guarantee that the attacks of oil targets would have an appreciable effect during the initial stages of Overlord." Anderson did say that a campaign against the synthetic oil industry "would have a decisive effect within a period of about six months." Since he was concerned about the immediate problems associated with putting an army into France and keeping it there, Eisenhower came down against the proposal. RAF Chief of Staff Air Marshal Sir Charles Portal found a compromise with the proposal that such a campaign would be mounted by both Eighth Air Force and Bomber Command once the Allied armies were firmly in Normandy and any German counterattack had been blunted.

Since the Fifteenth's bombers were not involved in the invasion, Spaatz was able to convince Tedder to allow him to mount a mission against Ploesti shortly after Eisenhower's decision. The results were so good that Tedder allowed the Fifteenth to make repeated attacks between early April and late June 1944, which saw the Romanian oil fields and refineries severely damaged and oil production severely curtailed. The Axis would lose all access to Romanian oil at the end of August 1944, when the country surrendered in the face of the Soviet advance.

With the demonstrated success of the Ploesti campaign Spaatz once again asked Eisenhower for permission to bomb the synthetic oil refineries. When Eisenhower told him to wait till the end of summer, an argument broke out between the two that was so intense it was rumored Spaatz had threatened to resign. Eisenhower relented by authorizing the Eighth to attack on two days in May when weather over France prevented bombing of rail targets.

On May 12, 886 bombers were sent to bomb a complex of synthetic oil plants in central Germany; the mission was strongly opposed. The 352nd's John Meyer almost became someone else's score during an escort mission to bomb the synthetic oil plant at Prenzlau. Spotting a combat wing of Fortresses rocked by explosions and taking two 487th Squadron flights to investigate, Meyer saw several parachutes in the air, then spotted three gaggles of enemy aircraft. He quickly lost the first two that he had spotted in the heavy haze, but one Bf-109 from the third flight failed to reach the sanctuary of the haze and Meyer set it on fire with one burst. After watching it crash, he spotted an airfield with bombers on it and made a run in which he destroyed a He-177. As he pulled up, a Bf-109 bounced him and he only managed to escape with a series of violent maneuvers taken at such a low altitude that he thought for a moment he might crash. Meyer was able to return to Bodney to complete the last mission of his first tour of duty with claims that raised his score to 15.5, including 8.5 aerial victories.

The Eighth lost 46 bombers on the May 12 missions. Altogether, the aerial battles had been one of the worst days for the Jagdwaffe, with the *Jagdgeschwadern* reporting a total of 61 fighters lost. Albert Speer wrote of the strike in his memoirs, stating, "On that day, the technological war was decided." A week later he told Hitler that if the enemy persisted in these attacks over the summer, Germany would have no way to prosecute the war by fall.

Speer had authorized top priority to repairing the synthetic oil refineries and crews worked 24 hours a day. On May 28 and 29, the Eighth's bombers returned to hit the newly repaired facilities while the Fifteenth hit Ploesti with its biggest attacks. ULTRA intercepts in June confirmed that gasoline production had been cut in half. With the invasion a week away, the campaign would have to await victory in Normandy before it could be concluded. Strategic bombing had finally found the target it could hit that would change the war.

By mid-June, with the Allies now firmly ashore at Normandy and the Germans unable to mount a successful counterattack due to Allied air superiority and destruction of the transportation network, General Spaatz renewed his request to Eisenhower that the Eighth be allowed to resume the attacks on the synthetic oil industry. He received written permission that allowed him to divert from direct support of the invasion on days when there was good weather over Germany and there were no missions against "Crossbow sites" (the German V-1 launch sites) or infantry support. The Germans had begun launching V-1s against London the week after D-Day. The politics of London again coming under attack were such that the attacks against the launch sites in northern France that had been started before the invasion were increased, but without effect; the British people would face the V-1s until ground troops took the launch sites in early September.

The oil campaign that was fought in the summer of 1944 was the first true test of the idea that daylight precision bombing could disable the German economy. The Eighth Air Force flew 28 days in June, 27 in July, and 23 in August – so fast that some bomber crews completed their tours in only a few months – with the majority of missions against the synthetic oil industry. The plants were located near coal deposits in the Ruhr, Silesia, and around Leipzig. They converted coal to gasoline and other petroleum products through the Bergius process, using hydrogen under high pressure and extreme heat to turn brown coal into high-grade gasoline and aviation fuel. These plants produced 75 percent of Germany's total liquid fuel supplies – 85 percent of high-grade diesel and gasoline and all aviation gasoline. Nearly one-third of this production was concentrated in the massive Leuna plant in Silesia outside Merseburg and Politz, just over the Polish border, 70 miles northeast of Berlin. Five other plants located in central Germany produced another third. After the war, Albert Speer told his interrogators that if the Allied air forces had made these plants their sole objective during the summer of 1944, they could have forced a German surrender in eight weeks, which would have allowed the airmen to achieve their dream of winning the war themselves. As it was, what was accomplished likely shortened the European war by six months.

The Leuna plant's 250 buildings covered three square miles and employed 35,000 workers – 10,000 of them slave laborers or POWs. A facility that size should have been easy to hit with precision bombing, but the German defenses involved greasy black smoke sent up from hundreds of small ovens that ruined visibility; additionally, decoy buildings were constructed outside the plant that were bombed as much as the plant itself. The plant was protected by 600 radar-directed 88mm antiaircraft cannon, while several Luftwaffe fighter units were based nearby. Second Lieutenant Tom Landry, who would later become head coach of the Dallas Cowboys, flew most of his missions in the oil campaign, and remembered that the sky over the city and the plant was filled by "an angry black cloud of exploding flak."

The American bombers primarily dropped 250-pound bombs, which were not strong enough to destroy the reinforced concrete blast walls protecting the storage tanks, compressors, and other machinery. The lighter bombs also made German firefighting easier because the fires were less intense and long-lasting as compared to the destructive effect of the RAF 4,000-pound "cookies." For most of the summer, poor weather prevented the bombers returning to a target quickly. The Germans were able to get plants back into production at lowered rates within four to six weeks; toward the end of the campaign, Air Force planners using increased photo reconnaissance were able to time attacks to coincide with the production resumption. In the end, the oil campaign was won by carpet bombing the plants, causing simultaneous damage to several plants that was beyond the means of the German repair organization to return them to even a modest percentage of pre-campaign production. By the end of summer, synthetic oil production would be 9 percent of what it had been in May, and the Ploesti oilfields were in the hands of the Soviets. The German aircraft industry achieved its highest monthly production total in September, but the overwhelming majority of the airplanes produced never flew for lack of fuel.

Over the 78 days of the summer of 1944, the Eighth lost almost half its operational bomber strength – 1,022 B-17s and B-24s – as well as 665 P-38s, P-47s, and P-51s of its normal fighter strength of 900. Even though the loss rate was 1.5 percent over 30 missions as compared to 3.6 percent during the "Battle of Germany," an aircrewman in the Eighth still had a one-in-three chance of being killed or made prisoner during his tour.

The first Eighth Air Force attack of the oil campaign was mounted against the huge plant at Politz on June 20, 1944. The 4th provided target withdrawal support, and got involved in a massive air battle when 50 ZG 76 Me-410s intercepted the bombers, some carrying massive 50mm tank cannons to use against the formations. The Zerstörers were escorted by Bf-109s. The Germans admitted the loss of 12 of the twin-engine fighters to the Eagles and other groups. The day also saw the loss of Jim Goodson, who led his 336th Squadron in his brand-new P-51D with its big bubble canopy, when the group strafed the airfield at Neubrandenburg on the way home. As he picked out a Do-217 on the field, Goodson's fighter took a hit in the vulnerable radiator. With the engine temperature soaring, Goodson crash-landed on the airfield and was quickly captured when he got out. The Mustang looked undamaged from the air, so other members of the squadron strafed it as Goodson and his captors threw themselves on the ground. At the time of his loss, Jim Goodson was VIII Fighter Command's leading ace, with 14 aerial victories and 15.5 ground kills; he would remain top ace of the 4th.

The attack against the synthetic oil plants in eastern Germany and Silesia saw the Eighth finally mount the first "shuttle" raid from England; the bombers and their escorts flew from England to Soviet bases in now-liberated Ukraine. Four shuttle raids against Ploesti were flown by the Fifteenth Air Force in June from their bases in southern Italy. Air Force planners had long looked forward to mounting such missions, which were organized as Operation *Frantic*. The original plan, agreed to by Stalin at the Tehran Conference, would have had three USAAF bomb groups permanently based in the USSR; in the end, only 1,300 Americans went to provide support for the airfields at Piryatin, Mirgorad, and Poltava, Ukraine. While the missions did bring previously untouchable targets into the range of the bombers, the operation ended when the Soviets began their August offensive into Romania, which knocked the country out of the war by the end of August.

The Eighth's first *Frantic* mission was flown on June 21. The target was the synthetic oil plant outside the city of Ruhland. The 1st Air Division contributed 163 B-17s; their escort to the target was performed by 72 P-38s of the 364th and 55th groups, and 38 P-47s of the 353rd Group. The Eagles, flying three 16-plane squadrons reinforced by 16 P-51s from the 352nd's 486th Squadron, led by Don Blakeslee, rendezvoused with the bombers before they hit the target and flew with them on to Ukraine, a flight of 1,600 miles.

Shortly after the Eagles picked up the bombers over Lezno, Poland, 30 Bf-109s attacked the bombers over Siedlice. Captain Frank Jones and First Lieutenant Joseph Lang each got one Messerschmitt, making both aces. Unfortunately, the 335th's First Lieutenant Frank Sibbett was shot down and killed. Blakeslee led the group on across Poland and Ukraine, navigating – as he was later proud to say – with four maps and a wrist watch, to bring the group to Poltava where they landed at 1450 hours, his exact ETA; ever after, he considered leading the flight across Europe his greatest achievement of his wartime career. Ralph Hofer, who had wandered off on his own again, was unable to rejoin the group and got lost. He landed unexpectedly at Kiev, where he was closely interrogated by the Russians before they let him fly over to Poltava the next day.

Unknown to the Americans, the force had been shadowed by a Ju-88 after the formation broke away from the main force and headed on east. That night, the Luftwaffe staged one of their last large-scale bombing missions. The Poltava airfield was hit, destroying 43 B-17s – half of those on the field – but left the Mustangs undamaged.

The redoubtable Major "Chili" Childress from the 27th Photo Squadron also set a record on June 22. Assigned to fly a bomb damage assessment mission for the *Frantic* force, he had to fly a very precise mission to stretch his fuel sufficient to make the 1,600 miles from

Mount Farm to Poltava. He later remembered, "My route was just south of the Baltic, to get photos of the airfields in northern Poland and the Baltic states which we had never been able to photograph before due to the distance, as well as bomb damage assessment photos of the synthetic oil plant in Ruhland they'd bombed." His strategy was to fly till each drop tank went dry and the engines stopped, to ensure he used all the fuel:

> I ran the first one dry over Schleswig-Holstein, and dropped it. Then near the Polish border, I ran the left tank dry, and hit the jettison switch. Nothing happened! I worked it again and still nothing happened. I tried a third time and accompanied that with a nose up pitch, to put some Gs on the tank and pull it off. It came loose and the next thing I knew, it somersaulted over the wing and hit the leading edge of the horizontal stabilizer, putting quite a dent in it!

Having flown too far to turn back, and with the engines still running and the airplane flying all right, "I kept on with the mission and got the photos, then flew on to Poltava."

Childress arrived at Poltava the day after the German raid. "I spent an extra day there while they took sheet aluminum from the burned-out B-17s and made a patch for my tail. After it was fixed I took off and flew over Czechoslovakia and southern Germany, bringing back the photos of those eastern front airfields I'd gotten on the way over to Russia."

Over the next 20 days, the Eagles would have quite an adventure before they returned to Debden. After three days of visiting Soviet units at other fields to promote Allied camaraderie, they flew escort for the bombers to Brodye in Poland, where they were to bomb the oil refinery at nearby Drohobycz. The Mustangs turned south and crossed Yugoslavia, headed for Italy where they landed at Lucera.

On June 29, Ralph Hofer and three other pilots who had remained behind at Piryatin with mechanical problems departed Poltava to rejoin the group in Italy. Hofer went off on his own, got lost over the Adriatic Sea, and was finally shepherded by a passing flight of RAF Spitfires he hooked up with to Malta. He flew up to Lucera the next day. The group was getting tired of Hofer and his irresponsibility. His squadron commander, Deacon Hively, had taken away his personal P-51B,

"Salem Representative," before the shuttle mission when Hofer had refused to get his shots for the trip.

The 4th flew a sweep over Budapest in advance of a Fifteenth Air Force bombing mission on July 2. Both the Luftwaffe and the Hungarian air force responded, and the 45 P-51s engaged 80 German and 18 Hungarian Bf-109s over the city in swirling fights. The result was the destruction of eight enemy fighters, including a triple by the 334th's CO, Deacon Hively. The mission also saw the loss of Ralph Hofer. For many years, it was thought he had been shot down during the battle over Budapest, and might possibly have been one of the four 4th Group P-51s scored that day by top ace of history Hauptmann Erich Hartmann of JG 52. The truth would not be learned until 2003: Hofer's element leader, First Lieutenant George Stanford, had been unable to drop his tanks, but had stayed for the fight. On the return, he ran out of gas and crash-landed in Yugoslavia. Hofer buzzed Stanford to see if he was all right, but then discovered he had a Bf-109 on his tail. Hofer managed to shake his opponent, but then strafed Mostar-Sud airfield, where 4.Batterie/Flak Regiment 9 "Legion Condor" hit Hofer's P-51B and the 15-victory ace crashed to his death. The 4th was running short of "characters."

After providing target withdrawal support for a bombing mission to Arad, Yugoslavia, on July 3, Blakeslee brought the group and the B-17s they had gone to Russia with home on July 5 by way of an escort mission to bomb the marshaling yards in Beziers, southern France. When they arrived back home, 52 Mustangs of the 61 that had taken off on June 21 were back at Debden.

The 56th was among the VIII Fighter Command groups sent out to greet the 4th's Mustangs and the B-17s returning from Italy. The Wolfpack found Bf-109s over Évreux and shot down eight. Among them was the Bf-109 credited to Gabby Gabreski, who had tied Bob Johnson's score on June 27; this was number 28 and made him the ETO leading ace. His tour was set to expire at the end of July and he planned to return home and marry his fiancée Kay Cochran; Oil City, Pennsylvania, had raised $2,000 as a wedding present for the hometown hero.

As American bomber formations had grown in size and striking power after the first Schweinfurt mission in August 1943, Reichsmarschall Göring ordered that, if necessary, fighter pilots must continue their attack on a bomber formation to the point of ramming. The Jagdwaffe did not adopt this as an intentional tactic until Major Hans-Guenther von Kornatzki persuaded the Oberkommando der Luftwaffe (OKL, the air force high command) to form Sturmstaffel 1 (1st Storm Squadron) and develop deliberate ramming of enemy bombers as a tactic.

Kornatzki's special unit was formed in December 1943 and attached to I./JG 1 at Dortmund in January 1944. While different attack methods were developed, a pilot was only expected to ram a bomber as a last resort in exceptional circumstances, and then only if he could bail out before impact; they were called *Rammjäger* but this was not the German *kamikaze*. Of pilots who did ram, half were reported to have escaped by parachute uninjured. Oberleutnant Zehart knocked down a B-17, the unit's first victory, on January 11. Future *Rammjäger* ace Unteroffizier Willi Maximowitz scored his first, a B-24, near Hannover on January 30.

In late April 1944, IV./JG 3 was selected to take the success of von Kornatzki's *Sturmstaffel* to the next level: the unit became the first *Sturmgruppe* (Storm Group, close attack), led by Hauptmann Wilhelm Moritz. Based at Salzwedel, it was equipped with the special Fw-190A-8/R7. Known specifically as the *Rammjäger*, the fighter carried a 20mm MG 151 cannon in the wing root and a MK 103 30mm cannon outboard in each wing with two 13mm machine guns in the fuselage, with the cockpit specially armored. Only three 30mm hits was sufficient to shoot down a B-17; the heavy armor protected the pilot while he attacked the bombers from the rear, which gave him time to concentrate on a single victim, an impossibility in the Twelve O'Clock High head-on attack.

Of course, the heavy *Rammjäger* could not survive against P-47s or P-51s; the heavy armor made it some 25 percent heavier than a standard Fw-190. The *Sturmgruppen* had to be escorted by Bf-109 fighters for protection while forming up and approaching the bomber stream, when it was at its maximum vulnerability to the American escorts.

The bombers and their escorts began to repeatedly meet the Fw-190s of the *Sturmstaffeln* beginning in late June. IV./JG 3 achieved its first success on July 7, when 1,129 B-17s and B-24s were sent to bomb aircraft factories in Leipzig and the synthetic oil plants at Boehlen, Leuna-Merseburg, and Lützkendorf. Escorted by the Bf-109-equipped I. and III./JG 300 led by Oberst Walther Dahl, Hauptmann Moritz led the *Sturmgruppe* in an attack on a formation of 492nd Bomb Group B-24s which were temporarily without fighter cover. The German fighters swarmed the bombers and within a minute 12 B-24s of 18 in the lower squadron were shot down. The fighters claimed 28 and were credited with 21, the majority credited to IV./JG 3. This action led to Moritz's award of the *Ritterkreuz* on July 18. Nine Fw-190s were shot down and five pilots killed; by the standards of the time, the mission was considered an outstanding success. With this success, the Fw-190-equipped II./JG 300 was ordered to convert to the *Sturmgruppe* role, while Major Kornatzki was given command of II./JG 4, which was created specifically for that role.

The next day, the P-38s of the 55th and 20th groups were part of the escort for the force of B-24s that bombed the factories around Leipzig at Halle and Bernburg. The Jagdwaffe rose in substantial numbers to defend the vital targets. The formation was opposed by large gaggles of rocket-carrying Me-410s and Fw-190s, which were covered by Bf-109s. The 20th Group scored seven destroyed while the 55th had its best day ever: Captain Orville Goodman led the 338th Squadron into a fight where they scored eight Fw-190s and three Bf-109s, while Lieutenant Colonel John D. Landers, a Darwin and New Guinea veteran ace with the Forty-Niners, led a flight from the 38th Squadron that bounced a gaggle of 20 Me-410s and claimed three destroyed and four damaged in a 20-minute battle. The 55th claimed a total score of 18 destroyed for no loss. In total, the P-38, P-47, and P-51 escorts claimed 77 destroyed, including six credited to the 56th.

The 353rd "Slybird" Group was over Holland returning from the mission when group commander Colonel Glenn Duncan spotted aircraft on an airfield below. Leading the 350th Squadron down for a strafing run while the 351st and 352nd squadrons stayed high for cover, Duncan took hits in his engine and put it onto the ground just beyond the airfield perimeter. He managed to walk away from the crash and the next day met a farmer who put him in touch with the Dutch Underground. He remained hidden in Holland until the country was finally liberated in 1945, when he returned and resumed command of the group.

The 20th Group also lost Jack Ilfrey, commander of the 79th Squadron, when his P-38J was shot down over an airfield in northern France after he spotted aircraft and led the squadron to strafe. Ilfrey bellied the

Lightning in and got away into the nearby woods before German troops on the ground could get to the fighter. After hiding from search parties for a day, he managed to make contact with a French farm family who hid him until late July after the major battles in the area were over. The local Resistance helped him make his way to the Allied lines, disguised as "Jacques Robert, Cultivateur," a peasant who had been made deaf in a bombing raid and was thus unable to hear anyone and respond. After being picked up by an Allied infantry patrol and convincing them he was an American when he pulled his identification out of the hiding place in the heel of his boot, he managed to get a ride back across the Channel and returned to King's Cliffe in early August. Following his "death in action," his personal gear had already been packed up and sent to Gatwick Airport to be returned to his family. He managed to get to Scotland a day before the plane carrying his gear was to leave, and retrieved it. He then returned to King's Cliffe and transitioned to the P-51s the group had begun operating two weeks earlier.

When VIII Fighter Command's Lightning-equipped groups began re-equipping with P-51s, the 20th turned out to be the most successful with a score of 89 shot down for 87 losses. The 55th and 364th groups had suffered more losses than victories. The two senior Lightning groups flew their first P-51D missions on July 19 and 20, respectively.

After July 7, with the majority of the Jagdwaffe in Normandy, missions over Germany did not find opposition until July 18. The 352nd was escorting bombers to targets in Peenemünde and Zinnowitz when it encountered a mixed force of about 40 Me-410s and Ju-88s, with a top cover of 20 Bf-109s that was stalking the bombers. Outnumbered, the 486th and 487th squadrons attacked the gaggle of Zerstörers, quickly dispersing them while the Bf-109 cover was engaged by the 328th Squadron.

George Preddy, whose run of victories had taken off in late June when he exchanged his P-51B "Cripes A'Mighty II" for one of the newer P-51Ds, which he named "Cripes A'Mighty III," claimed two Ju-88s destroyed, a third as a probable, and two more "damaged," along with a Bf-109 destroyed. With that, his score of aerial victories rose to 14.5 and he was recognized as the group's leading ace.

The rest of Preddy's squadron also did well. First Lieutenant Charles Ellison, who had flown 70 missions without any claims, had the most exciting day of his tour, when he caught four Ju-88s and sent down three of them in quick succession. Lieutenants William Fowler and Sanford Moats claimed two Bf-109s and a single, respectively.

Of the seven victories claimed by the 486th Squadron, five were credited to young pilots who had only joined the squadron in May and June. Lieutenants Ernest Bostrom, Robert Miller, and David French were each credited with an Me-410, while Lieutenants Marvin Stoll and David Reichman scored a Ju-88 apiece. Squadron commander Major Willie Jackson claimed a Ju-88 and a Bf-109 destroyed.

The 328th's Captain Henry White and Lieutenants Frank Kebelman and Earl Smith scored a Bf-109 each, while the squadron also lost Lieutenants John Galiga and James Burr shot down and killed.

On July 19, the 4th ran across Bf-109s that were airborne in large numbers over Munich. The 336th's Lieutenants Ira Grounds and Francis Grove got two and one, respectively, though the 335th's Second Lieutenant Kermit Dahlen was killed when a 109 exploded his Mustang.

First Lieutenant Curtis Simpson was lucky when it turned out he was over neutral Switzerland when his 335th Squadron P-51B lost its glycol after being damaged during the fight. He later recalled that:

This particular escort flight was the sixth straight flight that we had made to Munich in six days, but it was the first one where there was any opposition. We were jumped by a group of '109s and fought all the way into Austria. I was on full throttle for far too long a time and my electrical system on the coolant shutters went out. When they closed, the engine overheated and I lost all of my coolant. If I hadn't been so close to Switzerland I would have ended up as a Prisoner of War or dead. I was looking for a place to land, since I did not want to jump. I found this very short meadow that had some white signs on it so I thought that I should try it. I had no other choice. I used full flaps with no power from the engine and I landed slightly on the tail wheel. There was no one there when I landed, but as soon as I stopped, here they came. The Swiss had helmets similar to the Germans, and I was not sure where I was. I stood up in the cockpit with my hands raised and asked if they were Swiss. Luckily they said yes!

Simpson's Mustang was later repaired and taken on charge by the Swiss Air Force.

On the morning of July 20, having reached the 300-hour limit on his tour extension, Gabby Gabreski was waiting for a ride to Gatwick to catch a trans-Atlantic flight home. Learning that a bomber escort mission to Russelheim where there was a possibility of running across the Luftwaffe was scheduled for takeoff in an hour, he requested "just one more." The enemy failed to make an appearance. Gabreski spotted several He-111 bombers parked on the airfield at Niedermendig as they flew home. Rather than fly on further before returning, he dived to strafe the field, encountering only light flak. Dissatisfied with his first run, he reversed for a second pass. When he saw his tracers going over the parked bomber, he dropped the Thunderbolt's nose and the propeller clipped the runway, bending the tips. With the engine vibrating violently he crash-landed at the far end of the field and managed to run into the nearby woods where he eluded capture for five days. Gabreski spent the rest of the war at Stalag Luft I. No other pilot in the ETO would match his score.

August saw the Eighth's bomber force begin to standardize on the B-17. The B-24 had proven itself more vulnerable to fighters and not as able to survive being damaged as the B-17, which also had a higher operating altitude than the Liberator. On August 1, the 486th and 487th bomb squadrons, which had exchanged their B-24s for B-17s ten days earlier, flew their first B-17 missions. Crews had at first resented the changeover, since established loyalty to the "known devil" was not easily dropped, but the pilots had soon recognized how much easier the B-17 was to fly in formation than the B-24 with its heavy controls, while navigators and bombardiers found the B-17's nose compartment roomier without a manned nose turret to compete for space; the crew in back came to appreciate the B-17's superior heating system.

On August 6, the 357th Group provided escort for the second, and last, of the Eighth's shuttle missions to the Soviet Union. The group picked up the B-17s of the 390th Bomb Group after they hit the Focke-Wulf assembly plant at Rahmel. The bombers had been escorted by the 55th Group, led by new group commander John D. Landers in its first P-51 operation; the mission to Gydina and back to England covered 1,595 miles in seven flying hours and set the record for any group flying from England.

Over Poland, nine Bf-109s from the Eastern Front *Geschwader* JG 51 went after the bombers, but First Lieutenant Robert Shaw's flight cut them off. Shaw shot one down in flames while element leader First Lieutenant "Bud" Nowlin chased the fighter flown by Hauptmann Gunther Schack, *Staffelkapitän* 7.III./JG.51. Schack split-S-ed with Nowlin in pursuit. A burst hit the 109's radiator and brought a spray of coolant before it slowed so dramatically that Nowlin overran it. Pulling alongside Schack, he realized he had to preserve fuel. He waved and climbed away, not discovering for 40 years that shortly after Schack bailed out. Two other Yoxford boys chased a Ju-88 that dived so steeply they were credited with downing it.

On August 8 the group flew to Foggia, Italy, via Ploesti. Captain Bill Overstreet scored what was likely the strangest victory by an VIII Fighter Command pilot during the war. Since there was no expectation of meeting enemy fighters, Overstreet made some trades for vodka, which he stored in the ammo bays. Inevitably, Bf-109s were sighted over Romania; when they quickly broke for home, Overstreet turned onto one's tail, when to his amazement, the pilot bailed out. Overstreet was the nearest and could have been given credit, but he decided not to make a claim. The group returned home from Italy on August 12.

August 6 also saw the return to combat of Captain John Godfrey, who had found himself out of place on the publicity tour with Don Gentile. He later described his "escape" from the tour while they were at Mitchel Field in New York in late July: "I cadged a flight up to Maine, where I got another ride to Scotland on a C-54. I then convinced an RAF pilot to give me a ride down to Debden, where I walked into Colonel Don's office and asked if I could come back." Blakeslee was in need of an experienced pilot, now that so many of the Eagles had either finished their tours and left, or been shot down, so he worked out the paperwork and Godfrey – promoted to major – took command of his old squadron, the 336th; less than a year before, he had arrived at Debden as a 21-year-old second lieutenant. He returned with the goal of becoming "the number one ace," which he later wrote was nearly his undoing.

During a target support withdrawal mission for the day's Berlin raid, Godfrey shot down an Me-410. During the group's return, he led the squadron to strafe an airfield, where he took a hit in the coolant system. Jettisoning the P-51C's Malcolm hood, Godfrey was ready to bail out when Captain Fred Glover advised him to pump fuel into the engine, which would lower the temperature. Glover escorted Godfrey as he flew back to England, constantly priming the engine. By the time he landed at Beccles, the first airfield he came across, he had worn through his flying glove and bloodied his palm.

While Godfrey was making his perilous way home, George Preddy had his best day ever as a fighter pilot. When the group had been informed the night before that the August 6 mission would be scrubbed for weather, Preddy had spent the night drinking and shooting craps; he got gloriously drunk and won $1,200. Finally going to his room, he had been asleep an hour when he was awakened with the news that the mission was on. Not only did he have a major hangover, but he was supposed to lead the mission! He spent 30 minutes in his cockpit breathing pure oxygen to clear his head, but even so he vomited in his cockpit while flying across the Channel.

Ninety minutes later, the bomber stream was approaching Hamburg when a gaggle of 30 Bf-109s were spotted stalking the bombers. Preddy led White Flight to bounce the enemy from the rear. He later reported, "I opened fire on one near the rear of the formation from 300 yards and got many hits around the canopy. The enemy aircraft went down inverted and in flames. At this time, Lieutenant Doleac became lost while shooting down an Me-109 that had latched onto Lieutenant Heyer's tail." Preddy and Heyer continued their attack. Preddy got behind his second victory and got hits around the wing roots, setting the 109 on fire. "He went spinning down and the pilot bailed out at 20,000 feet." Heyer shot down another Bf-109.

The enemy formation stayed together with the pilots taking practically no evasive action as the formation tried to maneuver to attack the bombers. "We continued our attack on the rear end and I fired on another at close range. He went down smoking, and I saw him begin to fall apart below us." Another flight of P-51s joined the fight. "I fired at another '109, causing him to burn after a short burst. He spiraled down in flames." Still the Germans stayed together as they made a left turn to attempt another attack. "I got a good burst into another one, causing him to burn and spin down. The enemy aircraft were down to five thousand now." One pulled off to the left in an attempt to engage Preddy. "I was all alone with them now, so I went after this single '109 before he could get on my tail. I got in an ineffective burst, causing him to smoke a little. I pulled up into a steep climb to the left above him and he climbed after me. I pulled it in as tight as possible and climbed." The enemy pilot opened fire ineffectively as Preddy out-climbed him in a zoom. "He fell off to the left and I dropped astern of him. He jettisoned his canopy as I fired a short burst, getting many hits. As I pulled past, the pilot bailed out at seven thousand feet. I had lost contact with friendly and enemy aircraft, so I headed home."

George Preddy had just shot down six enemy fighters in one battle. It would be the ETO record. The group returned claiming 12 destroyed, including two from the 486th's Captain Henry Miklajcyk, flying the first mission of his second tour, and two to Lieutenant Charles Cesky of the 328th.

Preddy was still suffering the aftereffects of the epic drinking bout the night before when he landed. When he shoved open his canopy, everyone wanted to know his score. His first words were "NEVER AGAIN!" With this, his score was 28, 24 scored in the P-51 to make him the leading Mustang ace. He was awarded the Distinguished Service Cross for his record mission, and given 30 days' leave back home.

As the Fw-190 *Sturmböck* (battering ram) became more effective, VIII Fighter Command's response was to send fighter groups ahead of the bombers to find and break up the *Sturmgruppen* formations. By mid-August, this was so successful that the Germans were losing a fighter pilot killed for each bomber shot down; the Jagdwaffe couldn't stand such a level of attrition. By early September, the *Sturmgruppen* Fw-190s were the only ones committed to the defense of the Reich, while the other units recuperated from the terrible losses in Normandy.

On August 15, the newly designated *Sturmgruppe* II./JG 300 attacked the 303rd "Hell's Angels" group when it found the bomber stream that was headed for Wiesbaden near Trier. The Sturmböcken popped out of the clouds and shot down nine B-17s from the low formation. Minutes later, Bf-109Gs from I./JG 300 found the 466th Group's B-24s near Meppel and shot down four. The defending gunners claimed four Fw-190s and nine Bf-109s, respectively. On August 16, IV./JG 3 attacked the 91st Group near Halle and claimed six B-17s in trade for six Fw-190s lost to the defenders' fire in the four-minute battle.

The 91st's veteran B-17G "Outhouse Mouse" was hit by the Sturmböcken and fell away from the formation, only recovering from the dive 2,000 feet below. Just after recovery, its crew were introduced to the Luftwaffe's latest aerial weapon when tailgunner Sergeant Robert Loomis spotted a swept-wing aircraft approaching at great speed from the rear. He alerted pilot First Lieutenant Walker Mullins who skidded the bomber back and forth to throw off the attacker's aim. The strange airplane was identified as an Me-163 as it shot past "Outhouse Mouse." Its pilot, Leutnant Hartmut Ryll, died when the airplane was shot down moments later by two P-51s of the 359th Fighter Group. The Me-163 was from I./JG 400, which had flown its first operational mission on August 6, when two of the rocket-propelled fighters claimed to have shot down three Blue Noser P-51s. Four other Me-163s from the *Gruppe* also attacked a 1st Air Division wing near Bohlen. The rocket fighters closed with 200 yards, opened fire briefly, then broke away and dived for the ground at high speed.

August 24 saw the loss of Major John T. Godfrey in a freak "friendly fire" incident. Leading the 336th Squadron as they escorted B-24s returning from a mission to "Mercilessburg," they spotted many Ju-52/3m transports on the airfield at Nordhausen. Godfrey led the strafing attack and shot up four of the trimotored transports while his wingman, First Lieutenant Melvin Dickey, shot up three. The light flak was intense and Godfrey jinked to make himself a difficult target. In so doing, he flew into Dickey's line of fire as he opened up on a fourth ground target. Godfrey's P-51 was hit in the engine and the coolant system. With the temperature gauge "off the peg" as he later recalled, Godfrey bellied in beyond the field and managed to get out of the airplane as it caught fire and reach cover before the enemy troops arrived, despite suffering cuts to his head and leg. At the time that he went down, Godfrey was tied with Jim Goodson as leading ace of the 4th, with 29.88 air and ground victories. After three days on the run in Germany and walking 13 miles, he tried to catch a ride in a boxcar of a train outside Nordhausen, but was captured by railway guards. He later wrote that being captured and spending eight months as a POW was "the best thing that could have happened to me," since he had been obsessed with becoming the top ace of the ETO. "Prison taught me what was really important in life."

September 11 saw the strongest Jagdwaffe reaction to a bombing raid since May 28. It also saw the third and final Eighth Air Force *Frantic* mission, in which 75 B-17s of the 96th and 452nd Bomb

Groups bombed Chemnitz; as the others returned to England, they were escorted by the 20th Group. There was no enemy response, but the force did have to pick its way through heavy weather to land at Piryatin. The bombers hit targets in Hungary on their way to Italy and the full force was back in England by September 17.

The other escort groups saw plenty of action. The main force of bombers was headed for the Leuna factory in Merseburg. Seven JG 400 Me-163s attacked one formation and claimed three B-17s shot down in the vicinity of Leipzig. The "Bloody Hundredth" 100th Bomb Group was lagging, and got hit by an entire *Sturmgruppe*; 11 B-17s went down in the five-minute battle. Had it not been for the timely arrival of the 339th Group's Mustangs, the result might have been worse, but the P-51s shot down 15 enemy fighters. The 92nd bomb group was also hit, losing eight, with four others so badly damaged they made emergency landings at Allied airfields in France. They were rescued by the 55th and 359th groups, which claimed 28 and 26 shot down, respectively. The US fighters overall claimed an incredible 116 victories for the day.

The next day the bombers went after the synthetic fuel factory outside Magdeburg. The Jagdwaffe again made a strong showing and the bomb groups reported a total loss of 23. The 493rd Group, newest unit in VIII Bomber Command, was flying its mission as low box in a combat wing. The I./JG 300 Bf-109s found them and shot down seven of the B-17s to which they had recently converted. Overall the Eighth lost 43 bombers on the mission. Despite their successes, the American fighters returned with claims for 125 shot down. On the following day, the Mustangs and Thunderbolts claimed 150 shot down. The famous names in the fighter groups from the previous year were gone, returned home at the end of their tours or shot down, but their replacements were demonstrating the result of the strong training program that had been created in the previous two years back in the United States.

Responding to the success of IV./JG 3 and II./JG 300, Adolf Galland proposed that one *Gruppe* of each *Geschwader* be re-equipped with the Sturmböcken and turned into a *Sturmgruppe*. II./JG 4 had taken such duties at the end of August. This was fortunate, since IV./JG 3 had been caught over their home airfield on August 20 by P-51s and 15 pilots died in their shot-down *Sturmböcken*. IV./JG 4 came across the veteran

445th Bomb Group, considered the best B-24 unit in the Eighth on September 27, when 37 of the group's B-24s led 315 2nd Air Division B-24s to bomb the Henschel plant in Kassel. The 445th's bombers took a wrong heading at the Initial Point and moved them far enough from the rest of the formation to attract enemy attention. Rather than bombing Kassel through the overcast, their bombs fell on Göttingen, a university city in Lower Saxony, 20 miles from Kassel. Believing they were over the right target, the group executed their withdrawal plan, which put them ten minutes behind the rest of the Liberators. As they flew over Eisenach, three waves of Fw-190 Sturmböcken attacked from their rear. The Fw-190s were then followed by the Bf-109s of I. and III./JG 4, for a total of 90 attackers. The 445th lost 25 of their 37 B-24s, with the rest suffering varying degrees of damage, before the yellow-nosed P-51s of the 361st Fighter Group came to their rescue. Two of the damaged planes had to put down in France, while two others made it to crash-landings at Manston and a fifth got home to Tibenham where it crashed on the runway. The next day, the group was able to put up ten Liberators that all returned safely this time from a repeat mission to Kassel. Overall, the Eighth reported a total of 49 bombers lost on the 27th.

The loss of regular supplies of aviation gasoline due to the continuing destruction of the synthetic oil factories was the reason that the Luftwaffe could only put in occasional appearances, after the *Geschwadern* were able to collect sufficient gas to mount a mission. The next major Jagdwaffe response was on October 6, when the Eighth made another assault on Berlin. The 3rd Air Division was 1,000 feet below a cloud deck. Unknown to the bombers, the Sturmböcken of both II./JG 4 and II./JG 300, covered by Bf-109s of I./JG 4 and III./JG 300, were hidden above them by the clouds. The German controllers spotted the 395th Bomb Group, flying in the high position, as it lagged behind the rest when the bomber stream turned toward the target, and ordered the fighters to dive through the clouds; they surprised the 549th Squadron's bombers in the high position of the high group, just below the clouds. The defenders had no warning before the fighters were among them and 11 B-17s went down. The next day, 1,455 B-17s and B-24s went after the synthetic oil factories near Leipzig. IV./JG 3 came out of the clouds and ambushed the 94th Group, which lost 12 Fortresses in eight minutes. While these losses were "low" in the overall scheme of missions flown with more than 1,000 bombers, the losses were devastating to the individual groups.

Galland later wrote of the oil campaign:

From September on, the shortage of petrol was unbearable. The Luftwaffe was the first to be hit by this shortage. Instead of the minimum of 160,000 tons monthly, only some 30,000 tons of high-octane could be allotted. Air Force operations were thereby made virtually impossible! The raids against the oil industry was the most important of the combined factors that brought about the collapse of Germany. With only 5,166 tons of bombs, they had scored a bull's-eye against Germany's resistance.

The Jagdwaffe failed to appear during the rest of October. Eighth Air Force planners worried that the enemy was conserving their force to mount a huge attack on the bombers and inflict as many as 1,000 losses. As it turned out, Adolf Galland was planning exactly such a blow. His *Grosse Schlag* (Great Blow) envisaged a force of 2,000 fighters hitting the bombers and exacting a toll even higher than the Eighth's planners expected. Galland wrote, "Now it was a question of awaiting favorable weather. Good weather was one of the essentials of the mass action."

# 23

# THE ROAD TO *BODENPLATTE*

By early September, Zemke felt he had changed the 479th Group. He later wrote that when he first arrived and examined the group's records, "They had scored ten victories and lost 35 pilots in the nearly three months they had been on operations." Things changed on August 29 when he took the group on a mission that included strafing an airfield full of enemy aircraft on the way home. The pilots returned to claim 43 aircraft destroyed for the group's most successful mission to date.

Captain Robin Olds, who was as close to Army Air Forces "royalty" as could be, the son of Major General Robert Olds, one of the creators of the USAAF and a "father" of strategic bombing through his prewar work to develop the B-17, was one of the pilots in the 479th. As a child, Olds had gone flying with family neighbors Hap Arnold and Carl Spaatz. He later remembered Zemke's influence on the group:

Prior to Hub's arrival, we had tasted success in small measure, we had been blooded in large measure; we were learning both to survive and to cope. But what we really wanted was to achieve, to succeed, to earn the respect of the older units in VIII Fighter Command. We wanted a bigger piece of the action; someone to get us there. Then came The Hub. You could feel things changing; a presence, a leader.

On August 15, Olds shot down two Fw-190s, then he and his wingman got involved in a fight during an escort mission on August 25 with 50 Bf-109s near Rostock. "Hub had led us there, a member of my flight spotted them, two of us attacked, I knocked down three and my wingman two. This time Hub was really proud but put out, too, because I was so green, so excited, I couldn't give clear readings on location, heading and altitude." With that, Robin Olds became the group's first ace and would remain its leading ace through the rest of the war.

The first week in September saw JG 26 back inside Germany for the first time since May 10, 1940. The ground crews experienced the worst of the retreat from Brussels, their vehicles caught up in the endless stream of trucks, and even horse-drawn wagons. One *Feldwebel* recalled the nightmarish scene, with burning vehicles to either side of the road and everyone worried that the next minute would see Allied fighter-bombers appear.

At the beginning of September, when JG 26 and the other Western Front *Geschwadern* found refuge inside Germany, the Allies found they had outrun their supply lines. General Patton fumed that he could see the Siegfried Line through his binoculars, unoccupied, with his Third Army unable to advance for lack of gasoline. Many on the Allied side thought the German retreat from France presaged an early end to the war, perhaps by Christmas. General Eisenhower was caught on the horns of a military-political dilemma. There were supplies for one advance into Germany, and he had two candidates who both thought their records demonstrated that they should command the advance.

They were firstly General Patton, whose Third Army had surged out of Normandy at the end of July and swept across northern France. On the other was British Field Marshal Montgomery, hero of Alamein and victor over Rommel, whose army had broken out of Normandy and liberated Belgium. Britain felt the strain of five years of war: reserves were thin; the army was reducing a division from three to two regiments because manpower reserves were no longer sufficient.

Montgomery's plan was audacious: the Allied First Airborne Army would seize the three major bridges in Holland; the final one at Arnhem would bypass the Siegfried Line and allow his army to cross the Rhine. The US 82nd and 101st Airborne Divisions, and the British 1st Airborne, would provide the striking force. Patton proposed that Third Army smash through the Siegfried Line and strike into central and southern Germany. He even promised to liberate Berlin ahead of the Russians. Eisenhower was forced to play the politics of coalitions;

he accepted Montgomery's proposal. The unfortunate result meant that the war likely lasted four to six months longer than it might have had he decided not to support Operation *Market Garden*.

Wayne Coleman's days as new-boy-wingman ended on the evening of September 9. The 78th Group dive-bombed targets in the Giessen-Frankfurt-Fulda area at 1750 hours. Coleman was Yellow Four when White Flight found eight locomotives while the others hit Giessen airfield. White Flight was coming off its last strafing run when Yellow One spotted four Fw-190s take off and head for White Flight. The number four 190 had just tucked its gear when Coleman hit it from the rear; the fighter nosed over, hit the ground, and exploded on impact. A second Fw-190 came at him head-on; when it broke sharp left, it flipped into a spin and crashed. Spotting another Fw-190 chasing a P-47, Coleman fired to distract the enemy pilot; the two went through a few turns until the German realized Coleman was gaining and turned to run. Engaging his water injection, Coleman slid onto the enemy fighter's tail and fired a burst into the wing root and cockpit area. The 190 chandelled to 200 feet, rolled twice, then went straight in and exploded on impact. In his first aerial combat, Wayne Coleman scored a triple. He soon became an element leader.

The next day, the Thunderbolts scored 40 Ju-88s and He-111s destroyed on Mainbullau and Gernsheim airfields. The 83rd Squadron's Captain Raymond Smith became a "strafing ace in a day" with five He-111s. The cost was high: three pilots killed by flak and three who bailed out and were captured. That night, the pilots learned they would be involved in *Market Garden*.

Montgomery's plan suffered a roadblock when General Lewis Brereton, the USAAF officer commanding the First Airborne Army, refused to schedule more than one airlift a day for each division due to a claimed shortage of C-47s. Rather than land at full strength, the paratroops would not be strong enough at the outset to overcome opposition with missions to deliver all troops spread over three days. The drops would be in daylight, owing to the problems encountered with night drops at Normandy. Because of flak at Arnhem to defend the Rhine bridge, the British were dropped far from their target bridge.

Operation *Market Garden* began on September 17. Two hundred Thunderbolts of the 56th, 353rd, and 78th Fighter Groups provided support for the drop. Wayne Coleman later remembered, "Our job was to go in before the C-47s got there, and knock out the flak guns. Colonel Myers sent one flight down to make a low pass. When they took fire, the rest of us attacked." The P-47s used 260-pound fragmentation bombs on the gun emplacements. They followed up by strafing, destroying 16 multi-gun sites and damaging 37 others. Despite their effort, ten C-47s were lost to guns they hadn't spotted.

The three *Gruppen* of JG 26 were closest to the landings and were heavily engaged. Like all the other German units, they were unsuccessful getting through the escorts to attack the C-47s. I./JG 26 claimed three Spitfires west of Nijmegen for one pilot lost, while II./JG 26 engaged Mustangs, claiming five while losing two from 8.Staffel.

III./JG 26 suffered a ruinous loss. *Gruppenkommandeur* Major Mietusch led 15 Bf-109s to the landing zones that afternoon. The weather turned bad; there was continuous cloud at 15,000 feet over the battle zone. Mietusch spotted four P-51s through a break in the clouds, and led the bounce.

The Mustangs were the tail-end formation of the 361st Group's 376th Squadron, led by First Lieutenant William L. Beyer. He happened to glance back and saw the Bf-109s pop out of the clouds so quickly that his element leader and wingman went down before they could take action. Beyer reversed as the 109s flashed past, and got on the leader's tail. "The rest disappeared back into the clouds. We made many violent high-G maneuvers with wide open throttles." Beyer suddenly realized that his opponent had "stopped in mid air." Pulling his throttle to idle and dropping flaps and landing gear, Beyer fishtailed and weaved to stay behind his opponent. "This was repeated three times, and once I almost cut his tail off, we were so close."

The German pilot made a series of steep dives. "The last one was at a thousand feet, with flaps down. It was deadly and nerve-wracking. He went straight down, hoping I couldn't pull out. If I pulled out early, he could come in behind, so I stayed with him. We pulled out so low that if we'd had our gear down, we'd have been on the ground." At that moment, Beyer got his sights on his opponent and fired a burst. "I must have hit him with the first burst, because he kept turning and went in and broke up. Knowing the caliber of this opponent, I am sure if I had fired at him at any time before, he could have shot me down or made a getaway. My other combat victories were not nearly as spectacular as this."

Beyer's opponent was Mietusch. His loss hit hard; he had been a "Schlageter" pilot since joining the unit in 1938 at age 19. He made his mark as a member of then-Leutnant Joachim Müncheburg's 7.Staffel, which changed the air war over Malta in the spring of 1941. He had been shot down ten times and wounded four times. He never turned down a mission, and logged 452 combat sorties. His 72 victories, all scored on the Western Front and Malta, resulted in his posthumous award of the Oak Leaves to his *Ritterkreuz*. He was two months past his 25th birthday at the time of his death.

The afternoon of September 18, Lieutenant Colonel Oberhansly led the 78th to Arnhem, escorting supply-dropping B-24s. The Thunderbolts knocked out 12 flak sites and caught a large truck convoy they put out of action. The weather closed in with a 500-foot cloud ceiling forcing them low and flak killed one while four bailed out. Gunners on the ground could see them through the haze, while the pilots had difficulty spotting the guns. The 56th sent out 39 Thunderbolts and lost 16 to flak; eight landed in Allied territory. Every Thunderbolt was damaged. It was the group's blackest day.

While the Thunderbolts took a beating, JG 26 ran afoul of the 357th's Mustangs in what one of the German pilots remembered was an eerily lit purplish-blue sky. The low-altitude battle resulted in claims by the Yoxford Boys for 20 Bf-109s and five Fw-190s in exchange for five, including one squadron commander. JG 26 claimed five Mustangs, including one flight of four by Leutnant Gerald Vogt's 5.Staffel from II./JG 26.

On September 19, bad weather kept nearly all fighters in England grounded. With no fighter-bombers, the German defenders surrounded the British. The 56th and the 353rd groups did manage to put in an appearance; the Slybirds claimed six while Dave Schilling found 20 Fw-190s northwest of Nijmegen; the Wolfpack claimed 15 shot down for three, with Schilling claiming three. I./JG 26 managed get into the battle zone and shot down 20 of the C-47s and Stirlings towing gliders lost that day, without loss. "Old hare" Oberleutnant Fred Heckmann claimed four C-47s for victories 66–69.

The weather cleared on September 20 and the Thunderbolts returned to provide air cover, not knowing it was the day Arnhem was lost. The 78th and 353rd groups provided cover on September 23 and 25 for supply drops to the 101st Airborne at the Nijmegen bridge. Overall,

VIII Fighter Command lost 73 fighters, 45 of them P-47s, supporting Operation *Market Garden* between September 17 and 25. The 78th flew 237 sorties, resulting in award of the Distinguished Unit Citation.

With the failure of *Market Garden*, the Western Front stabilized in the face of the coming winter. The Germans remained secure behind the Rhine River and the Siegfried Line, which was now fully equipped and manned. JG 26, JG 2, JG 27, and JG 53 defended the Western Front. The situation would not change until spring as Europe shivered through the coldest winter in over a century.

On September 15, the three fighter wings in VIII Fighter Command were separately assigned to the three air divisions. The 65th Wing, with the 4th, 56th, 355th, 361st, and 479th groups, became part of 2nd Air Division; the 66th Wing, with the 55th, 78th, 339th, 353rd, and 357th groups, joined 3rd Air Division; the 67th Wing, with the 20th, 352nd, 356th, 359th, and 364th groups, went to 1st Air Division. In effect, each division was now its own air force, able to put up over 500 bombers and a similar number of fighters. VIII Fighter Command gave up full operational control on October 15.

By mid-September, the 479th received enough P-51s to re-equip the 435th Squadron, while the 434th and 436th kept their P-38s. On September 26, the group ran across a large formation of Bf-109s east of Arnhem. Flying his new Mustang, Zemke used the K-14 sight to shoot down a Bf-109 with a 40-degree deflection shot. He recalled that the fighter did not appear to be hard hit, but it immediately rolled over and the pilot bailed out. He then mistook his wingman for a Bf-109 and attempted to out-fly him for five minutes, but Second Lieutenant Billy Means stuck with Zemke despite his best efforts to lose him. He spotted a fight and headed toward it. One Bf-109 dived away and he followed, opening fire at 400 yards with a 20-degree deflection, hitting the enemy fighter in the fuselage. The canopy immediately flew off and the pilot bailed out while the airplane plunged into a field and exploded on impact. On return, the group claimed 29 destroyed for the loss of one P-38 and its pilot. Five pilots had shot down two each and two from the 434th Squadron shot down three each. By early October, the group was able to bid the P-38 farewell and the Lockheed fighter was no longer part of VIII Fighter Command.

Erprobungskommando 262, the first test unit for the Me-262, was created in July 1944, based at Lechfeld. On September 26, it was disbanded and Kommando Nowotny was formed to take the jet into combat. The commander was Major Walter Nowotny, a 258-victory *Experte* with JG 54 on the Eastern Front. The unit moved from Lechfeld to Achmer and began transitioning pilots to the new technology.

The experience of these early pilots was similar to that of Leutnant Jorg Czypionka, who flew the Me-262 with the night fighting unit Kommando Welter in the spring of 1945. He never forgot the first time he saw the aircraft. "It was absolutely breathtaking. It looked like it was going fast standing there! I looked at it and just knew I was looking at the future. I couldn't wait to get a chance to fly it."

Considering what a technological advance the Me-262 was over everything before, transitioning was almost off-hand. Czypionka recalled:

I sat in it for an hour and memorized where everything was, how to operate the throttle controls. That was the really hard part. If you operated the throttles too fast, the turbos would flame out. It took both hands to work them, which was why people got in trouble if they had an engine problem while they were flying. You had to baby them. For me, I had been flying gliders and light planes for so long, I was used to controlling the airplane with my flight controls. Many other pilots, who had a lot of time in high-powered machines, were used to controlling the airplane with a throttle that reacted quickly. You really had to have a feel for it as a flying machine to have any real chance in it.

Czypionka's first flight happened late in the afternoon:

It was the last light of day, already toward sunset. It was hard to get the engines started; the mechanic had to use these little two-cycle starter motors in each, and then you had to baby the turbo once it started. I closed the hood and it was so silent! So smooth, no vibration at all. I got out on the runway and applied power and it was so fast! Just straight down the runway, I didn't have to touch the rudder pedals at all like with every other airplane, and then I was off and climbing. It was the best flight I ever had.

Kommando Nowotny was declared operational on October 3, equipped with 40 Me-262A-1a fighters. They soon realized that they were highly vulnerable during landing and takeoff, when the pilot could not change throttle settings. III./JG 54, which had been withdrawn to Germany in mid-August to become the first unit to re-equip with the new Fw-190D-9 and was declared operational on October 12, was assigned to airfield defense. Oberleutnant Wilhelm Heilmann, a 34-victory *Experte*, took 9./JG 54 to nearby Hesepe airfield while 12./JG 54 under Leutnant Hans Dortenmann was based at Achmer.

The new fighter, which came to be known as the *Dora-9* or the *Langnasen-Dora* due to its longer engine cowling, was the result of designer Kurt Tank's attempt to improve high-altitude performance. Tank wanted to substitute the DB 603 liquid-cooled engine for the BMW 801, but was forced to use the Junkers Jumo 213A, an engine used for bombers. At first, pilots were uncertain about the airplane, since Tank called it "an interim type," while he continued to fight for the DB 603, but most had the same response as Peter Crump, who called it "The best airplane I ever flew." Allied pilots who flew it after the war considered it the best German fighter to reach combat.

October saw the 78th finish their assignment as fighter-bombers and return to providing escort to the heavy bombers over Germany. On October 6, Lieutenant Colonel Myers led a mission to Leipzig. At 1220 hours, Major Richard Conner received a warning from Fighter Control of high-speed bogies approaching from the rear. He spotted them at 14,000 feet and identified them as two Me-262s. He led his flight down from 24,000 feet but was unable to close the distance to the two jets to open fire.

The group flew to Osnabrück on October 15 and found more jets. The 84th's Captain John Brown and his new wingman, Second Lieutenant Huie Lamb, had just strafed a marshaling yard when Lamb spotted an Me-262.:

I called it in to John, but he didn't see it. He told me to go for it and he would cover me. I dove at him. I was indicating over 500 miles an hour as I closed. I knew they could outperform us, so I opened fire out of range, hoping to hit him but all that did was warn him I was there. He started a turn away and I hit the water injection – the only time I ever used it – and picked up about 25 miles an hour, which allowed me to close on him. He was turning wide and I opened fire again and hit him in the forward fuselage. He flipped over, then straightened out and went lower. I closed in to around a hundred feet right behind him. I only had two inner guns that still had ammo after the strafing. I hit his left engine and he fell off to the right and went in and exploded on impact.

As flak tracers surrounded him, Lamb realized he was right over the enemy airfield:

I'd been so close to him they couldn't open fire, but as soon as he went in, every gun on that field opened up on me! I got hit in the rudder, and it jammed for a minute. John radioed me to go lower and I went across that field at maximum speed and so low I must have nearly hit the ground with my prop. It was all a blur. I got out of there and pulled up. John joined up and told me I had a lot of hits in my plane. It was my first victory and I had promised myself before that I would do a victory roll when that happened, but I decided I'd just worry about getting on the ground in one piece, which is what I did.

That same day, Hub Zemke's flight of P-51s had a run-in with another of the Kommando Nowotny jets. His flight of four was at about 20,000 feet when a lone Me-262 appeared at five o'clock high. Zemke went into a hard right turn just before the jet came into firing range and he flashed past the P-15 with his guns firing. The Me-262 then made a wide climbing turn ready to position for another pass. Zemke pushed his throttle fully forward for maximum power and kept circling inside his opponent's turning circle, but eventually the enemy pilot was able to initiate another pass. Zemke turned to meet the jet head-on and both opened fire but again neither hit their target. The Mustang and the jet made two more frontal passes. Zemke was worried how much longer his overheated engine would continue giving him full power. The jet turned a little wide, then suddenly broke away in a fast shallow dive to the east, departing as quickly as he had appeared. Zemke reported that he had generated a good sweat, fired off all his ammo, and nearly blown a good engine in the fight, which clearly demonstrated the superior performance of the Me-262.

As if writing *finis* to an era, the two strongest American personalities among the fighter leaders were removed from the scene within days of each other. On October 30, Hub Zemke led an escort mission in which the weather turned out to be much worse than forecast. The fighters entered what turned out to be an enormous line of thunder cells just west of Celle in western Germany. They were tossed around like leaves. Zemke was thrown inverted; the P-51 hit a downdraft and the right wing came off. He suddenly found himself in his seat, in mid-air, after the airplane disintegrated. Falling through the storm, he opened his parachute some 500 feet above the ground. After three days on the run, he was captured by local farmers on November 2.

The same day that Zemke was captured, the 4th's indomitable Don Blakeslee led an escort to Hamburg, his first mission since returning from a 30-day leave back in the United States. He had just stepped into his office after landing when the phone rang. It was General Jesse Auton, commander of the 65th Fighter Wing. "I can't lose both of you. You're grounded. Effective immediately." While most pilots were glad to leave at the end of a 250-hour tour, Blakeslee had flown combat continuously since May 1941. He logged time leading new groups as "training" and used other devices to avoid being taken off operations. It is estimated he flew approximately 1,200 combat hours, more than any other American pilot.

Where Zemke was a professionally trained officer, Blakeslee was a talented amateur who "played it by ear," in the words of Jim Goodson. Both men sacrificed popularity to gain group cohesiveness and discipline. Both commanded deep loyalty from those they led; both "led from in front." They commanded the two most successful American fighter units ever to enter combat.

Only small numbers of enemy fighters had been encountered during October, as Adolf Galland began conserving the Jagdwaffe for his "Grosse Schlag"; however, that came to an end on November 2, which would be remembered as one of the most successful days of the war for VIII Fighter Command. The Leuna synthetic oil factory was the target of 683 B-17s. The 3rd Air Division, escorted by 420 P-15s, arrived at the Initial Point just after noon; enemy fighter formations were seen all around. Major Eugene Ryan, leading the 55th Group, split his force when 75–100 Bf-109s and Fw-190s were spotted heading for the bombers. The Mustangs broke up the formations, claiming 19 destroyed for one P-51. At the same time, 15 JG 400 Me-163s were spotted. Nine managed to streak through the escort screen to attack unsuccessfully.

Twenty minutes later, the 1st Air Division, covered by 200 P-51s from the 20th, 352nd, 359th, and 364th groups, encountered the strongest opposition as they arrived over "Mercilessburg" at 1221 hours. Major George Preddy, now commanding the 328th Squadron, led his Mustangs into a force of 50 Bf-109s while the other two Blue Noser squadrons hit other enemy formations. Over the next 15 minutes, the 328th pilots claimed 28 destroyed, the highest score yet for a single fighter squadron. Preddy's single victory made him the leading active Eighth Air Force ace, with 24.5 aerial victories and five ground kills. Captain Don Bryan, leading the 328th's Yellow Flight, was involved in 15 different combats, claiming five victories. Overall, the Blue Nosers returned to Bodney with claims of 38 destroyed, a new record.

The largest enemy force, estimated at 200–250, attacked two groups of B-17s that were off-course and straggling. The 20th Group intercepted; it claimed 28, including three by group commander Lieutenant Colonel Robert Montgomery and another triple by First Lieutenant Ernest Fiebelkorn, who at six feet four inches and 225 pounds was the biggest Mustang pilot in the USAAF.

The overall claims of 134 destroyed, three probables, and 25 damaged was the second-highest by the Eighth's fighter force. The battle raged around the Leuna factory for 40 minutes and involved a total of 300 Jagdwaffe fighters from ten *Gruppen*. Despite their best efforts, they could only claim 26 B-17s and eight P-51s.

Early winter rains at the end of October severely restricted operations from Duxford's grass field. Two P-47s were unable to take off on October 25 after they became mired in mud while waiting their turn. The rains continued into November and turned Duxford into a quagmire, too soft and muddy for flight operations, forcing a move to the 91st Bomb Group's base at Bassingbourn. Army engineers laid down a 4,500-foot by 150-foot pierced-steel-plank (PSP) runway.

On November 6, the 357th's Captain Chuck Yeager, who had successfully evaded capture when he was shot down back in March and became an "ace in a day" on October 12, engaged three Me-262s from Kommando Nowotny. He later reported, "I was leading Cement White flight north of Osnabrück when we spotted three Me-262s. We headed the last man off and I got a hit or two before he accelerated away." The three enemy jets disappeared in the hazy undercast; Yeager dived through and emerged in clear air where he met them head-on. He split-S-ed and got behind the leader. "I was indicating 430 miles an hour and I fired two bursts and hit him in the fuselage before he pulled away into the haze and I lost him."

Yeager found a large airfield – which later turned out to be Achmer – and flew around it looking for jets:

I spotted a lone 262 that was approaching the field at about two hundred miles an hour. I dived on him and was doing 500 miles an hour when I caught him at 500 feet. Very thick, accurate flak started coming up. I got hits on him with a couple bursts and then broke straight up. I looked back and saw him crash-land about 400 yards short of the field.

On November 7, Walter Nowotny shot down a B-24 from a formation that he attacked in his Me-262. The next day, four jets were ordered to take off – Leutnants Erich Büttner and Franz Schall from Hesepe, and Nowotny and Leutnant Günther Wegmann from Achmer. Only Schall and Wegmann managed to take off after Büttner punctured a tire while taxiing and Nowotny's engines wouldn't start. After some delay, Nowotny took off on his own. By this time, Schall and Wegmann were landing at Hesepe after sustaining battle damage. Minutes later, Nowotny radioed that he had shot down a B-24 and a P-51. A moment later he made a final garbled transmission containing the word "burning." Pilot Helmut Lennarz later stated he heard Nowotny say "I'm on fire – it's burning!"

Nowotny was claimed separately by the 20th Group's Ernest Fiebelkorn and the 357th's First Lieutenant Edward "Buddy" Haydon, who both claimed that they spotted the Me-262 east of Hesepe after he shot down the 364th's Second Lieutenant Richard W. Stevens. Several witnesses in the air and on the ground saw Nowotny's "White 8" dive vertically out of the clouds and crash east of Hesepe.

During the month that Kommando Nowotny was operational before its commander's death, the unit claimed 22 enemy aircraft shot down for a loss of 26 Me-262s. Galland considered the poor performance to be lack of experience in operating the jet and the poor quality of the engines, which were troublesome throughout the Me-262's career. Shortly after Nowotny's death the unit was redesignated III./JG 7, when that *Geschwader* was formed as the first jet-equipped fighter group on November 19.

With Blakeslee now gone from the 4th, the question of permanent leadership was important. In his absence, the group had been led by Lieutenant Colonel Claiborne Kinnard from the 355th Group. He had managed to get off on the wrong foot with the pilots when he told them they were "going to join the Army now," and tried to stamp out many of the unit's RAF-based traditions. Surprisingly, he had at first refused to have the spinner and nose of his P-51 painted red, the 4th's color, leaving it in the 355th's white. He also brought flight leaders from the 355th to help with his effort to remake the group. The result was a severe drop in morale and performance.

In mid-November, Lieutenant Colonel Sidney Woods became the Eagles' new commander. He was one of the veterans of the 49th Fighter Group – the Forty-Niners – who had learned their trade the hard way as the first USAAF fighter unit to deploy from the United States in the aftermath of Pearl Harbor, arriving in Australia where they faced the Japanese at Darwin. Joe Kruezel –who had advanced from deputy group commander to group commander of the 361st Group following the August death in action of his fellow Philippines escapee Thomas J.J. Christian – led the Green Dragon Flight of the 9th Squadron at Darwin; the two junior wing men were John D. Landers and George Preddy. After his arrival in the ETO in March, Landers became commander of the 55th Group that summer and was just completing a successful tour as commander of the 357th Group. Preddy now led the Blue Nosers' 328th Squadron as the Eighth's leading active ace.

All of these Pacific veterans shaped the units they served with in VIII Fighter Command. Woods was deputy group commander of the 357th, then deputy commander of the 479th, where he had so impressed Hub Zemke that he was recommended to take command of the group until Colonel Riddle returned from evading capture in France and was restored to command following Zemke's loss. Woods commanded the 4th through the final six months of the war; while he was no Blakeslee, he restored morale and led the group's return to its glory days.

On November 16, the 78th's commander, Colonel Gray, held a meeting at the Duxford base theater, where he announced the P-47s would depart at the end of the month, to be replaced by Mustangs. When Gray pointed out that the P-51 would have the range to "get to the fight," one wag replied, "Yes, but the P-47 will get you home!" The 356th Group had replaced its Thunderbolts with Mustangs on November 10; the 78th was the last Eighth Air Force P-47 group to change over to the North American fighter, leaving only the 56th still flying the Thunderbolt.

While the 78th began re-equipping, and the 4th changed leadership, JG 26 did much the same. II./JG 26 was withdrawn for two weeks to re-equip with the Fw-190D-9, followed by I./JG 26 in early December. Klaus Mietusch's place at the head of III./JG 26 was taken by Hauptmann Walter Krupinski, an *Experte* who was one of the few left with experience in the Polish and French campaigns, the Battle of Britain, and three years on the Eastern Front with JG 52. Krupinski, known as "Count Punski," a play on his name that acknowledged an addiction to puns in his voluble sense of humor, had 177 victories. Unfortunately, by October 1944, he was as tired of the war as were the men he commanded; the unit continued the decline that had begun under Mietusch.

This was demonstrated in the experience of 19-year-old Unteroffizier Georg Genth, whose father had flown Gotha bombers in attacks on London in 1917. He was proud to be chosen to fly as *Rottenflieger* to the 12.Staffel's *Staffelkapitän* on the first mission led by Krupinski. He later recalled that when they spotted Spitfires, his commander pulled up into the clouds overhead so sharply that he could not follow, and disappeared. "Callously, that tired warrior had abandoned the formation." A battle broke out and Genth surprised everyone by being the only one to score a victory. What he found most shocking was that on return to base, the *Staffelkapitän* also showed up; Krupinski did nothing to the man for abandoning his squadron in the face of the enemy.

On November 25, while escorting bombers to Koblenz, pilots of the 78th were the first to spot V-2 ballistic missiles being launched, with one of the three close enough that the Thunderbolt pilots could see it rise to 30,000 feet before it disappeared on its way to England.

On November 26, the bombers went after synthetic oil plants in Hannover, defended by 400 German fighters. 78B provided cover for the 1st Air Division's mission to Osnabrück. The 82nd Squadron was vectored onto 40 Bf-109s over Rheine. Lieutenant Donald Hart hit one; Lieutenant Harold Liebenrood caught another from six o'clock and set it afire. Lieutenant Manfred Croy chased another to low level, where it crashed and exploded. Lieutenant John Hockery's flight chased others that broke through the screen. He hit one with a deflection shot, then chased another to the deck and shot it down over an airfield; three Fw-190s flown by better pilots than he expected chased him. "My water injection ran out and they started to catch me, so I turned to fight. Just as I got strikes on one, an explosion blew off part of my wing and I crashed into a field." He got to a ditch before the 109s strafed the P-47, and became a POW shortly thereafter. The 83rd's Lieutenant Robert Bonebrake caught an Fw-190 over Dummer Lake; it rolled inverted and spun into the ground.

The 339th Group was escorting B-24s of the 2nd Air Division when it caught a gaggle of 40–60 Fw-190s from I./JG 301 at 24,000 feet just east of Hannover. Second Lieutenant Jack Daniel, flying his first mission, shot down five to become an "ace in a day." The group claimed 29 shot down in a battle that ranged from 24,000 feet to the ground, for one loss. That loss was Bert Stiles, who had completed his 30-mission tour with the 401st Bomb Squadron at the end of August. Turning down an assignment as a flight instructor, he volunteered for a second tour as a fighter pilot. After conversion training, he went to the 339th Group's 505th Fighter Squadron in October. The escort to Hannover was Stiles' 16th mission. He was seen to shoot down one Fw-190 and was last seen chasing another. Both planes slammed into the foothills of the Deister ridge line near the town of Springe, southwest of Hannover. Apparently, he became disoriented in the low-level fight and crashed due to target fixation. He was three months past his 24th birthday. Among the personal effects returned to his mother in Denver was the typewritten manuscript of a memoir he had composed while with the 401st. First published in 1947, *Serenade to the Big Bird* is still in print.

The 78th's Mustangs arrived at Duxford on December 16. The terrible weather that day masked the Wehrmacht's attack in Luxembourg's Ardennes Forest that became the Battle of the Bulge. The bad weather didn't let up until December 19, giving the enemy three crucial days to attack the unprepared American units in the Ardennes without fear of Allied fighter-bombers.

Over the previous two weeks, pilots had checked out in the war-weary P-51Bs that were brought in for conversion training. Frank Oiler remembered the transition:

Fighter pilots were creatures of habit and most everyone in the 78th agreed they wouldn't give up flying the P-47 for anything in the world. We had been forewarned it was coming. All the pleading and complaining in the world didn't change a thing. Even though we dug in our heels, they began to pull our P-47s from our icy cold fingers and ferried them to the Ninth Air Force. We received what felt like a demotion: Mustangs. Our brothers in the 56th Fighter Group must have had all the luck in the Air Force – they got to keep their Jugs!

Wayne Coleman remembered an item of great importance to a pilot:

The P-51's cockpit was smaller and tighter than the P-47. In the winter, all bundled up in a fleece-lined flying suit over a wool uniform and longjohns with flying boots and flying gloves on, we filled up the Mustang's cockpit. I used to be sure I answered nature's call before I went flying, but one time I was surprised to hear from her while I was at 10,000 feet. It took ten minutes to get down through all the layers to use the relief tube, and halfway through it froze up and by the time the overflow reached me, it was damn cold!

On December 19, the group flew its last big combat mission with the P-47, which the 83rd and 84th squadrons were still flying. With calls for support in the face of the all-out Wehrmacht assault, the 78th was the only fighter unit in England to get airborne in the atrocious weather. The target was Trier. Shortly after the bombers came off the target, ground controllers warned of incoming fighters but nothing was spotted in the cloudy skies; the squadrons strafed the railroad after aborting an attack on Baben-Heusen airfield.

As they pulled up from the attacks, the pilots of the 83rd Squadron spotted 30 Bf-109s. Pursuing them, they were engaged by 20 Fw-190D-9s. John Kirk fired at a Bf-109 that went straight in, then was engaged by a Langnasen-Dora. As Kirk out-turned the enemy pilot, he suddenly rolled his Dora-9 and bailed out. Lieutenant Francis Harrington hit one of the 109s; it went straight in inverted and exploded on impact. Harrington then went after three Fw-190s. One dived away and he followed; it caught fire, mowing down trees and starting a forest fire when it crashed. Robert Bonebrake got into a fight with three 109s, hitting one in the cockpit that went straight in as the pilot threw himself out and opened his parachute so close to the ground that he only swung a few times. Captain Frank Fish chased four Bf-109s and hit one which blew up when he hit it after the pilot bailed out.

The Battle of the Bulge was so intense that Ninth Tactical Air Command requested additional support from the Eighth Air Force. On December 23, the Blue Nosers flew to Airfield Y-29 at Asch in Belgium, where they would operate for the next two months, living in cold tents; the first night there, many of the pilots thought they would freeze to death. While the weather closed in over England, it was still clear enough, though cloudy, for operations over the Ardennes battlefield. Asch itself was close enough to the front lines that aircraft in the landing pattern sometimes took fire from enemy flak.

The Eighth was able to mount the largest mission of the war on Christmas Eve, when 2,000 bombers were sent against 20 Luftwaffe airfields in western Germany. Only 12 failed to return, and only one was the victim of a German fighter. Over the last six days of December, missions were flown against transportation targets as the weather became better.

On Christmas Day, the weather was flyable and the 352nd had two missions. George Preddy led his 328th Squadron on the second, an escort mission for B-17s flying from England. Preddy's wingman, First Lieutenant Gordon Cartee, later recalled, "After stooling around for a while with no action, we were vectored toward Koblenz, where some enemy aircraft had been spotted." When they got in the area, Preddy spotted two Bf-109s below. Cartee later reported:

Preddy got in a Lufbery with the first '109. Neither were gaining much advantage when all of a sudden another '109 cut in front of him. He eased up on his controls just enough to give it a short burst. It caught fire and he resumed pursuit of the first one. That guy lost his concentration when he saw his buddy flamed, and Preddy nailed him.

Moments later, Preddy and Cartee were vectored to an area southeast of Liège, where enemy aircraft were strafing ground troops. They were joined by First Lieutenant Jim Bouchier from the 479th Group, who had lost his unit. Preddy saw an Fw-190D-9 over the trees some distance away and accelerated toward it. The three Mustangs were in trail at 500 feet as he closed on the Dora-9.

They approached the village of Langerwehe, where Sergeant Harold M. Kennedy and Corporal Elmer L. Dye from the 104th Infantry were manning an observation post in the village church's bell tower.

They saw the three Mustangs approach at high speed. Suddenly tracers flashed up from a wooded area where the 12th Anti-Aircraft Group had guns set up.

Cartee saw "a whole field of golf balls" from the intense barrage. Ahead, Preddy's Mustang appeared to take hits and he started a chandelle to the left to get away:

> As we went over the woods I was hit by ground fire. Major Preddy apparently noticed the intense ground fire and light flak and we broke off the attack with a chandelle to the left. About half way through the maneuver, and at an altitude of about 700 feet, his canopy came off and he nosed down, still in his turn. I saw no 'chute and watched his ship hit.

The flak was still thick. Bouchier took hits and his engine began smoking heavily. He rolled over and fell out, pulling his 'chute immediately. He landed safely among nearby British troops. Cartee "went balls out and got out of there." US troops found George Preddy dead in his cockpit.

Back at Asch, Christmas dinner was being served. A keg of beer had been delivered for the celebration. When Cartee returned and made his report, the dinner and beer were forgotten.

The leading ace of the Eighth Air Force had been shot down and killed by "friendly fire." His friend and fellow pilot John C. Meyer described him as "the greatest fighter pilot who ever squinted through a gunsight; he was the complete fighter pilot."

The fog over East Anglia finally broke on December 28 and Colonel Gray led a P-47 mission with the 84th Squadron to Koblenz. On December 29, the 78th divided into three: first off at 0940 hours was the 84th Squadron which put up 32 P-47s as 78C, while the 32 P-51Ds from 82nd and 83rd squadrons flew their missions as 78A and B, respectively. The Thunderbolts went to Malmedy while the Mustangs escorted bombers to Frankfurt.

Huie Lamb, newly promoted to captain, had a very close call:

> We as a group were not that knowledgeable about dealing with technical difficulties with the Mustang at that time, which may have led to my problem. I was element lead with John Chiles as my wingman. As we approached Frankfurt, John's radio went out and

he aborted, which meant I had to return with him. We flew out over Holland. As we passed the coastal flak belt, we let down and suddenly my temperature gauge started climbing. I was on automatic control and went to manual control and opened the radiator door. The temperature came back into the green arc. I closed the door and continued on. We were headed for landfall at Orfordness. About halfway across, the temperature went into the yellow, close to the red arc. I opened the door again, but it had no effect. I throttled back, hoping to make it to the coast, but the engine overheated and caught fire. I unfastened my shoulder harness to bail out and slid the canopy back, but it jammed. When I finally got it open I was too low to jump. I was going to have to ditch, and all I had was the seatbelt.

I slowed, dropped flaps and used the surface chop to head into the wind. I stalled out just as I touched down, but my left wingtip hit first and I cartwheeled. I hit the gunsight and broke a tooth and cut my lip pretty bad. The airplane came to a quick stop and I stood up to get my dingy. The water in the cockpit was quickly up to my knees and the airplane was sinking fast. I threw the dingy out and inflated my Mae West and got out just as the airplane went down.

The water was really cold; they told me later it was 40 degrees. I inflated the dingy, but I couldn't get in and it floated away. John saw my predicament, but he couldn't radio for help. We didn't know it, but John Crump from the 357th Fighter Group was doing an air test and he saw me go in and radioed a Mayday. John Chiles flew to Martlesham Heath and saw a Walrus taxying to the runway; they were responding to Crump's Mayday. John landed and told them he would lead them to me. He said it seemed to take forever for the Walrus to get off, then he had to circle to stay with it. He flew to where I was, and circled until the Walrus landed, then had to leave since he was almost out of gas. The Walrus aircrewman had a hell of a time pulling me out, since my clothes were waterlogged and I was close to unconscious from exposure. They shut down the engine so they could pull me in the rear hatch, then they had trouble getting it started, but finally they managed to take off. Twenty minutes later they had me in the hospital; I was suffering from exposure. When I came to, the doctor told me my body temperature was so low when I got there that if I had been in the water another five minutes I would likely have died.

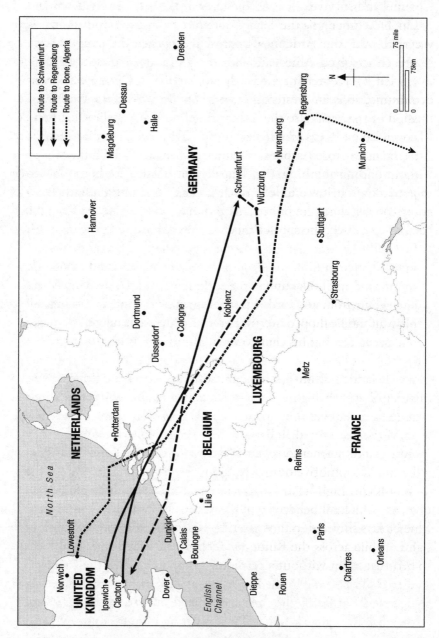

MAP 3: Operation *Bodenplatte*

Lamb was one of the few Mustang pilots to ditch a Mustang in the Channel and survive.

On December 30, the 84th Squadron put up 32 P-47s that were vectored over the Ardennes battlefield in chases above the clouds that each involved Allied aircraft. The other two squadrons sent 35 P-51s led by Lieutenant Colonel Myers to escort bombers targeting communications in western Germany. On New Year's Eve, the last mission of 1944 was also the last mission in the P-47 when Captain Pat Maxwell led 13 P-47s on a freelance fighter sweep to the Hamburg area. After being vectored around Bremen, Hannover, and Dummer Lake without finding anything, the Thunderbolts turned for home. Maxwell spotted a train below and led his wingman on a strafing run, but he was going too fast when he pulled out and only damaged it. As he climbed back to 2,500 feet, he spotted an Fw-190 at 1,500 feet:

> I peeled off after him. My closure was very fast from dead astern. He spotted me and broke up to the left. I put the dot on the canopy and opened fire from 400 yards with 80 degrees deflection. His belly tank blew up and he flipped over and fell like a rock. The pilot tried to bail out at 200 feet but his chute opened just as he hit the ground.

Maxwell landed from his final mission of his second tour, the final mission of a 78th Fighter Group squadron in the Thunderbolt, to be awarded a silver beer mug by Colonel Gray honoring the group's 400th victory, the last scored in a P-47. The group had closed out the final month of the momentous year 1944 with no pilot losses, eight aerial kills, and a locomotive destroyed.

That night, Eighth Air Force units in England celebrated the coming of 1945, which all believed would see the end of the war. At Asch, the Blue Nosers shivered in their sleeping bags inside their tents as snow fell lightly, while across the Rhine in Germany, the Jagdwaffe's pilots went to bed that night without a celebration.

# 24

# DEATH OF THE LUFTWAFFE

In a meeting held on November 20, 1944, regarding the Jagdwaffe's disastrous performance on November 2 – when only 80 American bombers had been shot down for a German loss of 90 fighters – Adolf Hitler overruled Adolf Galland's plan for his *Grosse Schlag*, stating that the enemy was now too strong in the air for such an operation to have a chance of success. Instead, he directed that the fighters be deployed to western Germany to support a coming operation. Only the anti-bomber Jagdgeschwadern 300 and 301 were held back for action against bombing attacks.

*Case Bodenplatte* (Operation *Baseplate*) was originally planned to commence with the Wehrmacht offensive in the Ardennes. That required bad weather to prevent Allied fighter bombers from operating; the Luftwaffe managed to launch 500 aircraft on December 16, but operating in such bad weather proved to be beyond the capability of most units and operations were canceled. Still, over the eight days when weather conditions allowed operations between December 17 and 27, the Jagdwaffe lost 644 fighters with 227 damaged. This included 322 pilots killed, 23 captured, and 133 wounded. On the three clear days between December 23 and 25, 363 fighters were lost. As a result, none of the fighter leaders expected a large-scale air operation.

The clearing skies brought the German offensive to a halt as Allied fighter-bombers returned. Despite running short of gasoline – the result of the Allied oil campaign in the summer and fall – the Wehrmacht attempted to launch *Unternehmen Nordwind* (Operation *Northwind*) and restart the offensive. *Bodenplatte* was meant to support this. The plan called for a surprise strafing attack against 17 Allied airfields in Belgium, the Netherlands, and France. Every *Geschwader* was involved. Bf-110s and Ju-88s acted as pathfinders for the Bf-109s and Fw-190s. Over the previous week, Ultra picked up Luftwaffe messages instructing bomber units to coordinate with fighter units – to provide navigational assistance in the attack – but this was mistaken for possible use of these with the fighters against Allied bombers.

Secrecy was so tight that not all German units were informed of its timing; the planners blundered by setting flight paths that took several units over the V-2 launch sites around the Hague, which were protected by 267 heavy and 277 medium or light antiaircraft artillery (AAA) batteries, in addition to 100 Kriegsmarine AAA batteries along the Dutch coast. The result was that one-quarter of the attacking units lost aircraft to "friendly fire."

The 352nd Fighter Group had provided early morning patrols over the front lines since its arrival from England, which had proven fruitful in combating Luftwaffe activities. Pilots were eager to be assigned due to the increased chance of finding the enemy. The group kept at least one squadron available throughout the day for front-line operations.

At midnight on January 31, Lieutenant Colonel John C. Meyer, recently promoted from command of the 487th Squadron to deputy group commander when Colonel Jim Mayden took command of the Blue Nosers, was interrupted while planning the first dawn patrol of 1945 by orders from "Football" – IX Air Force headquarters – directing the 352nd to prepare a "maximum effort" escort mission the next day. This meant there would be no early morning patrol. Meyer immediately informed Colonel Mayden and the three squadron commanders. All were dismayed, since there had been so much Luftwaffe fighter activity over the front lines and the patrols had been so effective. They examined the order, looking for a way to comply and also provide the patrol. Calls to headquarters to modify the order were unsuccessful. Frustrated, Meyer turned in with orders to wake him at dawn, in case things changed.

Dawn found Y-29 covered in thick fog, which would delay operations. At 0800 hours, Meyer called again, asking for a change in orders – could they put up three 12-plane squadrons, leaving 12 for patrol? He was told to wait 20 minutes; the response was negative. Not one to give up when he believed he was right, Meyer placed a direct call to General Pete Quesada. This time, Meyer mentioned the possible threat of enemy attack while taking off for the escort mission as reason to have a patrol. Quesada put Meyer on the spot: would he personally state the fighters were needed for patrol because of a threat, and take responsibility for anything that happened if the order was changed? With Meyer's yes, Quesada approved the patrol at 0845 hours.

By 0900 hours, the weather was clearing. The patrol would fly to St Vith, the logistical bottleneck for Wehrmacht activity on the front after their failure to take Malmedy and Bastogne; the Mustangs would return in time to provide cover for the escort takeoff. "Transport" (radio code for the 487th) Red, White, and Blue flights would make up the patrol. Meyer would lead as Transport White One. The pilots readied for start-up when the fog lifted sufficiently to allow takeoff.

Finally, at 0915 hours, the fog lifted; eight Ninth Air Force P-47s from the 390th Squadron of the 366th Fighter Group took off, disappearing in the ground haze. The 12 blue-nosed P-51s taxied to the runway. As Meyer accelerated for takeoff, he saw black puffs from antiaircraft gun explosions and tracers from machine guns whip the sky ahead. When he asked the control tower what was happening, they replied there was nothing. But the flak bursts got thicker as he passed the halfway point and spotted black specks low on the horizon.

A moment later, one speck turned into an Fw-190 that seemed to fly directly at Meyer, who could only continue accelerating to flying speed. The enemy fighter opened fire and Meyer momentarily ducked. Then he realized that he wasn't the target when he saw the C-47 parked next to the runway take hits. When his airspeed indicator hit 100 miles per hour, Meyer hauled the Mustang off the runway and immediately retracted his landing gear. He pulled the trigger and saw tracers hit the Fw-190's engine. It swerved toward him, then nosed down. Meyer flew over the stricken fighter so close collision was missed by inches.

Observers saw the Fw-190 explode when it hit the ground; for a moment, it was unclear if they had collided. Then Meyer banked away beyond the rising cloud of black smoke.

The fog was now a strong haze, making it difficult to identify shapes in the sky. Below, other Mustangs lifted off and tucked their gear. Reaching 2,000 feet, Meyer saw two indistinct shapes ahead. Closing, he momentarily took them for P-47s, then recognized them as another pair of Fw-190s. He closed on the wingman. When its wing span filled the sight reticle, he opened fire. He spotted a Bf-109 curve in on his left rear, still out of range. The Fw-190 ahead took hits but he couldn't hold fire on it as he bounced in the propwash.

Suddenly the Fw-190 ahead split-S-ed from 3,000 feet. Meyer turned hard left as the 109 fired and missed him. An instant later, a blue-nosed P-51 turned onto the 109's tail and opened fire; the enemy pilot turned away. Meyer saw streamers swirl from the Fw-190's wingtips as it pulled out so low it seemed to hit the trees. He dived to finish the fight but was suddenly hit by antiaircraft fire! A hole opened in the Mustang's wing. Meyer took another hit; he banked away from the "friendly" fire. The 190 started climbing and Meyer opened fire. The enemy pilot banked, looking to crash-land. As he touched down, he caught a wingtip and the fighter somersaulted, broke up, and exploded. Meyer departed the battle area, knowing he was too low on ammo to get in a third fight.

The eight P-47s that took off just before Meyer were the first to run into the JG 11 fighters closing on the field. The Thunderbolt pilots shot down two as they flashed through the enemy formation, distracting the enemy pilots at just the right moment.

Meyer's wingman, First Lieutenant Alex Sears, remembered:

We had just taken off when we were bounced by 40 or 50 Me-109s and Fw-190s. One Me-109 came at me head-on and we made several passes at each other, both of us firing. On the third pass I got some strikes on his engine and shot part of the tail section away. He started burning and went down in a lazy spiral and crashed.

Meyer's element leader, White Three First Lieutenant Ray Littge, shot down an Fw-190 as he lifted off. He chased another that took hits but kept on going, emitting huge clouds of black smoke. Littge kept shooting until he was out of ammunition, following it until the pilot bailed out in the vicinity of Paris.

Littge's wingman, Second Lieutenant Alden Rigby, shot an Fw-190 off Littge's tail, then turned onto another 190.

I dropped down on his tail and my gunsight went out, so I fired a long burst until I noticed hits on his wing roots. He started pouring black smoke and lost altitude until he crashed into the trees. I immediately returned to the field and noticed a P-47 in a Lufbery with a '109. The P-47 fired a short burst and I noticed a few strikes on the '109. He tightened his turn; as the P-47 mushed, I came in and fired a long burst. He crashed in an open field.

Nearly out of ammo, Rigby circled to land, but ran across another fight between two P-51s and a Bf-109. "The '109 broke in my direction and I fired the remainder of my ammo at him, scoring at least one hit in the cockpit. The enemy aircraft dived straight into the ground." Rigby claimed two Fw-190s and two Bf-109s, one possibly shared with an unidentified P-47 and the other possibly shared with an unidentified P-51. He would not get full credit for the two Bf-109s for 55 years.

Major Bill Halton's Yellow Flight followed White Flight into instant combat. Dodging enemy fighters on takeoff, element leader First Lieutenant Sanford Moats shot down four Fw-190s while his wingman, Second Lieutenant Henry Stewart, scored three Bf-109s. Flight leader Halton and his wingman, Second Lieutenant Dean Huston, got an Fw-190 each.

By the time Captain Bill Whisner's Blue Flight got airborne, the sky was filled with enemy aircraft; he scored his first while climbing from takeoff. He later reported: "I ran into about 30 Fw-190s at 1,500 feet. I picked one out and pressed the trigger. Nothing happened. I reached down and turned on my gun switch and gave a couple of good bursts." As Whisner saw number one hit the ground and explode, he felt hits:

A '190 was about 50 yards behind me, firing away. As I was turning with him, another P-51 attacked him and he broke off his attack on me. I then saw that I had several 20mm holes in each wing and another round hit my oil tank. My left aileron was also out and I was losing oil, but my temperature and pressure were steady.

Whisner was aggressive enough that, despite the damage, he turned toward a big dogfight and quickly caught another Fw-190. "After I hit him with several bursts, the pilot tried to jump. Just as his canopy came off I fired again and the '190 rolled over, crashed and exploded." He then came across a flight of Bf-109s and engaged one. "We fought for five or ten minutes and I finally managed to get behind him. I hit him good and he went down. At this time I saw some 15–20 fires on the ground from crashed airplanes."

The field was still under attack as Whisner turned back:

I saw a '109 strafe the northeastern portion of the strip. I started after him and he turned into me. We made two head-on passes and on the second I hit him in the nose and wings. He crashed and burned. I chased several more bandits, but they evaded me in the clouds. By now my windshield was covered with oil, so I headed back to the strip and landed.

Whisner, already an 11-victory ace, had just become "an ace in a day" fighting over his own airfield.

The attack on Asch was assigned to JG 11. I./JG 11 had only 16 Fw-190s on strength and six pilots. The lack of numbers was made up from III./JG 11, which had more pilots than aircraft. Only 41 Fw-190s – four from the Stab; six from I./JG 11 and 31 from III./JG 11; and 20 Bf-109s from II./JG 11 took part in the attack. The plan called for a strafing attack by the more heavily armed Fw-190s, with the Bf-109s flying top cover. While crossing Allied lines, four fighters were lost to antiaircraft. Their path took them directly over the Allied airfield at Ophoven, three miles from Asch and home to the Spitfire XIV fighters of No. 125 Wing RAF; 30 Fw-190s and Bf-109s attacked the field in the mistaken belief it was Asch.

The 45-minute battle at Y-29 went into the record books as "the Legend of Y-29," the wildest fight any Eighth Air Force fighter unit ever engaged in. The pilots of the 487th were credited with 24 destroyed. No P-51s were lost; two were damaged and one was damaged on the ground. The 366th Fighter Group lost one P-47 and was credited with eight destroyed while the airfield ground defenses claimed seven. JG 11 reported the loss of 28 Fw-190s and Bf-109s. Four pilots made it back to German territory, while four were captured and 20 killed. JG 11 *Kommodore* Oberstleutnant Günther Specht and III./JG 11 *Gruppenkommandeur* Hauptmann Horst-Günther von Fassong were among those killed.

The 487th Squadron's performance was so impressive that it was the only Air Force fighter squadron ever awarded the Distinguished Unit Citation. Distinguished Service Crosses were awarded to John

C. Meyer (his third); Bill Whisner (his second); and Sanford Moats. Major William Y. Halton, Captain Henry M. Stewart, and Lieutenants Raymond Littge and Alden Rigby were each awarded the Silver Star. For John C. Meyer, this was his last fight; he was injured in a jeep accident a week later and hospitalized for the rest of the war. He later wrote of New Year's Day, 1945:

> For the first time in my experience in the European air war, American fighters had neither the advantage of superior tactical position, numbers or equipment. For the first time there was no measurement involved in the final determination other than the relative skill and initiative of the pilots. It was no time for leadership or organization. It was man against man.

Only 11 of the Luftwaffe's 34 fighter *Gruppen* attacked on time with surprise. A total of 900 Luftwaffe fighters participated in *Bodenplatte*. JG 3's *Kommodore*, Major Heinz "Pritzl" Bär, led the attack on Eindhoven airfield. He claimed two Typhoon fighter-bombers that were just taking off. His long-time *Rottenflieger*, Oberfeldwebel Leo Schumacher, was badly damaged by defending antiaircraft fire and belly-landed his aircraft inside the German lines, sustaining slight injuries.

The Jagdwaffe claimed 400 Allied aircraft destroyed on the ground, 79 destroyed in the air, and 100 damaged. Actual Allied losses were 290 aircraft destroyed and 180 damaged. The cost to the Jagdwaffe was 143 pilots killed or missing, 70 captured, and 21 wounded. Among the losses were two *Geschwaderkommodoren*, six *Gruppenkommandeuren*, and 14 *Staffelkapitänen*. The Allied aircraft destroyed on the ground were replaced within a week. The German pilot losses were never replaced. For the Luftwaffe, *Case Bodenplatte* was the air force's death knell. Oberstleutnant Johannes Kogler, *Kommodore* of JG 6, who survived being shot down, confessed to his American interrogators, "Whatever we did was too soon or too late. One almost felt ashamed to go out in Luftwaffe uniform at home." Adolf Galland wrote in his diary, "An offensive in the West was senseless. I knew that the insufficient training and lack of experience of our unit commanders meant the Jagdwaffe was doomed to failure."

Despite the attacks, nearly 1,500 heavy bombers flew strikes against oil installations and numerous road and rail targets in western and central Germany later that morning. The Sturmböcken of JG 301 scrambled from their base at Stendal, 60 miles to the west of Berlin, to intercept several small formations of B-17s. One Fortress was claimed by 9.Staffel's Feldwebel Willi Reschke, who was badly shot up by the defenders, forcing him to bail out; this was his seventh and last bomber victory. Minutes later, 10.Staffel's Oberfeldwebel Josef "Jupp" Keil shot down a B-17 near Stendal. The losses were a drop in the bucket to the Americans.

Following Hitler's cancellation of Galland's *Grosse Schlag*, the only Fw-190 units left in Germany assigned to anti-bomber operations were the *Sturmgruppen* JG 300 and 301. All other *Jagdgeschwadern* equipped with Fw-190s of any type were based in western and central Germany, where they spent the war's final months engaged in tactical air combat against the fighter-bombers and medium bombers from the Allied tactical air forces. Outside of occasional encounters, the Würger's battle against the *Viermots* (four-engine bombers) was over.

Two weeks after *Bodenplatte*, on January 14, the last big battle in the defense of the homeland occurred, when 25 *Jagdgeschwadern* were unsuccessful in their attempts to intercept 900 B-17s and B-24s. The claims of 24 American fighters shot down paled against the admitted loss of 107 pilots killed or missing and 150 aircraft shot down by the P-51s. The Reichsverteidigung was no more. JG 300 and 301 lost 54 pilots, including five experienced *Staffelkapitänen*. The *Sturmgeschwadern* would never recover. After this failure, the inexorable advance of the Red Army into eastern Germany became a greater threat than the bombing by the Western Allies. As had happened in Normandy, the surviving fighters of Luftflotte Reich's *Jagdgruppen* were now sent east. The veteran JG 301 recorded its first losses to Soviet fighters on January 18.

Galland visited the fighter units on the Western Front during the week between Christmas and New Year. He was shocked at the attitudes he found among the pilots. His report stated, "Everywhere I went I found shortcomings basically due to insufficient training and lack of experience on the part of the unit commanders. Added to this was the considerable indignation about the leadership's desultory manner of allocating responsibilities and expecting unit commanders to lead from their desks." The report was his downfall.

Bomber leader Generalmajor Dietrich Pelz and Oberst Hajo Herrmann – the bomber pilot who had created the *Wilde Sau* (wild female boars, the most dangerous animal in the German forest) freelance night fighter units – had been working on Göring since the cancellation of Galland's *Grosse Schlag*, convincing the *Reichsmarschall* that redundant bomber pilots could be retrained to fly all-weather jet fighter-bomber missions. This was despite the experience of former bomber pilots assigned to Me-262 bomber units like KG 51, who had demonstrated they were unable to deal with flight operations at the speed associated with the jets.

On January 10, Galland received what turned into a two-and-a-half-hour telephone call from Göring, in which he was told that the *Reichsmarschall* had decided to fire him. Galland later wrote in his diary:

> Göring tried to blame me without really having a clear opinion himself. Amongst other things, he reproached me for having a negative influence on fighter tactics, a lack of support and failure to enforce orders, for having created my own empire in the fighter arm, a wrong staff policy, the removal of people I did not like and my responsibility for the bad state of the Jagdwaffe. I was not permitted to say a word in my defense. At the end, Göring expressed his gratitude, saying that after my leave, he would appoint me to an important position within the leadership. I said that this was not acceptable since under no circumstances would I want to be in a leading position now that the Jagdwaffe's collapse was imminent. I again requested to be employed operationally on the Me 262, not as a unit leader, but simply as a pilot. A decision was to be made during my leave.

On January 23, Göring met with senior fighter leaders at a meeting later called "the Revolt of the Kommodores." Led by Oberstleutnant Günther Lützow, the second German fighter pilot to be credited with 100 victories, they included Oberst Gustav Rödel, former *Kommodore* of JG 27; Oberst Günther von Maltzahn, former commander of fighters in Italy; Oberstleutnant Johannes Steinhoff, most recently *Kommodore* of JG 7; and Oberst Hannes Trautloft, former *Kommodore* of JG 54. They represented the cream of the Jagdwaffe, and demanded the reinstatement of Galland, but Göring announced that Galland would be replaced as *General der Jagdflieger* by his greatest enemy, General Gordon Gollob. The fighter leaders were sidelined for "cowardice"; Lützow was exiled to Italy; the others were placed in "inactive" status along with Oberstleutnant Heinz Bär, who had risen to command JG 3 after incurring Göring's wrath a year earlier; he was made commander of the Me-262 training unit III./EJG 2.

Galland was under virtual house arrest in Berlin with his car taken, his phone tapped, and Gestapo agents following him. Gollob planned to finally get rid of the man who had exposed his incompetence by making Galland *Staffelkapitän* 4./JG 54, flying support missions for German forces trapped in the Kurland peninsula in the Baltic States. If he refused, he could be charged with cowardice in the face of the enemy. Before the order could be given, Galland was summoned to the *Reichskanzlerei*, where he was informed by Hitler's Luftwaffe adjutant, Oberst von Below, that Göring had requested an investigation of him by the *Sicherheitsdienst* (Security Service), which had been stopped by Hitler after intervention by Albert Speer. He was then informed that Hitler had decided he was to establish a unit equipped with the Me-262 and demonstrate that his claims for the aircraft were right.

Three days later, Galland met Göring at his Carinhall estate, where both could hear Red Army artillery across the Oder River. Göring did not know of the meeting with von Below, and told Galland he had silenced the accusations. Göring stated that Galland had failed him, but that he would allow his former fighter commander one last chance:

> I was to set up a small unit to demonstrate that the Me-262 was the superior fighter I had claimed it was. It was to be a small unit – a *Staffel*. It was not to be under the command of any division, corps or air fleet; I was to be totally independent. I would have to find the aircraft myself. Oberst Steinhoff, whom he considered to be a "sad case," could be made available, and Oberst Lützow, if I wanted him. I was to submit my proposals as soon as possible.

Thus was born *Jagdverband* (Fighting Group) 44, which would come to be known as "the squadron of aces."

When he was interrogated after the war, Göring stated that he had recalled Galland because the weak air defense of southern Germany concerned him. "Mustangs were practically doing training flights over Bavaria. I recalled Galland in order to stop that nonsense."

Galland established his unit at Brandenburg-Briest, 30 kilometers west of Berlin, which was already the base for III./JG 7 and protected by strong flak defenses. On February 25, Jagdverband 44 was formally established with a strength of 16 Me-262s and 15 pilots.

Steinhoff was Galland's first recruit. He later recalled:

While we "mutineers" pottered around the field, my old unit JG 7 was under orders not to recognize our existence. The early days of JV 44 were far from being days of plenty. Our transport consisted of a single jeep and my tiny 90cc DKW motorcycle. The general, however, had influential friends, and we soon found ourselves on the receiving end of a swelling supply of equipment – aircraft, spares, and weapons. We even got a second jeep.

Steinhoff drew up a list of pilots he considered adept enough to quickly convert to the Me-262; it was a "who's who" of the leading *Experten*. Gollob later recalled:

At exactly the moment when Galland and everyone else in the Luftwaffe knew that there was a shortage of experienced formation leaders, this gentleman in no way held back from requesting for himself – without exception – our aces. But he only got those I let him have, and a few that he organized for himself by roundabout methods, among them those who, unfortunately, were in disgrace or those who, for other reasons, could not or did not wish to remain with their units.

In fact, many of those Galland recruited were exhausted men recovering from long periods of combat. Walter Krupinski checked himself into a rest home after III./JG 26 was disbanded by Priller for its poor performance. In 1984 he said, "By then, I was almost of no use to myself, let alone anyone else." Nevertheless, he responded to Galland's call. A steady trickle of the Luftwaffe's leading pilots found their way to JV 44 in the next several weeks.

Not all were famous *Experten*, but all were experienced. Unteroffizier Johann-Karl Müller, a ground attack pilot, came from *Schlachtgeschwader* 10 (10th Ground Attack Wing); Feldwebel Otto Kammerdiener was a flight instructor; Oberfeldwebel Leopold Knier had been shot down and captured by the Soviets, whom he convinced to let him go on his promise to steal a Bf-109 and fly it back to them;

Oberfeldwebel Rudolf Nielinger had scored 20 victories against the RAF in Tunisia before being wounded and becoming a flight instructor. Oberfeldwebel Josef Dobnig, who had flown with JG 26 before being wounded and assigned to instructor duties, remembered, "At first we were speechless, because this was Adolf Galland's elite unit. We'd heard that the *Ritterkreuz* was virtually a part of their uniform. And now we simple soldiers were to go there. But it was a much better prospect than fighting enemy tanks."

At first, pilots were given twin-engine training on Siebel Si-204 utility transports. JG 11's Feldwebel Franz Steiner accepted Galland's offer because he wanted to fly the Me-262:

> I have to say that flying the Me-262 was the high point in my flying career. When you first got off the ground and had attained height and speed, you couldn't help but feel a sense of absolute elation and wonderment. In my view, the only weak point was the engines. Engine failure during takeoff, which, unfortunately, was all too common, almost always meant certain death for a pilot. You would have felt safer with rocket-assisted takeoff. In flight, especially in a shallow dive, you had to adjust for the sensitivity of the engines too much.

As Feldwebel Steiner and many others discovered, the Me-262 was difficult to fly, since it could not be easily controlled by changing power settings due to the difficult throttles, and it did not have airbrakes. In March, Galland discovered that the best formation was a *Kette* (the old prewar formation of three – leader and two wingmen) of three aircraft, rather than the four-plane *Schwarm*. "We reverted to the *Kette*, and flew this way with slightly less intermediate spacing than we would have flown with conventionally engined aircraft – about 100 meters [330 feet] apart when climbing, and thereafter about 150–180 meters [500–600 feet] in level flight. These reduced intervals made it easier for the formation to keep together."

Steinhoff led a *Kette* with Leutnant Klaus Neumann and Oberleutnant Blomert on the first JV 44 combat operation in late March. The three flew over Berlin and then toward Frankfurt on the Oder where they ran into light flak approaching the front lines. Turning for home, they encountered a formation of Soviet fighters.

Steinhoff spotted a formation of Il-2 *Shturmoviks* strafing a German transport column. He reported:

> As I bent forward to look through the sight, I noticed that I had too much speed again. The trees and fields were flashing past beneath me and the shape of the last fighter-bomber loomed alarmingly in the sight. The burst of fire was very short. The *Shturmovik* started leaving a trail just as I pulled up over it, the tips of the tall pines almost seeming to brush the Me-262's wings. The fighter-bomber hit the ground not far from the edge of the forest, bouncing along on its belly, throwing up a gigantic fountain of powdery snow. Blomert was still having trouble keeping up and on the way back he told me he was running short of fuel. We reached Brandenburg on the last of our reserve.

In early April, JV 44 relocated to Munich. Galland chose München-Riem, a major civilian airfield nine kilometers (five and a half miles) east of Munich between the villages of Riem and Feldkirchen. Importantly, it could accommodate the extended takeoff of a fully loaded Me-262. They used an abandoned orphanage in nearby Feldkirchen as headquarters and mess hall.

The move put JV 44 squarely in the Ninth Air Force's bulls-eye as the Seventh Army pushed into Bavaria. Once the jets were discovered, the field was under constant surveillance by Allied fighters. JV 44 needed its own *Platzschutzstaffel* (airfield protection squadron), and formed it in mid-April. The unit came to be known as the *Papageistaffel* for its radio call sign "*Papagei*" (Parrot). The three Fw-190D-9s and one Fw-190D-11 were commanded by Leutnant Heinz Sachsenberg, son of World War I ace Gotthard Sachsenberg. His sense of humor was shown by the slogans painted on the airplanes: his Fw-190D-9 *Rot Eins* (Red 1) carried the slogan *Verkaaft's mei Gwand 'I foahr in Himmel* (Sell my clothes, I'm going to heaven!); Leutnant Karl-Heinz Hofmann's Fw-190D-9 *Rot Drei* (Red 3) carried *Im Auftrage der Reichsbahn* (By Order of the State Railway, a reference to the manner by which a shot-down German pilot could return to his unit via the railroad); Hauptmann Waldemar Wübke's Fw-190D-11, *Rot Vier* (Red 4) carried *Der nachste Herr, die selbe Dame!* (The next man, the same woman!); Oberleutnant Klaus Faber's Fw-190D-9 *Rot Dreizehn*

(Red 13) carried *Rein muss er und wenn wir beide weinen!* (In he goes and then we both cry!) The double-entendre can still bring a smile – whether or not one understands idiomatic German. The four had the most dramatic markings of any in the *Galland Zirkus*, as JV-44 was called by its members: the lower surfaces were painted red with white stripes, to convince the light flak gunners they were friendly at a glance, as they pursued Allied fighters. Galland recalled:

> Sachsenberg was a good pilot, and we felt safer when his aircraft were in the air. They surrounded the airfield – not in any formation – but usually just in pairs. We tried to get them into the air just as we took off and also when we came in to land, but often it didn't work because conditions were becoming impossible both on the airfield and in the air. Once up, they escorted us around the airfield.

Walter Krupinski made his first Me-262 flight without the benefit of twin-engine training. He remembered:

> Steinhoff was standing on the port wing. He said, "The most difficult thing with this type of aircraft is to start the engines – I'll do that for you." There was no reading any manuals or anything like that. There was no training program. He just gave me some basic information – enough to get started.
>
> Actually, I found taking off in the Me-262 was fairly easy because the nose wheel rolled smoothly, but the problem was that the engines didn't accelerate fast enough. You needed the whole length of the airfield before you reached an adequate takeoff speed. I prepared myself – I closed the canopy, threw a quick glance over the instrument panel and slowly, like a lame duck, the bird began to roll. But then the end of the runway, as I predicted, came towards me very quickly. A glance at the speed indicator told me I was moving at 200 kilometers per hour [125 miles per hour].
>
> Pulling gently at the stick, I got into the air. No drag, and she climbed swiftly. Landing gear up. Throttle lightly back to 8,000rpm. I climbed and the speed grew and grew – 350, 400, 500, 600 kilometers per hour [220, 250, 370 miles per hour] – there seemed to be no end to its speed. Still I climbed – it was fantastic! I leveled out, my speed slowly approaching 900 kilometers per hour [560 miles per hour].

He spotted a formation of P-38s, but when he attempted an attack, he overshot due to his high speed. Realizing he could not turn quickly, he broke away and used his speed to escape the Lightnings.

Over the next few days, JV 44 pilots had run-ins with Allied fighters, but their attacks were ineffective as they discovered that the jet's speed made aiming difficult. They were soon equipped with R4M rockets, with which one hit guaranteed destruction of the target. Steinhoff later remembered, "The rockets were the perfect weapon to destroy the bombers, but they arrived at 'five minutes to midnight,' too late. And there were too few of us to use them." On April 6, the unit had only 18 Me-262s, with only seven operational.

On April 9, 228 B-17s bombed the airfield in an attempt to destroy the unit. The field was cratered and 50 personnel, including two from JV 44, were wounded. The next day, a strafing attack by 353rd Group P-51s destroyed three Me-262s and damaged three others. Over the course of the day, 13 Me-262s were delivered to JV 44, but late afternoon attacks destroyed 11.

On April 12, Galland used the R4M missiles to shoot down two B-26 Marauders from the 322nd Bomb Group. Six days later, on April 18, bomber formations from the Eighth, Ninth, and Fifteenth Air Forces were over Bavaria. JV 44 put up six Me-262s, three armed with R4Ms. The two *Ketten* were led by Galland and Steinhoff, and included Franz Stigler and Walter Krupinski. It was a formation unlike any other: one *Generalleutnant* and five pilots with 550 victories and four *Ritterkreuzen* in their records. The first *Kette* took off successfully, but halfway down the field, Steinhoff's jet hit debris on the field at nearly takeoff speed. He swerved toward Krupinski, who was able to haul his jet into the air and avoid collision. Krupinski felt an explosion and when he glanced back, Steinhoff's jet was wrapped in flame. As Steinhoff struggled to get out, he was badly burned but managed to finally stagger onto the wing and jump to the ground before the jet exploded. He was taken to the hospital, where he remained the rest of the war. In the meantime, the five jets failed to contact any enemy formation.

That afternoon, Leutnant Hans Buch and other pilots of *Kampfgeschwader* 51 (KG 51, 51st Bomber Wing) delivered their Me-262As to JV 44. Many years later, Buch recalled this was the closest he had gotten to combat with the "Edelweiss" Geschwader.

"We had lost half our force trying to attack the Remagen bridge the month before and the unit was shot." Buch remained with the ground force supporting JV 44, and eventually was put in charge of one of the satellite airfields where the jets were dispersed as Allied attacks on their main field increased.

April 20 saw JV 44's greatest success; three *Ketten* attacked Marauders of the 323rd Bomb Group. The R4M rockets proved deadly, knocking down three and damaging seven B-26s. Unteroffizier Ernst Schallnoser tried to open fire, but his guns didn't work; he had failed to open the firing switch. While he attended to that, the jet got so close to the bombers that he collided with Lieutenant James M. Hansen's 455th Squadron B-26. The Me-262 rolled over and nosed down, streaming black smoke. Hansen was able to keep his bomber in the air, despite the propeller blades on the right engine having been bent back, and returned to base successfully. Schallnoser managed to bail out and parachuted into what turned out to be his mother's garden in Lenzfried-im-Allgau! Limping from a blow to his knee when he bailed out, he gratefully accepted the plate of pancakes his bewildered mother fed him.

On April 21, US troops made contact with the Red Army at Torgau, cutting Germany in two. Galland called his troops into the orphanage dining hall. He told them that in his view the war was lost militarily, but he was willing to continue to fly with any volunteers. He told the ground personnel that any who wished were free to return to their homes. Klaus Neumann recalled, "We stayed together and we flew. We had nothing else to do. We couldn't win the war – we did it just to prove that the Me-262 was a fighter." The next day, Heinz Bär arrived with his wingman Leo Schumacher and others from *Ergänzungs-Jagdgeschwader* (EJG 2, 2nd Training Fighter Squadron). Several other leaders of Me-262 units also showed up as it became known that JV 44 was staying in the fight.

Two days later, Galland met with Hermann Göring for the last time at his hideout in the Obersalzberg. Galland recalled that the *Reichsmarschall* was cordial, asking how his unit was faring. At the end, he told his former fighter leader, "You were right about it all." When he returned to Munich, Galland received orders from Albert Speer not to allow Göring to use any aircraft, since it was believed he was attempting to flee Germany.

On April 24, Günther Lützow led 11 Me-262s to intercept a raid on Schwabmünchen by Marauders of the 17th Bomb Group. Five B-26s were hit with R4Ms and three went down. That afternoon, Lützow led Krupinski and Neumann to intercept another raid. The *Kette* attacked B-26s from the 344th Bomb Group, escorted by P-47s from the 365th "Hell Hawks" group. Two P-47s dived on the jets, and Lützow pulled away from the others. He managed to avoid the Thunderbolts until Captain Jerry Mast got on his tail and put in a burst. Mast's wingman, Second Lieutenant William H. Myers, closed in and opened fire. At that moment, Walter Krupinski saw an explosion against the mountains; "Lützow didn't respond to my calls." The loss of the well-respected pilot hit the rest of the unit hard.

By April 26, JV 44 had accumulated 43 Me-262s. At 1130 hours, Galland led four *Ketten* to intercept a large force of Marauders from several bomb groups. The 12 Me-262s were all carrying R4Ms. Thirty minutes later, 60 Marauders were spotted, escorted by 60 P-47s; the bombers had just aborted their run due to increasing clouds. The jets approached the formation from ahead. Unteroffizier Schallnoser fired his rockets, which hit two B-26s, damaging one and sending the other down on fire.

Galland led his *Kette* around for an attack from the rear. When he pressed the trigger to fire the R4Ms, nothing happened; he had forgotten to arm the switch. While his attention was on arming the switch, he flew into range of the formation's tail gunners. He realized he was too close and opened fire, exploding one B-26 as he flew through the formation with the turret gunners all firing at him. The Me-262 was hit and trailed smoke. Technical Sergeant Henry Dietz, a former gunnery instructor manning the turret aboard the lead aircraft, recalled: "I had never seen a jet before. Galland slowed down to the speed of the B-26. I thought 'Dummy!' He was flying low, right into the sights of my machine gun. I shot a burst. Nothing happened. A little higher, a little lower, I just kept shooting." The other Me-262s made a total of five passes, all from different directions. Carnage spread in the Marauder formation and only one of the four squadrons came through without loss.

First Lieutenant James Finnegan was leading Green Flight of the 50th Fighter Group, one of four escort groups. He saw two jets flash through the bomber formation and went after one trailing smoke. "I caught up and put a burst into him, then he fell away." Finnegan claimed the jet "damaged." Galland remembered:

> A hail of fire enveloped me. A sharp rap hit my right knee, the instrument panel with its indispensable instruments was shattered, the right engine was also hit – its metal covering worked loose in the wind and was partly carried away – and now the left engine was hit. I could hardly hold her in the air.

The other jets claimed five Marauders shot down. In fact they got six and damaged more. Galland found one engine wouldn't respond to the throttle. He cut both as he came over the runway threshold and landed. He saw enemy fighters circling the field. As soon as the Me-262 came to a stop he jumped out. The Thunderbolts roared down on a strafing run. At that moment, a ground crewman arrived on a *Kettenkrad* (a motorcycle/halftrack). Galland jumped aboard and they took off across the field while his jet exploded when it was smothered in bullets. With shell fragments in his knee, Galland's war was over.

Heinz Bär took operational command of JV 44, and shot down a Marauder on April 27, bringing his score in the Me-262 to 16. The next day, American armored units were outside Munich and JV 44 flew their jets to Innsbruck, Austria. They eventually surrendered at Salzburg.

At the same time Galland and the last of the Luftwaffe were fighting their final battles, Oberleutnant Kurt Welter, who had formed the only Me-262 night fighter unit – Kommando Welter – in March, concluded the war was lost. Lieutnant Jorg Czypionka recalled, "Welter had collected every Me-262 he came across, including four two-seaters with radar we never used, since we were a *Wilde Sau* unit. He informed us we were to fly the airplanes to Schleswig-Holstein, where we would then trade them to the Allies in return for good treatment." The British took the airfield with Welter's prizes the first week in May. Welter then negotiated a deal in which his men would teach Allied pilots how to fly the airplanes, in return for not being sent to POW camps. As Czypionka related years later, "All the Me-262s the British and Americans tested after the war came from us. All the Me-262s you find these days in museums, came from us." While Welter's men worked with the British, he made arrangements with the commander of a nearby POW camp, for his men to check in, stay a few days, then be released with proper papers. "Welter had collected more than jets, which was how he could do that. When the whole operation was over that summer, the British commander told Welter he was sorry we would all have to go to POW camp. We showed him our papers and walked off the field!"

Hans Buch was among those who arrived in Austria:

> We sat there for a week, doing nothing. Then one day an American tank approached the field, but the country lane was so narrow they went off it and got stuck. We went out and asked if they wanted help. That sergeant was the first American I ever met; he had some words that I had never heard before during six years of English instruction, but he was glad of the help. We had a half-track, and we towed him out of the ditch back onto the road.

The Americans set up on the far side of the field and left Buch's men alone:

> After the surrender, an American officer asked if we would become military police for them. It meant we got to eat, and they gave us papers that told other American groups who we were. We had a big open Mercedes and were told to drive around Austria and pick up any German soldiers we found who had walked back from Italy. We were supposed to pick them up and take them to a detention center. I never took one. I figured if a guy had managed to come that far, he had a right to get home, so we would give them a ride in the direction they were going, then let them off and leave.

# 25

# A CLEAN SWEEP

The last four months of combat in Europe produced the climax of the greatest sustained aerial campaign in history. Those months saw US fighters appear in ever-growing numbers, roaming every corner of Germany, strafing airfields, shooting up trains and other targets as the whole country became a combat theater.

The month of January 1945 saw the 78th Group continue to deal with learning their new fighter. Converting to the Mustang brought more problems for pilots than that experienced by Huie Lamb. Following the biggest snowstorm in England that any Americans had seen on January 8, five P-51s ground-looped attempting to take off on the icy wood plank runway that covered the PSP runway at Duxford, which caused the cancellation of the mission. Bad weather continued. On January 10, Lieutenant Peter Keillor of the 84th Squadron ran into the piled snow beside the runway while taking off and knocked off a gear door; Lieutenant William DeGain found that the snow still on his wing spoiled the wing's lift and he ended up in a heap at the end of the runway. The solution was to widen the cleared area and to scrape it down daily.

January 14, 1945, would be remembered in the 357th Fighter Group as "Big Day." It turned out to be the last big air battle against the Reichsverteidigung *Geschwadern*. The sky was crystal-clear over the Continent, perfect conditions to send 950 B-24s and B-17s from the 2nd and 3rd Air Divisions against synthetic oil factories and storage sites in northwestern Germany.

The 3rd Division's bombers flew over Schleswig-Holstein just south of the Danish border, then turned toward Berlin, where their targets were in Derben, Stendal, and Magdeburg. The Yoxford Boys provided escort, positioned at the head of the bomber stream. Approaching Berlin from the northwest, they spotted enemy fighters ahead at 28,000 feet. These were Fw-190A-8/R2 Sturmböck bomber-destroyers from I. and III./JG 300, with cover from Bf-109Gs of II./JG 300 at 30,000 feet. Group commander Colonel Dregne led the 364th Squadron to bounce the enemy. The Fw-190s broke and dived away, pursued by the 363rd Squadron. The 362nd Squadron engaged the Bf-109s that belatedly dived into the fight.

Colonel Dregne later recalled:

The '190s broke formation and scattered, some of them rolling, some split-S-ing, but the majority broke right and then went into a Lufbery. I got my sights on a '190 and started firing, observing strikes on the fuselage and tail. He broke left and then went into a spin. I broke left, finding myself in a Lufbery with eight or ten Fw-190s. I started a tight climbing spiral, the '190s following, but I was able to out-climb them. I noticed a bomber box under attack so I started climbing toward it. When I got to the box the fight was over and the Huns had left. I picked up a P-51 and told him to be my wingman.

Lieutenant Colonel Andy Evans was flying that Mustang; he had just shot down one of the Fw-190s, after shooting down a Bf-109, then flown an Fw-190 into the ground and climbed after a third Fw-190, which collided with another 190 to become an "ace in a day." After they joined up, Dregne spotted a Bf-109 below and dived on it. A burst set it afire; the 357th's group commander was now also an ace.

Over the next 30 minutes, the enemy pilots demonstrated no lack of fight, being very good at evasive tactics. 364th Squadron commander Major John Storch shot down an Fw-190 in a wild dive from 24,000 to 12,000 feet, then spotted a fight below and headed toward it:

I singled out an Fw-190 on the outside of the scrap and he went for the deck. I followed, and at this point my wingman observed an Fw-190 firing at us and he had to break off to take care of him. In the meantime, my Fw-190 was going balls-out on the deck. I had enough excess speed to pull up behind him and fired for some time with no effect. I finally managed to get close enough so I couldn't miss and saw the strikes on the fuselage and left wing. He burst into flames and suddenly snap-rolled, and large pieces flew off. I overshot, and he went into the ground burning. I did not observe the pilot get out. I pulled up and my wingman pulled off his '190, and we rejoined.

Storch then sighted two Bf-109s and went after them. They separated and hit the deck:

I picked one and chased him for about five minutes. I finally caught him and he went into a turning circle. My gunsight had burned out and I was a picture of confusion trying to turn, fire, fix my sight, put down flaps, pull up flaps and work my throttle. Finally, I got close enough so I couldn't miss and got strikes – coolant and smoke came from the enemy aircraft. He tried to belly in just short of a forest, hit and bounced almost over into a clearing but then struck the last few trees on the fringe of the forest.

Despite their willingness to stick around and fight and their two-to-one advantage in numbers, the enemy pilots were no match for the experienced Mustang pilots, who claimed 56 destroyed for a loss of three, a new high score for a single group. In the battle, four pilots became aces.

Clarence "Bud" Anderson and Chuck Yeager had been assigned as spares for the mission, but when no one aborted, they broke away to spend their final mission touring Germany. Heading south, they made a low-level run through the Alps along the German–Swiss–Italian border, playing with their airplanes in the stark blue sky after dropping their tanks in a meadow and strafing them to start a fire. They were the last to return to base. Anderson's crew chief, seeing the gunfire residue on his P-51D "Old Crow," asked him how many he shot down. When Anderson replied "none," his crew chief related what had happened over Germany. Years later, Anderson said it still made him "sick" to remember how he missed the group's greatest day.

Unfortunately, while this fight raged, JG 301's Sturmböcken were able to penetrate the bomber stream northwest of Berlin. While many of the *Sturmgruppe* pilots appeared inexperienced, the enemy were still able to inflict losses on the bombers. They found no success in their attempt to attack the 95th Group, with the Fortress gunners claiming five. The Bloody Hundredth also mounted a strong defense, with the group's gunners claiming eight attackers. The 390th Group was not so lucky. Its eight-Fortress low squadron was lagging owing to the formation leader experiencing supercharger problems, and the bombers were 2,000 feet below and half a mile behind the rest of the combat box. The Sturmböcken attacked in pairs from the rear, with many showing their inexperience by opening fire too far out. Still, over 30 minutes they managed to shoot down all eight B-17s in the squadron, plus a ninth from the lead squadron's formation. The 390th's gunners were credited with 14 victories, down from 34 claimed and likely still more than actual losses, but a good indication of the intensity of the battle. This marked the 390th's worst day of the war with the group's highest losses on a single mission. It was also the Jagdwaffe's final sustained assault on a bomber formation. The 20th Group latched onto the JG 301 fighters and chased them off before they scored more bombers shot down, with the Mustangs claiming 20 destroyed.

For the 78th Group, the day was memorable for scoring its first victories with the Mustang near Cologne as it escorted 3rd Division's withdrawal. The 82nd's Lieutenants Warren and wingman DeGain spotted 15 bandits below their altitude of 26,000 feet. Diving on them, they flashed through a second formation they had failed to spot. They headed on toward the first group, where Warren's first burst of fire killed the pilot of an Fw-190 that flick-rolled into the ground. DeGain blasted a Bf-109 whose pilot bailed out while Warren proceeded to use the K-14 sight to shoot a second Fw-190 off DeGain's tail with a high-angle deflection shot.

Major Leonard Marshal, leading 78C group, spotted what he at first identified as three bogies but turned out to be a P-51 chasing two Bf-109s at low altitude. Marshal closed on one 109 but the pilot spotted him and broke left, then tried to belly in; the fighter exploded on touch down. Marshal turned on the other 109 that his wingman Lieutenant Louis Hereford had engaged and the two made quick work of it.

The 83rd Squadron's Major Richard Spooner spotted 20 Bf-109s trying to form up for an attack; he led his flight into them and shot one down. He ran out of ammo chasing another, but when he closed to

100 feet the enemy pilot was so spooked he hit some power lines and somersaulted into the ground.

Frank Oiler reported:

> We dropped our tanks and split-S-ed down on them. Rainbow Squadron split up the gaggle and Turquoise Squadron attacked them as they split up into twos and threes. An Fw-190 went between my wingman and myself so I turned on his tail but lost him, then picked up a Bf-109 and two Fw-190s being chased by a P-51. I called the P-51 to take one and my wingman and I took the other. The Fw-190s broke in opposite directions and the Bf-109 went straight up. I got in a Lufbery with one Fw-190 at 1,100 feet and used my flaps to get on his tail in two turns. I got in a three-second burst at 35 degrees deflection, observed many strikes in the cockpit, and he did a half snap and went in upside down.

Lieutenant Willis Lutz headed home after discovering his guns wouldn't work. He spotted three aircraft he identified as Mustangs; when he dropped down to join up, he discovered they were Fw-190s! He saw three more coming down and tried to sneak away, but they caught him. Lutz pressed his trigger several times; finally four fired. He closed the circle on number three and hit it with a deflection shot that set the wing on fire; it went inverted at 100 feet and crashed. The other two came at him again and he out-turned them. One disengaged after he fired two bursts and ran out of ammo. Bluffing the second, he broke for home. Crossing Allied lines, he was hit by "friendly" light flak that set the engine on fire. He bailed out and was picked up by American troops. A second mission that afternoon saw the 83rd Squadron's Red Flight bounce four Fw-190s that they spotted over Diepholz airdrome. Peter Caulfield shot one down, bringing the day's score to 14. With this success, the pilots decided they liked the P-51D after all.

Altogether, the 331 66th Wing P-51s that provided escort for the 3rd Division's B-17s claimed 90 destroyed from nearly 200 enemy fighters that they caught approaching, over, and withdrawing from the targets, which were close to being repaired from previous attacks and badly damaged before they could return to production; German gasoline supplies were reduced even more.

The B-24s and B-17s of the 2nd Division also found the enemy willing to engage. The Wolfpack, flying one of their last missions in P-47Ds before transitioning to their new P-47Ms, engaged the Fw-190s over Dummer Lake. Captain Felix Williamson became an "ace in a day," scoring five of the 19 enemy fighters the group claimed.

The 352nd Group joined the action over Holland as the bombers withdrew. The 486th Squadron ran across an aggressive flight of 12 Fw-190Ds from II./JG 26. Eight Blue Nosers bounced the German fighters, which all stayed together in a descending Lufbery circle from 9,000 to approximately 5,000 feet, when some tried to break away. Within minutes four were shot down. Two were claimed by First Lieutenant William Reese, while Lieutenants Ernest Bostrom and Earl Mundell each claimed one, with Bostrom's victory making him an ace.

The battles of January 14 saw the Eighth's fighters destroy 161 enemy fighters for the loss of only 16 of their own, and the nine B-17s of the 390th Group. The Jagdwaffe would never again oppose a mission with such intensity.

Following Colonel Gray's departure to become Director of Fighter Operations at Eighth Headquarters, deputy commander Lieutenant Colonel Olin Gilbert took command of the 78th with Lieutenant Colonel Joe Myers moving up to deputy commander. Over 19 missions in January, the group scored 14 aerial victories and destroyed 21 locomotives. There were no combat losses, though six P-51s were lost in crashes and eight suffered engine failure.

The 78th finally made it to Berlin on February 3, 1945, flying target support. A year after Big Week, the Jagdwaffe made no appearance in defense of the German capital. Following its relief by the 4th, it broke up by squadrons to search out targets of opportunity. The 84th Squadron found a fully packed airfield at Luneburg. The defense was not caught napping and the Mustangs flew into what many later recalled as a "wall of flak." Two pilots bailed out and were captured, while the rest found safety in the low ceiling when they pulled up after their runs. Fifteen German aircraft were left burning on the field.

Captain Earl Stier's Mustang, WZ-Y "Bum Steer," took a direct hit in the rear cockpit and another in the vertical fin blew away the upper part of the rudder and damaged the elevators as he made his run across the field. The P-51's left wingtip hit the treetops, but momentum allowed him to recover. "Bum Steer" corkscrewed through the air, trying to fall off on the left wing, for the entire two and a half hours it took to return to Duxford, where he had the choice of bailing out or attempting to land. "Bum Steer's" crew chief Sergeant James Aicardi remembered, "He came in low, flying very unsteady and trailing smoke. We thought his hydraulic system was gone and he would have to belly-land, not a good thing in a P-51. But the gear came down and he made a very rough landing with the meat wagon following him down the strip." The P-51 was tougher than the Thunderbolt pilots had expected.

On February 22, the 78th took part in Operation *Clarion*, an all-out assault on the enemy's rail and road communications. Colonel Gilbert was joined by former group commander Gray in a two-group sweep; railroads across western Germany were shot up. Back at Duxford, new group commander Lieutenant Colonel John D. Landers met them on landing. Landers, who three years earlier had flown the "Brereton Route" from Brisbane to Darwin as a 21-year-old second lieutenant fresh out of flight school, hoping not to become one of the crashed P-40s he had been told he could follow for navigation, had volunteered for an unprecedented third tour as an Eighth Air Force fighter group commander.

At the end of the month, the 18 missions in February saw seven pilots killed while ten became POWs and four evaded. The Luftwaffe had been entirely absent in the air, with 15 ground kills credited destroyed along with 103 locomotives.

Landers led the group to Berlin on March 2. Between Berlin and Magdeburg, 24 Bf-109s were spotted forming up for an attack. Landers led the attack out of the sun. The enemy flight leaders were experienced and aggressive, but the rest were novices who bailed out eagerly after one or two strikes; at one point nine parachutes were counted. Landers shot down four Bf-109s whose pilots bailed out, while his wingman Jack Hodge scored a fifth. Back at Duxford, Landers termed all four victories freaks. The 83rd Squadron claimed 13 destroyed for the loss of Lieutenant Henry Staub, who became a POW.

On March 7, 1945, the US 9th Armored Division found the Ludendorff bridge over the Rhine at Remagen still standing after a German attempt to blow it up failed. With the bridge in Allied hands, air battles heated up as the Luftwaffe attempted to finish the bridge's destruction through bombing. Control of the bridge allowed American troops to enter Germany's industrial heart in the Ruhr.

On 19 March, the 78th flew withdrawal support for the 3rd Air Division's return from Ruhland. As the 82nd Squadron approached Osnabrück, Captain Dick Hewitt spotted four Bf-109s at 8,000 feet. As he led the bounce, more enemy aircraft appeared. They had stumbled on all of JG 27. The 83rd and 84th squadrons piled in as the enemy gave no appearance of wanting to run. Hewitt was momentarily surprised when his engine cut out, then realized he had dropped his underwing tanks without switching fuel feed. Switching quickly, he regained power and closed in behind a Bf-109 whose pilot bailed out after several hits. Element leader Lieutenant Walter Borque turned on a 109 that dived on him and blew it up with a hit in the fuel tank.

Newly promoted Captain Huie Lamb spotted several Bf-109s below:

Just as I was closing on them, I glanced over my shoulder and there were four '190s diving on us! It was a trap. I was flying a P-51 that wasn't mine, that had the tail warning radar, and the light kept flashing red on the panel. I got into several head-on passes with the '109s. The radar warning would go on and off, and I figured it was my wingman and thought he was doing a pretty good job of staying with me. I hit a 109, then called to the rest of the flight; they said they were out of there. I realized those radar warnings were Germans on my tail! I got the hell out of there.

Landers caught a 109 as it split-S-ed out of the fight while his element leader Howard Seeley out-turned two 109s in succession, exploding both. The battle raged for 20 minutes, from 24,000 feet to the deck. All in all, the 78th had scored one of the biggest single mission scores in the group's best day of the war: 32 destroyed, two probables, and 16 damaged, for the loss of two killed and three POWs.

On March 21, Major Richard Conner led 43 Mustangs to Ruhland, where they found Alt Lonnewitz airfield with many planes, including several Me-262s. Conner was hit when he strafed three Me-262s waiting to take off. He turned east and crashed east of the Oder River, in no-man's land. Eventually found by the Soviets, he was sent to Lvov, Poland, then Poltava, Ukraine, before going on to Moscow; he returned to Duxford three days after VE Day. Two other Me-262s were shot down in the air, with the pilots firing at extreme long range and thanking the K-14 sight for its accuracy. Leading 82nd Squadron, Captain Winfield

Brown spotted three Me-262s taking off from Giebelstadt airfield. Diving from 14,000 feet, he hit one but flak forced him to break off; his wingman finished off the jets. Walter Borque climbed toward what he thought were three P-51s with wing tanks that turned out to be Me-262s. He closed on number three and hit it solidly, sending it down out of control. Robert Anderson fired on the third Me-262 of the group taking off. Despite flak hits, he hit the jet at 50 feet; it exploded on impact. The final score was five Me-262s shot down or destroyed on the ground.

On March 30, John Landers spotted an Me-262 at 1,000 feet, approaching Rendsburg. He caught up to the jet as the pilot made shallow turns. Landers and his wingman took turns shooting the jet, which crashed and burned short of the runway at Hohn.

The next day, newly promoted Captain Wayne Coleman, now Red Flight Leader in the 82nd, spotted two Me-262s flying parallel to the formation, in and out of clouds, near Stendahl at 15,000 feet; he then saw a third 262, which disappeared into a smoke cloud. When it emerged moments later Coleman winged over in a full power dive with the airspeed indicator reading close to 500 miles per hour; he set the K-14 on the jet's cockpit, scoring strikes in the cockpit and right engine. As he broke left, the jet rolled right and went straight in, exploding on impact.

The Mustang had revived the 78th's fortunes, with 25 missions in March that scored 54 aerial victories, four ground victories, and nine locomotives destroyed; losses were high, with nine killed, four made POW, three evaders, and three wounded. Dick Hewitt had gone from shavetail replacement in the summer of 1943 to commanding the 82nd Squadron.

While the P-51D was reviving the fortunes of the 78th Fighter Group, the 56th was tearing its collective hair out, trying to fix the problems of the latest Thunderbolt, the P-47M. The group could have been the second VIII Fighter Command unit to re-equip with the Mustang a year earlier, and that would have happened had Hub Zemke not been in Washington DC at the time the decision was made, unable to make the decision himself; he had no loyalty to any particular piece of equipment, only to its usefulness in achieving the goal. This was not the way Dave Schilling thought. As acting group commander in January 1944, he had turned down the P-51 in favor of the P-47, and was supported in that by the majority of the pilots. The 56th had literally "tamed the beast," and had an emotional attachment to the airplane. Additionally, many pilots knew they were alive and "at home" because of the toughness of the Thunderbolt. They would have agreed with a staged photo taken in the 78th Group in December 1944, in which ten pilots are seen dragging another pilot, kicking and screaming, from his P-47 to a nearby P-51.

The Wolfpack's belief in the Thunderbolt was sorely tested by the P-47M.

It had been obvious by the summer of 1943 that – even with the technical fixes Republic was coming up with – the P-47 would always be outperformed by the Fw-190 as an air superiority fighter at the altitudes where most combat occurred. Republic's answer was the XP-47J, developed in 1943 to use the C-series R-2800-57 engine; the engine could give 2,800hp at 2,800rpm at 35,000 feet in war emergency power – 133 percent of rated power. Using this engine, the XP-47J was capable of a top speed of 507 miles per hour at 34,300 feet. At "military power," the XP-47J hit 470 miles per hour, and could achieve 435 miles per hour at 81 percent of rated power. Not only was the new sub-type faster than any other piston-powered fighter, it had a sea level climb rate of 4,900 feet per minute, and 4,400 feet per minute at 20,000 feet, an altitude it achieved in four minutes and 15 seconds, with time to 30,000 feet only six minutes and 45 seconds. Not only could it fly and climb fast, it had a range of 1,075 miles, perfect for an escort fighter. And all was achieved with a full eight-gun armament. Had the XP-47J been in service when the Me-262 appeared, with its critical Mach of .83, it could have chased down the German jet with a shallow dive, using the advantage of its superior service ceiling of 46,500 feet. Unfortunately, the USAAF saw the XP-47J as little more than a technology demonstrator; putting it into production would have disrupted the output of Thunderbolts, while the P-51 was able to provide the necessary range for a fighter escort in the European Theater.

Concurrent with the development of the XP-47J, Republic stuck a C-series R-2800-57 in a P-47C to see what kind of extra performance could be achieved making minimum changes to the basic airframe. The performance increase was such that it led to further development of what ultimately became the "hot rod" P-47M. This performance increase was needed when it was found that the P-47D did not have a performance lead over the Fi-103 "buzz bomb" or the new Me-163 and Me-262 fighters. Four P-47D-27-RE airframes were taken off the Farmingdale production line and given R-2800-57(C) engines and larger CH-5 turbosuperchargers. The new engine provided war emergency power of 2,800hp at 32,500 feet using water injection. The aircraft also had the anti-compressibility dive flaps introduced on the P-47D-28. They were designated YP-47M.

The performance was sufficiently superior to the P-47D that the new engine and airframe combination entered limited production in September 1944, with the last 130 P-47D-30-REs delivered by Farmingdale fitted with the different engine and redesignated P-47M-1-RE. Performance included a 400 miles per hour maximum speed at 10,000 feet, 453 miles per hour at 25,000 feet, and 470 miles per hour at 30,000 feet. The initial climb rate was 3,500 feet per minute at 5,000 feet and 2,650 feet per minute at 20,000 feet; range without drop tanks was 560 miles at 10,000 feet. While this was nowhere close to the XP-47J, it was vastly superior to the P-47D series.

The first P-47Ms were delivered in December 1944 and rushed to the 56th Fighter Group, with the first ones arriving on January 3, 1945. The 61st Squadron quickly converted to the new Thunderbolt; the men immediately started experiencing the same kind of engine problems they had confronted with the P-47C in January 1943. By the middle of February, three crashes due to engine failure, one fatal, led to the P-47M being grounded, which put the Wolfpack out of business. Dave Schilling's extended tour as group commander had ended on January 27, and his replacement, Colonel Lucian Dade – who had been one of the original pilots in the 56th and had served as squadron commander, group operations officer, and deputy group commander – had to deal with the engine problems. War-weary P-51Bs soon arrived for conversion training, but Dade was able to stave off the dread Mustang when it was found that the engines had been incorrectly "pickled" for overseas delivery, and the electrical harnesses had been corroded by exposure to salt air; this was the same problem that happened with the first P-47Cs. With all engines completely overhauled by March 24, 1945, the group was ready to re-commence operations.

With only a few weeks of combat left, the 56th demonstrated that the P-47M was indeed a "hot rod" that made the Thunderbolt an air superiority fighter. On March 14, two of the new Ar-234 jet bombers were shot down, one by 62nd Squadron's First Lieutenant Norman D. Gould and the other shared by First Lieutenants Sandford N. Ball and Warren S. Lear. Four Me-262s were shot down by Wolfpack pilots in P-47Ms. On March 25, 63rd Squadron commander Major George Bostwick and his wingman, Second Lieutenant Edwin M. Crosthwait, shot down an Me-262 over Parchim airfield. The Wolfpack's final aerial victory was an Me-262 of III./JG 7, shot down on April 10 by the 62nd Squadron's Second Lieutenant Walter J. Sharbo near Wittstock, Germany. Moments before Sharbo's final score, Captain William F. Wilkerson shot down the wingman. Polish ace Mike Gladych also claimed an Me-262, which was not officially credited to the 56th.

The Wolfpack also scored with ground attacks. They were chosen to test the new T-48 incendiary round, designed to explode the low grade/high flash point fuels that the Germans were using, which resisted ignition by normal .50-caliber strikes. In April, they flew a series of airfield strafing attacks using the new round. On April 13, Dade led 49 P-47Ms to Eggebek airdrome, where 150–200 aircraft were parked on the main field and two nearby satellite strips. While the 62nd Squadron flew top cover at 15,000 feet and the 61st Squadron orbited at 10,000 feet, the 63rd Squadron initiated the attack. After a pass to suppress what turned out to be limited ground fire, the squadron made 140 individual passes, claiming 44 destroyed. The 61st then made 94 passes and claimed 25 destroyed; finally, the 62nd made 105 runs and claimed 26. The only loss was the 63rd's First Lieutenant William R. Hoffman who was shot down and killed when his parachute failed to open.

The group was credited with 95 aircraft destroyed and 95 damaged. The top scorer was the 63rd's Second Lieutenant Randall Murphy; following review of his gun camera film he was credited with ten destroyed. Another strafing mission on April 16 saw the group take its final combat loss when Captain John W. Appel of the 62nd Squadron was shot down; he successfully returned to Allied lines the next day. With this, the group closed out its wartime combat with a total score of 992.5; its 664.5 aerial victories made its pilots VIII Fighter Command's top guns. The Wolfpack's final mission was flown April 21, 1945.

The Wolfpack's closest competitor from the beginning was the Debden Eagles of the 4th Fighter Group. The unit had found new life under the leadership of Colonel Everett Stewart, who became permanent commander on February 21. Stewart, like Sidney Woods – who dropped to deputy group commander, replacing Jack Oberhansly – was a veteran Forty-Niner who had commanded the 355th Group since the previous November. Throughout the winter and early spring, the 4th's red-nosed Mustangs had ranged across Germany; by the end of February, their score stood at 800, only a few behind the 56th. The Eagles had taken such casualties in ground strafing that the prospect of assignment to Debden was viewed with alarm by new pilots arriving in England that spring. Facing the guns on the ground was the most dangerous part of an Eighth Air Force fighter pilot's life. When a plane was hit, if the pilot was lucky, he managed to get out alive to become a POW. The 4th's boogie-woogie ace Pierce McKennon changed that story on March 18, 1945.

McKennon was the last of the ex-RAF Debden Eagles still flying with the 4th, and had become commander of the 335th Squadron the previous May. On March 18, McKennon led the 4th's B group on an escort to Berlin. Again, there was no air opposition. On the return to Debden, McKennon took his group to Neubrandenburg airfield, where enemy aircraft were spotted on the ground. McKennon made a low pass to check the situation and set up the attack. His P-51D, "Ridge Runner II," took a hit in the oil line. He held it together long enough to get away from the airfield, then bailed out three miles west of Penzlin. The pilots of the other 26 Mustangs watched him land in the same field in which his P-51 crashed and exploded. At this point, McKennon's luck appeared to have finally run out and he was now headed to join his other old friends in POW camp.

McKennon's wingman, First Lieutenant George Green, decided otherwise. He had been troublesome since he joined the squadron the previous fall. McKennon had grounded him four times for infractions including damaging his plane and borrowing McKennon's jeep – which the Arkansan used when hunting rabbits on the field at night without permission. On at least eight occasions McKennon had threatened to toss him out of the squadron. Green's saving grace was that he was a talented and aggressive pilot; McKennon gave him a final chance, making Green his own wingman in order to keep him under close supervision.

Green spotted two men and a dog headed for McKennon in the field. He dropped down and made a low run at them, firing a few rounds that convinced them to back off. McKennon watched, amazed, as his rule-breaking wingman circled and dropped flaps and gear. Spotting other German troops entering the field, Green called the others down and they strafed the enemy troops while Green landed on the rough field. Attempting a "pick up" was strictly forbidden by regulations. Green managed to brake the Mustang before hitting the fence, then turned and taxied back to position himself for takeoff.

McKennon sprinted across the field as Green climbed out and tossed his parachute and dingy on the ground. The six-foot Green pulled his commander onto the wing, then pushed him into the cockpit, climbed in and sat on top of the smaller McKennon. Gunning the Merlin, Green accelerated across the field, yanking the airplane into the air at the last moment and spraying foliage with his prop as the Mustang passed low over a treetop.

Once in the air, McKennon radioed, "Horseback is airborne again. Okay fellas, form up and let's go home." Getting out of Germany, they had to fly at 18,000 feet because of the weather. McKennon passed out from lack of oxygen; Green revived him and they shared his oxygen mask. When they finally landed at Debden, McKennon had to be pulled out of the cockpit since he had lost circulation in his legs with Green atop him.

Several weeks later, General Auton was asked why Green had not been court-martialed. He responded, "I heard that story, but everyone knows it's impossible for two pilots to get into a P-51 cockpit." When Green was asked why he did it, he replied, "I figured I owed the guy a favor." By the time the war ended, Pierce McKennon had 505 combat hours in his logbook and had gone through two P-47s and seven P-51s while scoring 11 aerial and 9.5 ground victories over 27 months on operations with the Eagles.

On March 21, Sidney Woods became the only 4th group pilot of the war to be an "ace in a day." Over Berlin, he spotted four Fw-190 fighter-bombers headed toward the Soviet lines east of the city, dived on them and shot down number four with a short burst, then spotted another flight of four enemy fighter-bombers and shot down the trailing one. Two Fw-190s were chasing a P-51; Woods closed in and shot down the wingman, at which time the leader split-S-ed and broke away. As he circled to return to the group, he saw a third group of fighter-bombers and dived on them. The enemy pilots saw him and salvoed their bombs, but the fourth fighter was slow in breaking away and Woods hit it with a burst. The fighter rolled over and the pilot fell out, deploying his parachute. The entire fight had lasted less than 20 minutes. First Lieutenant William Reidel claimed two Fw-190s destroyed; Captain Hagan and Lieutenants Jahnke, Farrington, and Davis claimed one each.

After a week of bad weather, the 78th flew another Berlin mission on April 7 that saw its last aerial victories of the war. North of Dummer Lake, 83rd Squadron's Blue Leader, Francis Harrington, spotted three contrails that became Bf-109s; after shooting down one, he spotted Fw-190s and got one that rolled over and went straight in. Yellow Leader Captain Robert Green chased Bf-109s heading for the bombers. The leader was hit by defensive fire and collided with a B-17. Green shot off another's elevators; it spun into the ground, taking the pilot with it. The fourth victory came when Lieutenant Richard Kuchl hit a Bf-109 whose pilot bailed out quickly.

That same day, the 479th's 22-year-old Major Robin Olds scored his final aerial kill when he led the group escorting B-24s that bombed an ammunition dump in Lüneburg. The mission saw the only combat appearance of Sonderkommando Elbe, a squadron formed by Hajo Herrmann to ram Allied bombers. The Mustangs were south of Bremen when Olds noticed contrails above a bank of cirrus clouds, which he saw came from aircraft flying above and to the left of the bombers. The strangers paralleled the bomber stream for five minutes. Olds then saw several pairs of Me-262s dive toward the Liberators in an attempt to lure the Mustangs away from the bombers. A Bf-109 of Sonderkommando Elbe shot down a B-24. Olds pursued the fighter through the formation and shot it down.

The 479th attacked airfields at Lübeck Blankensee and Tarnewitz on April 13, and Reichersberg airfield in Austria on April 16. Olds was credited with destroying six planes on the ground. He later reflected on the hazards of such missions: "I was hit by flak as I was pulling out of a dive-strafing pass on an airfield at Tarnewitz, up on the Baltic. Five P-51s made a pass on the field; I was the only one to return home." Arriving back at Wattisham, Olds tested the stall characteristics of his P-51D "Scat VI," and found it quit flying just over 175 miles per hour and rolled violently into the right wing, where the flap had been blown away and two large holes knocked in the same wing. "Bailout seemed the logical response, but here's where sentiment got in the way of reason. That airplane had taken me through a lot and I was damned if I was going to give up on her. Why the bird and I survived the careening, bouncing, and juttering ride down the length of the field, I'll never know."

Two years out of West Point, Robin Olds had been promoted to major and given command of his squadron on March 25, age 22. He finished the war with credit for 13 aerial and 11.5 ground victories. He was the only pilot to become an ace in both the P-38 (5) and P-51 (8), and was one of four West Point graduates to become an ace during the war.

On April 16, the 4th had its best day of the war. Group A, commanded by Lieutenant Colonel Woods, and Group B, under Major "Red Dog" Norley, flew an escort to Rosenheim and Prague; they followed this with strafing attacks on airfields around Karlsbad, Salzburg, and Prague. The 335th Squadron devastated Gablingen airfield. When McKennon radioed he saw no flak, all sections pulled up in line abreast and made the first pass from southwest to northeast. Norley later reported, "We pulled up to starboard and came in for the second pass. On my third pass, I observed several columns of smoke and several more beginning to burn." A total 50 ground victories were later claimed.

Meanwhile, at Prague/Kbely airfield, the 335th and 336th squadrons found targets. First Lieutenant Harold Fredericks reported, "There were about a hundred ships parked on the Prague/Kbely airfield. There were also 15 parked at adjacent fields. It seemed to be a receiving point for all types of aircraft." Lieutenant Colonel Woods was hit during his third pass; he radioed he was bailing out, and became a POW. A total of eight pilots were lost. McKennon's new "Ridge Runner III" was hit by a 20mm round that exploded in the cockpit and wounded his eye, but he nursed his Mustang home. The wound put him off operations for what remained of the war. The cost to the enemy was staggering, with 51 at Prague/Kbely and 110 for the entire day.

As if that were not enough, a few hours later the 78th Group arrived over Prague and upped the 4th's score. After covering 760 1st and 2nd Air Division B-17s and B-24s bombing bridges and marshaling yards in the Regensburg-Straubing-Platting-Landshut area, Colonel Landers sent 82nd Squadron hunting targets. When they struck Straubing airfield, many of the parked aircraft wouldn't burn due to lack of fuel.

Landers then turned toward Prague. Arriving at 1530 hours, Landers spotted 80 aircraft at Cakowice airfield north of the city. He lit up four He-177s on his first pass and torched two more on his second. After four passes by 83rd and 84th squadrons, 50 fires were counted, with only three aircraft on the field unharmed. The 82nd's Blue Flight exploded those for a 100 percent score.

Other pilots hit Prague/Letnany airfield; after the third pass, the flak was silenced and the Mustangs flew a left-hand gunnery pattern for 25 minutes. Again, many aircraft wouldn't burn for lack of fuel. With ammunition nearly completely exhausted and enough fuel to return to Duxford, the group left 135 aircraft smashed and burning, the record high strafing score of VIII Fighter Command in the war; the group received a second Distinguished Unit Citation. Lieutenants Donald DeVilliers, Dale Sweat, Duncan McDuffie, Gene Doss, Danford Josey, and Dorian Ledington qualified as ground kill "aces in a day." This mission lasted seven hours and 40 minutes, unthinkable a year earlier.

On April 20, Eighth Air Force banned further strafing attacks. This frustrated the 78th the next day when its pilots spotted 20 Me-262s on the *Autobahn* southeast of Munich, which were likely from Adolf Galland's JV 44. Returning home, the weather became progressively worse. By the time the men of 84th Squadron fought their way through rain and thunderstorms, they were at 2,000 feet west of Koblenz, where they hit a solid front with zero ceiling and visibility. Four pilots were lost. Four days later on April 25, the 78th flew their last mission, escorting 11 Lancasters of 617 Squadron that bombed Hitler's Berchtesgaden "Eagle's Nest" with 12,000-pound "Tallboy" bombs. The final victory total for April was 202 ground victories in 18 missions, for seven pilots killed and six POWs.

On April 25, Colonel Stewart led the 4th on a sweep to the Linz-Prague area, where the 334th's First Lieutenant William Hoelscher spotted an Me-262 over the field. He scored strikes all over the jet, but was hit by a 40mm round over Prague/Ruzyne airfield that tore off his left elevator and he bailed out. Fortunately, he landed among a group of Czech partisans. As the end of the war descended into chaos, he hitched rides on motorcycles and jeeps before catching a ride at Munich in a C-47 that returned him to England. He walked in the Debden main gate on May 12, four days after the end of the war. The 4th recognized Hoelscher's Me-262 as its last victory of World War II. With that, the

Debden Eagles, originally formed from pilots who couldn't qualify to join the USAAF, became the most successful American fighter group in history, with a combined air and ground total of 1,015.5 air and ground victories, including 583 aerial victories.

Mission 968, flown April 25, 1945, was the final heavy bomber mission of the war in the European Theater. Six B-17s were lost to flak. There was no appearance during the mission by any Jagdwaffe fighters. The bloodiest air campaign in history was over.

# BIBLIOGRAPHY

Arthy, Andrew, "Ton-Up Debut," *Aeroplane Magazine*, May 2021

Bucholtz, Chris, *Fourth Fighter Group – The Debden Eagles* (Osprey Publishing, 2011)

Bucholtz, Chris, *Mustang Aces of the 357th Fighter Group* (Osprey Publishing, 2012)

Caldwell, Donald L., *JG 26: Top Guns of the Luftwaffe* (Orion Books, 1991)

Correll, John T., "The Cost of Schweinfurt," *Air Force Magazine*, February 2010

Correll, John T., "The Third Musketeer," *Air Force Magazine*, December 2014

Courter, Robert W., "How the Mustang Trampled the Luftwaffe: The Role of the P-51 in the Defeat of the German Air Force in World War Two," Louisiana State University, Unpublished Master's Thesis, 2008

Craven, Wesley Frank and James Lea Cate, *The Army Air Forces in World War II; Vol. I: Plans and Early Operations, January 1939 to August 1942* (US Air Force History Division, 1948)

Craven, Wesley Frank and James Lea Cate, *The Army Air Forces in World War II; Vol. II: Europe: Torch to Pointblank, August 1942 to December 1943* (US Air Force History Division, 1949)

Craven, Wesley Frank and James Lea Cate, *The Army Air Forces in World War II; Vol. III: Argument to VE Day, January 1944 to May 1945* (US Air Force History Division, 1950)

Davis, Richard F., *Bombing the European Axis Powers: A Historical Digest of the Combined Bomber Offensive 1939–45* (Air University Press, 2006)

Dorr, Robert F., *Mission to Berlin* (Zenith Press, 2011)

Forsyth, Robert, *Jagdverband 44, Squadron of Experten* (Osprey Publishing, 2008)

Freeman, Roger A., *The Mighty Eighth: A History of the US 8th Army Air Force* (Doubleday, 1970)

Freeman, Roger A., *The 56th Fighter Group* (Osprey Publishing, 2012)

Freeman, Roger A., Alan Crouchman and Vic Maslen, *The Mighty Eighth War Diary* (Motorbooks International, 1990)

Gentile, Don S., told to Ira Wolfert, *One Man Air Force* (Pickle Partners Publishing, 2013)

Godfrey, John T., *The Look of Eagles* (Random House, 1958)

Hall, Grover L., *One Thousand Destroyed: The Fourth Fighter Group in World War II* (Aero Publishers, 1978)

Hammel, Eric, *Aces Against Germany: The American Aces Speak*, Vol. II (Pacifica Publishing, 1993)

Hess, William N., *354th Fighter Group* (Osprey Publishing, 2002)

Howard, James H., *Roar of the Tiger* (Crown Publishers, 1991)

Ivie, Tom, *352nd Fighter Group* (Osprey Publishing, 2002)

Ivie, Tom and Paul Ludwig, *Spitfires and Yellowtail Mustangs: The US 52nd Fighter Group in World War II* (Stackpole Books, 2013)

Johnson, Robert S. and Martin Caidin, *Thunderbolt!* (Ballantine Press, 1959)

Knoke, Heinz, *I Flew for the Führer* (Frontline Books, 2012)

Kucera, Dennis C., *In a Now Forgotten Sky: The 31st Fighter Group in WW2* (Flying Machines Press, 1997)

Lacy, Lee, "Command Decision: Leadership Lessons from the Strategic Air War Against Germany," *Journal of Military and Strategic Studies*, Vol. 16, Issue 4, 2016

Ray, Levon L., "Fifty Missions in a B-17," personal diary

Rogers, J. David, "Doolittle, Black Monday and Innovation," Missouri State University, Unpublished Master's Thesis, 2014

Russell, Ernest E., *A Mississippi Fighter Pilot in World War II* (Trafford, 2007)

Sims, Edward H., *American Aces* (Harper, 1958)

Smith, Jack H., *The 359th Fighter Group* (Osprey Publishing, 2002)

Stanaway, John, *P-38 Aces of the ETO/MTO* (Osprey Publishing, 1998)

Stout, Jay A., *The Men Who Killed the Luftwaffe: The US Army Air Forces Against Germany* (Stackpole, 2010)

Stout, Jay A., *Fighter Group: The 352nd Fighter Group in World War II* (Berkley Caliber, 2013)

Stout, Jay A., *Hell's Angels: The True Story of the 303rd Bomb Group in World War II* (Berkley Caliber, 2015)

Tillman, Barrett, "Back to Schweinfurt," *Air Force Magazine*, August 31, 2018

Zaloga, Steven J., *Operation Pointblank 1944: Defeating the Luftwaffe* (Osprey Publishing, 2011)

Zemke, Hubert "Hub," as told to Roger A. Freeman, *Zemke's Wolfpack* (Orion Books, 1989)

Interviews:
Donald J.M. Blakeslee
Hans Buch
Wayne Coleman
Walter Cronkite
Jorg Czypionka
Adolf Galland
James A. Goodson
Richard E. "Dick" Hewitt
Gladwyn Hill
Walter Krupinski
Hughie Lamb
Jackson "Barry" Mahon
Walker M. "Bud" Mahurin
Elmer L. "Mac" McTaggart
Spiros "Steve" Pisanos
Gunther Rall
Ernest E. "Ernie" Russell
Robert "Bob" Wehrman
Walter "Chili" Williams
Charles E. "Chuck" Yeager
Hubert M. Zemke

# GLOSSARY

The list below contains German terms and abbreviations that are used repeatedly within the text.

## GERMAN TERMS

| | |
|---|---|
| *Experte(n)* | lit. "expert." German term for "ace," though it was not merely based on how many planes were shot down, but by a judgement of the skill used by the pilot. |
| *Fliegerkorps* | air corps |
| *Geschwader(n)* | wing(s) |
| *Geschwaderkommodore* | wing commander |
| *"Grosse Schlag"* | "Great Blow" (A planned attack of 1,000 Luftwaffe fighters with the goal of shooting down 800 bombers. Never happened because Hitler cancelled it for Operation *Bodenplatte*). |
| *Gruppe(n)* | group(s) |
| *Gruppenkommandeur* | group commander |
| *Inspekteur der Jagdflieger West* | inspector of day fighters in the West |
| *Jabostaffel(n)* | fighter-bomber squadron(s) |
| *Jagddivision* | fighter division |
| *Jagdflieger* | fighter pilot(s) |
| *Jagdgeschwader(n)* | fighter wing |
| *Jagdverband* | fighting band |
| Jagdwaffe | German Fighter Force |
| *Kannonenboot(e)* | gunboat |
| *Kette(n)* | prewar formation of three aircraft: leader and two wingmen |
| *Luftflotte* | air fleet |
| Luftwaffe | German Air Force |

| | |
|---|---|
| *Nachwuchs* | lit. "new growth," a new recruit later in the war |
| *Rammjäger* | ramming fighters |
| *Ritterkreuz* | Knight's Cross |
| *Rotte* | formation |
| *Stab* | staff |
| *Staffel(n)* | squadron(s) |
| *Staffelkapitän* | squadron commander |
| Reichsverteidigung | lit. Defense of the Reich, overall organization in charge of aerial defense of Germany |
| *Rottenflieger* | wingman |
| *Rottenführer* | element leader |
| *Schwarm* | flight |
| *Sturmböck* | battering ram |
| *Sturmgruppe(n)* | close-in attack group |
| *Sturmstaffel(n)* | close-in attack squadron |
| *Würger* | butcher bird |

## ABBREVIATIONS

| | |
|---|---|
| AAA | antiaircraft artillery |
| AAF | Army Air Forces |
| AVG | American Volunteer Group |
| DFC | Distinguished Flying Cross |
| ETO | European Theater of Operations |
| FBI | Federal Bureau of Investigation |
| GM | General Motors |
| KIA | killed in action |
| MAAF | Mediterranean Allied Air Forces |
| MIT | Massachusetts Institute of Technology |
| NAA | North American Aviation |
| NAS | Naval Air Station |
| PCBW | Provisional Combat Bomb Wing |
| POW | prisoner of war |
| RAF | Royal Air Force |
| RCAF | Royal Canadian Air Force |
| SHAEF | Supreme Commander Allied Expeditionary Forces |
| USAAF | US Army Air Forces |
| USSTAF | United States Strategic Air Forces |

# INDEX

Note: page numbers in **bold** refer to illustrations.

85, 102, 133, 263, 265, 279, 290, 314, 317, 343, 350, 354, 356, 358, 364, 368, 394, 404, 422; JG 27: 339, 396, 420, 438; JG 51: 87, 383; JG 52: 102, 404; JG 53: 396; JG 54: 364, 397, 420; I./JG 54: 350, 351; II./JG 54: 351; III./JG 54: 350, 351, 354, 358, 398; JG 77: 330; JG 300: 412, 419; I./JG 300: 379, 386, 388, 432; II./JG 300: 432; III./JG 300: 379, 389, 432; *Sturmgruppe* II./JG 300: 380, 386, 388, 389; JG 301: 412, 419, 433–434; I./JG 301: 405; JG 400: 388, 400; I./JG 400: 387; Jagdkorps I (XII Fliegerkorps) 99; JV (*Jagdverband*) 44: 421–429, 447; *Platzschutzstaffel* (airfield protection squadron) 424; Sonderkommando Elbe 445; Staffeln 122, 368; 2./JG 26: 265; 2./JG 54: 351; 3./JG 26: 286; 4./JG 11: 123, 177, 267; 4./JG 26: 63, 353; 4./JG 54: 421; 5./JG 11 (2./JG 1) 25, 122–123, 124, 155, 157, 160–161, 175, 252–253, 267, 282, 320; 5./JG 26: 58, 60, 62, 269, 279–280, 286, 395; 6./JG 11: 123, 177, 267; 6./JG 26: 280; 7./JG 26: 82, 83, 265, 286, 395; 7./JG 51: 384; 8./JG 26: 57, 394; 9./JG 26: 63, 82; 9./JG 54: 398; 9./JG 301: 419; 10./JG 26: 358; 10./JG 301: 419; 11./JG 26: 314–315, 357, 358; 12./JG 26: 263, 292, 404; 12./JG 54: 398; Sturmstaffel 1: 379; Zerstörergeschwader (Heavy Fighter Groups): ZG 1: 307; ZG 26: 307; ZG 76: 307, 375; I./ZG 76: 96–97; III./ZG 76: 274 *see also* Luftwaffe, the
Japanese raid on Darwin, the 192
Jenkins, Col Jack 206, 334
Johnson, Capt Gerald 162, 166, 207
Johnson, Kelly (Clarence) 30–32, 169
Johnson, Second Lt Robert S. 52, 67, 113, 118, 126–127, 131, 132, 183, 207, 209, 235–236, 268, 302, 303–305, 311, 325, 338–339, 360, 378

Kammerdiener, Feldwebel Otto 422
Kammhuber, General Josef 99, 100
Kammhuber Line, the 100, 138
Kartveli, Alexander 34, 35, 171
Kellerstadt, Armorer Warren 346, 348
Kelsey, First Lt Benjamin S. 30, 31, 32–33
Kennedy, Sgt Harold M. 407–408
Kepner, Brig Gen William 167, 190, 199, 212, 231, 232, 233, 327, 329, 339, 362–363
*Kette* air formation, the 423, 426, 427
Kindelberger, James H. "Dutch" 38, 39, 40
Knoke, Leutnant Heinz 25, 96, 122–123, 124, 128–129, 140, 155, 157, 160–162, 175–178, 208–209, 252–254, 264, 267, 270, 282–283, 319–320
Koontz, Flight Off Glenn 22, 23, 136–137, 183
Kordasiewicz, Flight Sgt Maria 82
Kornatzki, Major Hans-Guenther von 379, 380
Krupinski, Hauptmann Walter 102, 103–104, 404, 422, 425–426, 428

Lamb, Capt Huie 398–399, 408–411, 431, 438
Landers, Col John D. 192, 380, 383, 403, 437, 439, 446–447
Lang, Hauptmann Emil "Bully" 364, 369
leadership qualities and skills 43, 47, 87, 91, 99, 102–103, 108, 114, 130, 163, 196, 197, 227, 321, 330, 403, 419
Ledington, Lt Dorian 352, 447
Lee, Maj Morris 50, 65, 66
LeMay, Col Curtis 27, 104–105, 106, 146, 148, 155–156, 157, 158, 180, 279
Lemp, Leutnant Helmut 74, 75
Lend-Lease military matèriel 65, 73, 130, 343
Leuna synthetic oil plant, Poland 374, 388, 400–401
liberation of Paris, the 367–368
Littge, First Lt Raymond 415, 418
Lockheed Corporation 31, 170, 336
London, Capt Charles P. 20, 24, 84, 92, 112, 129, 135, 137
"Lord Haw-Haw" (William Joyce) 13, 269–270
losses of matèriel 21, 24, 25, 50, 53, 60, 61, 62, 72, 82, 83, 85, 86, 87, 89, 92–93, 96–98, 124, 131–132, 134, 137, 140, 143, 149, 155, 158, 160, 162, 163, 166, 167, 172, 177, 183, 186, 187–188, 205, 206, 207, 208, 210, 212, 215, 216, 221, 235, 260, 262, 265, 267, 269, 270, 272, 274, 277, 278, 279, 283–284, 287, 288, 291, 297, 307, 308, 309, 322, 331–332, 339, 341, 349, 355, 357, 359, 364, 368, 369, 373, 375, 386, 388, 389–390, 394, 395, 396, 401, 402, 412, 417, 418, 419, 426, 434, 436, 446, 448
Lowell, Maj John 308, 309
Loyd, Second Lt Daniel 352
Luftwaffe, the 29, 31, 65, 77, 78, 80, 99, 110, 141, 145, 146, 164–165, 216, 229, 241, 242, 247, 251, 252, 257, 277, 309, 310, 311, 321, 346, 368, 378, 390; Kampfgeschwader (Bomber Wings): KG 51: 365–366, 420, 426; Kommando Nowotny 397–398, 399, 401–402 *see also* Jagdwaffe, the
Luksic, Second Lt Carl 337–338, 341
Lützow, Oberstleutnant Günther 420, 421, 428

MAAF (Mediterranean Allied Air Force), the 229
Mahon, Barry 71, 72
Mahurin, Capt Bud 162, 207, 210, 268, 309, 311, 317, 322–323
maneuverability 21, 51, 96, 97, 111, 136, 170, 198, 199, 202, 203, 207, 226, 304, 313, 334, 343
Martin, Lt Col Harold 196, 197, 200, 202, 212, 215, 255, 257, 272, 274
Mason, Col Joe 193, 234, 340, 341
Massa, Vincent 348, 352
Mayer, Major Egon 56, 84, 131, 302
McClure, Capt John 111, 112, 114
McCollom, Lt Col Loren 110, 126, 131, 162, 190
McColpin, Maj Carroll W. "Mac" 77, 178